In a Cardboard Belt!

Books by Joseph Epstein

In a Cardboard Belt!

ESSAYS PERSONAL,
LITERARY, AND SAVAGE

•

Joseph Epstein

HOUGHTON MIFFLIN COMPANY
BOSTON • NEW YORK
2007

For information about permission to reproduce selections from
this book, write to Permissions, Houghton Mifflin Company,
215 Park Avenue South, New York, New York 10003.

Library of Congress Cataloging-in-Publication Data
Epstein, Joseph, date.
In a cardboard belt! : essays personal, literary, and savage
/ Joseph Epstein.
p. cm.
Includes bibliographical references (p.) and index.
ISBN-13: 978-0-618-72193-1
ISBN-10: 0-618-72193-2
I. Title.
PS3555.P652715 2007
813'.54—dc22   2007008515

Book design by Melissa Lotfy

Printed in the United States of America

MP 10 9 8 7 6 5 4 3 2 1

The essays in this book previously appeared in *Commentary,* the *New Criterion,* the *Hudson Review, Poetry,* the *American Scholar,* and *Nexus.*

The author is grateful for permission to quote from the following:
    Correspondence of W. H. Auden to Chester Kallman: the Estate of W. H. Auden. Copyright by the Estate of W. H. Auden; reprinted by permission.
    Lines from *Collected Poems* by W. H. Auden: "Who's Who" copyright 1937 and renewed 1965 by W. H. Auden; "Letter to Lord Byron" copyright 1937 by W. H. Auden; "Brussels in Winter" copyright 1940 and renewed 1968 by W. H. Auden. Used by permission of Random House, Inc.
    Lines from "The Orators" by W. H. Auden: Copyright 1932 by W. H. Auden, reprinted by permission of Curtis Brown, Ltd.
    Poems and writings of Karl Shapiro: The Estate of Karl Shapiro, c/o Wieser and Elwell, Inc. Copyright by the Estate of Karl Shapiro; reprinted by permission.
    Correspondence of Truman Capote: Copyright © 2004 by the Truman Capote Literary Trust; reprinted by permission.

FOR ARNOLD EPSTEIN

Yo, bro

The profession of letters is the only one
in which one can make no money
without being ridiculous.

—JULES RENARD, *Journal*

Look at me now! Look at me now!
I'm wearing a cardboard belt!

—ZERO MOSTEL, in *The Producers*

Contents

III. Attacks

IV. The Intellectual Life

Introduction

SEVENTY. Odd thing to happen to a five-year-old boy who only the other day sang "Any Bonds for Sale," whose mother's friends said he would be a heartbreaker for sure (he wasn't), who was popular but otherwise undistinguished in high school, who went on to the University of Chicago but has long ago forgotten the dates of the rule of the Thirty Tyrants in Athens and the eight reasons for the Renaissance, who has married twice and written books nineteen times, who somewhere along the way became the grandfather of three, life is but a dream, sha-boom sha-boom, seventy, me, go on, whaddya, kiddin' me?

A funny age to turn, seventy, and, despite misgivings, I am about to go ahead and do it, yet with more complex thoughts than any previous birthday has brought. Birthdays have never been particularly grand events for me; my own neither please nor alarm me. I note them chiefly with gratitude for having got through another year. I have never been in any way part of the cult of youth, nor delighted to be taken for younger than I am, nor proud that I can do lots of physical things that men my age are no longer supposed to be able to do: twenty-six chin-ups with gila monsters biting both my ankles. I have always thought I looked — and, as mothers used to instruct, always tried to act — my age. But now, with seventy about to arrive, I notice that for the first time I am beginning to fudge, to hedge, to fib slightly, about my age. In conversation, in public appearances, I describe myself as "in my late sixties," hoping, I suppose, to be taken for sixty-seven. To admit to seventy is to put oneself into a different category: to seem uncomfortably close to, not to put too fine a point on it, Old Age.

At seventy, middle age is definitely — and definitively — done. A wonderful period, middle age, so nondescript and imprecise, extending perhaps from one's middle thirties to one's late sixties, it allows a person to think him- or herself simultaneously still youthful though no longer a kid. Forty-eight, fifty-seven, sixty-one, those middle-aged numbers suggest miles to go before one sleeps, miles filled with potential accomplishments, happy turnabouts in one's destiny, midlife crises (if one's tastes run to such extravaganzas), surprises of all kinds.

Many ski lifts at Vail and Aspen, I have been told, no longer allow senior-citizen discounts at sixty because so many people continue skiing well into their sixties. With increased longevity, it's now thought a touch disappointing if a person dies before eighty-five. Sixty, the style sections of the newspapers inform us, is the new forty. Perhaps. But seventy, seventy, as the punch line of the joke about the difference between a virgin and a German Jew has it, seventy remains seventy. One can look young for seventy, one can be fit for seventy, but in the end there one is, seventy.

W. H. Auden, who pegged out at sixty-six, said that while praying we ought quickly to get over the begging part and get on to the gratitude part. "Let all your thinks," he wrote, "be thanks." One can look upon life either as a gift or as a burden, and I happen to be a gift man. I didn't ask to born, true enough, but, really, how disappointing not to have been. I had the additional good luck of arriving in 1937, in what was soon to become the most interesting country in the world, and to have lived through a time of largely unrelieved prosperity in which my generation danced between the raindrops of wars: a child during World War II, too young for Korea, too old for Vietnam, but old enough for the draft, which sent me for twenty-two months — useful as they in retrospect seem — off to Missouri, Texas, and Arkansas. My thinks really are chiefly thanks.

As for my decay, what the French call my *décomposition générale,* it proceeds roughly on schedule, yet for the moment at a less than alarming rate. I have had a heart bypass surgery. Five or so years ago, I was diagnosed with autoimmune hepatitis, which caused me no pain, and which side-effectless drugs have long since put in remission. I am paunchless, have a respectable if not abundant amount of hair atop my head (most of it now gray, some of it turning white), retain most of my teeth (with the aid of expensive dentistry). I have so far steered clear of heart attack, dodged the altogether too various menacing cancers whirling about, and missed the wretched roll of the dice known as aneurysms. (Pause while I touch wood.) My memory for unimportant things has begun to fade, with results that thus far have been no more than mildly inconvenient. (I set aside ten minutes or so a day to find my glasses and fountain pen.) I have not yet acquired one of those funny walks — variants of the prostate shuffle, as I think of them — common to men in their late sixties and seventies. I am, though, due for cataract surgery. I'm beginning to find it difficult to hear women with high-pitched voices, especially in restaurants and other noisy places. And I take a sufficient number of pills — anti-this and supplement-that — to have made it necessary to acquire one of those plastic day-of-the-week pill sorters.

Suddenly I find myself worrying in a way I never used to do about things out of the routine in my life: having, for example, to traverse major freeways and tollways to get to a speaking or social engagement. I take fewer chances, as both a driver and a once intrepid jaywalker. I find myself sometimes stumbling over small bumps in the sidewalk, and in recent years have taken a couple of falls where once I would do an entrechat and a simple pirouette — a Nureyev of the pavement — and move along smartly. I walk more slowly up and down stairs, gripping the railing going down. I have, in sum, become more cautious, begun to feel, physically, more fragile, a bit vulnerable.

Sleep has become erratic. Someone not long ago asked me if I watched *Charlie Rose,* to which I replied that I am usually getting up for the first time when *Charlie Rose* goes on the air. I fall off to sleep readily enough, but two or three hours later I usually wake, often to invent impressively labyrinthine anxieties for myself to dwell upon for an hour or two before falling back into aesthetically unsatisfying dreams until six or so in the morning. Very little distinction in this, I have discovered by talking to contemporaries, especially men, who all seem to sleep poorly. But this little *Iliad* of woes is pretty much par for the course, if such a cliché metaphor may be permitted from a non-golfer. That I shall arrive at seventy without ever having golfed is one of the facts of my biography to date of which I am most proud.

"Bodily decrepitude," says Yeats, "is wisdom." I seem to have accrued more of the former than the latter. Of wisdom generally, I haven't all that much to declare. I find myself more impressed by the mysteries of life and more certain that most of the interesting questions it poses have no persuasive answers, or at least none likely to arrive before I depart the planet. I haven't even settled the question of whether I believe in God. I try to act as if God exists — that is, the prospects of guilt and shame and the moral endorphins that good conduct brings still motivate me to act as decently as I'm able. I suffer, then, some of the fear of religion without any of the enjoyment of the hope it brings. I don't meanwhile have a clue about why there is suffering in the world, whether there is to be an afterlife, or how to explain acts of truly grand altruism or unprofitable evil. You live and you learn, the proverb has it, but in my case, You live and you yearn seems closer to it.

But, then, I must report that at seventy even my yearnings are well down. I have no interest in acquiring power of any kind, and fame beyond such as I now pathetically possess holds little interest for me. My writing has won no big prizes, nor do I expect it ever to do so. ("Tell them," the normally gentle and genteel ninety-two-year-old William Maxwell said to Alec Wilkinson and another friend on the day before his death, "their fucking honors mean nothing to me.") I am ready to settle for being known as a good writer by thoughtful people.

I would like to have enough money so that I don't have to worry, or even think, about money, but it begins to look as if I shan't achieve this either. Rousseau spoke of feeling himself "delivered from the anxiety of hope, certain of gradually losing the anxiety of desire." I've not yet lost all my desire, and suspect that to do so probably is a sign of resigning from life. Although I'm not keen on the idea of oblivion, which seems the most likely of the prospects that await, I like to think that I have become a bit less fearful of death. One of the most efficient ways to decrease this fear, I've found, is to welcome death, at least a little, and this growing older can cause one to do so, or at least it has me, sometimes.

Seventy poses the problem of how to live out one's days. To reach seventy and not recognize that one is no longer living (as if one ever were) on an unlimited temporal budget is beyond allowable stupidity. The first unanswerable question at seventy is how many days, roughly, are left in what one does best to think of as one's reprieve. Unless one is under the sentence of a terminal cancer or another wasting disease, no one can know, of course, but I like the notion of the French philosopher Alain that, no matter what age one is, one should look forward to living for another decade but no more. My mother lived to eighty-two and my father to ninety-one, so I'm playing, I suppose, with decent genetic cards. Yet I do not count on them. A year or so ago, my dentist told me that I would have to spend a few thousand dollars to replace some dental work, and I told him that I would get back to him on this once I had the results of a forthcoming physical. If I had been found to have cancer, I thought, at least I could let the dentistry, even the flossing, go. Turning seventy, such is the cast of one's thoughts.

At seventy one encounters the standard physical diminutions. I am less than certain how old I actually look, though have no doubt my dashing youthful looks are gone. My intellectual and cultural stamina are also beginning to deplete. A younger friend in California writes to me that, in a restaurant in Bel-Air, Robin Williams, Emma Thompson, and Pete Townshend (of The Who, he is courteous enough to explain) walked by his table. I write back to tell him that I would have been much more impressed if

Fred Astaire, Ingrid Bergman, and Igor Stravinsky had done so. My longing to meet Robin Williams, Emma Thompson, and Pete Townshend is roughly the same, I should guess, as their longing to meet me.

I don't much mind being mildly out of it, just as I don't finally mind growing older. George Santayana, perhaps the most detached man the world has known outside of certain Trappist monasteries, claimed to prefer old age to all others. "I heartily agree that old age is, or may be as in my case, far happier than youth," he wrote to his contemporary William Lyon Phelps. "I was never more entertained or less troubled than I am now." Something to this, if one isn't filled with regret for the years that have gone before — and I am not, having had a very lucky run thus far in my life. At seventy it is natural to begin to view the world from the sidelines, a glass of wine in hand, watching younger people do the dances of ambition, competition, lust, and the rest of it.

Schopenhauer holds that the chief element in old age is disillusionment. According to this dourest of all philosophers, at seventy we have, if we are at all sentient, realized "that there is very little behind most of the things desired and most of the pleasures hoped for; and we have gradually gained an insight into the great poverty and hollowness of our whole existence. Only when we are seventy do we thoroughly understand the first verse of Ecclesiastes." And yet, even for those of us who like to think themselves illusionless, happiness keeps breaking through, fresh illusions arrive to replace defunct ones, and the game goes on.

If the game is to be decently played at seventy, one must hark back as little as possible to the (inevitably golden) days of one's youth, no matter how truly golden they may seem. The temptation to do so, and with some regularity, sets in sometime in one's sixties. As a first symptom, one discovers the word "nowadays" turning up in lots of one's sentences, always with the assumption that nowadays are vastly inferior to *thenadays,* when one was young and the world green and beautiful. Ah, thenadays — so close to "them were the days" — when there was no crime, divorce was unheard of, people knew how to spell and everyone had good handwriting, propriety and decorum ruled, and so on and on into the long boring night. Start talking about thenadays and one soon finds one's intellectual motor has shifted into full crank, with everything about nowadays dreary, third rate, and decline and fallish. A big mistake. The reason old people think that the world is going to hell, Santayana says, is because they believe that, without them in it, which will soon enough be the case, how good really can it be?

Seventy brings prominently to the fore the question of Big D, and I don't mean Dallas. From seventy on, one's death can no longer be viewed as a surprise; a disappointment, yes, but not a surprise. Three score and ten, after all, is the number of years of life set out in the Bible; anything beyond that is, or ought to be, considered gravy, which is likely to be high cholesterol, so be careful. Henry James, on in his deathbed, in a delirium, said of death, "So here it is at last, the distinguished thing." I wonder why. Few things are less distinguished than death, that most democratic of events and oldest of jokes that comes to each of us afresh.

At seventy, one more clearly than ever before hears footsteps, as they say a wide receiver in the NFL does who is about to be smashed by an oncoming pass defender while awaiting a pass at midfield. The footsteps first show up in the obituary pages, which I consult with greater interest than any other section of the newspaper. Not too many days pass when someone I know, or someone whom someone else I know knows, does not show up there. A few weeks ago the anthropologist Clifford Geertz and the novelist William Styron conked out; neither was a close friend, though as fellow members of an editorial board, I spent a fair amount of time with them. The other day the tennis player Ham Richardson appeared on the obit page. I was a ball boy for an exhibition he and Billy Talbert put on with two members of the Mexican Davis Cup team at the Saddle and Cycle Club in the 1950s in Chicago. I was surprised to learn that Richardson was only three years older than I. I am fairly frequently surprised to discover that the newly deceased are only a little older than I.

Along with footsteps, I also hear clocks. Unlike baseball, life is a game played with a clock. At seventy, the relentless ticking is always going off in the background, I have decided to read books I've missed or those I've loved and want to reread one more time. I recently reread *War and Peace,* my second reading of this greatest of all novels, and I ended it in sadness, not only because I didn't wish to part from Pierre, Natasha, Nicolai, and the others left alive at the novel's end, but because I know it is unlikely I shall return for another rereading. I've been reading Proust's *Jean Santeuil,* his run-up to *Remembrance of Things Past,* which I'd like to have time to read for a third and last time. I wonder if I shall be in the game long enough to reread *Don Quixote* and Herodotus and Montaigne — reread them all deeply and well, as they deserve to be read but, as always with masterworks, one suspects one failed to do the first and even second time around.

Seventy ought to concentrate the mind, as Samuel Johnson said about an appointment with the gallows on the morrow, but it doesn't, at least it hasn't my mind. My thoughts still wander about, a good part of the time forgetting my age, lost in low-grade fantasies, walking the streets daydreaming pointlessly. (Tolstoy, in *Boyhood,* writes: "I am convinced that should I ever live to a ripe old age and my story keeps pace with my age, I shall daydream just as boyishly and impractically as an old man of seventy as I do now.") Despite my full awareness that time is running out, I cheerfully waste whole days as if I shall always have an unending supply on hand. I used to say that the minutes, hours, days, weeks, months seemed to pass at the same rate as ever and it was only the decades that flew by. But now the days and weeks seem to flash by too. Where once I would have been greatly disconcerted to learn that the publication of some story or essay of mine has been put off for a month or two, I no longer am: the month or two will now come around in what used to seem like a week or two.

I hope this does not suggest that, as I grow older, I am attaining anything like serenity. Although my ambition has lessened, my passions have diminished, my interests narrowed, my patience is no greater, and my perspective has not noticeably widened. Only my general intellectual assurance has increased. Pascal says that under an aristocracy "it is a great advantage to have a man as far on his way at eighteen or twenty years as another could be at fifty; these are thirty years gained without trouble." To become the intellectual equivalent of an aristocrat in a democracy requires writing twenty or so books — and I have just completed my nineteenth.

Still, time, as the old newsreels had it, marches on, and the question at seventy is how, with the shot clock running, best to spend it. I am fortunate in that I am under no great financial constraints and am able to work at what pleases me. I don't have to write to live — only to feel alive. Will my writing outlive me? I am reasonably certain that it won't, but — forgive me, Herr Schopenhauer — I keep alive the illusion that a small band of odd but immensely attractive people not yet born will find something of interest in my scribbles. The illusion, quite harmless I hope, gives me I won't say the courage, for none is needed, but the energy to persist.

The fear of turning seventy for a writer is that he will fall too far out of step with the society that he is supposed, in essays and stories, to be chronicling. I recently wrote a book on friendship, but was I unqualified to do so, as one or two younger reviewers politely suggested, for not knowing how friendship really works among the young today? I continue to read contemporary fiction, but not with the same eagerness with which I once read the fiction written by my elders and people of my own generation. In his sixties, Edmund Wilson, describing himself as "a back-number," announced his loss of interest in much of the writing of the day. A time comes when one loses not merely interest but also curiosity about the next new thing. How intensely, at seventy, must I scrutinize the work of Jack Black, Sarah Silverman, Dave Eggers, and Sacha Baron Cohen?

I have never attempted to calculate the average age of my readers. When I am out flogging a new book or giving a talk, the audiences who come to hear me are generally as old as I, and some a bit older. Perhaps the young do not wish to spend time attending such nonevents. Perhaps they feel I haven't much to say to them. I do receive a fair amount of e-mail from younger readers (in their twenties and thirties), but many of these readers have literary aspirations of their own, and write to me seeking advice.

But the feeling of being more and more out of it begins to sink in. The news of the new movie stars, comedians, hotshot bloggers usually comes to me a little late. My pretensions as a writer of nonfiction have been toward those of cultural criticism. Older men and women — Henry Kissinger, Jeanne Kirkpatrick, James Baker — can stay in the foreign policy game almost unto death. But how long can a writer commenting on the culture be expected really to know the culture? In fact, there can even be something a little unseemly about writers beyond a certain age claiming to share the pleasures of the young. I recall Pauline Kael, who was eighteen years older than I, once comparing a movie to "your favorite rock concert," and I thought, Oh, poor baby, how embarrassing to see her whoring after youth. I much like the Internet, adore e-mail, and probably use Google seven or eight times a day. But must I also check in on YouTube, have a posting on MySpace, and spend a portion of my day text messaging? At seventy, the temptation is to relax, breathe through the mouth, and become comfortably rear guard.

By seventy, too, one is likely to have lived through a fair amount of cultural change, so that traces of disorientation tend to set in. Chateaubriand (1768–1848), whose dates show that he lived through the ancien régime, the French Revolution, Napoleon, the Restoration, the Second Republic, and died just before the revolution of 1848, wrote: "Nowadays one who lingers on in this world has witnessed not only the death of men, but also the death of ideas: principles, customs, tastes, pleasures, pains, feelings — nothing resembles what he used to know. He is of a different race from the human species in whose midst he is ending his days." In my youth one could go into a drugstore and confidently ask for a package of Luckies and nervously whisper one's request for condoms; now things are precisely reversed.

I have of course lived through nothing so cataclysmic as did Chateaubriand. But I was born on the far side of the rock 'n' roll curtain: some of that music (the less druggy Beatles songs) seems to me charming, but none of it for me is charged with real meaning. More important, I was born in a time when there still existed a national culture, so that the entire country grew up singing the same songs, watching the same movies, and later the same television shows. The crafty marketers had not yet divided the country and its culture into Kid Culture, Black Culture, and scores of other Ethnic Cultures. Something like the old *Ed Sullivan Show*, which might have a comedian, an animal act, a tenor from the Met, a young popular singer, a foreign dance troupe, a magician — something, in short, for all the family — is no longer possible today.

I also grew up at a time when the goal was to be adult as soon as possible, while today — the late 1960s is the watershed moment here — the goal has become to stay as young as possible for as long as possible. The consequences of this for the culture are enormous. That people live longer means only that they feel they can remain kids longer: uncommitted to marriage, serious work, life itself. Adolescence has been stretched out, at least into one's thirties, perhaps one's early forties. At seventy, I register with mild but genuine amazement that the movie director Christopher Guest's father played keyboard for the Righteous Brothers or that the essayist Adam Gopnik's parents, then graduate students, took him in their arms to the opening of the Guggenheim Museum. How can anyone possibly have parents playing keyboards or going to graduate school! *C'est impossible!*

I of course hope for an artistically prosperous old age, though the models here are less than numerous. Most composers, with the notable exception of Stravinsky, were finished by their sixties. Not many novelists have turned out powerful books past seventy. Matisse, who is a hero of culture, painted up to the end through great illness, though his greatest work was done long before. There are the models of Rembrandt and Yeats. Rembrandt, in his richly complex self-portraits, recorded his own aging with great success, and Yeats — "That is no country for old men" — made aging, if not Byzantium, his country: "An aged man is but a paltry thing, / A tattered coat upon a stick, unless / Soul clap its hands and sing, and louder sing / For every tatter in its mortal dress."

Rembrandt died at sixty-three, Yeats at seventy-four. I had better get a move on.

As I reread the essays in this book, I recognize that they are none of them the work of a young, or even younger, man. My subjects identify my age: the death of a father, retirement from teaching, reading the obits, dismantling a personal library, roads not taken. My literary tastes tend more and more toward those of an exquisite (Valéry, Proust, Auden, Beerbohm, Lord Berners); my impatience with intellectual fraudulence grows greater; my cultural observations tend to be those of the wily veteran, someone a little distanced and perhaps no longer fully engaged with the life he is observing but still finding it amusing.

Rereading these essays, I also discover myself far from displeased with them. *In a Cardboard Belt!* is my tenth book of essays, and I like to think that I have not yet grown worse. My point of view has been steady, my craft not noticeably diminished. I often laugh at my comic touches. (After all these years, I may have found my own best reader, and he turns out to be me.) The passion, however transmuted by time, is still there. As I turn seventy, and now see the barn off in the middle distance, I hope to be able to maintain this same passion all the way home.

I
Personal

Oh Dad, Dear Dad

I T WILL SOON be seven years since my father died, leaving me, at a mere sixty-two, orphaned. He was ninety-one when he died, in his sleep, in his own apartment in Chicago. Such was the relentlessness of his vigor that, until his last year, I referred to him behind his back as the Energizer Bunny: he just kept going. I used to joke — half joke is closer to it — about "the vague possibility" that he would predecease me. Now he has done it, and his absence, even today, takes getting used to.

When an aged parent dies, one's feelings are greatly mixed. I was relieved that my father had what seems to have been an easeful death. In truth, I was also relieved at not having to worry about him any longer (though, apart from running a few errands and keeping his checkbook in the last few years of his life, he really gave my wife and me very little to worry about). But with him dead, I have been made acutely conscious that I am next in line for the guillotine: *C'est,* as Pascal would have it, *la condition humaine.*

Now that my father is gone, many questions will never be answered. Not long before he died I was driving him to his accountant's office and, without any transition, he said, "I wanted a third child, but your mother wasn't interested." This was the first I had heard about it. He was never a very engaged parent, certainly not by the full-court-press standards of today. Having had two sons — me and my younger brother — had he, I suddenly wondered, begun to yearn for a daughter?

"Why wasn't Mother interested?" I asked.

"I don't remember," he said. Subject closed.

On another of our drives in that last year, he asked me if I had anything in the works in the way of business. I told him I had been invited to give a lecture in Philadelphia. He inquired if there was a fee. I said there was: $5,000.

"For an hour's talk?" he said, a look of astonishment on his face.

"Fifty minutes, actually," I said, unable to resist provoking him lightly. His look changed from astonishment to bitter certainty. The country had to be in one hell of a sorry condition if they were passing out that kind of dough for mere talk from his son.

Was he, then, a good father? This was the question an acquaintance put to me at lunch recently. When I asked what he meant by good, he said: "Was he, for example, fair?"

My father was completely fair, never showing the least favoritism between my brother and me (a judgment my brother has confirmed). He also set an example of decency, nicely qualified by realism. "No one is asking you to be an angel in this world," he told me when I was fourteen, "but that doesn't give you warrant to be a son-of-a-bitch." And, as this suggests, he was an unrelenting fount of advice, some of it pretty obvious, none of it stupid. "Always put something by for a rainy day." "People know more about you than you think." "Work for a man for a dollar an hour—always give him a dollar and a quarter's effort."

Some of his advice seemed wildly misplaced. "Next to your brother, money's your best friend" was a remark made all the more unconvincing by the fact that my brother and I, nearly six years apart in age, were never that close to begin with. On the subject of sex, the full extent of his wisdom was "Be careful." Of what, exactly, I was to be careful—venereal disease? pregnancy? getting entangled with the wrong girl?—he never filled in.

My father and I spent a lot of time together when I was an adolescent. He manufactured and imported costume jewelry (also known as junk jewelry) and novelties—identification bracelets, cigarette lighters, miniature cameras, bolo ties—which he sold to

Woolworth's, to the International Shoe Company, to banks, and to concessionaires at state fairs. I traveled with him in the summer, spelling him at the wheel of his Buicks and Oldsmobiles, toting his sample cases, writing up orders, listening to him tell — ad infinitum, ad nauseam — the same three or four jokes to customers. We shared rooms in less-than-first-class hotels in midwestern towns — Des Moines, Minneapolis, Columbus — but never achieved anything close to intimacy, at least in our conversation. His commercial advice was as useful as his advice about sex. "Always keep a low overhead." "You make your money in buying right, you know, not in selling." "Never run away from business." Some of it has stuck; nearly a half century later, I still find it hard to turn down a writing assignment lest I prove guilty of running away from business.

My least favorite of his maxims was "You can't argue with success." In my growing-up days, I thought there was nothing better to argue with. I tried to tell him why, but I never seemed to get my point across. The only time our arguments ever got close to the shouting stage was over the question of whether or not federal budgets had to be balanced. I was then in my twenties, and our ignorance on this question was equal and mutual — though he turned out to be right: all things considered, balanced is better.

When not in his homiletic mode, my father could be very penetrating. "There are three ways to do business in this country," he once told me. "At the top level, you rely heavily on national advertising and public relations. At the next level, you take people out to dinner or golfing, you buy them theater tickets, supply women. And then there's my level." Pause. Asked what went on there, he replied: "I cut prices." His level, I thought then and still think, was much the most honorable.

He appreciated jokes, although in telling them he could not sustain even a brief narrative. His own best wit entailed a comic resignation. In his late eighties, he made the mistake of sending to a great-nephew whom he had never met a bar mitzvah check for $1,000, instead of the $100 he had intended. When I discovered the error and pointed it out to him, he paused only briefly, smiled, and said, "Boy, is his younger brother going to be disappointed."

Work was the place where my father seemed most alive, most impressive. Born in Montreal and having never finished high school, he came to America at seventeen, not long before the Depression. He took various flunky jobs, but soon found his niche as a salesman. "Kid," one of his bosses once told him, so good was he at his work, "try to remember that this desk I'm sitting behind is not for sale." Eventually, he owned his own small business.

He worked six days a week, usually arriving at 7:30 A.M. If he could find some excuse to go down to work on Sunday, he was delighted to do so. On his rare vacations, he would call in two or three times a day to find out what was in the mail, who telephoned, what deliveries arrived.

He never had more than seven or eight employees, but the business was fairly lucrative. In the late 1960s I recall him saying to me, "The country must be in terrible shape. You should see the crap I'm selling." In later years, a nephew worked for him; neither my brother nor I ever seriously thought about joining the business, sensing that it was a one-man show, without sufficient oxygen for two. One day, after he had had a falling-out with this nephew, my father said to me, "He's worked for me for fifteen years. We open at eight-thirty, and for fifteen years he has come in at exactly eight-thirty. You'd think once—just once—the kid would be early."

"I call people rich," Henry James has Ralph Touchett say in *The Portrait of a Lady,* "when they're able to meet the requirements of their imagination." Although not greatly wealthy, my father made enough money fully to meet the demands of his. He could give ample sums to (mostly Jewish) charities, help out poor relatives, pay for his sons' education, buy his wife the diamonds and furs and good clothes that were among the trophies of my parents' generation's success, in retirement take his grandsons to Israel, Africa, Asia, Latin America, the Soviet Union, New Zealand. At the very end, he told me that what most pleased him about his financial independence was never having to fall back on anyone else for help, right up to and including his exit from the world.

In my late twenties, my father, then in his late fifties, had a mild heart attack, and I feared I would lose him without ever getting to know him better. Having just recently returned to Chicago after a stint directing the anti-poverty program in Little Rock, Arkansas, I thought it might be a good thing if we were to meet once a week for lunch. On the first of these occasions, I took him to a French restaurant on the Near North Side. The lunch lasted nearly ninety minutes. I could practically smell his boredom, feel his longing to get back to "the place," as he called his business, then located on North Avenue west of Damon. We never lunched alone again until after my mother's death, when I felt he needed company.

At some point — around, I think, the time he hit sixty — my father, like many another successful man operating within a fairly small circle, ceased listening. A courteous, even courtly man, he was, please understand, never rude. He would give you your turn and not interrupt, nodding his head in agreement at much of what you said. But he was merely waiting — waiting to insert one of his own thoughts. He had long since mastered the falsely modest introductory clause, which he put to regular use: "I'm inclined to believe that there is more good than bad in the world," he might offer, or "I may be mistaken, but don't you agree that disease and war are Mother Nature's way of thinning out the population?" I winced when I learned that the father of a friend of mine, having met him a few times, had taken to referring to my father as "the Rabbi."

Although he did not dwell on the past, neither was he much interested in the future. He had an astonishing ability to block things out, including his own illnesses, even surgeries. He claimed to have no memory of his heart attack, and he chose not to remember that, like many men past their mid-eighties, he had had prostate cancer. "I'm a great believer in mind over matter," he used to say.

He also liked to say that there wasn't anything really new under the sun. When I would report some excess to him — for example, a lunch check of $180 for two in New York — he would say, "What're ya, kidding me?" Although he was greatly interested in human nature, psychology at the level of the individual held no attraction for him. If I told him about someone's odd or unpredictable or stupid behavior, he would respond, "What is he, crazy?"

Then, after his retirement at seventy-five, my father began to write. His own father had composed two books — one in Hebrew and one in Yiddish — for which my father had paid most of the expense of private publication. Offering to sell some of these books, he kept a hundred or so copies stored in our basement. This turned out to be a ruse for increasing the monthly stipend he was already sending my grandfather: each month he would add $30, $45, or $50, saying it represented payment for books he had sold. Then one day a UPS truck pulled up with another hundred books and a note from my grandfather, who had grown worried that his son's stock was running low.

And now here was I, his eldest son, also publishing books. My father must have felt — with a heavy dose here of *mutatis mutandis* — like the Mendelssohn who was the son of the philosopher and the father of the composer but never had his own shot at a touch of intellectual glory. So he, too, began writing. His preferred form was the two- or three-sentence *pensée* (he would never have called it that), usually pointing a moral. "Man forces nature to reveal her chemical secrets" is an example of his work in this line. "Nature evens the score because man cannot always control the chemicals."

In the middle of the morning my phone would ring, and it would be my father with a question: "How do you spell 'affinity'?" Then he would ask if he was using the word correctly in the passage he was writing, which he would read to me. I always told him I thought his observations were interesting, or accurate, or that I had never before thought of the point he was making. Often I tossed in minor corrections, or I might suggest that his second sentence didn't quite follow from his first. I loved him too much to say that a lot of what he had written bordered on the common-place and, alas, often crossed that border. I'm not sure he cared all that much about my opinion anyway.

He began to carry a small notepad in his shirt pocket. On his afternoon walks, new material would occur to him. Adding pages daily — hourly, almost — he announced one day that he had a manuscript of more than a thousand pages. He referred to these writings offhandedly as "my stuff," or "my crap," or "the *chazerai* I write." Still, he wanted to know what I thought about sending them to a publisher. The situation was quite hopeless; but I lied, said it was worth a try, and wrote a letter over his name to accompany a packet of fifty or so pages of typescript. He began with the major publishers, then went to the larger university presses, then to more obscure places.

After twenty or so rejections, I suggested a vanity-press arrangement — never using the deadly word "vanity." For $10,000 or so, he could have 500 copies of a moderate-size book printed for his posterity. But he had too much pride for that, and after a while he ceased to send out his material. What he was writing, he concluded, had too high a truth quotient — it was, he once put it to me, "too hot" — for the contemporary world. But he kept on scribbling away, flagging only in the last few years of his life, when he complained that his inspiration was drying up.

Altogether, he had ended up with some 2,700 pages — his earnest, ardent attempt to make sense of the world before departing it. Although he had no more luck in this than the rest of us, there was something gallant about the attempt.

Becoming aware of our fathers' fallibilities is a jolt. When I was six years old, we lived in a neighborhood where I was the youngest kid on the block and thus prey to eight- and nine-year-olds with normal boyish bullying tendencies. One of them, a kid named Denny Price, was roughing me up one day when I told him that if he didn't stop, my father would get him. "Ya fadda," said Denny Price, "is an asshole." Even to hear my father spoken of this way sickened me. I would have preferred another punch in the stomach.

World War II was over by the time I was eight, but I remember being disappointed that my father had not gone to fight. (He was too old.) I also recall my embarrassment — I was nine — at seeing him at an office party of a jewelry company he then worked for (Beiler-Levine, on Wabash Avenue), clownishly placing his hand on the stomach of a pregnant secretary, closing his eyes, and predicting the sex of the child.

He was less stylish than many of my friends' fathers. He had no clothes for leisure, and when he went to the beach (which he rarely did), he marched down in black business shoes, socks with clocks on them, and very white legs. He cared not at all about sports — which, when young, was the only thing I did care about. Later, I saw him come to wrong decisions about real estate, worry in a fidgeting way over small sums he was owed, make serious misjudgments about people. He preferred to operate, rather as in his writing, at too high a level of generality. "Mother Nature abhors a vacuum," he used to say, and I, to myself, would think, "No, Dad, it's a vacuum-cleaner salesman she abhors." At some point in my thirties I concluded that my father was not nearly so subtle or penetrating as my mother.

What do boys and young men want from their fathers? For the most part I think we want precisely what they cannot give us — a painless transfusion of wisdom, a key to life's mysteries, the secret to happiness, assurance that one's daily struggles and aggravations amount to something more than some stupid cosmic joke with no punch line. Oh, Dad, you have been here longer than I, you have been in the trenches, up and over the hill; quick, before you exit, fill me in: does it all add up, cohere, make any sense at all, what's the true story, the real *emes*, tell me, please, Dad? By the time my father reached sixty, I knew he could not deliver any of this.

But, now past sixty myself, I cannot say I expect to do better. Besides, the virtues my father did have, and did deliver on, were impressive. Steadfastness was high on the list. He was a man you could count on. He saw my mother through a three-year losing fight against cancer, doing the shopping, the laundry, even some of the cooking, trying to keep up her spirits, never letting his own spirits fall. He called himself a realist, but he was in fact a sentimentalist, with a special weakness, in his later years, for his extended family. (He and his twin brother were the youngest of ten children, eight boys and two girls, my father being the only financial success among them.) He had great reverence for his own father, always repeating his sayings, marveling at his wisdom.

We may not have reverenced him, but we certainly paid him obeisance. He was of the last generation of fathers to draw off the old Roman authority of the paterfamilias. The least tyrannical of men, my father was nevertheless accorded a high level of service at home because of his role as head of the household and efficient breadwinner. Dinner always awaited his return from work. One did not open the evening paper until he had gone through it first. "Get your father a glass of water," my mother would say, or, "Get your father his slippers," and my brother and I would do so without quibble. A grandfather now myself, I have never received, nor ever expect to receive, any of these little services.

My father lived comfortably with his contradictions — another great virtue, I think. He called himself an agnostic, for example, and belonged to no synagogue, yet it was clear that he would have been greatly disappointed had any of his grandsons not had a bar mitzvah. He always invoked the soundness of business principles, yet in cases of the least conflict between these principles and a generous impulse, he would inevitably act on the latter: loaning money to the wrong people, giving breaks to men who did not seem to deserve them, helping out financially whenever called upon to do so. To bums stopping him for a handout he used to say, "Beat it. I'm working this side of the street," yet he gave his old suits and overcoats to a poor brain-fozzled alcoholic who slept in the doorways on North Avenue near his place of business.

Not long before my high school graduation, my father told me that he would naturally pay for college but wondered if maybe I, who had never shown even mild interest as a student, might not do better to forget about it. "I think you have the makings of a terrific salesman," he said, though he let me make the decision. I chose college, chiefly because most of my friends were going and I, still stalling for time, was not yet ready to go out into the world.

But, then, my father allowed me to make nearly all my own decisions. True, he had insisted that I go to Hebrew school, on the grounds, often repeated, that "a Jew should know something of his background, about where he comes from." But apart from that, my brother and I decided what we would study, where we would go to school, and with whom. He never told me what kind of work to go into, offering only another of his much-repeated apothegms: "You've got to love your work." He never told me whom or what kind of woman to marry, how to raise children, what to do with my money. He let me go absolutely my own way.

Only now does it occur to me that I never sought my father's approval; growing up, I mainly tried to avoid his disapproval, so that I could retain the large domain of freedom he permitted me. For starters, he was unqualified to dispense approval where I sought it: for my athletic prowess when young; for my intellectual work when older. Then, too, artificially building up his sons' confidence through a steady stream of heavy and continuous approval—the modus operandi of many contemporary parents—was not his style. "You handled that in a very businesslike way," my father once told me about some small matter I had arranged for him, but I cannot recall his otherwise praising me. I would send him published copies of things I wrote, and he would read them, usually confining his response to "very interesting" or remarking on how something I said had suggested a thought of his own.

In my middle thirties I was offered a job teaching at a nearby university. In balancing the debits and credits of the offer, I suggested to my father that the job would allow me to spend more time with my two sons. "I don't mean to butt in," he said, before proceeding to deliver the longest speech of his paternal career, "but that sounds to me like a load of crap. If you're going to take a teaching job, take it because you want to teach, or because you can use the extra time for other work, not because of your kids. Con yourself into thinking you make decisions because of your children and you'll end up one of those pathetic old guys whining about his children's ingratitude. Your responsibilities to your sons include feeding them and seeing they have a decent place to live and helping them get the best schooling they're capable of and teaching them right from wrong and making it clear they can come to you if they're in trouble and setting them an example of how a man should live. That's how I looked upon my responsibility to you and your brother. But for a man, work comes first."

In the raising of my own sons, I attempted, roughly, to imitate my father—but already the historical moment for confidence of the kind he had brought to fatherhood was past. For one thing, I was a divorced father (though with custody of my sons), so I had already done something to them that my father never did to me— break up their family. For another, I found myself regularly telling my sons that I loved them. I told them this so often that they probably came to doubt it.

True, I wasn't like one of those fathers who these days show up for all their children's school activities, driving them to four or five different kinds of lessons, making a complete videotaped record of their first eighteen years, taking them to lots of ball games, art galleries, and (ultimately, no doubt) the therapist. But I was, nonetheless, plenty nervous in the service, wondering if I was doing the right thing, never really confident I was good enough—or even adequate. The generation of fathers now raising children, I sense, is even more nervous than I was then, and the service itself has become a good deal more arduous.

Many are the kinds of bad luck one can have in a father. Being the son of certain men—I think here of Alger Hiss's son, Tony, who seems to have devoted so much of his life to defending his father's reputation—can seem almost a full-time job. One can have a father whose success is so great as to stunt one's own ambition, or a father whose failure has so embittered him as to leave one with permanently bleak views and an overwhelmingly dark imagination of disaster. Having too strong a father can be a problem, but so can having too weak a father. A father may desert his family and always leave one in doubt, or a father may commit suicide and leave one in a despair much darker and deeper than any doubt. Worst luck of all, perhaps, is to have one's father die of illness or accident before one has even known him.

"They fuck you up, your mum and dad," wrote Philip Larkin in a famous line that is not only amusing but, it is agreed, universally true. But need it be true? Ought one to blame one's parents for all that one (disappointingly) is, or that one (equally disappointingly) has never become? One of the most successful men I know once told me, without the least passion in his voice, "Actually, I dislike my parents quite a bit" — which didn't stop him, when his parents were alive, from being a good and dutiful son. (We are, after all, commanded to honor our parents, not necessarily to love them.) Taking the heat off parents for the full responsibility for the fate of their children throws the responsibility back on oneself, where it usually belongs. "I mean, I blame for every fuckups in my life my parents?" asked Mikhail Baryshnikov, who had a horrendously rough upbringing. His resounding answer to his own question was "No."

The best luck is, of course, to love one's parents without complication, which has been my fortunate lot. Whether consciously or not — I cannot be sure even now — my parents gave me the greatest gift of all. By leaving me alone, while somehow never leaving me in doubt that I could count on them when needed, they gave me the freedom to go my own way and to become myself. Of the almost cripplingly excessive concern for the proper rearing of children in our own day, in all its fussiness and fear, my father's response, I'm almost certain, would have been: "What're they, crazy?"

Talking to Oneself

I HAVE BEEN KEEPING a journal for more than thirty years, and if you were to ask me why I continue to do so, the best answer I can offer is that I cannot stop now. I consider scribbling a paragraph or two each morning in the notebooks that constitute my journal part of my intellectual hygiene. That the entries are made in the morning is important; I suspect that if I wrote late at night, when tired, my entries would be spiritually darker and, I prefer to think, less true to life, or at least my life, which has been a lucky one.

As for the contents of my journal entries, they generally have to do with events, incidents, thoughts (more like notions) of the day before, though I am not above writing something genuinely vicious about something I've read, someone I've met, or some piece of gossip I've heard. A day's entry rarely runs longer than two paragraphs of six or seven sentences each, and seldom takes me more than fifteen minutes to compose. I also try to be charming, if only to charm myself. The trick, I have discovered, is not to make the keeping of a journal into a chore. My advice on journal-keeping is, as Cosima Wagner neglected to instruct Richard, keep it light.

I began keeping my journal when I was thirty-three years old. I had attempted one earlier, but found that it was too filled with complaint and depression. The complaint chiefly had to do with the world, ignorant beast, not recognizing my obvious talent. But by thirty-three the rug of this complaint — a small Sarouk with a medallion pattern — had been pulled out from under me by the world's modest acceptance, and so I knocked off the complaint and the depressive tone, and on September 25, 1970, began:

> This is to be a writer's notebook. In it I intend to put down everything I find of interest about writing generally and about my own personal development and problems as a writer. Everything I put into this notebook shall be written out with a fair amount of care, for I half-hope that it will be published some day — an expectation that assumes, of course, that before I go to my grave I shall have accrued a respectable amount of fame. False modesty will not be one of this notebook's strong strains.
>
> I believe I am entitled to call myself a writer at all for two reasons: I publish with a decent regularity in almost all the O.K. American magazines; and if I did not have writing to look forward to, I could only imagine the years ahead as flat and joyless.

My earliest entries, read today, do not make me ashamed. They are about the writer's — this writer's — need for praise, about the death of an important novelist (John Dos Passos), about my own small reputation among editors, about placing and losing a $100 bet on a Detroit Lions–Chicago Bears football game. About the latter, I wrote:

> Screwing is nice, so is food, booze I can do without, drugs scare the hell out of me — so my vice, I suppose, however inconstantly practiced, is gambling. It affects me on every level, not least the physiological . . . Win or lose, when it's over I'm exhausted; having won, I am briefly elated; having lost, I am remorseful, though, somehow, better concentrated on my own inadequacy. It is awful and I can scarcely wait to do it again . . .
>
> Since the ordeal of gambling is by and large unpleasant, since the money is not of primary significance (after all, thirty successive $100 wins would hardly make me a free man), what's

the big attraction? I think it has something to do with the need for venturing forth, for striking out against routine, for wanting an altogether unearned, wholly illicit reward out of life. If you win, you feel that you have beat the system a little — earned easy money on your nerve, while the masses down below have to sweat in the sun for it. If you lose, well, that is a rotten shame, but at least you made the attempt. But to break even, to have geared yourself up without financial consequences — that is to know true impotence.

Another thing about gambling is that it is a marvelous antidote against the most dread disease there is: fear of living.

My early entries tend to be essaylets of this kind. They are on such subjects as the political lines of magazines, the filter that choosing to become a writer places on one's experience, the pleasures as a writer of attacking the rich and famous while being oneself poor and obscure. On the latter subject, I conclude that only a versatile prose style makes this possible, and that "less democratic theory and more English prose needs to be taught in the public schools."

But soon enough I run out of these general — and generalizable — subjects, and my journal descends to the more personal: I write about acquiring a literary agent, about a close relative who has to go into therapy, about choosing not to do a piece on Wilhelm Reich for the *New York Times Magazine,* about an older English writer telling me that something I have written is "valuable because it is percipient." My entries are still not complaint-free. I record that "I cannot recall what it is like to have no one dependent upon me." I ask if "one ever really gets over relationships that have busted up." I wonder if one's depressions "are the few unmerciful moments of truth in one's life, and that all the rest of one's conscious life is made up of periods in which one is allowed the mercifully false notion that one has, in some loose sense, 'prospects.'" I then go on to add that "it is not permitted, for minds like my own, to delve into such matters too deeply or too long." As I wrote capping this rather dark entry, "Enough discontent and a little more civilization, please." As the writer of a journal, I was beginning to gain my tone.

Reading back in the early years of my journal, I am surprised to learn that I was better at handling some problems then than now. Insomnia, notably. I report that, after rolling around, maddeningly for the first hour or two,

> I laze into it, luxuriate in it. I recall old relationships, the wounds and felicities they brought, think about my present situation, consider the possibilities for the future. I introspect, but in a rambling way, nothing neither systematic or deep about it. Somewhere Wm. James talks about the dues that it is necessary to pay the self, if personality's delicate economy is not to break down. During such hours as these, I pay my dues, and it is a great pleasure.

These were years, too, when I began to discover one of my forms: the "piece in which I take a subject and attempt to illuminate it in some rough way through the light of my own particular experience." I also attempt to set out my motives for accepting a writing assignment: "1. Can this be used in a book someday? 2. Is there something about the subject I really want to say? and 3. Do I need the money?" To which I add, "All three questions seem to elude any suspicions of high motive behind my writing." Just so.

Emerson asked himself why his diary contained no jokes, and answered, "Because it is a soliloquy and every man is grave when alone." A sign of my deep shallowness perhaps, but not true of me. I was, even talking to myself, an ironist young. On June 6, 1971, I wrote:

> Every so often I will see a woman coming out of a high-rise or shopping on Michigan Avenue. She is generally small and good-looking, in a dark and somewhat cute-ish way. Sometimes she will be walking a small dog down Sheridan Road, or along Lake Shore Drive. "Ah," I will say to myself, upon sighting these various women, "here is the kind of woman I should now be divorced from."

On occasion I rise — or is it lapse? — into aphorism: "Five years ago I found much about life absurd; nowadays I find many of the same things merely sad. It would be good to be able to regress a little in this sphere." How's this for cut-rate La Rochefoucauld: "Vanity without foundation in either physical beauty or true talent is one of the most pathetic of human spectacles." And this, which shows perhaps too great bookishness to qualify for real originality: "To have a silly judgment from someone one cares about is to understand the accuracy of E. M. Cioran's remark that love is merely an agreement on the part of two people to overestimate each other."

In 1969 I left a job as a senior editor at *Encyclopaedia Britannica* and took up a new one working with my friend Ivan Dee at Quadrangle Books, which was later bought — and soon thereafter wrecked — by the *New York Times*. After a little more than a year at Quadrangle, I decided to leave to write full-time. My journal entry for August 6, 1970, reads:

> Today is to be my last day at Quadrangle Books, and hence the end of still another short segment of my professional life. As an editor in publishing I think, overall, I have been a failure. Not because the publishing business is corrupt — though in many ways it is — not because I thought myself too good for the job, or my standards too high, or my sensibility too fine. No, I have been a failure because of my inability any longer to work up a modicum of excitement for a cooperative venture, or for that matter for anything that I don't find useful for my own writing. It is in this sense, then, that there is truth in the remark that a writer, an authentic writer, always cheats his boss.

Then an odd thing happens: a hiatus of sixteen months occurs during which I do not write a word in my journal. When I return to my scribbling, I do not explain why I left off — and even now cannot recall why I did so. Looking at this gap today, I feel about it as I might a bruise on my leg the origin of which I cannot remember. But when I return, on December 15, 1972, I decide that this journal is "worth keeping — and keeping up — as a record of my various states of mind." I then go on to describe my current state of mind as "fatigued but tiring fast." The reason is that I am more than halfway out to sea in my first book, about which I descant a bit on the difference between writing pieces and writing at much greater length, concluding that the latter allows so much more time "for confusion, self-hatred, and deep doubt."

My not being able to recapture why I didn't write in my journal for more than a year reminds me of another of the reasons I am grateful for having kept a journal. Doing so is perhaps the greatest of all aids to memory, especially as one grows older and life begins to seem more than a touch dreamy. Impressions of places visited on foreign travels became a regular feature of my journalizing, and they become the only hard evidence I have that I spent, say, a week in Ghent. At some point, I begin to note each movie I see and concert I attend; at the back of each notebook I make a list of the books I have read and the date on which I finished reading them. I have fairly often gone back to check on these various items of which my journal is the only record, especially now that I have reached the stage of memory where I can see *The Pelican Brief* as if afresh every two years without remembering anything of its plot from my last viewing.

In my early years, I wasn't at all bad at marking down my own shortcomings. One among them was the habit of what I call "moral vanity," which entails the "need always to appear on the correct side of every issue, relationship, etc. On the way to wriggling myself into the morally correct position, I am quite prepared to do the selfish, the brutal, or otherwise immoral thing." This observation was made in connection with an article I wrote attacking the politics of people who were in fact my friends, and the entry closes by my noting: "A case, clearly, of my cutting off someone else's nose to spite my own face." One of the few regrets in rereading one's journal is the realization that one was sometimes a lot smarter then than now.

In early 1973 the great intellectual event of my life occurred: my meeting, through Saul Bellow, Edward Shils, the most extraordinary human being I have known or ever expect to know. Later in my journals I noted various of his amusing remarks and observations. I only wish I had, Boswell-like, recorded more. When the son of a friend of his at Cambridge committed suicide, leaving a note saying that he found life meaningless, Edward responded, rather angrily at the waste, "Of course it is meaningless, but most of us are fortunately too busy to dwell on its meaninglessness."

I am pleased with myself for being intelligent enough, at thirty-six, to know that I was in the company of a great man. On April 13, 1973, I wrote:

> Dinner last night with Edward Shils . . . For me E. S. is a most pleasant reminder that the intellectual life is still possible, if one stands ready to shuck off certain temptations: joining factions, seeking publicity, reneging on unrenegable principles. Hard to do in our day, but still the only way. E. S.'s face, which late at night, after a long day at the desk and in the classroom, can become quite beautiful, radiant with wit and strength of character, is an indication that such austerities do not go altogether unrewarded.

On June 5, 1973, a sloppily written entry begins: "Chicago essences — a Lincoln Continental Mark (I believe) III driven by a white pimp in a striped shirt — three black women in back down Sheridan Road at (roughly 3:00 A.M.). God bless him, too."

After a paragraph break, I add: "As may be clear from handwriting and syntax, the author is reasonably drunk — an aberration, to put it calmly." This is the only record I have of having been DWW, or drunk while writing, and it shows.

I also used my journal for mentioning the possibility of literary essays I might write, few of which I actually got round to writing. One is about the peculiar memory of writers, or memory shaped by imagination, which I claim to be "one of the most magnificent of instruments of intellection" but "not to be trusted for accuracy." Another is for a piece about things that call up what I refer to as "transient emotions." Yet another is occasioned by first reading Willa Cather's *A Lost Lady,* which suggests to me the subject of what happens when women act quite as brutally as men in the sexual realm. After sketching in a paragraph or so on this, I write that this "would be an almost purely literary essay, or one that starts from literature and goes, as most literary studies should, to life."

Less pretentiously, I sometimes note small items in my journal simply because I feel they oughtn't to go unrecorded. The other day, visiting the graves of my parents, I passed and noted in my journal a gravestone that read, "Rex Salem Wilk, 1930–1992, A Gentle Man." So much suggestion in those last three words. A neighbor dies, a woman weighing perhaps five hundred pounds, and in my journal I wonder what mortuary complications this will present. I also write down, shamelessly, what I take to be my own witticisms. While listening to the Romanian pianist Radu Lupu, I wrote in my concert program that "the Rumanians are the wogs of Europe," which I wrote again in my journal, adding that I think it a remark that my friend Edward, with his unending interest in nationalities, would have enjoyed.

Many years earlier, an older man who lives on my block seems, I report in my journal, "askew: his evening paper was not properly folded, his coat was open, he did not seem quite in control of his open umbrella." When I came in closer range, it was clear he was drunk. "Sir," he said, and at first I thought he was going to upbraid me for something, "how would you like me to suck your peter?" When I ask if he's all right, he reports that he is upset. But before entering his building, he turns to say, "If you want me to do it, I will." I conclude: "In fine, a nice reminder of the madness that sometimes lurks beneath the tranquil appearance of life nowadays — and no doubt always."

Recording the deaths of relatives and friends has become a more regular part of my morning journalistical task. In my sixties, I am not yet in the condition of having more dead than alive friends, but soon it may be close, then tilt the other way — that is, if I am lucky enough to stay alive myself. At my age, I can no longer achieve dying young, which is, as we say in Chicago, fine by me. I especially feel the need to record the deaths of relatives, friends, and acquaintances whose death may not be noted in newspaper obituaries or in memorial services. It cannot matter much to them, I realize. Yet to me it matters a lot, though it is perhaps mere writer's vanity: no one, I feel, should depart the planet without a few of my sentences to accompany him.

As for departures, what, when I make my own, will become of this journal? Who will want it? I still hope, of course, for some form of posthumous publication. I have tried to drop as many names as possible in it, for a namey journal can be greatly amusing. But I have met mostly artists and intellectuals, a few politicians, but not enough people from the great world to give my name-dropping proper zing. No royalty, no movie stars appear in my pages. Much as I should have liked to have done, I cannot report that the Duchess of Windsor goosed me at Ascot or that Grace Kelly promised to return to the screen if I would write a scenario for her. I am more in the league of recording that Irving Howe once told me he never got over the fact that, behind his back, a woman intellectual in his circle had described him as "another Jew-boy in a hurry." My journal is also notably unsexy, both figuratively and literarily. Unlike Edmund Wilson in his journals, I do not report on my bonking, domestic and otherwise. Nor do I report on sexual fantasies, which for me would, I have to report, cover the "otherwise" in my previous sentence. A bit of occasional gossip on sexual alliances or someone announcing he or she is homosexual is about as far as I go, and less and less of this crops up in recent years.

The forty-two notebooks that constitute my full journal must by now run to nearly a million words. To the question of who is ever likely to publish them, the short — and I suspect definitive — answer is: no one. Edmund Wilson is perhaps the last American writer to have his journal published so extensively — in six volumes, one each for five decades and another devoted to his life at his family's Talcottville house in upstate New York. I much enjoyed reading the Wilson journals as they appeared, though they were not without their longueurs: exceedingly boring patches of landscape writing, trial runs for his not very engaging fiction, and the adventures of what he at one point refers to as his "large pink prong," which are a lot less amusing than those of the Pink Panther. Wilson's journals are best when he writes about his meetings with other artists and intellectuals; and since he never for a moment seems to have felt himself intellectually inferior to anyone — not to André Malraux, to Isaiah Berlin, and certainly not to John F. Kennedy — he is usually quite good at taking their measure.

Edmund Wilson aside, everyone who has ever written a journal or diary at some point seems to have had doubts about the usefulness of doing so. "Possibly," writes Ned Rorem, in *Lies,* a recently published volume of his diary, "the Diary is a red herring. The author seeks to guide readers away from the essential, which even he ignores." The Romanian writer Iosif Hechter, who wrote under the name of Mihail Sebastian, in the best modern journal I have read in many years, wrote, "In the end, there is something artificial in the very fact of keeping a private diary; nowhere does the act of writing seem more false. It lacks the excuse of being a means of communicating just as it lacks any immediate necessity." Jules Renard put the matter more straightforwardly: "What is the good of these notebooks? No one tells the truth, not even the one who writes it down."

We know all autobiographies are public lies. Are journals, then, nothing more than private lies? "What a pack of lies intimate journals are," declared Charles Ritchie, a Canadian diplomatist who kept a journal during World War II, "particularly if one tries too hard to be truthful." I have just read — quickly, the more quickly the further I got into them — the published journals of Alfred Kazin, a writer who had all the deep humorlessness and badgering moralizing of Thoreau with none of his feeling for nature, and almost every word in them is devoted to self-justification (no small project), self-dramatizing, and attacks on enemies. Truth, like Godot on stage, never appears on page.

I wonder if those journals aren't best that steer clear of deep innermost thoughts, which probably are better worked out through formal writing or in works of literary art. When Alan Bennett began keeping his diary in 1974, he decided straightaway not to record his emotions and thoughts, because "they make you cringe when you read them again." Byron felt rather the same, claiming he couldn't read his own journal over, noting: "If I am sincere with myself (but I fear one lies more to one's self than to anyone else) every page should confute, refute, and utterly abjure its predecessor." I seem to have solved this problem in my own journal by having almost no innermost thoughts, let alone a subconscious; as for my unconscious, I suspect it might best be described the way Edward Shils, as noted in my journal, once described Mexican food: "mostly mud and peppers."

Despite all the drawbacks that journals present, they also provide advantages no other form of literature offers. Mihail Sebastian's account in his journal of the events in Romania between 1937 and 1945 has a day-to-day freshness that neither autobiography nor written history can ever hope to capture. Along with filling in history, in the manner of Sebastian, a journal is often the best way to encounter a strong mind. I've recently read an English translation of a selection from *The Journals of Jules Renard* (1864–1910), which is filled with useful information of a kind that is unlikely to have fitted into any other form. Nice to learn from Renard, who was in a position to know, that the poetry of Mallarmé is "untranslatable, even in French." Or that "any writer who is polite, who acknowledges a letter or the receipt of a book, does not believe himself to be famous." And, in the spirit of its taking one to know one: "The profession of letters is the only one in which one can make no money without being ridiculous."

Although Jules Renard wrote novels and for the theater, he is among those writers whose claim on posterity — of which he noted, "Why should people be less stupid tomorrow than they are today?" — is owing almost wholly to his journals. The Goncourt brothers, Edmond and Jules, are two others. André Gide's novels today seem less interesting than do his journals. The same holds for Harold Nicolson's diaries over his rather thin histories and biographies. Without his journal, we should not have known of the high quality of Delacroix's mind. Another painter, Benjamin Robert Haydon, would be unknown today without his journals and their valuable comments on his more famous contemporaries: Keats, Wordsworth, Byron, Shelley, Hazlitt, Lamb, & Co. Alice James's diary is her proper claim on the attention of posterity. Kierkegaard's journals, while of lesser importance than his major philosophical and theological works, embellish, enhance, and help explain that work, and thus have a key place in his oeuvre. Giacomo Leopardi's *Zibaldone*, or notebooks, which run to 4,562 pages, hold an even more central place in that poet's life. "The *Zibaldone*," writes Iris Origo in her fine biography, "is Leopardi himself." Tolstoy made a similar claim — "My diaries are me" — but in his case they aren't; they were chiefly him in his mood of self-flagellation, filled with accounts of his youthful whoring and carousing. He showed the diaries to his young wife — was there ever a genius more stupid than Tolstoy? — which got their marriage off on just the wrong note.

The young Countess Tolstoy was clearly not the ideal reader for her husband's diary. But who is the ideal reader for a journal or diary? Harold Nicolson laid it down that "the purely private diary becomes too self-centered and morbid. One should have a remote, but not too remote, audience." Nicolson thought this would be one's (still unborn) great-grandson. Chips Channon, the Chicago-born English politician, was one of the great snobs of the past century. He adored royalty, and once, overstimulated by having two actual queens in his house, got so drunk that he had no memory of the event. "I sometimes wonder why I keep a diary at all," he wrote. "Is it to relieve my feelings? Console my old age? Or to dazzle my descendants?" Dawn Powell, who had no descendants beyond her retarded son, wrote, "The reason I write is because there is no one to talk to and I might as well build up a completely private life."

In the ideal journal or diary, one is talking to oneself but with the understanding that others are welcome to eavesdrop, after one is dead. Eavesdropping would normally be the last thing one

would think one would want, given the ostensibly private nature
of journals and diaries. In melodramas, it used always to be a serious violation to read, without their awareness, young women's diaries. Nowadays they try to publish them and as soon as possible.

Some of the best entries from published diaries and journals appear in a splendid anthology, *The Assassin's Cloak,* edited by Irene
and Alan Taylor. The Taylors are Scots, both of whom have put in
time working in libraries. Their title derives from the entry of one
of their book's most interesting contributors, William Soutar, a
Scottish poet whose life was brought to a too early close, after a
lengthy invalidism owing to a spinal disease, at age forty-five. "A
diary," Soutar wrote, "is an assassin's cloak which we wear when
we stab a comrade in the back with a pen."

The Taylors have also found a useful method for organizing an
astonishingly large and multivarious body of material. They have
set out entries, from the seventeenth through the late twentieth
century, organized chronologically by day through the 366-day cal-
endar year, so that for January 10 one gets entries written on that
day in their own diaries and journals by Henry Crabb Robinson
(1824), the Reverend Francis Kilvert (1872), Sir Allen "Tommy"
Lascelles (1914), Count Harry Kessler (1920), Chips Channon (1945),
Jean Cocteau (1953), Roy Jenkins (1979), Alan Clark (1984), and the
rock musician Brian Eno (1995). This organization gives a nice feeling for the variety of human response to private and public experience both in and through time.

"Are all Brits bisexual," a recent cartoon in *The New Yorker* has
one woman asking another, "or just the ones who publish their diaries?" From *The Assassin's Cloak* we can now answer confidently
that only half the Brits are bisexual, and of these all publish their
diaries. The comprehensiveness of the Taylors' anthology is impressive. The only large names left out of this excellent book that I
know are those of Renard, Edmund Wilson, and Ned Rorem;
there is only a single entry by Emerson and too many by Thoreau.
In recompense, a number of the contributors to the Taylors' anthology are new to me, among them W.N.P. Barbellion, Roy

Strong, Etty Hillesum, Joan Wyndham, and Charles Ritchie, all of whom wrote consistently interesting things in their journals and diaries.

What impresses about this assemblage of journal and diary entries is the sheer richness of human possibility. In 1644 in London, Samuel Pepys goes out to attend the hanging of a man named Turner ("A comely-looked man he was, and kept his countenance to the end: I was sorry to see him"). In 1821 in Ravenna, Lord Byron goes out to make love ("Somewhat perilous, but not disagreeable"). In 1978 in New York, Andy Warhol, despite a lot of appointments, decides to "stay home and dye my eyebrows." Different folks, as the old saying has it, different strokes.

Some diarists seem to get things wonderfully wrong in the passion of the moment. Lord Longford, for example, is certain that Lady Diana Spencer is perfect for her husband, and at her marriage to the Prince of Wales he writes that it will bring "lasting benefit to the nation in a renewed sense of unity." (Yeah, as the kids say, right, sure!) Beatrice Webb has a very poor impression of her future husband Sidney on their first meeting. Others get it wrong not sometimes but every time: see any entry by Simone de Beauvoir on America. Still others are amusingly wrong, such as Stendhal, who thought that "an efficacious remedy for love" was to "eat peas." (I haven't actually kitchen-tested this.) Stephen Spender has a taste for telling mildly demeaning stories about himself in his journal, one about his flatulence, another about being recognized by a clerk at the Seattle airport as "a near-celebrity." The editors use a number of entries from the diaries of Virginia Woolf, which don't, cumulatively, redound to her greater glory, but instead show her to be rivalrous, anti-Semitic, intensely in need of praise, even for that most praise-guzzling of animals, the writer.

One of the especial pleasures of reading journals and diaries is that one gets to glimpse historically interesting experience freshly recorded — almost on the scene. The English actor Charles Macready, in 1833, hears Paganini play at Drury Lane. Joan Wyndham recounts being set upon by a (predictably) drunken Dylan Thomas in a cab: "It was rather like being embraced by an intoxicated octopus. I tried to tell myself I was being kissed by a great poet but it was a relief when the taxi finally stopped." Noël Coward, after going to a Beatles concert, reports that "they were professional, had a certain guileless charm, and stayed on not too long." But the audience gets to him: "Personally I should have liked to take some of those squealing maniacs and cracked their heads together. I am all for audiences going mad with enthusiasm after a performance, but not incessantly during the performance so that there ceases to be a performance."

Alone among literary works, journals and diaries do not benefit from revision. Chips Channon claimed never to reread his diaries and mentions what a mistake it is to dictate a diary, which tends to cut down on its spontaneity and scandalousness: "What is more dull than a discreet diary? One might just as well have a discreet soul." Cocteau advises the editor of his diary to "cut what I jot down for reference and the repetitions which occur because I don't remember if I've already described the things I've described," but otherwise to let 'er rip and print what he wrote. Editing for libel and slander needs be done in some journals and diaries — some of the best, my guess is.

Dullness is a regular worry of all diarists. "My life is really too empty for a diarist," Evelyn Waugh writes. "The morning post, the newspaper, the crossword, gin." Fanny Burney, in 1768, writes: "Alas, alas! my poor Journal! how dull, unentertaining, uninteresting thou art!" and wishes for a journal-worthy adventure to record. Two centuries later, Tallulah Bankhead remarks: "Only good girls keep diaries. Bad girls don't have time." The prize diary entry in the dullness sweepstakes belongs to Kafka, who on June 1, 1912, records: "Wrote nothing."

Journals and diaries are often nowadays used as part of psychotherapy. One wonders about the value of doing so. Some benefits may accrue from setting out, in the plainest, least self-dramatizing prose, one's troubles, if only to gain greater clarity about them. But it makes for dreary reading. Kafka, a great writer, is, for precisely this reason, often a dreary diarist; when not complaining, he is endlessly analyzing his weaknesses. "One stops being a child," Cesare Pavese wrote in his diary, "when one realizes that telling one's troubles does not make it better." Yet it remains true that, in troublous times, people tend to diarize. (I hope I may be forgiven this back-formation verb, but I take my inspiration here from Evelyn Waugh, who, in one of his diary entries, availed himself of "to lesbianise.") Perhaps the largest single category of diary entries in *The Assassin's Cloak* is made up of those written during, and having to do with, World War II.

A journal provides one with that best of audiences, that most loyal supporter, that closest and most understanding and greatest goodhearted of friends — oneself. One can say to it things one wouldn't dare to say to anyone else. James Lees-Milne, contemplating a passport photograph of himself at the age of sixty-nine, writes: "My God, how absolutely hideous I have become. Sad really, when you think. As long as I keep clean. I suppose all I can do is maintain that one standard." One can hazard speculations in a journal or diary one wouldn't dare write in, so to say, the public prints. In his diary, Noël Coward blames the death of Marilyn Monroe on Arthur Miller: "Poor silly creature. I am convinced that what brought her to that final foolish gesture [her suicide] was a steady diet of intellectual pretentiousness pumped into her over the years by Arthur Miller and 'The Method.'" Coward is perhaps the most unfailingly charming diarist of all, a man who, after a splendidly rich life, looked forward to oblivion: "I cannot really feel that oblivion will be disappointing. Life and love and fame and fortune can all be disappointing, but not dear old oblivion. Hurrah for eternity!"

Finally, though, there is something slightly deceitful about keeping a journal or diary, especially if one never shows it to anyone else. James Lees-Milne notes in his diary that "if a man has no constant lover who shares his soul as well as his body he must have a diary — a poor substitute but better than nothing." The excellent W.N.P. Barbellion, an English naturalist, takes this a step further when, in his journal, he writes that, for an engaged or married man, there is something suggesting infidelity in keeping such a "super-confidante," and he wonders if his own "journal habit [isn't] slowly corrupting my character."

Keeping a journal or a diary, once begun in earnest, becomes more an addiction than a habit. I cannot now imagine abandoning mine. I continue to scribble in it each morning, living my life at a second remove, with nothing in it quite real until it has been scrawled out in my increasingly poor handwriting. "When all is said and done," Siegfried Sassoon wrote, "a good life is better than keeping a good diary." No doubt, but please note that Sassoon makes this observation in his diary. You may think this essay has at least come to its conclusion, but it will really only be done tomorrow morning, when, in my journal, I write, "Finished essay on journals and diaries. Am, as usual, uncertain of its quality."

Goodbye, Mr. Chipstein

MY INTEREST IN university teaching was initially aroused by the leisure it promised. "Every century has its cushy profession," the English poet Philip Larkin said. "It used to be the church. Now it's academe." Larkin was right. Do the math: assuming one does not teach in the summer — and the vast majority of professors do not — college teaching is roughly a six- or seven-month job, and during those months one generally goes into the office two or three days a week. Not bad, not bad at all.

I was thirty-six years old, and after holding a number of mid-grade editorial and government jobs, I had begun writing as a free-lance, a phrase the reality behind which comes nowhere near matching the dash and romance it seems to suggest (freelance: d'Artagnan off on a long weekend). I had never held a job for more than four years, and did not so much plan my new jobs as flee my old ones.

Among the magazines I had written for was *Dissent*, the quarterly edited by the critic Irving Howe, and in the early 1970s, when Howe came out to give a talk at Northwestern University in Evanston, he dropped by my apartment. Talking about my brilliant career, he suggested that teaching might not be a bad idea; it would give me health insurance and other benefits, and make it possible not to have to scribble under full financial pressure. The combination of teaching and writing, he said, had worked well for him. He offered to do what he could on my behalf.

Before Howe left town, I had a call from the chairman of Northwestern's English department, asking if I would speak to the faculty and graduate students. It was to be an audition of sorts. I hacked together a half-hour's worth of talk on the subject of the Man of Letters. Although I blew no one away with my brilliance, neither did I utterly disgrace myself, and soon there came an offer to teach six courses over three of the four quarters of the next academic year at a salary of $20,000. I would have the title of lecturer. On the day I accepted, I called my mother to let her know I would now be teaching at Northwestern University. "That's nice," she said, with her typical sang-froid, "a job in the neighborhood," and we moved along to more important topics.

Howe probably told the chairman of the department that I was a comer, and therefore a future ornament to the university. I held no degree more advanced than a B.A. *in absentia* from the University of Chicago, and although I had published a fair amount of intellectual journalism and written a book that was about to be published on the subject of divorce, I had no real scholarly qualifications. Irving Howe's must have been an impressive sales job.

The year I started teaching was 1973. The student revolt was over, at least in its to-the-barricades phase, but the more long-lasting effects had begun to kick in in earnest. A new air of informality had become almost de rigueur. Teachers called students by their first names, and some students returned the favor. Among the faculty, now the objects of routine written evaluations by their students, pedants were out, democrat-activists in. Soon after I started, I asked a colleague if many professors slept with their students. "You mean," he answered with a perfectly straight face, "many don't?"

Out of sheer nonconformity, I chose to teach in a jacket and tie. I also decided to call my students by their last names, preceded by Mr. or Miss (later, more hissily, Ms.). These two items set my general tone, which was slightly formal, maintaining a distinct distance between teacher and students. My thought was that if you're wearing denim and calling your students Chip and Muffy, it might be difficult to ask with a properly serious face what Nietzsche meant when he said God was dead and man faces the abyss. I preferred to keep that properly serious face, among other reasons because it offered a much better launching pad for irony, oblique insights, even jokes.

No training is available for teaching at the university level. One strains to remember one's own best teachers and to borrow from them what one can. At Chicago, many of my most memorable professors had been Europeans; they had about them a grandeur that was foreign (in every sense) to their American colleagues, who had to fall back on precision and, among a lucky minority, wit. Some of my teachers deployed an impressive erudition, a commodity I did not happen to possess, and some a no less impressive passion for their subject, which I thought I could muster. I asked a friend who had been teaching for a decade or so if he had any advice. "Yeah," he said, "never let 'em go outside. When the weather gets warm, they'll want to hold class on the lawn, as in those sappy photographs in the brochures. Don't let 'em do it." In thirty years of teaching, I followed this sound advice to the letter.

I was never given a class of more than forty students, and so I rarely had to lecture for a full period, filling the remainder of the time instead with questions to stimulate (the hope was) interesting discussion. I was grateful for this, for even at the start I sensed that the national attention span had somehow diminished, and that short of relying on a whoopee cushion, setting oneself aflame, or establishing an atmosphere of menace, to hold a class's attention through eighty minutes of a teacher's talk could not be done, at least by me.

I say eighty minutes because I was permitted to hold two such rather lengthy sessions on Tuesdays and Thursdays, an arrangement I much preferred to the standard three fifty-minute classes on Mondays, Wednesdays, and Fridays. I thought of myself primarily as a writer and only secondarily as a teacher, and the interval between Thursdays and Tuesdays would give me more time (or so I felt) for my real job.

Without the writing, would I have been a better teacher? I used to think so; at least I would have found more time to read up on my subjects, and more time to cultivate students outside class. But as the years went by, and my reputation as a writer began to grow a bit, I also came to realize that from it derived much of my authority as a teacher lacking in the usual scholarly qualifications. Some of my students seemed quite as thrilled as I to see my name in print.

I could never accustom myself to being called Professor. Wasn't the professor the little fellow in the derby who played the piano in a bordello ("Hit it, Professor!")? And to be called *Dr.* Epstein was even worse. When so addressed, I was always tempted to reply, "Read two chapters of Charles Dickens, get into bed, and call me if things get worse." Nor could I long forget that, university teacher though I might now be, I had never been much of a student myself. I had little memory of doing homework in high school, and in college, where I had made a greater effort, I fell just short of mediocre.

The problem was that my mind never wanted to stay in the expected academic groove but sailed on ahead, or sideways. (Today, of course, I love to read about authentic geniuses who did not do well in school.) A year or so into teaching, I began to see that my real education would take place as a teacher. I found myself reading books — chiefly novels, though also bits of criticism and philosophy — with a new concentration. In preparing for class, all the puzzling passages had to be puzzled out, the Latin tags and foreign phrases to be translated, other people's interpretations to be considered. I read not only intensively but defensively, to avoid being tripped up, embarrassed, made to look foolish.

I had heard stories of teachers, famously good ones, who were so nervous before a class that they had to make a quick stop in the nearest lavatory to throw up. The late Robert Nisbet, who was known as a riveting lecturer, told me that he never entered a classroom without real trepidation. I was not in this league, but I did tend to nervousness, especially at the beginning, when my greatest fear was that I would never be able to fill those eighty minutes with my mini-lectures and my too often less-than-stimulating questions. Occasionally I had nightmares — pure anxiety dreams — about contracting to give a lecture to a large audience on, say, Hungarian literature and showing up without a single topic sentence in my head. Or I would be late and unable to find the classroom, or would be bringing the wrong notes for a lecture to the wrong class.

Part of the reason for my anxiety must have derived from the worry that somehow or other, by my own incompetence or laziness, I would be made to look shoddy. If I were teaching the same novel two years in a row, I had to reread it fully each time lest I lose some small point that a student might raise to show me up (though none ever attempted to do so). As someone with his own low threshold for boredom, I also had a horror of communicating dullness to others. I worked up anecdotes, inserted bits of (to me) piquant literary history, told jokes where appropriate, and sometimes found myself doing goofy or slightly wild things. Once, in a class called "Advanced Prose Style," I wrote out the words "to walk" on the blackboard and asked if anyone knew how to split an infinitive. When no one answered, I let out my version of a martial-arts yelp, leaped in the air, and hit the board with a chop, afterward remarking that this was not how to split an infinitive. Whether I did this to stave off their boredom or my own is a genuine question.

The year after I began teaching at Northwestern, I was offered a plum: the editorship of *The American Scholar,* the quarterly journal sponsored by Phi Beta Kappa (of which I was not a member). The pay was set at half the salary of a full professor, in those days considered to be $40,000. I continued to teach full-time for a few more years, then cut back to half-time, which translated into three courses over two quarters.

From this point on, I locked into a permanent repertoire: separate courses in Henry James, Joseph Conrad, and Willa Cather, with one of the trio giving way in alternate years, and always a course called "Fundamentals of Prose Style," my hardy perennial, for would-be novelists, poets, and essayists. I taught graduate students only once, and did not find it — nor, my guess is, did they find me — very rewarding. Their minds were set, they were in possession of a jargon, they had lost their amateur (or lover's) standing.

I was able to teach what I wanted because, with the rise of literary theory — deconstruction, the new historicism, feminism, queer theory, and the rest — nobody else seemed interested in what interested me. Meanwhile, I had also become mildly notorious in the English department on account of two articles I had published — one in *Commentary*, the other in *Hudson Review* — on what I regarded as the betrayal of literature by university teachers. This led most of my colleagues to avert their eyes when I walked past them in the hallways. I was left to teach what I wanted, then, also because I was a minor pariah, which was fine with me. My real life was elsewhere.

I never had, or really wanted, tenure. Instead, each year I would receive a letter from whoever happened to be dean of the arts-and-sciences college, inviting me back and offering me a token raise. The smallest such raise was for $400, offered by a dean whom I had insulted in a remark that happened to get into the newspaper. In the course of a talk in Los Angeles I had said that there were two cultures in America, one composed of those who had elected Ronald Reagan president by a large majority and the other of those, many of whom resided in the best universities, who would sooner have voted for Louis Farrakhan than for Reagan. To illustrate the cast of academic thought in those years, I mentioned that my own university was just then trying very hard to acquire the services of a Marxist professor of English named Frederic Jameson, and in the hope of persuading him to leave his current position it had also offered his wife a teaching job. Then I added that, according to a rumor I had heard, the university was even willing to kick in another $18,500 a year for the Jamesons' dog to guard the gymnasium. That was what got into the *Los Angeles Times* and earned me my derisory raise.

Not having tenure meant not having to attend departmental meetings, which was no doubt for the best. I started teaching just as the ancien régime was giving way to the regime of the politicizers. The battle between the older guard and the young theorists of race, gender, and class came to be known as the culture wars, but the war was lost almost from the outset. Today, in most English departments, the two-penny Saint-Justes, Dantons, Marats, and real-life Madame Defarges reign without much interference, though no one any longer seems to care. My negative feelings for them were quite explicit, registered through occasional writings on the subject — a fact, however, that also failed to win me friends among those who were still holding on, for the most part fearfully and surreptitiously, to the values of the ancien régime. One way or another, collegiality was not something that would be part of my experience as a teacher at Northwestern.

And yet I found myself greatly engaged by some of my students. The English department had instituted something called independent studies, in which undergraduates selected teachers to work with them on subjects of special interest. One of the first to approach me was an attractive girl from West Virginia who wanted to explore the roots of her own extreme shyness; she wrote a beautiful essay that opened with an anecdote of how, in the laundry room of her building, when a man asked if she was finished with the dryer, she, unable to tell him that she wasn't, began to remove and fold her still completely wet clothes. Another young woman wrote an essay titled, after Mary McCarthy, "Memoir of a Half-Catholic Girlhood"; this was about growing up in an intensely Catholic Chicago suburb with six brothers and sisters, about the falling apart that took place after the reforms of Vatican II and the removal of her family to California, and about her own current tendency to wander into churches of various kinds — Buddhist, fundamentalist, you name it — in the all-but-lost hope of replacing the religious upbringing that had been so dear to her. Still another student wrote about the strains of alcoholism on exhibit in the fiction of F. Scott Fitzgerald, showing how Fitzgerald had traced with precision the phases and manifestations of a disease long before it became a subject of medico-scientific interest. I thought this essay so good I published it in *The American Scholar.*

Of the few thousand students who passed through my classes, thirty or forty impressed me with their seriousness and the heat of their desire to do intellectual or artistic work. Some of them went on to become journalists or editors or writers. Others, gifted in various ways but unable to decide what to do with their lives, drowned in what Kierkegaard called "the sea of possibility." Still others, I have to assume, did not want a literary career sorely enough. On an irregular basis, most have stayed in touch and have become friends. Some of the earliest are now past fifty. My friend Edward Shils, himself then in his early eighties, once told me of a visit from two former students of his, one of whom was then seventy-seven and the other seventy-five. "Nice boys," said Edward. Only now do I fully understand what he meant.

As a teacher I attempted to establish a setting of good will. I did not have it in me to be one of those tough guys—like the legendary Norman McLean during my own undergraduate days at Chicago—who can heighten the tension in a classroom through the application of useful fear. I say useful because fear is certainly one motivating element in education. If you ever want to test this proposition, just tell a class that you intend to give everyone an A, that attendance is not mandatory, and that no one need take careful notes. Things will fall apart on the instant.

My own modus operandi in the classroom was to be a (very) poor man's Socrates, shooting out questions—"Ve haf vays of making you talk," I would announce in my best Gestapo voice—but grilling students lightly, trying less to embarrass them than to engage them in the significance of the proceedings. I was very pleasantly amazed at how little my students seemed to have been affected by the current academic craziness. No student ever attempted to turn Derrida or Foucault on me. I was never accused of homo- or any other brand of phobia. For a brief spell in the early 1980s, I felt the feminist pronoun police on my trail, ensuring that every "he" was followed by a "she," every mention of Tolstoy accompanied by a nod to Virginia Woolf. One year, at the opening of my Conrad course, a student asked "how" we were going to read Joseph Conrad, by which she meant what suppositions we were going to bring to the task: Marxist, structuralist, deconstructionist, multiculturalist, and so forth. I said that we were going to try to discover what Joseph Conrad himself meant to convey in his novels and stories, and that this ought to keep us sufficiently occupied to fill out a quarter. All I really wanted was to convince them that there was something called the moral imagination and that, outside of the way it played in the world, it tended to be found most impressively highlighted in serious novels. Most of them seemed to buy it.

As for how successful I was as a teacher in general, I haven't the faintest idea. Among those who took my writing courses, I could measure progress by how quickly their prose gained fluidity, shed itself of the most egregious errors, started to reflect the requisite degree of care and self-consciousness. But then I would hear from some of them a few years later and their writing would bristle with everything I had tried to knock out of them. Sometimes a student would confide that I and another professor were his two favorite teachers at Northwestern — the other guy being, inevitably, someone for whose intellectual quality I had a well-developed contempt. A girl who had studied Henry James with me told me, "I loved that course, but then I've always been a romantic." Since James has not the least thing to do with romanticism, in either its historical or its emotional sense, I had to conclude that one of us had been asleep at the switch.

Student evaluations were of little help to me. In my thirty years, only one was technically useful: "He jiggles his keys." (No longer, kiddo, I would think as I slipped keys and loose change into my briefcase before every class.) Although the assessments were preponderantly enthusiastic, generous, even sweet, they were also vague: "entertaining," "knows his stuff," and — vaguest of all — "interesting." Only one of them sticks in my memory. It read: "I did extremely well in this course, for I would have been ashamed not to." Good to know that if I could not or would not instill fear, I could on occasion inspire shame, at least in the right sort of student. Alas, my evaluator neglected to tell me how the trick was done, or might be repeated.

By my final year of teaching I had concluded that, although I could make good students a little better, I could do nothing to improve the mediocre or the uninterested. In fact, I believe I made some of them a little worse, by confusing them with my high-flown talk. "The power of instruction is seldom of much efficacy," Gibbon wrote, "except in those happy dispositions where it is almost superfluous." At Northwestern, most of my students had already developed the habits of achievement, but even among them, with their high SAT scores and the advantages of their middle- and upper-middle-class homes, only a small minority burned with the flame that Gibbon calls a happy disposition. That disposition has to do not with IQ but with passion, the source of which remains a mystery.

I always taught to the best students in my courses. I knew no other way. Of the three writers I concentrated on during my last ten years or so — James, Conrad, Cather — all were highbrows, with Cather perhaps more accessible than the first two but, in novels like *The Lost Lady* and *The Professor's House,* formidable enough in her own way. Conrad's novels I used to describe as Henry James for people who like the outdoors. As the years went by, I lightened the load of the James course until I was omitting all the works of the so-called major phase — *The Ambassadors, The Wings of the Dove, The Golden Bowl* — and making do with something I thought of as Henry James Lite. James is the true test for the serious student of literature, and not many undergraduates nowadays seem able to pass it.

Received wisdom has it that each year our students are growing dumber; one sometimes hears that they no longer read at all, but only watch television and fiddle with their computers. This is hardly a new complaint. As early as 1937, in a lecture entitled "Our Destiny and Literature," Paul Valéry remarked that the thick air of distraction in modern life had done severe damage to "the powers of attention, meditation, and critical analysis." Today's professors nevertheless seem to believe that their students are possessed of some special ignorance, and love to tell stories that italicize this ignorance: "I asked the class what event marked the end of communism, and one of them said, 'The destruction of the Berlin Mall.'"

I preferred not to go in for this kind of thing, remembering my own genuinely impressive ignorance as a kid from an unbookish home. Had anyone at the University of Chicago asked me, in 1956, who or what Diaghilev was, I might have answered, my voice atremble with uncertainty, "A city in the Ukraine," while worrying that perhaps it was a trick question and that Diaghilev was really the name of a Polish sausage. College professors will now tell you that none of their students knows who Mussolini was. But, then, in the mid-fifties I did not know who General Foch was, I could not have told you anything about the Ottoman empire, and great swaths of American history were as hidden to me as the sun in January at the North Pole.

The chief difference between my day and now is that, though the ignorance may be commensurate, I do not sense the same embarrassment about it. Occasionally I would run a little cultural-literacy test, asking my students to name the dates of the Spanish Civil War or to identify Leon Trotsky, Gertrude Stein, and Nijinsky. What was sad was not the small number who knew but the even smaller number who seemed to care.

This seems to me to have something to do with the declining national attention span that I mentioned earlier. The more I taught my Henry James course, the fewer seemed the students who appeared able to stay alert even to the point of following the plot. The last time I taught James, I felt that only perhaps six out of a room of thirty could really return the master's brilliant American twist serve.

Toward the end of this course, I led off one of the three sessions devoted to *The Portrait of a Lady* by asking a nice young man to describe Gilbert Osmond, one of the richest characters in nineteenth-century fiction. "Well," he said, without any malice toward me or any intention of shocking his classmates, "he's an asshole." (I suppose this marked an advance over the student who, in a longish essay two years earlier, had consistently referred to Osmond as Oswald.) Shocked his classmates may not have been, but I have to confess I was. Something, I realized, had changed in the nature of civilized discourse in America. I decided right then never to teach Henry James again.

In his journals, the Romanian writer Mihail Sebastian, who during the Nazi occupation of his country had to earn his living by teaching, notes that "neither my students nor my 'colleagues' have taught me anything new." In a strict sense, I have to say the same, at least about my students. They taught me nothing. What they did do, though, was remind me of the surprise of human possibility. I have taught courses that, so low was the intellectual voltage in the room, I felt the dismaying truth of W. H. Auden's remark that a professor is someone "who talks in other people's sleep." (Another, more pervasively truthful definition of a professor is "someone who never says anything once.") But throughout my years as a teacher — and especially in my writing courses — I was taken by surprise by students who displayed qualities I would not have expected to find in them.

In my last quarter of teaching, one young woman, who wore punky reddish-pink hair and a razor blade on a silver chain around her neck, announced that she was tired of the nonsense of alternating feminine and masculine pronouns and in her own writing always used masculine ones — "and I make it a point to say 'mankind,' too," she added, "never 'humankind.'" She also wrote wonderfully and without the least hint of victimization about her complicated family, including an alcoholic father whom she had last seen when she was eleven. Another young woman with the innocent look of a Disneyland guide showed an astonishing mastery of language and could sustain an extended metaphor over four full pages. A young man who rode a motorcycle and was a practicing rock musician wrote with terse but uproarious comedy about the zany behavior of otherwise intelligent people when they enter hardware stores. Still another young woman, with a fine smile and an ebullient laugh, handed in an essay about the treatment of migrants at the New Mexico border that was filled with lucid and persuasive political rage.

These were four members of a class of twelve that, for the nine weeks it met, caused me to walk into and out of it with a dance in my step. During our time together they were lively and bright, cheerful and receptive — everything one could desire from the intelligent young. In my closing words I said that if they wanted their final essays returned they would have to leave an envelope with their address on it in my departmental mailbox. "And I'm not talking about a self-addressed envelope, either," I said, "for we all know, surely, that an envelope cannot address itself." At the moment, it seemed entirely appropriate to end my thirty-year teaching career with neither a bang nor a whimper but a small puff of pedantry.

On the Road Again, Alas

SEARCHING FOR

THE GREAT GOOD PLACE

I T IS 7 A.M. and I have just arisen, two hours later than usual. My wife and eleven-year-old granddaughter are still asleep in the second of this two-bedroom condominium we have rented on Sanibel Island, Florida, which also contains two bathrooms and three television sets, all with VCRs. I open a light drape, slide back a glass door, and step out onto a screened-in balcony. The view is of palm trees, shrubs trimmed to a topiary nicety, a swimming pool filled with warmish, turquoise-colored water. Beyond are more palm trees, and beyond that, at perhaps two hundred yards' distance, teal-colored at this early hour, is the gentle Gulf of Mexico. Walking along its white-sanded, shell-laden beaches yesterday I saw dolphins frolicking less than twenty yards from shore. The temperature has been in the eighties, sunny, with occasional breezes. I sigh and wish I were elsewhere.

"Have lotsa fun," says an older man, white-haired, tall, deeply tanned, as he loads the groceries in the back of my rented Nissan Altima. "Gilligan's," a sign on Sanibel's Periwinkle Way reads, "A fun place to eat"; I make a mental note never to stop there. The only thing worse than "a fun place to eat," in my view, are those places that advertise "family fun," two words that, lashed together, automatically force my foot down heavier on the accelerator. I am no fun guy and have, perhaps you are coming to gather, a fun problem.

More than a simple antipathy to what my countrymen have decided is fun is entailed. My problem runs deeper. I have — as I have only recently grasped — almost no vocation for vacation, and, to make matters worse, I am losing my taste for travel. In the morning hours, before the heat comes up, people on Sanibel are bicycling, rollerblading, smashing tennis balls, whacking away at golf balls, jogging, walking with grim looks of determination on their faces. I myself arrived in Sanibel with no golf sticks, skates, or tennis rackets with sweet spots twice the size of my fairly large head. Nor do I find any pleasure in card games, crossword puzzles, detective novels. For a week's stay I brought four books with me: Balzac's *Cousin Pons*, *The Collected Stories of J. F. Powers*, *A Short Life of Kierkegaard* by Walter Lowrie, and *Auden* by Richard Davenport-Hines. I alternate among the four, read none completely through, and instead spend a lot of my time making astonishingly small and dreary observations, most of them about myself: for example, how my very white legs, under water, look rather corpse-like. What fun!

Before going off to Florida, I discovered that I owned no shorts. I bought two pair: one of khaki at the Gap, the other, of a light-weight gray, at Foot Locker. I packed a Chinese-red beaked cap and several solid-colored polo shirts and a pair of "Rod Laver" tennis shoes from Adidas. Such comprise my "fun" clothes. Packing them, I was reminded of the generations of American men who owned no clothes whatsoever for leisure.

I remember my father walking down to the beach behind our apartment on Sheridan Road in Chicago wearing one of his ribbed undershirts, dark blue bathing trunks, black wingtips, and silk socks with clocks on them over legs the exact whiteness of mine today. Alfred Kazin described Edmund Wilson, on the beach at Wellfleet, arriving in stained Panama hat, cane, and long white shirt (of the kind Brooks Brothers used to sell), "sometimes flopping over the bulky stomach in Bermuda shorts." This was his get-up — what you saw was what you got. There wasn't one Edmund Wilson for work and another Edmund Wilson for play. Why do I find that so appealing? If you've developed a strong character, why dissipate it in games and goofy costumes. The idea of, say, Henry Kissinger on a golf course, or Colin Powell and Dick Cheney playing badminton, feels plain wrong, does it not?

This past summer I was invited to sit for three days in a hotel conference room in Big Sky, Montana, where I rattled away with ten or eleven other people on the subject of *The Decline and Fall of the Roman Empire*. I accepted the invitation because I love that magnificent book, and love quite as much that extraordinary, ironic little pudge who sat in his study in Lausanne chuckling away, as I like to think of him, while writing it. Montana, which I had not before seen, was part of what persuaded me to accept the invitation. I planned to travel west from there, to drive through Oregon, Washington, and parts of British Columbia, none of which I had seen before.

On that holiday, only Gibbon did not disappoint. Montana and the Northwest provided, as advertised, spectacular scenery: staggeringly dramatic mountains, lush redwoods, dense rain forests suggesting the prehistoric. A turn in the road and, lo!, an azure lake encircled by gigantic conifers. Such trees were everywhere, causing me, at the wheel, to sing: *You're nondeciduous now, so what're you gonna do?*

Yet the whole thing, I found, was a bit much: a much of a muchness, as the English say. Nature in the Northwest was relentless. A beautiful scene, I decided, pleases but does not excite me. Seeing them in such abundance, one after another, it occurred to me for the first time in my life that perhaps nature was overrated. I began to feel about nature as Groucho, when confronted by the contestant on his quiz show who mentioned that she had some improbably large number of children, said he felt about his cigar: it gave him pleasure, he said, but he didn't want it in his mouth all the time.

Few things are more pleasing than to find what one thinks

one's idiosyncratic views corroborated by someone whose mind one much admires. "The country here is dotted with the houses of second-rate writers and painters," writes W. H. Auden of Taos, New Mexico. "It's curious how beautiful scenery seems to attract the second rate. For me, I like it for a holiday, but I'd rather die than live permanently in a beauty spot, at least till I'm much older." I am much older than Auden then was, and it still doesn't do it for me.

I was only a week on Sanibel. I chartered a boat to take my granddaughter fishing—a great success; I sat out at the pool reading about poor Kierkegaard's troubles, which were manifold; I walked the beaches, looking for exotic shells and picking up snatches of mundane conversation: "It's a junk bond, what'd he expect?"; ". . . her sophomore year at Tufts"; ". . . they're crazy to give Bobby Knight a job." I pass a tallish man, the very type of a CEO, in an orange bathing suit, himself walking the beach, saying into his cell phone: "That's no problem. Refer it to Jim." The weather was perfect, untoppable. By the third day out I longed to be back at my desk.

"I do not know what I am looking for abroad," wrote Montaigne in Italy, "but I know well enough what I am escaping at home." Might it be that I like home too much and seek no escape from it? Everything there is near at hand, order reigns, all is familiar, nothing unpredictable. But might this, instead, be a sign of a hardening not of the arteries but of the imagination and spirit? This last is a hypothesis that, like the late Duke and Duchess of Windsor, must be entertained.

I have never been one of those for whom freedom has meant a hasty departure for foreign lands. All my foreign travel has been conventional, the most exotic being a few days in Turkey as part of a Swann's cruise of the Greek Islands. I find I do not long for travel outside Europe. Travel in the Third World holds few enticements for me. I have made a mental note to visit India and Pakistan as soon as England once again makes those countries part of its empire, which is scheduled to take place, I understand, roughly two weeks after hell freezes over. I find myself in the condition of Philip Larkin, who, its being known that he left England only twice in his lifetime, was asked by an interviewer if he wouldn't like to see China. "Yes, of course," Larkin replied, "if I could return home that night."

I have a friend, older than I, who has probably spent more time in Kathmandu than I have spent in Manhattan. He is always off, aloft, driving a Land Rover over rocky ground, high upon a Himalaya, or mounted on a French bicycle the mere sight of which is almost enough to make me want to consult a proctologist. He is pedaling away in Greece even as I tap out these lines. None of this is my idea of a good time. Have I become a dull boy? Or was I, possibly, always a dull boy?

My leading subject for anxiety dreams for some years now has been travel. In these dreams, decisive things are always going wrong. I show up at the airport without my tickets, or money, or wallet, or passport, or suitcase, or — in one notable instance — shoes; in the heavy traffic of people, I lose my wife, granddaughter, cat (though why I am traveling with a cat is unclear). I am late, the gates are closing, people I love are inside the plane, taking off without me. Where am I going, anyway? (Non-sequiturial Africa, perhaps?) And why?

Why, moreover, do I have such dreams when I have had very little serious difficulty in my years of flying? I was once forced to spend a night in a motel near La Guardia owing to bad weather in Chicago; another time a plane out of Oakland skittered badly on the runway before takeoff and had to return to the hangar; and we, the passengers, were put up for the night and flown out first class the next day.

Those incidents aside, flying has gone smoothly enough for me. Sometimes, true enough, flying, which should always be an astonishment, has come to seem a punishment, at least if one is flying economy or coach, which I almost always do. (So, recently, I read, has the King of Norway, on a flight between Oslo and Mallorca, earning him the title, in the headline of an Oslo daily, "The King of Tourist Class." I wonder if he sat aisle, window, or got stuck with the middle seat.) I envy the first-class passengers chiefly the width of their chairs. But the people who sit in first-class seats do not otherwise appear to be very first class; they seem to be mainly salesmen and middle managers with vast quantities of airline "miles" and rather too wealthy ninnies willing to pay an extra five hundred to two thousand dollars to avoid the rabble (which is to say, me). Nothing further can, nor need, ever be said about airline food. But something about the combination of close quarters, bad food, largish bags stuffed into smallish overhead compartments, and the rest of it has encouraged a phenomenon that has now been given the name "air rage," in which while aloft one somehow flips, goes bonkers, makes specific threats, causing airport police to take one in custody upon arrival. The added nuisance of security checks after 9/11 hasn't made things any jollier.

I do not much mind air travel. I enjoy the tumult of O'Hare, Heathrow, LAX. A *luftmensch* to begin with, I read well in the air; I used to fly with a copy of Pascal's *Pensées,* which never seemed more pellucid than at thirty thousand feet. Sometimes I watch bits of the movie without the aid of earphones. I nap, write in my journal. It is only upon arrival that I begin to grow edgy.

The jolt of dislocation that a new country presents has begun to throw me more and more off balance. There is the language and currency to get used to, of course, but in recent years I have become, while abroad, a poor sleeper. In Florence I spent night after night twisting in the sheets while listening to the Vespa scooters roar under our window on the street outside our hotel near the Duomo. Insomnia and jet lag make a dreary cocktail.

Might it be that I am no longer capable of travel fantasies? I have never been abroad alone, and have no yearning to be so now. The chief travel fantasies have to do with meeting elegantly accented and extraordinarily beautiful partners on trains, in cafés, in the corridors of posh hotels. Hazlitt, who didn't do all that much travel, captured the fantasy well when he wrote that "the soul of a journey is liberty, perfect liberty to think, feel, do just as one pleases." Graham Greene–ish, really — but these fantasies are more proper to a young person; beyond the age of, say, fifty, they become the fantasy of that fool like whom we are told there is no other, the old fool. The travel writings of V. S. Naipaul or Paul Theroux tend to have a reverse, or anti-aphrodisiacal, effect. How nice, I think as I read the complaining accounts of their travel, that they have gone to Indonesia — now I don't have to do so myself.

"An effect of traveling in distant places," wrote Auden, who did a fair amount of it in the 1930s (his itinerary included Iceland, China, and Spain during the civil war), "is to make one reflect on one's past and one's culture from the outside." True, but perhaps less true than it once was. Less true certainly if one is an American and the indigenes in the country you are visiting are wearing, say, Michael Jordan tank tops and Reebok gym shoes. As like as not, these same indigenes will be going about in American jeans. Israeli academics, fearful of intellectual isolation, are encouraged to travel, and the place they chiefly travel to is America. After two centuries of suffering cultural inferiority to Europe, America, for better and worse, is where the action now is. Europeans come to us.

Richard Davenport-Hines, Auden's biographer, remarks that, as of the 1930s, "he deliberately unsettled himself, and until the final years of his life was always a traveler or voluntary exile, spurred by the intellectual masochist's need of the neurosis of estrangement." Hope everyone picked up those words masochist and neurosis and estrangement, for travel has increasingly come to require a portion of all three.

Auden suffered under the belief that "exile and isolation had creative uses." They may have, for him — but not for everyone. I prefer the view of Ravel, who said that he obtained more, aesthetically, from an hour of joy than from a long stretch of suffering.

Still, the party line has long been that travel is good for the soul—so broadening, so widening—and for no souls is it better than for those of artists.

Goethe acquired substantial intellectual dividends from his trip to Italy. Byron was a great traveler and always went absolutely first class, taking along his own horses and a considerable library. Keats, on a much smaller budget, longed to travel and was able to do so only when at the door of death. "I am a poet," announced Kierkegaard, "I must travel." But he seems to have gone only to Berlin. "Would Italy have cured his melancholy," asks his biographer Walter Lowrie, "and perhaps quenched his peculiar talent?" Useful to recall that the Königsberg Flash, Immanuel Kant, discovered the categorical imperative without ever leaving town.

"In order to understand one's own country," said Somerset Maugham, "one should live in at least two others." Here I would underscore the word "live." I have never actually lived in a European country, by which I mean settled in one place for four or five months or more.

The closest I've come is a few years ago, when friends lent us their comfortable house in the village of Laconnex, twenty minutes outside Geneva. This took us out of the hotel-restaurant flow of foreign travel—although during the better part of the days, apart from shopping for food, we remained tourists: listening to lectures at Madame de Staël's charming house at Coppet, museum-going, shopping, and the rest of it.

But it's one thing to live in a country, another to visit it. The visiting, I contend, is wherein the pain resides. Consider, to begin with, the people whom Henry James, prescient fellow, more than a century ago referred to as "one's detested fellow pilgrims."

A problem with foreign travel, if I may say so, is that one finds the great centers are infested by so many people like oneself. Often they are older and rather wealthier than oneself, though lacking, it goes without saying, one's intrinsic charms. But they are there for the same things one came for: as yet unseen works of art, fresh landscapes, different food.

They remind me in some ways of my father, who traveled scarcely at all, and then, upon retirement, set out to see the world and did a fairly impressive job of it. Up to that point an armchair traveler, seeing the world through PBS documentaries, he embarked in earnest at seventy-five to see it in the flesh. He first went to Israel. Africa south of the Sahara was next. He toured Norway and Denmark and Sweden. He visited Thailand, Hong Kong, and stuck a toe in China. He visited the Soviet Union and saw it again when it was once more Mother Russia. He went to Ecuador and Peru. He traveled to India under the auspices of — believe it or not — the B'nai B'rith. Seeing Alaska and the Panama Canal and much of the Caribbean by ship, he did more cruising than Captain Ahab and Christopher Isherwood combined.

His wife, my mother, though a highly intelligent woman, had almost no geographical curiosity. She had long before arrived at where I seem to be tending. She went with her husband to Israel, and together they flew to Paris on the Concorde, returning from London on the *QE2*. On many of his trips he took his still young grandsons, though on some he went alone. My father took almost no photographs and said very little about these trips on his return. What the motive behind all this expensive travel was remained unclear; I saw him mentally ticking off each continent and country he visited, as if it were his goal to see as much of this planet as possible before departing it. His need — make that his compulsion — for travel approached mania; he seemed genuinely happy only when getting ready to set off on yet another journey. And when, in his ninetieth year, he became too ill to set forth again, something in him died. "See this world before the next" was one of his standard joke lines. Now that he is in the next, I hope he is seated in first class.

I'm not sure what my father got out of all his travel. But, then, I'm no longer sure what anyone does. I suppose those who are committed to traveling feel a need to fill in the blank spots: to see those wonderful Velázquezes at the Prado, those charming Lorenzettis in Siena, those magnificent lion statues at Delos, taste that fantastic risotto in Ravenna. But the crowds — Germans, Japanese, Americanos, detested fellow pilgrims all — make it less than easy. "I hereby sentence you," runs a standard judge-and-defendant cartoon in a recent *New Yorker*, "to the Vermeer show on a Saturday afternoon."

Not funny, McGee. Not if you have, as I have, woken in the Jan Luyken Hotel in Amsterdam at 4 A.M. to drive to The Hague to stand in line in the cold drizzle of a Dutch morning to get tickets to see twenty-six paintings by Vermeer as part of a crowd that was even more wall-to-wall than the carpeting. One of the problems with the world, I begin to discover, is that there are too many people in it just like me.

"No hidin' place down here," the old gospel song has it, and it's beginning to seem so in connection with travel. One must be both rich and clever to find what Henry James called "The Great Good Place." In the late 1940s, W. H. Auden bought a house on Ischia, an island in the Bay of Naples, and thought he had found it. But in ten years' time too many Englishmen arrived to spend their holidays, and so he moved on to buy another in the bleaker landscape of Hirchstetten, near Vienna. Elizabeth Bishop thought she had found her great good place in Key West, Florida. Soon enough, something similar had happened to her: too many second-class poets and critics showed up, and so she moved on to Brazil where she lived with her friend Lota de Macedo Soares. But in Ischia and in Key West, Auden and Bishop were really the advance guard of the despoilers, their presence helping to make their retreats fashionable.

I have not been in either Ischia or Key West, but I have been in Mystic, Connecticut, and Santa Fe, New Mexico, and neither seems anything close to the great good place to me. Great good places are declared with some regularity — Aspen, Colorado; Jackson Hole, Wyoming; Big Sky, Montana — but as soon as they are so declared they cease to be either great or good but just places where people keen on the fashionable like to squat. The artists arrive first, then the wealthy, then the tourists; imprinted T-shirts and baseball caps follow. (Life is not easy for me, being a snob and a reverse snob simultaneously.)

While I stood in the great church of St. Mark's in Venice, all I could think of was what a vast clutter all this significance made. Walking through the Old City in Jerusalem, I kept an eye peeled for the serious shenanigans of the PLO. The site of Troy, now in Turkey, left me disappointed. Malcolm Muggeridge once wrote that he thought about God all the time, except when in an Anglican church. Parts of Greece and Flanders Field in Belgium excepted, I fear I am in something of the same condition with regard to visiting the great historical and religious sites.

"I am not one of those who go to Venice to experience an emotion," wrote Jules Renard in his journal. I take his — and he makes my — point. People such as Renard and I, who live mostly in our minds, don't require travel as an expensive lubricant for the imagination. If anything, some of us do better without travel. I think of Wallace Stevens, that most cosmopolitan of poets, who never went to Europe, but wrote letters to Mademoiselle Paule Vidal, his art dealer in Paris, asking her to acquire paintings for him with an amusing unspecificity of detail combined with strong general advice: "I should definitely like you to buy one of the paintings of René Renaud . . . Whether to buy a Morning or an Evening, a Bay or a Port, I must leave to you, merely reminding you that I like things light and not dark, cheerful and not gloomy, and that above everything else I prefer something real but saturated with the feeling and imagination of the artist." Why Stevens never went to Europe is something of a mystery — lots of talk about having to stay home owing to Mrs. Stevens's dahlias — but it's far from clear that the Europe of his imagining wasn't much more vivid than any actual Europe could have been.

The great century of travel for Americans was the nineteenth. You had to have money, though it could apparently be done without scads of it. In the nineteenth century Europe was more open, less tumultuous, and everyone wasn't rushing about as if waiting for the twenty-four-second shot clock to go off. With the exceptions only of Thoreau, Whitman, and Emily Dickinson, all the important American writers traveled abroad. Some went farther than others: Charles Eliot Norton, looking after his family's shipping interests, spent more than a year in India. Most Americans traveled to widen their culture among the monuments of Europe and the (presumably) more refined manners of the English, French, and Italian superior classes. "It is for want of self-culture that the superstition of traveling . . . retains its fascination for all educated Americans," wrote Emerson, whose best book, *English Traits*, came out of his stay in England.

But no American got more — aesthetically, morally, spiritually — out of his travels than Henry James, who at various times referred to himself as "the passionate pilgrim," "the visionary traveler," and "the sentimental tourist." Born in 1843 to a traveling family, James first went abroad at the age of six months and, in later years, claimed to have a memory even from that age "of the admirable aspect of the Place and Colonne Vendôme." The Jameses returned to Europe when Henry was twelve and again when he was seventeen; and they did not, you may be sure, go on the fourteen-day whirlwind tour but stayed for two or three years each time. In 1869, at the age of twenty-six, Henry James took up permanent residence there.

The international subject — of Americans in Europe, but also of Europeans in America — was one of the chief benefits of Henry James's travel experience. He had of course internationalized himself as no other American. T. S. Eliot said that James had turned himself into "a European but of no known country." Europe was, for James, as he himself put it, "ever so many things at once, not only beauty and art and supreme design, but history and fame and power, the world in fine raised to the richest and noblest expression."

He spoke excellent French, but finally never quite, as he might say, "appropriated and took possession" of France. He loved Italy above all European countries, and two of his greatest novels, *The*

Portrait of a Lady and *The Wings of the Dove,* owe much of their power to their tapestried Italian settings. A character touring Italy in one of his stories, upon remarking regretfully about not being Catholic to another character, says, "What a different thing this visiting of churches would be for us, if we occasionally felt the prompting to fall to our knees."

But it was in England that Henry James settled, and of England that in his journal he wrote: *"J'y suis absolument comme chez moi."* In the same journal entry, after cataloguing all that is wretched about London—"the fogs, the smoke, the dirt, the darkness, the wet, the distances, the ugliness, the brutal size of the place, the horrible numerosity of society, the sense in which all this senseless bigness is fatal to amenity"—he ends by concluding that for him "London is on the whole the most possible form of life." In 1915, with England at war, the year before his death, as a sign of his deep spiritual allegiance to the country, he became an English citizen.

Yet for all Henry James's cosmopolitanism, when he came to write his story "The Great Good Place," that place, though never pinned down geographically, turned out to be not "that happy land—far, far away," but "in the beloved British Islands and so near as we are to Bradford." The place turns out to be great and good because in it "The Great Want [is] Met." The great want is for liberty, tranquility, comfort, simplification. The burden of success may be set down there, and also the weight of failure. It is likened to a retreat, but with the exercises of piety subtracted. Taste everywhere is perfect; servants, though always inconspicuous, are omnicompetent; it is also likened to a club, but without any newspapers or bores about. One's fellow guests are all exquisitely simpatico. It extracted all the things in modern life it "was such rapture to be without."

The great good place replenishes the inner life and contains so many of the Jamesian grace notes: "the cool plash [of the fountain] in the stillness . . . the broad cloister of peace or some garden-nook where the air was light, a special glimpse of beauty or reminder of felicity seemed, in passing, to hover and linger." It is a place where the hero of the story "could read and write; there, above all, he could do nothing—he could live."

You will not be shocked, I suspect, to learn that the place, great and good though it is so designated, doesn't exist, either in life or even in the story itself. The great good place is the dream of the story's greatly overworked hero, who feels himself at the outset weighted down and all but plowed under by the trivialities of existence at the level of success, when one is most vulnerable to losing one's sense of life's point and purpose.

I have given up on discovering any great good place. I am fairly convinced that, should I find anything resembling such a place, I am likely to ask if there is a fax machine nearby and worry about my phone calls, mail and e-mail. I am a man who always thought he desired serenity, but (to apply some roller-coaster-like prepositions here) when you come right down to it, I am not really up to it.

Tourism is said to be a condition of moral rest, but I have never quite found it so. Tourism chiefly makes me edgy, morally uncomfortable. Might it be that the loss of a taste for travel is the price paid by people who love their work too much? I begin to see that, for me, such serenity as is available won't come with a background of blue water and palm trees, mountains shimmering majestically in the distance. It probably won't come at all. Anywhere you go, an old saying has it, there you are. And here I am. With so many miles on me already, I am terribly late in making this discovery.

Memoirs of a Cheap and Finicky Glutton

EATING OUT — I can recall when those words were filled with promise, and what was promised was swell food, an interesting scene, dressing up, a festive feeling, an occasion. The first serious restaurant I was taken to as a child was a Romanian-Jewish steak house on Roosevelt Road in Chicago called Joe Stein's. It was an upstairs joint and had large parrots in cages along its walls. The *spécialité de la maison* was lengthy strips of skirt steak and wonderful fried potatoes, both brought to the table, family style, on platters; also bowls of pickles, pickled tomatoes, and ice-cream-scoop-shaped balls of chopped liver that one spread on heavily textured dark bread. Flatfooted, world-weary, damp, slightly soiled towels over their arms, pencils behind their ears, the waiters had strong greenhorn accents and seemed to come out of classic Jewish waiter jokes: "Vich of you gentlemens vants the clean glass?" "Sorry, sir, dey heppen to be out of cream in de kitchen, vill you take it mit out milk?"

My first time at Joe Stein's, I remember, I asked our waiter if he had any soda pop. "Ve got pop," he said, deeply uninterested. "What kind do you have?" I asked. "Ve got red," he said, shifting smoothly from boredom into mild disdain, "and ve got brown."

I must have been five or six when this visit occurred. People did not then — in the mid-1940s — go often to restaurants with young children. People did not then go often to restaurants, period. Certainly not as casually and frequently as they do today, when they not only eat out all the time, but do so in odd places. A recent marketing survey in Washington state found that more people ate in their cars than any other place, including home. Drive-in restaurants, one of California's great gifts to Western civilization, were chiefly for adolescents, but now that no one is required to depart adolescence until heavy dementia sets in, why not eat with one's own children in the old haunts of the formerly young?

My own youthful gastronomic range was greatly limited. My mother, the best of all mothers, was the least adventurous of cooks. Although not Orthodox, nor even synagogue-going, she would not let certain — though not all — foods outlawed by Leviticus into her kitchen. No pork in any form was served, though shrimps were. Rare, even unto the lightest pink, beef was unknown; kosher chickens were, for reasons never made clear, thought to have more flavor than unkosher ones. Iceberg lettuce in those days held a monopoly greater than any dreamed of by Bill Gates. In our house, most vegetables and many desserts — peas, beans, corn, pears, fruit cocktail — came out of the can. Good at baking though my mother was (also at soups), Jell-O in exotic combinations was a fairly frequent dessert; so, too, bananas and sour cream.

When we went to restaurants, it chiefly meant one steak house or another, for Chicago in those years was still the site of the stockyards, and beef in all its forms was the *spécialité de la ville.* The standard "deluxe" meal for midwesterners in those years began with a shrimp cocktail, followed by a wedge of iceberg lettuce with Thousand Island dressing, then either a steak or prime rib and a baked potato for a main course, with strawberry shortcake or pie à la mode for dessert. All this, of course, was long before awareness of cholesterol, the first of many snakes to have crept into the American gastronomic Garden of Eden. Diets were not up for discussion. People didn't seem much to mind being overweight — "a little heavyset" was a frequently hauled-out euphemism of the day. The carcinogenic, far from being a terrifying factor, was not even a known word.

We were once taken out, with an extensive cousinage, by a wealthy and high-rolling uncle of my father's, a bootlegger in Prohibition days, to a steak house, where I, a boy of perhaps nine, ordered a T-bone steak. This turned out to be a vast wedge of beef, flopping over the sides of the plate and causing some attention because of its monstrous largeness. On the drive home, my mother, normally so gentle to her spoiled older son, upbraided me, saying that I had embarrassed her; in the future, when taken out by other people, I must never order the most expensive item on the menu. I hadn't noticed the price. Apparently, there was a slightly complicated etiquette — even an ethics — to dining out. One didn't always order exactly what one wanted.

My boyish dining out on my own chiefly involved hot dogs (with mustard, onions, piccalilli, never ketchup) and small bags of french fries, the two together costing a quarter. I first tasted pizza in my freshman year of high school, at a joint called Laurie's, and thought I had gone to heaven. Fried shrimp, at a stand called Davy Jones's Locker, nicely situated in the middle of a parking lot, was my next gastronomic thrill. I can even now recall the pungent smell of Polish sausage cooking out of doors on Maxwell Street — polio sausage, a pal called it, lending it a touch of danger during those years when polio was still a threat. Not long after, I was taken to the basement of a great Chicago restaurant called the Berghoff, where for less than half a buck (a phrase, John O'Hara once said, never used by any woman who graduated from high school) I was served a handsomely unbalanced meal of pot roast, German potato salad, and noodles, with a large stein of root beer.

Driver's licenses were available at fifteen years old in the Chicago of my youth, and a driver's license meant freedom, access to a large city with many secrets, not a few of them gastronomic. In our fathers' cars, we tested the claims most of us had until then only heard about. The best ribs in those days were thought to be at a place called the Tropical Hut, with its hokey Polynesian decor, twenty miles away in Hyde Park; the best pizza was Pizzeria Uno, its sausage being especially splendid; the best shrimps were those at a takeout place on Grand Avenue called Al's Fishery.

Viewed from today, when I find I can eat only one substantial meal a day, I am much impressed by my youthful capacity. (A contemporary recently observed to me that, as he grows older, the only activity at which he isn't worse is drinking.) My aim was always to eat as much as possible; satiety was not a notion I knew. After a light breakfast (two fried eggs, orange juice, toast), for lunch at a store near our high school called Harry's I would eat two bacon-lettuce-tomato sandwiches slathered in mayo, fries, and a chocolate square, washed down by a Pepsi-Cola. (Who, I wonder, invented the BLT? His or her identity ought to be known, for that person brought much more happiness into the world than any modern poet.) At home that evening I might eat four or five chicken breasts with a mound or two of mashed potatoes.

After a night out roving with the barbarian band that constituted my dearest friends, we generally stopped at an open-all-night delicatessen called Friedman's, where it was not uncommon to sup on a bowl of kreplach soup, a jaw-expanding corned beef sandwich on a kaiser roll, and another Pepsi or the drink known as a chocolate phosphate, with coffee to follow. Then it was home for eight or ten chocolate chip cookies, perhaps two or three fingers of salami, a few soup spoons of ice cream eaten out of the carton, and then eight or ten hours during which I slept as soundly as a monk.

When I was young, putting on weight wasn't a consideration. Despite my locust-like appetite, I remained thin. A. J. Liebling, still my favorite writer about food, said he grew up during a period when a diplomat weighing less than 250 pounds was not to be trusted. (Recall the deviousness of the "lean and hungry" Cassius.) I grew up at a time when stocky, burly, husky, portly, even stout were not insults; Moose was an approbative nickname; thick calves, heavy arms, and the beginning of a paunch were signs of manhood.

I ate less well in college, for the University of Chicago, that least hedonistic of institutions, provided chiefly brain food. Food somehow seemed, for that brief time, of tertiary interest. The United States Army was even worse, lean pickings for the finicky glutton I then was. On my way into the mess hall at Fort Hood, I recall asking a fellow enlisted man coming out what was for dinner. "I dunno," he memorably replied, "some red shit."

When I moved to New York in the early 1960s, my gastronomic range widened considerably. New Yorkers made demands of their restaurants that it would never occur to people elsewhere to make. In the simplest luncheonette on 15th Street, I heard a man order a sardine sandwich on rye toast, with a single leaf of lettuce, a very thin slice of onion atop it, and a light rinse of lemon over that — and then grumble because the counterman hadn't got it quite to his liking. In New York I learned about northern Italian food; I went to my first French restaurants; I shared a chateaubriand and roaring laughter with my friend Hilton Kramer at the Oak Room of the Plaza but couldn't bring myself to ask for a side order of peas at $5 (in 1963). I discovered great secret restaurants behind grocery stores in Hell's Kitchen — hell for the Italian immigrants who arrived there near the turn of the twentieth century to live in crowded tenements; heaven for me in the early 1960s.

Interest in food took a jump in the late 1960s and early 1970s with the rise of ethnicity. Suddenly everyone felt called upon to try the newest Thai, Afghan, Ethiopian, Symbionese restaurant. Food replaced movies as the interest of choice among the upper middle and so-called educated classes. One would go to a party and be asked, not what one thought of the latest Robert Altman or Woody Allen flick or (more important) what Pauline Kael thought of it, but if one had been to the recently opened bistro on Halsted Street or trattoria on Southport.

The age of competitive cooking had begun. During this time, I sat at dinner tables where a serious topic of discussion was lettuce. The phrase "just a touch of tarragon" seemed to come up with astonishing frequency. Ginger and dollops of sorbet were served between courses to refresh what were said to be "tired palates."

I enjoy pretentious talk about food; I recently met an acquaintance in Chicago for lunch, and he suggested a place that served, as he said, "a fairly reliable risotto." (Yeah, baby.) I don't, however, like to theorize about the deeper significance of food and the rituals surrounding its preparation and consumption. The secondary pleasures in life — food, sex, sport — are, in my view, better enjoyed for not being talked to death; besides, I've never met an anthropologist with a really good appetite.

"The French," one learns from Amy Trubek's *Haute Cuisine*, "invented the cuisine of culinary professionals." Trubek was set on her gastronomic path at the age of twenty by a meal at the first really serious French restaurant I had eaten in: Le Français, a restaurant not in France but in — of all places — Wheeling, Illinois, perhaps half an hour from where I live. Jean Banchet, its chef and owner, is everywhere acclaimed whenever anyone makes up a list of the ten best restaurants in the solar system, and, near as I can tell, rightly so. The food was expensive but — here is the bad news — worth it.

French cookery generally, in my view, has set a poor precedent, especially among the status-nervous upper middle class. French restaurants charging fixed prices of $200 and beyond feel wrong — and more than wrong when they charge more yet to seat you in the kitchen (as a place in Chicago called Charlie Trotter's does). I took a pass on the nouvelle cuisine stage of French cookery; I also took a pass on those French-inspired restaurants that bring food to the table in a vertical presentation; Viagra meals, the man who runs Morton's in New York calls them. I was in a Chicago restaurant called Avanzare, where a lunch companion was served such a meal and had to call upon the waiter to help him deconstruct it. Japanese is the most beautiful of all cuisines, but seems to me more elegant than good; and I feel about sushi, as the joke has it, that it is food fit only for castaways. But then between the raw and the cooked, I'll take the cooked every time: even sex tartare seems to me a bad idea.

In California, in Santa Rosa, I felt the French influence in what used to be a very sound restaurant when neither I nor any of the five other people at the table could identify more than two of the six main course dishes. One of the dishes was called Alphonsino. "What might Alphonsino be?" I asked the waiter. "Oh," he said, "it's a kind of red snapper." A kind of snapper, eh? I suggested that perhaps Alphonsino was the fish's first name. In New York, at the excellent Coco Pazzo Teatro, they threw the names of at least three pastas at me that I had never heard before.

I'm not keen, either, at having waiters break down the so-called specials to the cellular level. I've had enough of specials generally, and I have never met anyone who, when presented with more than four specials by a waiter, can recall the first two. I also dislike the new democratic chumminess of waiters: "Hi, my name's Zack." (Waiters telling you their first names has its dishonorable roots in the odious Playboy Clubs of unsainted memory, where the poor waitresses were instructed to begin by saying, "Hi, I'm your bunny, Karen.") I'm not keen either on Zack telling me what his favorite dishes are, that he has already tasted this evening's specials, or that he thinks I've ordered very intelligently. Take the order, bring the food, and bugger off, Zack.

At a Chicago restaurant called Ambria, the waiters not only bring out all the main courses at once, but lift the salvers from each with neatly timed simultaneity, a great *voilà*-ish flourish. At this same restaurant, when one of our table went off to the bathroom, a waiter appeared and took her dish out to the kitchen to keep it warmed until her return. Can one get too much service in a restaurant? Perhaps not. Still, things begin to seem a bit fussy in restaurants where the male waiters are more carefully coiffed than their customers, male or female.

Part of the pleasure of eating out, it seems to me, is to put a certain distance between oneself and everything to do with the preparation of the food one is served. Especially, if one is wise, does one want to avoid too much knowledge of what goes on in the kitchen. George Orwell, in *Down and Out in Paris and London* (1933), made nauseatingly plain the point that the more successful the restaurant, the more chaotic — and probably the dirtier — the kitchen.

Anthony Bourdain's *Kitchen Confidential,* the best book I have ever read about the nuts and bolts of running serious restaurant kitchens, doesn't speak to dirtiness but is brilliant on the tumult of running a kitchen that might turn out anywhere from two hundred to four hundred or so serious meals a night. His is also a book with much useful instruction to diners: you want to avoid brunches and buffets, which are outlets for previous days' uneaten food; because of delivery schedules, Tuesdays and Thursdays are the best nights to order fish in New York; much restaurant bread is probably recycled from someone else's table. Calling himself "a wrangler of psychopaths," Bourdain is particularly fine on the sociology of the wild, lost, occasionally admirable people who wind up working in the hellholes of restaurant kitchens, from head chefs to night porters. Bourdain has worked at the Rainbow Room and been executive chef at Coco Pazzo Teatro, and has been head chef at Brasserie Les Halles, but in his talk of food he is almost the reverse of pretentious. He's a wild old boy and a bit of a lost soul himself, and, being strongly anti-malarkey, utterly believable.

It didn't take me long to understand that serious fancy gastronomy was not for me. My own palate was a good bit less than refined. I don't think I am gastronomically disabled, but though I enjoy food immensely, I seem to taste things merely blatantly. Even though all the world's famous chefs seem to have been men — Brillat-Savarin, Dubois, Escoffier, and other famous culinary frogs — my sense is that in general women seem to taste food with greater sensory refinement than do men. (Perhaps women don't have the first-sergeant, kick-ass personality that is required to run a large kitchen staff.) "Men don't like complicated food," says one woman character to another in a Barbara Pym novel, and I believe there is something to it.

My wife can often tell with real precision what herbs and spices have gone into the preparation of a dish we have just eaten; I can only tell you whether or not I like it. And I like a lot, not least a lot of fairly coarse food. A Chicago specialty that gives me heightened pleasure, for example, is a sandwich called an Italian-beef-sausage combo, with peppers, a wet and dripping thing, the mechanics of the devouring of which would have stripped the dignity from General de Gaulle. It is a sandwich that takes three hands to manipulate, requires anywhere between fifteen and twenty-five small paper napkins, and costs $4.95, not including the dry-cleaning bill.

A man of selective cheapness, I don't like to spend too much money on restaurant food. I think of Flicoteaux, the restaurant mentioned in Balzac's *Lost Illusions,* favorite dining place of students and struggling writers during the first twelve years of the Restoration, which offered a three-course meal for 18 sous, a bottle of wine included, and "bread at your discretion." Today a meal that, apart from bar bill and gratuity, costs more than, say, $40 per person seems to me, somehow, morally excessive. Expense accounts long ago ratcheted up restaurant prices, but I, gluttonous and thrifty at once, still search for great meals at reasonable prices. In *Between Meals,* his account of his youthful dining in Paris, A. J. Liebling reports that the best bargains in food were those restaurants at which priests and prostitutes ate when they paid for their own meals. When I was a kid, the legend used to be that the best restaurants on the road were those at which truck drivers ate; perfectly untrue, of course.

I have all my days been searching for the excellent, reasonably priced Italian restaurant. While French cuisine may be architectonic, as Trubek argues in her book, my own preference is for Italian and Chinese food. An inexpensive Italian restaurant would perforce have to be a southern, or red-sauce, one. For years I tried the Italian restaurants around 26th Street, an old Italian Chicago neighborhood run by an alderman with the delicious name of Vito Marzullo, but with no great success. On Taylor Street the best Italian restaurants tended to be northern Italian. What I wanted was plain fare — properly cooked homemade pastas, fresh sauce, fiery sausages, bread that suggested spiritual nourishment — all for from $6 to $10 a serving. I despaired of ever finding such a place, until one day ten or so years ago in South Bend, Indiana, I walked into a place with the solidly cliché name of Sunny Italy. A sign at the cashier's counter read, "No credit cards." Behind the cash register sat a short dark man in his late seventies, complaining about the hopelessness of his grandchildren. El Dorado discovered at last. And so it turned out: solid, no-nonsense grub, fresh and good, large portions, the complaining owner's wife in charge of the kitchen. The only problem is that South Bend is 110 miles from where I live. I needed a Sunny Italy in the neighborhood.

Marcel Proust, the most complicated and impractical man in the Paris of his day, had the Ritz Hotel in his neighborhood, and used it to give lobster and champagne dinners for friends. He became such good friends with the maître d'hôtel that he had a key to the kitchen, and on occasion sent his servant and dear friend Céleste Alberet down, after the restaurant closed, for a very late night beer. I have in my neighborhood, all within a hundred yards or so of my apartment, a good enough Italian restaurant, a more ambitious restaurant that serves too many Viagra meals, a Nepalese restaurant, a Greek restaurant of the kind known among the cognoscenti as a Grecian spoon, and (a winner at last) a fine Spanish restaurant called Barcelona Tapas, an Irish restaurant, a French bistro, and a hot dog joint. A mile or so away is Kendall College, which has a culinary school at which I have eaten four or five times, but never with real satisfaction.

What's missing in the neighborhood — sorely, sorely missing — is a Chinese restaurant. Jews need Chinese restaurants. An old joke has it that Jewish civilization began nearly six thousand years ago, Chinese civilization nearly four thousand years ago, and so for nearly two thousand years the Jews went hungry. Jackie Mason, meanwhile, reports that though Chinese restaurants are filled with Jews, you never see any Chinese in Jewish restaurants. Quite so. This Jew finds he could, without any difficulty, eat Chinese food no fewer than three times a week, and to go more than two weeks without it makes him a touch cranky.

Not only is there no good Chinese restaurant within ten miles of where I live, but the great restaurant of my life, which once was in my neighborhood, has long ago closed down. It was called The Bird, in part because one of the chef-owner's signature dishes was a great delicacy that he called Crispy-Skinned Chicken, and in part because, phoenix-like, the restaurant had had many rebirths in different locations. I first heard of it from an English friend, then a visiting professor at Northwestern University. "It's rather pricey," he reported, "and not all that good." I didn't go there for a year. I shall always hold a grudge against this man, as would you of anyone who had deprived you of perhaps sixty or seventy grand meals.

Because the food from The Bird is no longer available to me, describing it, rather like recalling an old love, is painful, though I shall try. Ben Moy, the owner, is Chinese, but his cookery was so distinctive that I came to think of it as Moyan. He served courses one at a time, unlike the normal convention of American Chinese restaurants, where one's plate becomes a mélange. All his dishes were beautiful, without ever lapsing into the merely arty. The crispy-skinned chicken, a deboned chicken served on romaine lettuce with a dressing of subtle pungency, had a brown, burnished look, resembling nothing so much as the color of an old and precious violin. Mr. Moy could cut a walleyed pike into the most delectable morsels. A butcher in his earlier career, he always cooked his beef dishes to a perfect pinkness, and they sang with flavor. He taught me how to stop worrying and love squid — at least as he prepared it, in the most various ways, none of them rubbery or tasteless. He introduced me to green mussels. Every so often a hunter friend would bring him pheasants, the taste of which, with Mr. Moy's lovely touch added, made plain why Wallace Stevens once described great poetry as "a pheasant disappearing into the brush." None of it seemed expensive.

Food at The Bird was — how to say this in a single word? — honest. Mr. Moy went in for no exhibitionistic exoticism: no cheeks of veal, no head of pork, no *schwantz de boeuf.* His light sauces, piquant dressings, vegetable accompaniments, everything he did had only one end: to bring out the highest possible flavor in all he served. A great chef, he was a genius of a shopper. If he served a melon, it was, inevitably, the Platonic ideal of a melon. I was impressed upon learning, after we had become friends, that, with the exception of Chinese vegetables, he found most of his produce at the same supermarkets where I bought mine. Almost all other food, after Ben Moy's cooking, felt a little gross.

A year or so after I discovered The Bird, the restaurant did another of its phoenix turns, moving nearly twenty-five miles away to Melrose Park, a suburb west of Chicago, once the home of many of the city's Mafia middle managers. Twenty-five miles was not too far to go for Ben Moy's cooking, and I continued to dine there at least once a week for the next eight or nine years, with his annual Chinese New Year's banquets thrown in gratis. I would probably be dining there still, but an elderly gent, in a moment of mental lapse, put his heavy foot on the accelerator when he intended the brake and drove his Cadillac into The Bird's kitchen. The damage, Mr. Moy decided, was beyond repairing, and he packed his two enormous, magical woks and closed up shop.

The phoenix fluttered briefly one last time in a smaller location in Oak Park, where Ben Moy, who had all along given cooking classes, opened a cookery school, serving meals without a restaurant license to old friends, so to say, out of the back door. Another of these friends was Dale Clevenger, the first French horn for the Chicago Symphony. One night when I was there, Clevenger brought Pierre Boulez and a small party to dine. In the kitchen, Ben Moy, before carving a vast Lake Superior whitefish, announced that he wished to dedicate this fish to "two artists, Pierre Boulez and Joseph Epstein." I have photographs marking the event. Having a whitefish dedicated to one is not, I realize, the Nobel Prize, but it continues to please me hugely — and besides, unlike the Nobel Prize, I didn't have to share the whitefish with Sully Prudhomme, Saul Bellow, or Toni Morrison.

Not long after that, Ben Moy closed up for good, and like the Jews in the joke, I have been hungry ever since. Still, I shall always be grateful for the gift of more than a decade of superlative feeding.

I not long ago read the theory that when one is young sex is one's main preoccupation, when one turns to middle age that preoccupation changes to food, and in old age it is good sleep one most craves. To let you know exactly where I am on this spectrum, I find it a great pleasure to get a good night's sleep in which I have dreamt of eating course after course of Ben Moy's food. After a long career of eating out, I begin, I fear, to eat in.

Speaking of the Dead

IT'S ALMOST ALWAYS a mistake not to speak of the dead, especially when one has good things to say. I passed up a chance to do so a while back, and I continue to regret it. An acquaintance — one on the cusp of becoming a friend — died in his middle sixties. He was a widower and a painter, an abstract expressionist, who lived in the same building I do and earned his living as a designer — chiefly of children's toys. He was a quiet man, but he liked a joke, and whenever I ran into him in our building or the neighborhood I made it a point to tell him one. There was nothing of the showoff about him, and it was only gradually, after innumerable meetings, that I learned how much he knew: about jazz, about classical music, about modern literature. He was impressive in his gentle understatedness.

A few weeks after he died, a memorial service was held in an art gallery with perhaps a hundred people present. No music was played, and the element of religion — he was apparently a thoroughly secularized Jew — was entirely absent. Someone acted the master of ceremonies. Seven or eight people were designated to speak. Two of them read utterly negligible poems. Old friends told amusing stories, many of them about his ability to stand aside and coolly view scenes of domestic chaos. A few spoke of his earlier, bohemian days as a painter.

Listening to all this, I felt no one had come close to capturing his quality. This was an elegant and serious man, and no one seemed to have noticed, or at least thought it worth mentioning. The master of ceremonies, who wished to give the evening something of a therapeutic note, invited everyone in the audience to speak. I thought of doing so and then — out of a slight nervousness? out of fear of seeming unauthentic? out of a worry that it was not my place to do so? — decided not to. Whenever I think about him now, I feel a slight stab of guilt.

When my mother died, I felt I had to speak. The rabbi officiating at her funeral service simply did not know her well enough to talk about her in a penetrating or even mildly interesting way. When he did speak, it was, alas, in clichés of the sort that give no comfort. Whether I gave comfort to anyone other than myself I do not know, but I am pleased to have spoken about the extraordinary woman who was my mother.

I also once spoke at the memorial service of an older friend who I thought had a splendid gift for enjoying life: he loved travel, food and drink, the company of elegant women. He had as a son-in-law a rather dour clergyman for whom my friend's gift seemed a dubious one, and as it turned out, the son-in-law spoke less in clichés than in generalities: about the attractions of death, chiefly. He might have been talking about anyone, but certainly not about the remarkable man who was his father-in-law.

I was asked to speak at a memorial service for my friend Erich Heller, the literary critic, a man of great good humor, powerful learning, and more than a touch of intellectual snobbery. When I saw the program for the service, I could not but note that, of the five speakers, two were men whom Erich found, as he might have said, clownish in their pretensions and nonexistent in their intellectual qualities. If people do spin in their graves, then as the pair spoke — solipsistically and clownishly — about him, Erich must have been spinning in his.

I later learned that both these men had put themselves forward; they had not been asked but offered to speak. An axiom in these matters is that you never allow anyone to speak at a memorial service who too insistently offers, for he will almost certainly speak about himself, which is what these two men did, over, you might say, Erich's dead body. One of these men has since died, and a friend of mine has exacted from me the promise that the other not be permitted to speak at his memorial service, should he predecease me.

The memorial service is rather like live television — anything can happen, everything go wrong. I recall such a service for a Chicago publisher who had what I thought a needlessly complex sense of humor: quippy, overly ironic, frequently inappropriate, often missing its target. Five of the six people asked to speak all emphasized the poor man's sense of humor, furnishing, as I recall, no examples. (It was dangerously reminiscent of the joke about the funeral service for the man about whom no one has a good word. Finally, a man gets up to speak, clears his throat, and announces, "His brother was even worse.") Only the publisher's son saved the day by speaking about the man's genuine goodness as a father.

Recollection of such events is enough to turn one's attention to one's own memorial service — or, given the possibilities for minor disaster, to the question of whether one wishes to have such a service at all. I can think of three people I shouldn't mind speaking about me at such a service: one with a reputation for truthtelling, one with a fine ebullience whose comments are certain to remind any audience of life's delights, and one of whose love I am certain. I suppose I ought to make a note of this, and, while I am at it, choose the music I should like to have played: Mozart, Borodin, Ravel. Then again perhaps it might be better to forget the whole thing and instead leave a few thousand dollars to throw a party at which the word "death" is not permitted. This was what Randolph Churchill, son of Winston, instructed his heirs to arrange:

> I desire that my corpse shall be disposed of either in the churchyard of East Berghold or in the gardens of Stour [his home], as speedily as possible and with the least inconvenience to other people or expense to my Estate. Any of my friends who care to

attend my sepulture shall be entertained to baked meats and a cold collation at Stour and drink anything that may happen to be in my house. There shall be no memorial services. Bones (not my own) shall be provided for my dogs and bitches; but steps must be taken that the bones shall not be bones of contention nor treated like those of Jezebel.

"Of all the things in the world I think the least about," allowed Bernard B. Jacobs, in his day one of the two powers in the theater-owning and play-producing Shubert Organization, "it's what happens after you die. Dead is dead." Jacobs, who died in 1996 at the age of eighty, was nonetheless ushered out with a long obituary in the *New York Times* that spoke in a flattering way about his lack of pretentiousness. *Sub specie aeternitatis,* judged in the light of eternity, making a fuss over the dead doesn't seem to make much sense.

Quite right — and yet, and yet . . . One cannot help imagining what the world will make of one after one has shuffled off to some place rather distant from Buffalo. One knows justice is limited in life, but is it any greater afterward? Perhaps, but not, as a reader of obituaries I have come to suspect, immediately afterward.

In his foreword to *The Last Word,* a collection of obituaries from the *New York Times,* Russell Baker writes that "the obituaries are best left until last." They are the first thing I turn to in the *New York Times;* and, in fact, if it weren't for the obituaries, I probably wouldn't read the daily *Times* at all. Not that the obituaries are all that grand, but they do at least let me know who has been taken out of the game from those leagues — the arts, scholarship, intellectual life — in which I have an interest.

Sometimes the obits provide charming surprises. I like especially the modest ones. "Francine Katzenbogen, 51; Gave Cats the Lap of Luxury." Or: "Adelma Grenier Simmons, 93, Authority on Herbs, Is Dead." Or again: "Eldon W. Lyle, 89, a Fighter of Diseases Affecting Roses." And I seem to have kept the obit of a few years back whose headline read, "David Fleay, 85, Whose Specialty Was the Platypus." "Rest," I found myself muttering after reading it, "in Platypus."

For many years obituaries in the *New York Times* were written by Alden Whitman — the Angel of Death, as I came to think him — and most seemed to me perfunctory and some badly politicized (Whitman was a man of the left). I don't recall if any of his obituaries were actually vengeful, but if they were, it would not have been the first time that people have used the obituary as a weapon to kick an enemy who was already down. When the famous (in his day) agnostic Robert Ingersoll died, one newspaper couldn't resist noting: "Robert Ingersoll died yesterday. Perhaps he knows better now."

In recent years, however, the obituaries have improved as the *Times* began to interest itself in people whose lives had a charming oddity — people who did good works anonymously (a man who gave away gloves to the homeless), or invented things that you would have thought came into being on their own (the inventors of the Rolodex and the zoot suit, the designer of the Corvette, the promoter of the New York Marathon, the coach who started the huddle in football), or had a slightly silly success ("Bob Wilvers, 65, Ad Executive Put 'Plop, Plop' with 'Fizz, Fizz' in an old Alka-Seltzer Commercial"), or had fleeting fame (the little boy for whom Babe Ruth promised to hit a home run in 1926).

In death as in life, luck is an element. I seem to remember that the novelist John Dos Passos's obituary was demoted in importance because he happened to die on the same day as the Egyptian political leader Colonel Gamal Abdel Nasser. The *New York Times* nowadays tries, insofar as is in its power, to make death seem comprehensive through its selection of obits (a word that sounds, as Thomas Mallon has noted, like a snack food). On a characteristic day — Sunday, January 4, 1998, for example — it ran obituaries of a master grower of bonsai trees, a Green Beret leader in Vietnam, a former football coach at Rutgers, and the mayor of Scottsdale, Arizona, during the town's period of greatest growth.

Almost by their nature, obituaries tend to be skeletal (some metaphors are impossible to pass up). Usually not all that much space is provided: T. S. Eliot's Prufrock may have measured life with coffee spoons, but death is measured out in column inches. Facts must be fitted in, economical use of anecdotes and quotations made, and on to the next corpse. The *Times* usually assigns its obits to writers specializing in the deceased's own specialty: art critics on artists, military writers on famous soldiers and sailors, and so forth. But I have noted an interesting general-assignment obituary writer with the somewhat overloaded name of Robert McG. Thomas, Jr., who occasionally gets beyond the facts and the rigid formula of the obit to touch on — of all things to find in the *New York Times* — a deeper truth. Thus Thomas on one Fred Rosenstiel, "who spent his life planting gardens to brighten the lives of his fellow New Yorkers, and to alleviate an abiding sadness in his heart, died at Western Queens Community Hospital in Astoria. He was eighty-three." The sadness, we learn later in the obituary, derived from Mr. Rosenstiel's inability to "forgive himself for surviving the Holocaust, friends said." A fine touch.

If one reads the obituaries with a relieved sense of "there but for the grace of God go I (since I'm damn far from ready to go)," one also, as one grows older, tends to be dismayed by the deaths of people one's own age or even younger. Now that I am beyond sixty, I find it much more comforting to begin a day in which the obituary page lists three people who died in their nineties and one who made it to 105. It cheered me to read about "Gamblin' Rose Hamburger, a race track handicapper who beat all the odds by living to 105, precisely." On the other, sadder hand, William Vickrey, who won a Nobel Prize in economics in 1996, died, at eighty-two, three days after his prize was announced, which must have been extremely irritating.

Henry James somewhere says that, after the age of fifty, someone one knows dies every day. Not quite true, but nearly so: if one does not know the person who has died, one knows someone who knew him. Sometimes one is visited, in the obits, by figures out of one's past. On January 2, 1998, I read, "Richard Elman, Novelist, Poet and Teacher, Is Dead at 63." I knew Dick Elman in the early 1960s. He was afire with literary ambition in those days. It never worked out. He had, to begin with, the bad luck to have the same name (one *l* and one *n* short) as Richard Ellmann, the biographer of James Joyce and Yeats and Oscar Wilde, and those who didn't simply confuse the two tended to compare them — not to Dick Elman's favor. He was a leftist when I knew him, but the political element evidently grew stronger in him, so that, in his obituary, it is mentioned that he "described himself as a Socialist." His books never received much in the way of serious attention; and as he grew older, his publishers grew more obscure. He picked up teaching jobs at different universities. His first marriage went sour, he contracted another, had a daughter from each. The obit's photograph shows a man in dishevelment, bald with unruly long hair on the sides, squinting into the sun. Not an easy life, my guess is, with a higher than normal quotient of disappointment.

Am I reading too much into Dick Elman's obituary? Perhaps. But obituaries, which tend to summarize a life, also call out for such judgments. Sometimes they do this more quietly than at other times. The sentence "There are no known survivors" at the close of an obituary invariably suggests sadness to me. Reading the obituary of the Beat Generation figure Herbert Huncke — a man whose life was filled with drug addiction, petty crime, and squalor of various sorts ("he sold drugs at times and himself at others," his obit notes) — one wonders about the reaction of his sole survivor, "his half brother, Dr. Brian Huncke of Chicago." One remembers, too, that such lives, good copy though they make for the obituarist, represent vast heartbreak for their families.

Reading obituaries, one cannot help wondering about one's own. Will it appear at all? How many factual errors will it have? Will it contain something really stupid, as did a recent obituary of the Sicilian writer Danilo Dolci, who is described as "the Studs Terkel of Sicily" because he once produced a book of interviews? How brief will it be? (A woman calls the newspaper to place an obituary notice for her recently deceased husband and is told that they charge by the word. "Very well," she says, "I'd like it to read,

'Schwartz dead.'" The minimum fee, she is told, is $50, and for that you get five words. "Very well," she says, "make it, 'Schwartz dead. Cadillac for sale.'")

These are not questions that torture me as I try to sleep, but rather ones I think about from time to time when reading about the deaths of others. Besides, I am confident that, whatever might be written about me, I would be sure to find it inadequate. I hope its writer at least has the common decency to begin my obit, "Joseph Epstein, the writer whose works held great appeal to a small but select audience of highly cultivated readers, died last night of natural causes, a great-grandchild on his lap, while listening to the Schubert Octet in F Major. He was ninety-seven and in full possession of his faculties. Known for his suavity and charm, his penetrating intellect and amusing subtlety, Epstein . . ."

Writing one's own obituary reminds me of the only story I know about an obituarist, "The Cemetery," by J. C. Squire. In the story, a poet accepts a job in the obituary department at what must be the *Times* of London. Out of a natural curiosity, he checks the files for his own obituary and finds it all too brief and disappointing. So he adds a bit to it, and then, on other occasions, he adds more — in fact, quite a bit more, so that it eventually puffs up into a major article. Then one day he gets a bad conscience about what he has done and cuts his obituary back to the bone — making it even briefer than he originally found it. Feeling better, he goes off to lunch and, crossing the street, is hit by a car and instantly killed. The obituary is printed in its drastically cut version and generates outrage at what is felt to be the vast injustice visited upon the poet. His work is revived, his reputation restored, and his life proves posthumously a great success.

The editor of *The Last Word*, Marvin Siegel, closes his collection of obituaries on a thumping ironic note. The last five obituaries he reprints include one of a Brooklyn restaurant owner who was famous for his artery-clogging cheesecake but who himself lived till ninety-two; a seven-year-old girl who died piloting her own plane; a woman who lived a thousand days longer than she wished and had to undergo the full horror of life in a nursing home; a sixteen-year-old girl shot by a boy who didn't like the way she looked at him; and an account of burial at the potter's field on Hart Island, in New York City.

The point is, I assume, that the ugly customer, as Hazlitt referred to death, or the eternal Footman, as T. S. Eliot called him, isn't very discriminating in his choice of victims.

In his great book *The Ancient City*, Fustel de Coulanges writes about the founding of Greek cities around the gravesites of ancestors and reminds us how much of life in the ancient world was organized around the dead: "All antiquity," he writes, "was persuaded that without burial the soul was miserable, and that by burial it became forever happy. It was not to display their grief that they performed the funeral ceremony, it was for the rest and happiness of the dead." Maintenance of the gravesites, including elaborate rituals for remembering and even attempting to feed the dead, were central to the lives of the living.

Today, almost all the old pieties toward the dead have been vastly attenuated. Great numbers of people nowadays are cremated and do not even have graves. Churchgoing appears to be in decline, and so even when his family wishes to have religious funerary rites, more often than not the clergy do not really know the deceased and have nothing of note to say about him. Most people under fifty do not own graves for their own burial, in the way that earlier generations did; the majority assume, I take it, that they probably will not die in the city in which they currently live, but instead in — who knows? — California, Tuscany, or Paris. All this has made speaking well of the dead more significant than ever.

At a higher level than the obituarist is the memorialist, who writes under less pressure and usually at greater length. Unlike the obituarist, the memorialist may linger over the mysteries of character, attempting to tighten up loose screws, ravel back unraveled edges, explain the hitherto inexplicable — attempt, in short, to make sense of the life of the person who has died. The philosopher Isaiah Berlin, who himself died in 1997, did this very well. Thus far no one has provided a similar service for him, and most of what has been written about him has seemed exaggerated. Exaggeration is one of the great, perhaps the greatest, traps awaiting anyone who writes or speaks about the dead. The point is nicely made by the best joke I have ever heard about memorial services.

This is the joke about a Mr. Nussbaum, who goes to his rabbi to announce that his beloved dog Buster has just died and that he would be grateful if the rabbi would say a memorial service for the dog. The rabbi, after expressing his condolences, tells Mr. Nussbaum that Jews are not permitted to say memorial services for animals. Mr. Nussbaum informs the rabbi that he has no other family, that Buster meant everything to him, that he would be willing to make a serious contribution to the rabbi's special fund for working with inner-city children if he would accommodate him here. The rabbi, not an inflexible man, tells Mr. Nussbaum that, all right, he will do the service for Buster the next day in the small synagogue at 2:30. And so the following day, the rabbi goes through the service and speaks about the dog for roughly fifteen minutes. Mr. Nussbaum, alone in the audience, listens, tears in his eyes. When it is over, he approaches the rabbi, hands him a check for $5,000, and says: "Rabbi, I shall always be grateful to you for what you did for me and for Buster. It meant the world to me. And what you said about my beloved dog moved me greatly. Do you know, Rabbi, till this afternoon I had no idea how much Buster had done for Israel."

To have died without anyone's having captured the combination of one's idiosyncrasies, or understood the inner drama of one's life, seems a profound sadness. Lady Murasaki, in *The Tale of Genji*, notes that novels get written because "the storyteller's own experience of men and things . . . has moved him to an emotion so passionate that he can no longer keep it shut up in his heart."

Our experience of dead family and friends above all must not be kept shut up in the heart. We owe it to the dead and to ourselves to tell their story, to get it as straight as possible, to pass it along with sympathy reinforced by a dedication to truth. It is crucial that the last word not be — like that of Mr. Nussbaum's rabbi — a shabby, foolish, or false word.

Why I Am Not a Lawyer

I dreamed of a man with the greatest gifts — who would
do nothing with them, being sure he had them.

— PAUL VALÉRY

WHEN I WAS A BOY, growing up in a neighborhood
of distinctly on-the-make families, the phrase "professional man" — never, ever in those days "professional woman" — rang the success gong resoundingly. The neighborhood was Jewish, lower middle class ascending skyward, and
though there were a small number of fathers who were lawyers,
physicians, dentists, almost all had come of age during the Depression, when there wasn't always money for college, let alone
professional school.

In a strict historical sense, the professions include theology,
medicine, and law, but in the looser construction put on them in
our neighborhood, West Rogers Park in Chicago in the late 1940s
and early 1950s, the professions also included dentistry, at a stretch
accounting (at the CPA level), possibly at the very lower end phar-
macy, and I suppose veterinary medicine, though my guess is that
a Jewish veterinarian then was rarer than a Jewish coal miner is
now. Such was the allure of the "professional" that bright young
boys actually aspired to be dentists; the money was good, you were
allowed to wear a white smock, people called you doctor — hey,
what's so bad about that?

As an indifferent, in fact deeply uninterested student, I had no pressure put upon me by my parents to become a professional man. My father, who never finished high school, once told me that he thought I had the makings of a pretty good salesman, which is what he was, but he quickly inserted into the conversation that the main thing about work was that you had to love what you were doing or life could be hell. (Very sound advice, I thought then and believe even more strongly now.) Nonetheless, I have no doubt that if I told my parents I was keen to go to medical or law school, they would have been extremely pleased.

An old joke asks: What do you call a Jewish boy who can't stand the sight of blood? The answer: A psychoanalyst. The problem is that, even to become a psychoanalyst, at least in America, one needs to put oneself through medical school. When I finally roused myself to take an interest in things of the mind, science was not among them, or at least I found myself with small aptitude and even less background for it.

Accounting was far from enticing; I had a high school friend who evinced some interest in accounting, but when he told his immigrant and quite successful father about his possibly becoming an accountant, the old boy is said to have replied, "Lloydie, don't be a schmuck. You don't become an accountant — you hire an accountant." Dentistry was never a possibility for me. But law, law was possible.

The only lawyer in my parents' circle of friends — and he was out on the periphery — was a man with the good Jewish lawyerly name of Red Denenberg. He was always spoken of with the respect accorded a man who had insider knowledge, connections, someone who, if needed, could remove obstacles for you. Another family friend was a mild man named Joe Kaplan, who took a law degree but decided to forgo practice for the family plumbing supply business, where, I assume, the money must have been better and the combat less. Toward the close of his life, his family company went under, and Joe Kaplan fell back on his law degree, grinding out a living chiefly at Chicago traffic court on North LaSalle Street, where I once saw him, looking slightly dazed, searching out an errant client.

I had a much closer acquaintance with the lawyers in the movies of my youth. These were, inevitably, criminal lawyers: "smart mouthpieces," as they were generally referred to by the actors who played the crooks in these flicks. Many of them dressed like shysters: homburg, bespoke suit, boutonniere. The all-purpose smart mouthpiece from those movie days may have been a now nearly forgotten actor named Richard Conti, whose movie persona was that of the street-smart Italian, with a deeply dimpled chin, lots of black pomaded hair, squinting skeptical eyes, a dark double-breasted overcoat, and vast street smarts. The type was not without its appeal.

As a high school kid in Chicago, I believe I was already a fairly good mouthpiece in the making. I was aggressive — if not highly successful — in my attempts to pick up girls at Riverview Amusement Park, good at talking my way out of small jams, in the classroom much better at deploying words while on my feet than on paper.

At one point during my senior year in high school a friend and I decided, for want of anything better to do, to get a sweet little nebbishy freshman boy, heavily freckled and with braces, into our rather high-status social-and-athletic club on the sheer force of our arguments on his behalf. Each week during his semester-long pledgeship other members wanted to blackball the kid, and each week, chiefly through manufactured sob stories, we managed to talk them down. I usually spoke last. I had acquired a pair of horn-rimmed spectacles with window glass, which I removed in what I took to be a lawyerly manner, and addressed the jury on the kid's behalf. I hadn't yet heard the word, but what I believe I was engaged in was pure sophistry, which is to say adroit, subtle, and entirely specious argument. Need I add that it gave me immense pleasure, week after week, to bring it off, which I seem to have done?

"Live fast, die young, and have a good-looking corpse" is the motto of one Nick Romano, hero of the novel *Knock on Any Door* by Willard Motley. Nick, a tough street kid in Chicago, played in the movie version by a handsome young John Derek, lives up to his motto. But until his fall — he goes to trial for murder — his one protector, as I remember, is a lawyer, played by Humphrey Bogart, who attempts to save him by wise counsel and then in a court-room by bravura legal skill.

Although I enjoyed a mildly dissipated youth, by the time I was eighteen, I realized that my own motto was more likely to be "Live a little slower, die as old as possible, and let the funeral direc-tor worry about the look of your corpse." I realized, too, that I would live my life not by direct engagement but from the sidelines — looking on, not in on, the main action. Rather, you might say, like a lawyer.

The fact that I had begun to fall in love with literature might also have propelled me into a legal career. The law, I have long thought, ought to provide excellent training for the essayist or fiction writer. As a lawyer, one often sees clients in extremis, either in trouble or attempting to ward off trouble, filled with multiple motivations, loaded down with greed, anxiety, fear, anger, the hunger for revenge — in any event with human nature roiling away near the surface, and nicely italicized.

Not all that many lawyers have turned to the writing of fiction. John Mortimer, in England, has done so, with great commercial success, with his *Rumpole of the Old Bailey* and other crime novels. In America, Louis Auchincloss, through several narrators who are attorneys, usually in white shoe New York law firms, has investi-gated the demise of the old Eastern Seaboard upper class, into which he himself was securely born. Scott Turow, a Harvard-trained lawyer, has turned out novels with legal backgrounds, based in part on his own experiences as a lawyer in Chicago. Ste-phen Carter, a professor at the Yale Law School, has written a le-gal thriller called *Emperor of Ocean Park,* whose milieu is upper-middle-class African-American society, of which Carter is himself a part (he is a third-generation lawyer). John Grisham has written bestseller after bestseller with a legal setting.

But the best American writer about lawyers, James Gould Cozzens, was not himself a lawyer. In such novels as *The Just and the Unjust* and *By Love Possessed,* Cozzens wrote about law as a high calling, and with a genuine understanding of the inner drama of the legal life as one carrying a heavy burden of moral responsibility. Law, in Cozzens's novels, is never a job but a vocation, one that informs one's point of view, forms one's character, sets one's aspirations, imbues one's life with whatever quality it is likely to possess.

I did not read James Gould Cozzens until I was in my forties; had I done so two decades earlier, I might have seriously considered going to law school. When I went off to the University of Illinois in 1955, most of my high school friends, wishing to show their newfound seriousness as college men, decided to major in business. They took courses in accounting, marketing, corporation finance, and other grim fare. A number of them subsequently went to law school.

The city of Chicago was, and remains, loaded with law schools. At the top, judging by status, are the University of Chicago and Northwestern, then DePaul and Loyola, then John Kent and John Marshall, the latter two institutions, when I was young, providing night-school law courses. I have had friends attend all of these schools, and one friend who dropped out of Harvard Law School after a year, to become, eventually, a successful filmmaker. Some of the smarter people in the country seem to have done a Harvard Law degree and then chosen not to practice, beginning with the late sociologist David Reisman.

Having come alive intellectually, as an undergraduate I transferred to the University of Chicago. From there I probably would have had a shot at the University of Chicago Law School — which wasn't as difficult to get into then as now — and almost certainly would have been accepted at Northwestern. A major distinction obtained in those days between the two schools: Northwestern tended to feed young lawyers into Chicago's big law firms — Sidley & Austin, Kirkland & Ellis, and others. The University of Chicago sent lawyers all over the country and also created lots of law professors. The knock on the University of Chicago Law School in those days was that it was too theoretical, treating the law as an intellectual quite as much as a moneymaking endeavor.

Undergraduate education at the University of Chicago was itself as impractical as possible and immitigably highbrow: no second-rate books, no textbooks whatsoever, were taught. The underlying message of this education, the not so hidden agenda, was that the only things worth doing in life were art, science, and politics, the latter at the statesman level; if one couldn't do any of these three things, teaching them was the loophole that allowed one to think oneself not entirely worthless.

Had I decided to go to law school, and had I my druthers, I suspect that I would have chosen Northwestern over Chicago, not because it was better — I'm fairly sure it wasn't — but because by the time I was twenty-two I was eager to shed an academic atmosphere and get out into the world. But here I would have run into another problem, and this was that the great Chicago law firms to which Northwestern Law School was said to provide entrée were not welcoming — there is a nice euphemism — to what we might call (and here is another) Jewish-surnamed Americans. A few large Jewish firms did business in the city, but one had to have been especially brilliant to crash the gates of these others. A fellow I went to high school with, who did patent law, is said to have been one of the first Jews made a partner at Sidley & Austin.

I'm far from sure that I would have worked well in the context of a large law firm, even if invited to do so. My father's other piece of occupational advice to me was that "only a schmuck works for someone else." My wife's and my own family lawyer, a man a year or so older than I, went to Northwestern, briefly tried working for a firm, and soon departed to do the legal equivalent of what in medicine is, I believe, called "family practice." He does his clients' taxes, writes and executes their wills, handles their real estate closings, provides financial advice (if needed), does estate planning, and pretty much anything else he is asked to do. He hasn't opened his books to me, but my guess is that he makes a solid income from this.

Much as I appreciate having such a lawyer on my side, I am certain I myself could not have established and run such a practice. I am too egotistical, too frisky temperamentally to settle into such relentlessly detailed work, too impatient for clear victories and heady successes to work over such a long haul. What, then, do I see myself doing in the law?

Robert Frost spoke of "the road not taken," and I see that road, specifically, as Sheridan Road, leading out of Chicago to the expansive — and expensive — North Shore, the towns of Winnetka, Glencoe, Highland Park, Lake Forest (where Jay Gatsby's flame Daisy lived with her husband Tom Buchanan). I am driving a tan Mercedes convertible, top down; my own top is doing very well, thank you, in a $100 haircut; I am wearing a buttery soft cashmere jacket, the big wristwatch, am manicured, have what I call North Shore teeth (a $40,000 or so caps-and-implants job), and am headed home to a capacious house. I see a winter condo, perhaps in Palm Springs, possibly on Captiva Island. All this paid for, of course, by my highly lucrative law practice. But doing what?

Litigating, I like to think; a smart mouthpiece, after all, is what I am even now, except not on my feet in court but on my duff and on the page. Litigators are to law as surgeons are to medicine, or so, from the outside, it appears to me. I don't think I could exist for long on repetitive work, no matter what the line: I could no more do wills and trusts all day than I could check prostate glands or x-rays of the duodenum. Litigation — again viewed from the outside — seems sufficiently varied to hold my attention; the terror of losing and humiliating myself through poor preparation would be an immense aid. Guilt and the fear of shame have safeguarded me nicely thus far in my writing and teaching career, and I like to think that they would, as we nowadays say, "be there" for me in litigation, too.

But for whom would I litigate? On the side of under- or overdogs? A few years ago an attractive man in his early fifties showed up in one of my classes at Northwestern University; he was doing a midlife career shift, going from law to high school teaching. He had been trained at good schools — Notre Dame as an undergraduate, then Stanford Law School — and had more than made his nut as a lawyer. He'd earned enough, I gather, to allow him to end his life in (in effect) good works. One day over coffee he told me that behind his decision to teach was that he couldn't bring himself to defend another surgeon for sawing off the wrong leg.

Meanwhile, another lawyer I know, a man who had an early and successful career as a liberal alderman in the Chicago City Council, after losing an election for state's attorney, decided to do personal injury law, but of a left-wing, defending-the-rights-of-the-little-guy sort. He seemed to be making a decent go of it, but when I last met him he told me that, now in his late fifties, he was looking for another kind of work, perhaps as the head of a foundation or running a not-for-profit institution. He didn't say it straight out, but then he didn't have to: the law wasn't doing it for him.

Another, younger man I know, after going from Southern Illinois University to the Harvard Law School—a trip, measured in academic miles, slightly longer than that from Nizhni Novgorod to Miami Beach—could bear no more than a few years at a high salary at a large Chicago law firm after his Harvard years. He left for a job as a proofreader on the city's second newspaper and has since become a best-selling writer. The son of a friend, after Harvard and the Harvard Law School, put in a couple of years at the district attorney's office in New York City, then cut out for the coast and a job writing for *The Simpsons*.

Why is it that the law no longer seems able to hold bright and imaginative people? In his novel *Eve's Apple*, Jonathan Rosen has his young protagonist, still unsettled in life, note: "Law school was a word I kept lodged at the back of my mouth, like a cyanide tablet, *just in case.*" In another contemporary novel, Valerie Block's *Was It Something I Said?*, a young man dating a woman lawyer remarks that law is "an unimaginative choice as a career for a man," though still acceptable for a woman. Such squibs are not good news for the legal profession.

I have myself published two stories with lawyers at the center. The first is called "Coming In with Their Hands Up," and is told by a divorce lawyer about the intricacies of his trade during a time that society is falling apart. The title derives from a saying I once heard about two brothers with a divorce practice in Chicago, bachelors who dressed in homburgs, dandyish suits, and Chesterfield overcoats; it was said that if your wife hired them in a divorce dispute, "you might as well come in with your hands up" and you would be lucky to get away with your tickets to Chicago Bears games and perhaps a change of socks and underwear. No need to retell the story here, but its background is the nuttiness of a business, divorce, that seems to bring out the worst in everybody and in which lawyers rarely come out heroes.

The other story I've written is about a fix-it lawyer, also with a Chicago background, who has connections with the Mafia, the Teamsters, and Hollywood at the mogul level. Without ever going into courts, or even keeping a law book in his office, he is the kind of lawyer who could, as I wrote, "get the unions off your back, or get you a sweetheart contract, or get you a million-dollar loan out of union pension funds . . . He could get major zoning ordinances changed, or set in motion the gerrymandering of a congressional district. He could persuade all sorts of people in politics, show business, and sports not to be stubborn about deals and contracts. I heard it said — whispered, actually — that, should it be required, he was the man to see if you needed to have a business partner, or a wife or husband, removed in a quiet and completely efficient manner."

These are not the kinds of lawyers Alexis de Tocqueville might have imagined when he visited America for nine months between 1831 and '32. Tocqueville had many interesting and admiring things to say about lawyers in the United States. "The people in a democracy do not distrust lawyers," he wrote, "knowing that it is to their [the lawyers'] interest to serve the democratic cause; and they listen to them without getting angry, for they do not imagine them to have any *arrière-pensée.*" And: "If you ask me where the American aristocracy is found, I have no hesitation in answering that it is not among the rich, who have no common link uniting them. It is at the bar or the bench that the American aristocracy is found."

Tocqueville also knew that, where lawyers are absolutely needed, if only to guide people through the hopeless maze of laws they themselves have created, "they become increasingly separated from the people, forming a class apart. A French lawyer is just a man of learning, but an English or an American one is somewhat like the Egyptian priests, being, as they were, the only interpreter of an occult science."

How did lawyers go from America's natural aristocrats, from an almost priestly cast, to figures an increasingly large share of the population look upon as, chiefly, disastrously expensive to do business with, hopelessly pugnacious, and people for whom life is much better when they play no part in it. Something has happened to the practice of law over the past fifty or so years to cause it to lose its grandeur, and, in many quarters, even its dignity. To allow that one is a lawyer might nowadays even gain you the automatic contempt of strangers.

One sees something of the high glory of the law in the letters of Justice Oliver Wendell Holmes, Jr. Holmes was tremendously well rounded — and splendidly well read in all realms of civilized interest — but the center of his being was in the law; the essence of the man was that he knew the law, had practiced it, done scholarship in it, adjudicated upon it, lived with it day in and day out all of his adult years. To read Holmes in his letters is make one wish one had studied law. These letters — to Harold Laski, to Lewis Einstein, but above all to the English jurist Sir Frederick Pollock and to Felix Frankfurter — provide in bold relief what law as a calling used to be about and what serving that calling honorably does to polish and hone a man. Holmes could doubtless have served in the Department of Philosophy at Harvard with his friend William James or shone at some branch of science. But his engagement with law put him into the world. Fighting in the Civil War had made a man of the young Oliver Wendell Holmes, Jr.; the law made him a great man — perhaps, after Abraham Lincoln, the second-greatest American.

No Justice Holmeses in view today; nor any Louis Brandeises, nor Benjamin Cardozos, nor Learned Hands; nor any Clarence Darrows, either. Usually so wondrously prescient, Tocqueville was wrong about the trust in which Americans held lawyers, or at least he was wrong about that trust holding up. (Brutally rough lawyer jokes available on request.) O. J. Simpson's so-called "dream team" of lawyers—Johnnie Cochran, Alan Dershowitz, F. Lee Bailey, & Co.—would have been Alexis de Tocqueville's and Justice Holmes's nightmare team—as, I suspect, it was for many Americans.

How did the law as a profession seem to sink so profoundly over the past thirty or forty years? Do understand it was as a profession, specifically, that this happened, for during this time lawyers, in the view of those who have thought about it, became small (sometimes large) businessmen, entrepreneurs, operators, hustlers, lots of things that, whatever else may be said about them, are less than professional.

As long ago as 1934, Paul Valéry, speaking as a member of the Académie Française, gave an address called "Report on the Montyon Awards for Virtue." Valéry all but says the prizes for virtue are pointless, because virtue, the thing itself, has disappeared from civil discourse. "Virtue, gentlemen," he announced to his fellow academicians, "is a dead or at least a dying word," and he proposes that "such a word, through its very decline, can still teach us something: death confers a kind of supreme meaning on the dying term." Later in his talk, he adds: "We are witnesses to the extinction of various words and locutions which at one time described or designated what were considered the best or most valuable or most refined attributes of man viewed as a moral being." And he continues: "One scarcely ever hears it said of someone nowadays that he is 'upright'; *honor* itself is a thing of the past, for statistics are not in its favor. Expressions like 'an honorable man,' 'word of honor,' 'an insult to honor,' are not only dying but seemingly without substitutes in the language as it is currently used."

In this same talk, Valéry writes that he "should not be surprised if, within the next thirty years, the customs, the manners, the forms of social life practiced by half the human race underwent a change as radical as that wrought in the material world by the applied sciences." The changes he noted had to do with indulgent attitudes toward scandal, laxity in intellectual and artistic endeavor, the tendency to fall back on expedients in politics, commerce, and just about every other department of life.

The law has been hit particularly hard on this front. The reputation of lawyers depended utterly on their probity and rectitude; honor and uprightness and the practice of virtue are everything to them. Because of their privileged position, they were understood — and, quite as important, once understood themselves — to be held to a stricter code of behavior than everyone else in society, perhaps physicians only excepted. No one, I think, would argue that, as professionals, lawyers have been unable to maintain their former high standard.

Certain words that were once at the heart of the legal profession are currently unknown or have been so twisted out of shape that they have lost their core meanings. Consider the word "disinterested," which is now regrettably used as a synonym for "uninterested." Members of the legal profession, like judges, were thought to have a fine impartiality about them, the same impartiality implied in the word "disinterested." Fight for their clients though they might, there were things they wouldn't do; they didn't view their work as purely adversarial; and even when it was adversarial, they were felt to represent interests beyond those of their clients: they were "officers of the court," and they took that commission seriously; they had an investment in fairness, a deep respect for the law, a yearning for honor among fellow professionals. The most withering criticism a lawyer could receive was to be thought a hack among his fellow lawyers.

The word "partnership" also seems to have undergone a change in its legal context. In *The Betrayed Profession*, Sol M. Linowitz, in a philippic about the state of the legal profession that he loved, reports on how nearly sacred legal partnerships could be. He recounts that soon after World War II, the general counsel for American Airlines offered to bring the business of that immense company to the firm of Sullivan & Cromwell if the firm would make him a partner. Despite the enormous profits for everyone in the firm that would result from the deal, the offer was refused. Partnerships weren't for sale. During World War II, many partners who went off to fight continued to be paid their salaries by the firm.

Now partners in large, prosperous firms seem more like athletes under free agency. A better deal beckons and they are gone, taking their prosperous clients with them. Older partners, when they fail to produce at their old levels, are lopped off. Everybody apparently goes where the money is. Hourly billing is the name of the game.

Linowitz quotes Harrison Tweed, of the New York firm of Milbank Tweed, saying: "I have a high opinion of lawyers. With all their faults, they stack up well against those in every other occupation or profession. They are better to work with or play with or fight with or drink with, than most other varieties of mankind." It's not that lawyers had become worse than everyone else. It is that, like everyone else, their new credo seems to be "Show me the money," which makes them now seem no better. And no better makes them seem worse — worse because the nature of their work requires them to be better. If they are not better, they really aren't much damn good at all.

Some lawyers, resisting such arguments, point to the pro bono work that they or their firms do. Every nonlawyer nowadays probably has an evil-lawyer story, and mine has to do with pro bono. Seven or eight years ago, an African-American woman who worked one day a week for my wife reported to me that her nineteen-year-old grandson, whom she had raised, had been tried and found guilty of murder. Drugs were involved. He had been sentenced to up to thirty years. Was there, she wondered, anything I could do. The first thing I did was to call the boy's defense lawyer, who, I learned, had pled him guilty and charged his poor grandparents a $5,000 fee. I then called around to various law schools and law firms around the city to see if his case couldn't be reviewed, with the possibility of an appeal set in motion. No one at any of the places I called was in the least interested. They all did *pro bono* work, but only if it was, you should pardon the expression, "interesting"; that is, that it involved testing law or innovations in law or precedent-setting law. I don't know whether this boy was guilty or not, but up to thirty years hard time plainly wasn't interesting.

Perhaps because law has been increasingly stripped of its old and grand mystique, that of high intellect in the service of justice, in its own way one of the helping professions, as Sol Linowitz calls it, the very best people are no longer attracted to it; or when they are attracted to it, they soon feel lost and cheated, because the law is presented to them in its unadorned reality as business, an efficient form of moneymaking and not much more.

Had I become a lawyer, would I, I wonder, have stayed with it? Would I, now in my sixties, have felt mine a satisfying career or a mistaken one? As a lawyer, would I have had the character, which is to say the moral stamina, to practice law with the probity the profession has always required and without which it is no more than a used-car dealership without the burden of inventory? I like to think so, though I don't honestly know. Better, perhaps, that I became instead the writer that I am. It's a much easier job to be an investigator or critic of morality, which is what a writer does, than a lawyer, someone called upon to practice morality, relentlessly and at the highest level, day after day after day.

Books Won't Furnish a Room

AFTER MORE THAN a decade, our apartment is being re-painted. Rugs have gone off for cleaning. Furniture that we have had for more than twenty years is being re-placed. The sense of a new leaf is upon me, which has brought on the urge to live, somehow, differently than I have until now. No way could be more different than to remove vast quantities of books from this always book-crammed apartment. Books do, as the old saying has it, furnish a room, but, it has only recently occurred to me to ask, where is it written that they have to furnish *every* room?

"Of making many books there is no end," Ecclesiastes reports. Of collecting them it's even worse. Such were my thoughts before making the decision to cut back radically my library. At a rough guess, I would say that I owned perhaps two thousand books. I set out to prune this number back to four hundred or so. I've now done it, with the result that, like Henry James when he shaved off his beard at fifty-seven, "I feel forty and clean and light."

More than thirty years ago, I trimmed down a much smaller library. In my twenties then, I was moving from New York to Little Rock, and couldn't afford the expense of sending by movers the three hundred or so books I then possessed. So I called in the owner of a used-book store on Fourth Avenue. Off went almost all my books in a couple of shopping carts. I remember my sadness as I watched them go. Nothing fancy was included; it was chiefly the library of a young man, slightly Anglophilic, with literary aspirations: novels and poetry, some ancient and some British history, some philosophy. I had acquired most of these books during lunch hours when I worked on a political magazine on 15th Street; in those days I roamed the Fourth Avenue and University Place used-book shops, the intellectual equivalent of the drunken sailor in port, in Shanghai, after months at sea.

I did keep a small number of these books. Among them was a handsome Bodley Head edition in green covers of *Ulysses,* six or seven slender volumes of Max Beerbohm, and a six-volume edition of Macaulay's *History of England.* Until recently I continued to own these books — though, after letting them sit unread on my shelves for more than thirty years, I finally sent the six volumes of Macaulay's *History* off to my son. There I expect they will remain unread for thirty or so more years, at which time I hope he will pass them along to his son, who will go and do likewise.

I reacquired all the books I gave up and many hundreds more in the intervening years. Books long ago threatened to take over my apartment; and my guess is that, had I remained a bachelor, they would easily have done so. Any flat space is fair game to the book collector, and there are the stories of bachelor scholars — Harry Wolfson of Harvard among them — using ovens and refrigerators to store books.

My friend Edward Shils was too good a cook to permit that in his own apartment, where he kept some fifteen thousand books (with another five or six thousand in his house in England). But he did convert a small bathroom in his apartment into a book repository, having bookcases built around and over a bathtub and toilet and sink. Eight-foot-high bookcases lined the walls in all the rooms and all the hallways in his large apartment. Books, magazines, and manuscripts covered all the tables and chairs not in use.

You may have some nodding acquaintance with this library, because it appears in a spiteful portrait of Edward Shils in Saul Bellow's novel *Ravelstein.* "When you first came into his apartment," Bellow writes, "your respect for him grew. On his shelves there were full sets of Max Weber and all the Gumplowitches and Ratzenhofers. He owned the collected works of Henry James and of Dickens and the histories of Gibbon's Rome and Hume's England as well as encyclopedias of religion and masses of sociology books. Useful for propping up windows when the sash cord broke, I used to say." Not bad as far as it goes, though it doesn't go anywhere near far enough. It leaves out the delight acquiring these books gave their owner, who was not a passionate collector merely, but had read every book he owned and seemed to forget nothing about any of them.

As one of the trustees of Edward Shils's estate, it fell to me to dispose of this magnificent library. I hated to see it broken up, for it was in itself a work of art. But I finally sold it to a local bookseller who later, I am told, sold it to a small German university. There, presumably, it sits, used by earnest German undergraduates getting up various lengthy and heavily footnoted papers of a doubtless dour kind.

Alone in his empty apartment, surrounded by my friend's much-loved personal library, I would wonder about the purpose of laying in so large a supply of books. These books gave Edward Shils keen pleasure, and he put them to the highest use. Their pertinence was so much greater when he was alive to preside over them. Now they seemed inert, cumbersome, almost grotesque in their plenitude. Look on these tomes, ye learned, I thought, and despair.

The possibility of cutting back my own personal library first hit me with real force a month or so ago, when I visited the apartment of a new neighbor, a productive historian of America who had recently moved into our building. After he had shown me around his apartment, I asked, "But where do you keep your books?" To which he jauntily replied that, apart from some dictionaries and fairly standard reference books, he didn't have *any* books; with a good public and a large university library within three blocks, he didn't feel the need. His apartment seemed light, airy, much more spacious than mine, though it is in fact a bit smaller. And this man, please understand, wrote books that required serious research; he was no mere schmoozer, unlike another writer I know — me, who almost remained nameless.

An apartment without lots of books in every room? Was this possible? With the exception of our bathrooms and kitchen, every room in our apartment had at least one and usually two or three or more jammed bookcases. A small number of these books were my wife's, but the vast cumbersome majority were mine. The thought of living without books in our midst simmered in my low-fire brain for a week or so, and then, like a football team breaking with a resounding clap from a huddle, I said to myself, all exclamation marks: "Yes! Go! Do it! Now!"

Getting rid of most of my personal library comported nicely with my long-held fantasy of traveling light, existing with minimal encumbrance, living simply. A fantasy it has always been, for the longer I have lived, the heavier has my equipage grown. Neckties, spectacles, fountain pens, wristwatches, tuxedos, prints, small sculptures, and of course endless books — accumulation has gone on and on. I am a man who owns an electric shoe-shining machine. Far from simplifying, I have complicated my life; far from lightening up, I seem everywhere to have weighted myself down. But if I could toss off all these books, here, yes, was a felicitous start.

My library could have been much larger, you understand. Bulky though it seemed, I actually tried in recent years to keep it under control. At one point, when I edited a magazine that ran a book-review section, books arrived at my apartment in what it would not be imprecise to call profusion. Soon, though, discrimination kicked in, and I realized that I didn't need any books about the New Deal, let alone studies of the WPA, nor any on ecology, theology, technology, and a number of other large subjects. Still, I was a sucker for biographies of composers, the letters of poets, the memoirs of high-level European statesmen. Surely one couldn't have too many critical studies of Turgenev, or biographies of Matthew Arnold, or diaries of Mitteleuropean dilettantes, could one?

Turns out, one could, and soon I did. I began to weed things out, lest books threaten to take over, leaving me, like the poor fellow in Poe's "The Cask of Amontillado," completely bricked in — or, in my case, booked in. I began to tell myself that for every new book I allowed in, one had to go out. I ceased dropping into used-book stores, those pool halls for the bibliomane. I bought very few new books. Yet I continued to collect sets of books, such as the Yale edition of the works of William James in multiple volumes. Someone gave me the *Cambridge Modern History of Europe*, a mere thirteen vols. How could I turn it down? How could I not provide a home for four exceedingly well-edited volumes of the letters of Samuel Johnson? And so it went. My attempts to set up restrictions on the model of strict immigration quotas didn't come to much; the printed hordes could not be stopped.

How much of all this did I actually read? If I give the impression of a fairly well-read person, it is an impression merely. Much of what I have read has been in connection with things I have written. Like most writers, I am a slow reader; as a writer, when reading I try to discover how the better writers do it and, while I'm at it, steal from them what I can for my own scribbling. This tends to slow a fellow down. Gazing at my library, I realized that given all the hours I spend reading newspapers and magazines, I probably had more — much more — print on hand than I could hope to read in the time remaining to me on the planet. Getting rid of most of these books would be an earnest of my belief that life was finite, a fact in which I claimed to believe.

Having read a book, most people seem to feel it has become a part of their autobiography and thus must be saved, like an important family document. I am not among these people. Deciding which books to banish, I found an almost shocking absence in myself of such sentimentality.

George Orwell was a key figure in my education, but I was surprised to find myself able to let go his four volumes of collected journalism and letters without a whimper. Edmund Wilson was even more important, and I owned the two dozen or so of his squat books and four or five books about him. Those babies are out of here, and all I saved is a recently published volume of his uncollected writings (which I haven't yet read), *Night Thoughts* (his book of light verse and parodies), and *Shores of Light* (his first collection of book reviews). A. J. Liebling gave me more pleasure than any other journalist of my time, but at the moment this apartment doesn't contain a single baroque sentence of his. I also let go four volumes of Joseph Mitchell, though kept his *The Bottom of the Harbor,* because he sent me an inscribed copy. Orwell, Wilson, Liebling, Mitchell, these are writers whom I loved when young. That I so easily let them go will give you some notion of the ruthlessness of the man you are reading.

I tried to devise principles for keeping the books I did. Usefulness and rereadability were the best I could come up with. (Add to this pure pleasure: I couldn't let go of a small paperback of *The Lyrics of Noël Coward.*) I thought I had a few other principles under construction, but each of them, freshly devised, fell before my reluctance to let certain books go. No need for biography, I thought, but then I decided to keep a scholarly edition I own of Boswell's *Life of Johnson,* and also — why not? — Donald Frame's biography of Montaigne. I also kept a biography of John Dryden, because I've never read one. I let go biographies of Rousseau, Balzac, Hazlitt, Jowett, Emerson, Henry James, William James, Justice Holmes, Keynes, Edmund Gosse, Walter de la Mare, Vladimir Nabokov, Lord Berners, A. J. Ayer, and many others.

I sold off not only the recent biography of but all the books I owned by Isaiah Berlin — the complete run, I believe — even though over the years I think I learned a thing or two from his writings, especially about the great nineteenth-century Russian writers. Berlin put me onto Aleksandr Herzen, whose four-volume *My Past and Thoughts* I did not dispose of. I first read it in my late twenties, recall how rich it is, and dream of reading it once again before checkout time.

Yet having derived pleasure from a writer in the past didn't strike me as a good enough reason to keep his books forever. Not a scrap of H. L. Mencken is now in this apartment. I almost lost my nerve and saved the three volumes of Mencken's autobiography, my favorite among his works, but decided — steady, friend, steady — to be stern and let the old boy go without a tear.

Lots of history wound up on the book buyer's cart. I parted with 602 pages of *Russia in the Age of Peter the Great,* 654 pages of *Men, Women, and Pianos,* and a cool 1,018 pages of *A History of the Byzantine State and Society.* I kept mostly ancient history: Thucydides and Herodotus and Plutarch, the narrative *Alexander to Actium* by Peter Green, a few volumes of Theodor Mommsen on Rome. I sent off to a younger friend six volumes of the essays and lectures of Arnaldo Momigliano. No works on American history remain on the premises, apart from Tocqueville's *Democracy in America,* Henry Adams's histories of the administrations of Jefferson and Madison, and the historical volumes I have in the Library of America series.

I rid myself of six volumes of the plays of George Bernard Shaw without a flicker of doubt. The only plays I now have in the house are those of the three guys from Athens and the thirty-six written by the fellow with the receding hairline and large forehead from the river town in England. I'm not keeping a word of criticism about the man. But then I never have had much interest in the unremitting torrent of books of Shakespeare criticism — it is a Big Muddy into which I never cared to step, lest I come up, bespattered, in the fleshy-armed embrace of Professor Harold Bloom.

I watched the books of Walter Benjamin leave without registering the least fibrillation. Robert Musil's *The Man Without Qualities* accompanied them with the same equanimity in my breast. (I wish I had owned some of the French literary theorists, if only for the delight it would have given me to get rid of them.) I was not, overall, kind to German writers. I kissed poor Franz Kafka goodbye. I bid good day to Thomas Mann, keeping only *Joseph and His Brothers,* which I haven't yet read. I did keep a few items—in paperback—of Nietzsche and two of three promised volumes of a biography of Goethe by Nicholas Boyle, along with *Conversations with Eckermann.* Goethe is a writer I'd rather read about than actually read. I kept a few Schopenhauer items, including *The World as Will and Representation;* his unrelenting darkness for some reason charms me.

I shall genuinely miss a number of books I couldn't somehow justify keeping: Delacroix's *Journals* and Julius Meier-Graefe's *Vincent van Gogh,* though I felt no qualms about unburdening myself of ten books by E. H. Gombrich. I shall miss the amusing and highly idiosyncratic books on France and French culture by Richard Cobb. I gave up a deluxe paperback set of Anthony Powell's *A Dance to the Music of Time,* which provided much delight when I first read it. I gave up, too, the six volumes, in another deluxe paperback edition, of Casanova's memoirs, which I've never read and probably never will. Leaving the room in which they sat, I used occasionally to run my index finger across their spines and pose the query, "Yo, Giacomo, getting much?"

Asked if he read novels, the English philosopher Gilbert Ryle replied, "Yes, all six," by which he meant the six novels of Jane Austen. For someone who reads more novels and stories than anything else—"the biography you can make up," Peter Ackroyd once said, "the fiction has to be the truth"—I am not keeping all that much fiction. I did hold on to my Oxford University Press edition of Jane Austen. I kept a two-volume boxed edition of the stories of Somerset Maugham. I retained three volumes of Jorge Luis Borges—stories, poems, nonfictions—that astonishing blind man of Buenos Aires who, through the purity of his literary impulse, turned himself into a figure in world literature.

The Russians did not do well in this purge. I let go all the stories of Chekhov, plus two biographies and two collections of letters, even though he is a writer for whom I have great admiration; I kept a two-volume Penguin edition of *War and Peace,* but no

Dostoyevsky whatsoever. I retained the *Complete Stories of Vladimir Nabokov* and *Speak, Memory*, but not *Lolita*. In paperback, I've kept seven Balzac novels and *The Leopard* and *Confessions of Zeno*, the latter two swell continental novels that I love and hope one day to reread.

I retained books of poetry by Cavafy, Eliot, Stevens, Frost, Larkin, Leopardi, Auden, MacNeice, Betjeman, L. E. Sissman, Henri Coulette, Howard Nemerov, and Czeslaw Milosz, among others. I'm also holding on to that most impenetrable of modern books, *Finnegans Wake*, on the assumption that one ought to have at least one book, no matter how small one's library, that one will never quite get around to reading. Except for that by T. S. Eliot and Randall Jarrell, all criticism of poetry got the delete key.

Keep no writing about other writers, I announced early in the game, but then I found myself making a few exceptions. I couldn't let go of Samuel Johnson's *Lives of the Poets*. I kept Paul Valéry and Desmond MacCarthy on literature, Clement Greenberg on art, Edwin Denby on dance, and Donald Tovey on music. I seem to have written four books of essays on literature myself; these — you will be shocked to learn — were given special dispensation and have been allowed to remain; also nine other of my books, sacred and profane. I also kept the two copies each of two books in Yiddish that my grandfather wrote and that my father paid to have published. I hope my own grandson will one day be as kind to me.

I let go of nearly a full bookcase of books of music criticism and biography, though keeping two volumes of my late friend Samuel Lipman's essays on music. I hesitated about saving some Virgil Thomson, whose prose is always a good reminder of what lucidity looks like, but finally cut him loose. I had less compunction about seeing off the less than lucent books of Charles Rosen and the vastly more fluent ones of Ernest Newman. I have always enjoyed reading things by and about Stravinsky, but I retained only a slim book of his called *Memories and Commentaries*. I kept a book of Ravel's writings, because he is in my pantheon of modern artists, not alone for his elegant music but for saying that he got more artistic use out of an hour of joy than out of months of suffering. Lots of musical biographies will now have new homes. Was I ever really going to find time to read a five-hundred-plus-page biography of Gabriel Fauré? Not, I strongly suspect, in this life; and perhaps not in the next life, either. I had meant to keep a collection of pieces by Proust's friend the composer Reynaldo Hahn, but it got away.

Proust, however, didn't. I saved a full shelf of Proust, in a glass (if not cork-lined) bookcase, along with three fat Proust biographies. Proust is among a small number of writers whom I not only love to read but can endlessly read about. Henry James, Edward Gibbon, and George Santayana are three others, and I kept all of their books that I had (most of James's fiction is in my Library of America volumes). The works of these four writers, along with those of Max Beerbohm, fill one bookcase.

What does it say about me, I wonder, that after a lifetime of reading, these are the five writers about whom I care most? Three of the five were overweight. None was exactly a sexual conquistador. All took up a detached attitude toward the life of their times —the entire quintet produced no children—and cared tremendously about style. I would love to tell you what the deeper meaning of my love for them is, but I cannot because I gave away my six volumes of the *Collected Papers of Sigmund Freud,* and though I kept the two-volume *Principles of Psychology* by William James, I don't think he will be much help in this line.

I kept thirty or so reference books: French, Latin, Italian, and German dictionaries, *The Oxford Classical Dictionary, Bartlett's* and *The Oxford Dictionary of Quotations,* H. W. Fowler's *Modern English Usage, Chambers Biographical Dictionary,* a couple of music dictionaries, a French and an English grammar, the excellent *Brewer's Dictionary of Phrase and Fable,* and (my main man) *Webster's Collegiate Dictionary.* I once yearned to own the multivolume *Oxford English Dictionary,* but now that I have the use of it through my computer, I have ceased to long for its bulky, magisterial presence on my shelves. I had two sets of the *Encyclopaedia Britannica,* for which I long ago worked, and unloaded the later one, which

Mortimer J. Adler mucked up by dividing it into dreary things called Propaedia, Macropaedia, and Micropaedia.

I need a new coffee table, if only to support the small number of coffee table books I have kept. These include a volume of the drawings of Piranesi and another of those of Saul Steinberg and a third of the caricatures of Max Beerbohm and a fourth and fifth of the photographs of Henri Cartier-Bresson and Atget. Add to this a volume on Vermeer and a collection of the drawings and cartoons of Ralph Barton.

I have three different Bibles in the apartment—a work, the Bible, I've not yet read all the way through and tell myself I must before I am hit with a most unpleasant quiz administered at certain pearly gates. I unloaded Maimonides's *Guide for the Perplexed*, since I am myself far too perplexed on the subjects of which he writes to make much use of it. I let go two works on Jewish mysticism, reasoning that I am still a long way from mastering Jewish rationalism. I did keep one volume of Plato and two containing all of Aristotle. I also kept nine slender volumes, most of them in paperback, of Wittgenstein—not because I pretend to understand him or that he gives me solace but because I like the shape of his sentences, even in English translation. Of the French *moralistes*, I retained La Rochefoucauld and La Bruyère, but let Joubert and Chamfort go. I shall know where to find those boys if I need them.

I'm counting, really, on finding any books I need at my nearby libraries. One of the longstanding clichés of book owning is that, as soon as one gives a book away, one instantly has need of it. Doubtless it is fine to have all the books one requires at hand, so that one need only step into the next room to discover the precise phrasing of that quotation, date of that royal marriage, spelling of that place name. But the best way to arrange this is to move into the library, living the way certain wealthy retired men choose to do on the edge of a golf course.

I have almost as little desire to live in a library as I do on a golf course. I seek a compromise: living in a place where not every wall has a bookcase. I hope that by now the book collector's impulse is dead in me. With luck, I expect always to have the right books to keep my mind engaged, to put me gently to sleep at night, to be on hand to distract me during bouts of insomnia. I'm far from ready to go so far as Philip Larkin and say that "books are a load of crap." But in selling off my books I felt I was freeing myself in some way, entering another stage in life—though I'm not altogether clear what it might be. Behind my selling all these books was a longing to streamline my life a bit, make it feel less cluttered, encumbered, book-bound. In doing so, I feel as if I had gathered my desert-island books about me without actually having to sail off for the island.

Fine things, books, but perhaps the moment has come to stop taking them so seriously. Who was it said that people who are always reading never discover anything? I'm not sure if that is true, but I do know that reading and thinking are not necessarily the same thing. Sometimes reading supplies the most cunning of all means of avoiding thought. It would be good once in a while to try thinking without the stimulus of books, to become not an out-of-the-box—never, please, that—but at least an out-of-the-book thinker. Books may furnish a room, but there surely are other things quite as suitable for furnishing a mind. Time, I think, for me to attempt to find out what these might be.

II

Literary

The Intimate Abstraction
of Paul Valéry

Always demand Proof, proof is the
elementary courtesy that is anyone's due.

— VALÉRY, *Monsieur Teste*

T HE NAME PAUL VALÉRY carries its own music. For those
who know something of what lies behind it, the music
deepens, is suggestive, and always richly complex. ("Complex," said Ravel, about his own artistic aims, "never complicated.") To know Valéry only from his melodious but difficult poems — "Le Cimitière marin," "La Jeune Parque," and others — turns
out to be to know him scarcely at all. "Poetry," he wrote, "has
never been a goal for me — more an instrument, an exercise, and
its character derives from this — an artifice — product of will." Poetry provided him with fame, but he found his real intellectual
stimulation elsewhere.

Today, Valéry is perhaps best known for his aphoristic remarks,
inevitably both brilliant and running against received opinion.
Glimpse Valéry's name on the page and one knows something
immensely clarifying, possibly life-altering, awaits. "Everything
changes but the avant-garde" is one example. "The future, like
everything else, is not what it used to be" is another. "History is
the science of things which do not repeat themselves" is a third.

Without too much effort, one could record three or four hundred Valéryan remarks of equal charm and intellectual provocation.

"Remarks are not literature," Gertrude Stein is supposed to have said to Ernest Hemingway. She was wrong; all depends on the quality of the remarks. But then Stein's stricture would not much have bothered Paul Valéry, who did not think "literature" a purely honorific word. For him literature is a construct, made for entertainment, instruction, excitation, and many other things that are not quite the truth. "There's always a rather sordid side to literature," he wrote in his *Cahiers*, "a lurking deference to one's public. Hence the mental reservations, the ulterior motives basic to every form of charlatanism. Thus every literary production is an 'impure' product."

Although Valéry came to public notice as a young poet, what most interested him was the intellectual operation of the mind; the search for the truth about the way the mind works in cerebration, the mechanics of its functioning, was his main passion. He sought, as he himself late in life put it, "to know the substratum of thought and sensibility on which one has lived." In his *Cahiers*, again, he wrote: "I would like to have classified and clarified my personal forms of thought, and learned to think within them in such a way that each new thought bore the imprint of the whole system generating it and was unmistakably a modification of a well-defined system."

The way Valéry went about this enterprise is not the least astonishing thing about this extraordinary man. After a lustrous beginning as a poet — he met and early fell under the influence of that saint of modernism, Stéphane Mallarmé — he stopped writing poems for twenty years, beginning in 1892, when he was twenty-one. While making a living for a wife and children through employment with the French War Ministry and later as private secretary to one of the chief executives for the Paris financial conglomerate Agence Havas, he worked out his ideas, chiefly in private, in 261 notebooks, which he wrote during the early morning hours.

· · ·

Harry Kessler, in his journals, described the middle-aged Valéry as resembling nothing so much as a French marquis. French to the highest power though Valéry has always seemed, from the accent *aigu* in his name to the chill clarity that he invariably brought to matters of the highest abstraction — *C'est qui n'est pas clair, n'est pas français* — Valéry's father, a customs officer, was Corsican and his mother came of a northern Italian family. His upbringing was in the French Mediterranean seacoast city of Cette. He was, like Baudelaire, Henry James, and so many literary men who went on to have unconventional points of view, rather a poor student; most of his serious reading was done away from school. He thought of a naval career, but was washed out by his poor math; he went to law school at the Université de Montepellier, where he developed a serious interest in science and mathematics, and began writing poems. He met Pierre Louÿs, later the author of erotic novels written in a Hellenistic vein, who introduced him to the poetry of Mallarmé.

When Valéry sent Mallarmé a few of his poems, the older man returned them with the comment that "the gift of analogy along with adequate music are already yours and they are all that count." Mallarmé would later write that one of Valéry's early published poems "charms me." Valéry, meanwhile, after having moved to Paris, became part of the coterie of young poets and belletrists who met to discuss literary questions at Mallarmé's apartment on Tuesdays.

But on the night of October 4, 1892, in Genoa, Valéry had a vision, an epiphany, one doesn't quite know what to call it, but on that night he decided to forgo a standard literary career and instead concentrate his intellectual power on what one can only call pure thought. (He would later write that "there are few poets who do not go through a fundamental crisis between the ages of twenty and thirty, one in which the destiny of their gift is at stake.") He wanted to know how thought works, what it is based on, its underpinnings, the fundamental mechanisms of the mind itself. This did not mean that Valéry withdrew from society; not at all. He was something of a literary man about town. Nor did he cease publication altogether. He published a few poems. He wrote *An Evening with Monsieur Teste,* his portrait of a man coolly distanced from common concerns by his detached, scientific standards of truth, and *An Introduction to the Method of Leonardo da Vinci,* his study of perhaps the only man in history who did both first-rate science and art.

In a letter to his Harvard teacher J. H. Woods, T. S. Eliot remarks that there are two ways to make a great literary success in London. One is through ubiquity, to publish constantly and everywhere; the other is to publish seldom but, when doing so, always to dazzle by making "these things perfect in their kind." Eliot of course chose this latter path, and so, in a more extreme way, did Paul Valéry.

But, somehow, even with his greatly limited publication, everyone seemed to know about the brilliance of M. Valéry. André Gide was a close friend and a longtime correspondent. Valéry saw Cocteau and Degas and the publisher Gaston Gallimard regularly. His wife, whom he married in 1900 (and with whom he had three children), was the niece of Berthe Morisot and a cousin to Edouard Manet. He knew Ravel and Debussy. André Breton, the main figure in French surrealism, asked him to be best man at his wedding. "I think I met him [Valéry] for the first time in 1921 or 1922 at a reception by the Princesse de Polignac," Igor Stravinsky recalled in *Memories and Commentaries.* "He was small — about my own height, in fact — quick, quiet (he spoke in very rapid, *sotto voce* mumbles), and gentle. His monocle and *boutonnière* made him seem a dandy, but that impression dissolved as soon as he began to talk. Everything he said was instinct with wit and intelligence."

At the urging of Gide and Gallimard, Valéry returned to writing verse in 1912, and in attempting to round out a volume of verse for publication, he wrote "La Jeune Parque," a poem of 512 lines that made him a poet of great fame not only in France but throughout Europe. But fame is one thing; fortune, for a poet, quite another. In 1922, after the death of his patron Edouard Lebey, at Agence Havas, he had to scramble for a living. Scrambling meant becoming a literary man-of-all-work: giving talks, doing bits of teaching, writing introductions to other people's books, and the rest of it.

In 1925, Valéry was appointed to fill the seat at the Académie Française of Anatole France. In a dazzling ironic reception address upon ascending to membership, he lightly mocked his predecessor and made plain how the changing of the guard of literature had itself changed:

> Blessed are those writers who relieve us of the burden of thought and who dextrously weave a luminous veil over the complexity of things. Alas, gentlemen, there are others, whose existence must be deplored, who have elected to strike out in the opposite direction. They have placed toil of the mind in the way of its pleasures. They offer us riddles. Such creatures are inhuman.

Valéry was of course speaking of himself and his own difficult writing. He also got in a shot about a French society "notable for its inability to find for the intellectually gifted man an appropriate and tolerable place in its gigantic and crude economy." The French seem to understand such mockery and do not let it get in the way; they take it in stride, make no real changes, and move on, business as usual. For Valéry, this meant treating him very much as what used to be called an establishment figure, without his ever having an establishment financial base.

> Please include me [he wrote in connection with being asked to serve on yet another award committee] among those who are weariest of delivering oracles. In the course of this past week, I have spoken a dozen times before thinking. On one occasion, I was asked to name the most beautiful line of verse in our language; on another, I narrated the greatest day in my life; I offered opinions on State reform and on votes for women. I nearly even issued a pronouncement on the comma! The truth is, my good man, that I am past admiring my brain for all the wonderfully various things it had no idea it contained.

Honors continued to come to him until his death in 1945: presidency of the French PEN club, an honorary doctorate from Oxford, the post of administrator of the Centre Universitaire Méditerranéen de Nice, a leading member of the Committee on Intellectual Co-operation of the League of Nations and later of its Permanent Committee on Arts and Letters, professor of poetics at the Collège de France. He was long considered the unofficial poet laureate of France; he referred to himself, in 1932, as "a kind of state poet." His intellectual connections widened, and he knew people as diverse as Joseph Conrad and Rabindranath Tagore, T. S. Eliot and D'Annunzio, Pirandello and H. G. Wells. The wonder is how he managed to escape the Nobel Prize.

Valéry wrote no more poems after 1926. His two main periods of poetic production were from 1887 to 1892 and from 1912 to 1922. "After each period," Roger Shattuck has written, "came twenty years of highly active 'silence' in prose." Such was his intellectual skill that, despite his complaints about all the official hackwork he had to turn out, he was incapable of writing anything really dull. The source of this skill was in the daily work on his *Cahiers*. From his early twenties until his death, Valéry began each day, arising between 5 and 6 A.M., aided by coffee and cigarettes, in the act of cerebration, writing out those of his thoughts that he felt were worth preserving. Ultimately, these came to a body of work of twenty-six thousand pages, constituting twenty-nine volumes in a facsimile edition and two volumes in the Pléiade edition of his works.

Much of this material has never been available in English, though an enticing portion was published in the volume titled *Analects*, in the splendid sixteen-volume English-language edition of Valéry that Jackson Matthews edited for the Bollingen Foundation. Valéry has always been fortunate in his editors, and perhaps in none more than Matthews, who gave the better part of his adult life to making him available to the small number of readers who do not negotiate the French language with complete ease but who are capable of appreciating both the importance and the pleasure that Valéry's work gives.

An English-language version of the full *Cahiers,* under the title *Cahiers/Notebooks,* has at last begun to appear, scrupulously and skillfully edited by three Valéry scholars, Brian Stimpson, Paul Gifford, and Robert Pickering. The first two volumes are available in a handsome edition, issued under the aegis of the international publisher Peter Lang. Valéry seems to have struggled with the question of how to organize all this material in a systematic way, and even felt unsure at times whether it ought even to be published at all. Five volumes are planned for this English edition, the last three more scientific and philosophical (another word that was no honorific in Valéry's vocabulary) than these first two, which are more literary and, in a distant sense of the word, personal. The project is a genuine contribution to scholarship and even more to the history of thought in the twentieth century.

Rilke once remarked that what drew him to Paul Valéry's writing was the "finality" and "composure" of its language. His clarity on complex subjects is what excites; his ability to capture the essence of the questions, issues, and problems that the rest of us find puzzling, if not impenetrable, is what amazes — and that he was able to do so with an almost assembly-line regularity is itself astonishing.

What gives Valéry's prose its gravity, lucidity, and chasteness is what he excludes from it. He disliked irony except in conversation, and felt that it chiefly gave a writer an air of superiority, adding that "every ironist has in mind a pretentious reader, mirror of himself." He also had a distaste for eloquence, "because eloquence has the form of a mixture, adapted to a crowd. It has not the form of thought." He cared more for precision than profundity, and precision was only accessible through the utmost clarity: "the kind that does not come from the use of words like 'death,' 'God,' 'life,' or 'love' — but dispenses with such trombones." No trombones, no trumpets, no brass section in Valéry's prose; a solo cello, deep strings played under perfect control and superior acoustical conditions, is all we ever hear.

Add to this his intellectual contempt for politics, which he felt took on life en masse, or in its coarsest possible form. "I consider politics, political action, all forms of politics, as inferior values and inferior activities of the mind," he wrote. Politics is the realm of the expedient, the rough guess: "crude, vain, or desperate solutions are indispensable to mankind just as they are to individuals, *because they do not know.*" In politics, he wrote, "by a trick of inverted lights, friends see each other as enemies, fools look impressive to the intelligent, who in turn see themselves as very tiny indeed." Politics calls, inevitably, for the polemic, which carries its own peril: "that of losing the power of thinking otherwise than polemically, as if one were facing an audience and in the presence of the enemy." Valéry could think of nothing in the realm of thought "madder" or more vulgar "than wanting to be right," which is of course what politics is chiefly about.

He had no greater regard for history. "The *true character* of history," he wrote, "is to play a part in history itself." He thought of it as sheer storytelling, with the added danger of "invitation to plagiarism," which entails repeating earlier historians' stories, always "a fatal invitation." He wrote: *History teaches us . . . History will judge . . .* That's a myth in two nonsenses." He especially disliked the grand dramatizers of history — Michelet is a notable example — and he believed that "history finally leads to politics, just as Bacchus used to lead to Venus."

Although his own quest was sometimes described as philosophical, philosophy, too, was for Valéry yet another shaky enterprise; "hearsay," he called it, and pronounced metaphysics "astrology with words." Religion, he felt, "provides people with words, acts, gestures, and 'thoughts' covering the predicaments in which they are at a loss what to say, to do, or to imagine." A man tends "to deny what he is unable to affirm (express)," and so religion, inadequate as a mode of thought, at least provided a shield against our deep ignorance about the basic questions of existence. He was not averse to using the world "soul," though he said he was interested in collecting minds only. Valéry does not say much about his own views on religion, but he was prescient enough, more than half a century ago, to write: "The religious debate is no longer between different religions, but between those who believe that *belief* has some sort of value and those who don't."

Anyone who reads through these *Notebooks* and through Valéry's work generally will notice how seldom he quotes, or even mentions, other writers. In an essay called "French Thought and Art," he descants for thirteen pages with the mention of only a single name, that of Montesquieu, and this brought in only tangentially. This is another sign of the purity of his lucubrations. "Names," he wrote, "are only made to send us back to things, yet they too often save us the journey."

As by now will be evident, Valéry sought a position of maximum detachment for his own efforts to understand the functioning of the mind. "No one has stood back from everything and everyone more than I have." he wrote. "I'd like to turn them all into a spectacle — and rid myself of everything but my own way of looking." His *Notebooks* are neither journals nor a diary, nor even notebooks, in the sense in which most writers, Henry James perhaps primary among them, use notebooks to record impressions and ideas later to be used in one's novels, plays, or poems. "Here is no merely private record of personal hopes, fears, and aspirations, no chronicle of deeds and days, still less is it (as Journals from Rousseau to Gide had commonly been) the public confession of, or apology for, an intimate self," as Paul Gifford writes. Instead the *Notebooks* constitute, as Gifford accurately calls them, "a laboratory of thought." Valéry uses them to work through his intellectual dissatisfaction with modes of thinking that we have all inherited, and in the effort to break through them he attempts, in these many pages, to understand why, in their faultiness, they appeal to us.

Cool and impersonal though Valéry's *Notebooks* at first might appear, in the end it is difficult to imagine anything more personal than this work. T. S. Eliot said that poetry "is not the expression of personality, but an escape from personality." But the more impersonal serious writing attempts to become, the more personal it seems. This may be owing to the mystery of style, which is a way of looking at the world, and no one had a more original way of looking at the world than Valéry, which of course is what gave him his distinctive style. His is a style of thought rather than of manner, thought marked by skepticism, penetration, and a taste and talent for useful paradox. The deeper, the more abstract, his thought, the more intimate he could be.

Characteristically, Valéry disapproves of the words "deep" or "depth" to describe thinking. He held that "only what is on the surface can have meaning," by which he meant that if one has the intelligence to read the surface accurately, one will easily enough discover what lies beneath it. "Being 'deep,' getting to the bottom of things," he writes, "is nothing. Anyone can dive; some, however, are caught in the water weeds of their abyss and die there, unable to break free." In his *Notebooks,* sometimes one is required to put on the scuba-diving equipment. Behind his quest for the way the mind works was the deeper search for human potential — that is, only when we know how our mental operations work will we know of what we are capable.

"By scrutinizing the inner structures and workings of the self," Brian Stimpson writes in the introduction to the English edition of the *Notebooks,* "and by employing the most advanced tools of scientific analysis, [Valéry] might, so he hoped, at once free himself from the tyranny of ideas and emotions and formulate a unitary mathematically expressed model of mental functioning, a rigorous, comprehensive understanding of the mind and its products." Valéry didn't, no one will be shocked to learn, achieve this, or even come anywhere near close. "What Valéry has done, had to be attempted," said Henri Bergson, his very grammar acknowledging the element of noble defeat. Valéry himself came to have a more modest view of his own enterprise. "Personally," he wrote, "I regard thought as a sort of 'nexus of possibilities' which, operating between these two states [a question and an answer], and by means of certain disciplines, can render useful services as a catalytic." Reading through Valéry's works, I have come to regard him as both catalytic and prophylactic, simultaneously evoking thought and guarding against shoddy thinking and unearned intellectual confidence.

In a famous formulation, Valéry wrote, "The mind is a moment in the response of the body to the world." One might think that the triad of mind, body, and environment, and their effect on one another, would be easily enough plotted and traced, but they are not. And to raise the question of mind, of what is behind our thinking and how it really works, is, as Valéry knew, "to call everything into question." In a brief essay called "I Would Sometimes Say to Mallarmé," he wrote: "Why not admit that man is the source and origin of enigmas, where there is no object, or being, or moment that is not impenetrable; when our existence, our movements, our sensations absolutely cannot be explained; and when everything we see becomes indecipherable from the moment our minds come to rest on it." Valéry did admit it, and in his *Notebooks* he attempted to investigate why this was so.

Of the various divisions among thinkers, I have always been partial to that between thinkers whose strength is in their ideas (Marx, Freud, and, to a much lesser power, Orwell) and thinkers whose strength is in the texture and subtlety, the sensibility, of their minds (Montaigne, Henry James, Santayana). The former win their way in the world, then die out; the latter, always less dramatic in their presentation, are wiser and their work tends to last longer. Valéry is among the sensibility thinkers. "I don't construct a 'System,'" he reports in his *Notebooks*. "My system — is me." And later he writes: "Just think! — The stock of ideas on which the majority of 'cultured' people live is the legacy of a specific number of individuals, all of whom were moved and inspired by philosophic and literary vanity, and by the ambition to govern other minds and seek their approval and their praise." This may seem very radical, but Valéry would have viewed it as traditional, for, as he wrote, "in all great undertakings, tradition, in the true sense of the word, does not consist of doing again what others have done before, but in recapturing the spirit that went into what they did — and would have done differently in a different age."

If one doesn't read Valéry in the hope of finding yet another false key to unlocking the room containing all the world's mysteries, one does read him, or at least I read him, to remind myself what genuine thought looks like. I also read him because, as he writes, "From 1892 onwards I've felt and maintained a hatred and scorn for Vague Things, and have waged relentless war on them my whole life long. They are the things which cannot stand up to sustained attention, without being reduced to having no existence beyond the name which one thinks denotes them; things which either evaporate the more you think about them, or change into objects of thought for which quite different names are appropriate." If a few examples of such "things" are wanted, try, just for size, the Class Struggle or the Oedipus Complex. "I don't like those minds," Valéry wrote, "even vast and powerful ones, whose thoughts are incapable of being taken to a certain level of precision." Think of Ralph Waldo Emerson; now reverse him and you have Paul Valéry.

"My life's ambition," Valéry wrote, "has only ever been to stir a little interest in minds that are not easily satisfied." One hopes, of course, that one possesses such a mind. Another requisite for an appreciation of Valéry is a mind excited by style. Style, my guess is, functioned for him as a filter through which nonsense was strained. Karl Kraus once described a journalist as "someone who, given time, writes worse." So with Valéry: when he wrote longer he often wrote worse. His lordly lucidity is most impressive when most concise. "A machine is matter that has been trained," he wrote. "A lyrical poem is the unfolding of an exclamation," he wrote. "Optimists write badly," he wrote.

Valéry's was the art of precise formulation. His powers of formulation made him one of the great naturally aphoristic writers of the past century. Unlike other French aphorists, *les moralistes,* his aphorisms touch on serious and delicate matters but almost never on moral questions. "My son," he confided to his *Notebooks,* "I'll bring you up very badly for I'm incapable of giving you precepts that I don't understand." Elsewhere he added: "I know the value of *good* and *evil.* I feel very pleased when I do *good* because I recognize evil so strongly — and because I recognize even more strongly the irrelevance of these notions." By "irrelevance," my suspicion is, he meant his inability to do much about good or evil in the world. Valéry claimed to despise proselytizing, and there is no reason to disbelieve him.

His own mind operated above the level of ideas. You will find few words in Valéry that end in *ism,* and those that he does use he brings in only to mock. Symbolism is an example, for "Symbolist" was the label attached to the poets clustered around Mallarmé when he, Valéry, was young. "It is impossible to think *seriously* with such words as Classicism, Romanticism, Humanism, Realism, and the other -isms. You can't get drunk or quench your thirst with the labels on bottles."

Although Valéry tended to be less than impressed with the novel — "reading stories and novels helps to kill second- or third-class time" — his was in many ways the view of a superior novelist. In an essay called "Descartes," he wrote: "My own view is that we cannot really circumscribe a man's life, imprison him in his ideas and his actions, reduce him to what he appeared to be and, so to speak, lay siege to him in his works. We are much more (and sometimes much less) than we have done."

Valéry's formulations, brilliant in themselves, often provide the added pleasure of provoking useful disagreement. "Our most important thoughts are those which contradict our feelings." True enough though that seems, it seems even truer the other way round: our most important feelings are those which contradict our thoughts. "A writer is 'profound,'" Valéry claimed, "when what he says, *once translated from language into unambiguous thought,* compels us to think it over for a perceptible, and rewarding, period of time." Valéry's own writing passes that test again and again.

The only standard of truth that Valéry was able to invoke was that of science, especially mathematics. The man who when young was unable to set out on a naval career for want of mathematical ability later developed a passionate fascination for the beauty of mathematics and an intense interest in neuroscience. His personal library provides evidence that, as he grew older, he read more science than literature. Among his friends were Poincaré and Niels Bohr; Einstein was someone he met on a number of occasions. His heroes were men, beginning with Leonardo da Vinci, in whom thought and action were one, from Lord Kelvin to Napoleon. Although he was no more than a reasonably well-informed dilettante in scientific matters, scientists came to have a high opinion, as his niece Judith Robinson-Valéry has put it, of his "precise and strategic grasp of what is at stake in their own research." In early positing the inextricability of the triad of Mind, Body, and World in influencing human thought and conduct, Valéry can even be said to have anticipated much work in modern neurology that was still to come.

The task Valéry set himself was that of re-cognition — to "recognate, to rethink things afresh," and to work through them shorn of the conventional wisdom supplied by politics, history, and rhetoric. "'Opinions,' 'convictions,' and 'beliefs' are to me like weeds — confusions," he wrote. He claimed that he wrote "to test, to clarify, to extend, not to duplicate what has been done." He sought his own definitions, more precise than any to be found in dictionaries. "I notice in passing," he wrote to his friend André Gide, "that it is the vague idea that is most generally understood — and that a man is taken to be obscure as soon as he is precise." He also knew that in human beings "cognition reigns but does not rule."

Not everyone felt that Valéry's great project was worthwhile. Some even felt it an evasion. Stravinsky thought he was "altogether too fascinated by the process of creation" and too worshipful of the power of intellect, and regretted that he failed to spend more time at his poetry than in solitary cerebration. Invited to write about Valéry by Hubert Benoit, St. John Perse felt that Valéry had been mistaken not to set his thoughts in order "with a view to make definite statement of them," and instead "dissipated his gifts, for lack of real control and of ability to follow through, and also for lack of a really demanding vitality."

Valéry himself was far from thinking his enterprise a grand success. He was in the uncomfortable position of being everywhere revered yet knowing his own shortcomings. "I'm afraid," he wrote in the *Notebooks,* "I might be beginning to find a feeling of vanity in me — thinking I'm something — which until now was quite foreign to me." He goes on to say that this feeling is pleasant to the taste, "like certain kinds of poison," but that he knows he hasn't obtained "what I would have desired from the world." What he desired can only have been a lucid presentation of the function of the mind, a magnum opus, *The Art of Thinking,* he once called it, saying it was a book "which has never really been written; nor was anyone ever to write it."

Instead he left behind these 261 notebooks, filled with his thoughts on everything from the composition of poetry to the relation among body parts to recognition of the beautiful to the connection between dreams and intellectual discovery ("sleep and ye shall find") to negative hallucinations (not seeing things that are there), and a catalogue of other items, whose vastness I have been able only to hint at here. In the end, though, he understood that "the essential object of the mind is the mind. What it pursues in its analyses and its construction of worlds, what it tracks down in heaven and on earth, can only be itself."

Valéry was too wise not to know that, when his life was over, his work was incomplete. He had set out to do for intellection what Dante had done for the spirit and Balzac for men and women in society — to write, in fact, a Comedy of the Mind. People who put themselves to a reading of his *Notebooks* will recognize them as an unfinished masterpiece, but he would have thought otherwise and eschewed the word "masterpiece," for in an entry in those *Notebooks* he remarks that what other people judge a successful work may seem a defeat for the author; and he also believed that, though what he discovered was not without its importance, people were unlikely to be able to decipher it from his notes.

"Everything I've accomplished all my life since I was twenty consists of nothing other than a kind of *perpetual preparation, without purpose,* without end . . . without practical or external goal," he wrote. He also claimed that everything done outside his *Notebooks* was "my *artificial* work — the result of obligations and external impulses. And this must be understood if anyone wants to understand anything about me — there's nothing essential — or necessary — in any of it." But his every morning's work — "between lamp and dawn," as he once described it — sharpened his mind, so that even the least dutiful official talk he gave, introduction he wrote, journalistic query he responded to, shimmered with intelligence and was free of falsity.

Some minds, Valéry wrote, "have the merit of seeing clearly what all others see confusedly. Some have the merit of glimpsing confusedly what no one sees as yet. A combination of these gifts is exceptional." He was himself in possession of this combination, but, then, he was an exceptional man. Reading him gives you the sense of fog lifting. His writing makes you feel, as he himself wished to feel, that you see things no one but you (and he) has seen. One of the keenest pleasures of reading derives from being in the close company of someone more thoughtful than you but whose thoughts, owing to the courtesy of clarity, are handsomely accessible to you. Paul Valéry provides this pleasure more delectably than any writer I know.

Monsieur Proust's Masterwork

W HAT DO WE come away with when we read not merely a masterpiece but a masterwork of literature? The distinction between the two, masterpiece and masterwork, I take to be in favor of the latter, for a masterwork is not necessarily perfect of its kind, as a masterpiece ought to be, but of a significance beyond the question of mere (some "mere") perfection. Usually large, often sprawling, always the product of monstrous ambition, a masterwork is a key book, one that defines a historical era, or the culmination of a form, or a national literature, or Western thought itself. Robert Musil, in *The Man Without Qualities,* set out to produce a masterwork, but, despite his great brilliance, failed. Nothing short of genius is required to bring it off. The *Iliad,* the *Odyssey,* the *Aeneid, The Divine Comedy* — such are masterworks. Closer to our own time, books that qualify as masterworks, I should say, include *War and Peace, Ulysses,* and *Remembrance of Things Past.*

One of the qualities that mark a masterwork is the inability of readers ever to feel that they have quite grasped it, or at any rate grasped it in its entirety, its wholeness. Almost all masterworks fit into that select category of works that probably shouldn't even be read for the first time; they are works, in other words, that call for being not merely read but reread, two, three, maybe more times, for even the most percipient reader cannot hope to comprehend all that is going on in their pages. Such is their richness that they may yield up quite different and possibly equally persuasive interpretations at various ages in the same reader's life.

The modern masterwork at its most characteristic, in some ways the masterwork of all masterworks, is Marcel Proust's *Remembrance of Things Past.* Yet of the great works of modern literature, it is the one that offers the most obstacles. The first of course is its bulk, its length: more than a million words, 3,365 pages in the Terence Kilmartin reworking of the C. Scott Moncrieff translation. Much depends on the edition in which one attempts to read Proust. The C. Scott Moncrieff translation, which came in a boxed two-volume Random House edition, had wretched leading; the very want of space between lines makes dragging one's eyes across the page a physical difficulty in itself. And the language in Moncrieff has sometimes been thought too lush, the editing that is necessarily a part of the act of translation too lenient. Not that one wishes in any way to undervalue Moncrieff's achievement, which is immense.

Like any serious *proustolâtre* (as we Proust fanatics are called), I own both the C. Scott Moncrieff and the Terence Kilmartin editions; and I own, too, the Pléiade edition of *A la recherche du temps perdu.* Attempting to read Proust in French fairly quickly put paid to my pathetic pretensions as a reader of French. Proust presents difficulties enough in English. His long, looping sentences, interrupted by parentheses frequently more interesting than the sentences in which they are embedded, often held together by shaky syntax, sometimes require rereading. A stockpile of such sentences in a paragraph that itself runs four or five pages is not exactly what might be called, in the current cant phrase, reader friendly.

Lest one think oneself low on the learning curve for finding Proust difficult, one's spirits — and self-esteem — might revive slightly by the discovery that E. M. Forster found Proust no piece of (madeleine) cake. "I was hoping to find Proust easier in English than in French," Forster wrote, and do not. All the difficulties of the original are here faithfully reproduced. A sentence begins quite simply, then it undulates and expands, parentheses intervene like quick-set hedges, the flowers of comparison bloom, and three fields off, like a wounded partridge, crouches the principal verb, making one wonder as one picks it up, poor little thing, whether after all it was worth such a tramp, so many guns, such expensive dogs, and what, after all, is its relation to the main subject, potted so gaily half a page back, and proving finally to have been in the accusative case.

Much of this is owing to Proust's method of composition. Extravagance, in prose as in life, was not something he worried much about. Céleste Alberet, his housekeeper and friend of his last years, tells that Proust, whose skin, like so much else about him, was very sensitive, used to require several towels to dry his face. "He dabbed himself with each towel once, either to wash or to dry himself, and then threw it aside," thence to be sent to Lavigne, an expensive Paris laundry. With his towels, so with his prose: Proust was lavish in the extreme, rarely cutting, endlessly adding to his already vast manuscript. No believer in the modern dictum that less is more, he believed, au contraire, that more was plainly more and hence better, and he seems never to have had any trouble in finding more to add by way of new subordinate clauses, additional parentheses, and fresh codas to already vastly labyrinthine sentences.

This method, if method it was, can give Proust's prose a density and a difficulty that puts some readers off, but it also gives that same prose a richness and complexity that turns quite as many readers on. ("These, however, are the disciplines of Proust," Forster wrote, after the passage I quoted above. "No earnest sportsman would forego them.") The love of complexity in literature is an acquired taste. Joseph Conrad had it. And Henry James had it in excelsis, once saying that if he could make the pronunciation of his name more complicated, he would not hesitate to do so. The complexity of Proust is an acquired taste, but once acquired, it becomes an abiding love.

•   •   •

I have read *Remembrance of Things Past* two and one-seventh times. The first, or one-seventh, time was as an undergraduate at the University of Chicago, where *Swann's Way,* the first volume of *Remembrance of Things Past,* came near the end of one of those mad-hatter survey courses in the novel that young teachers put together, beginning with *The Princess of Clèves* and running through Henry Fielding, Stendhal, Jane Austen, Dostoyevsky, Proust, and ending with *Ulysses.*

What did a boy of twenty make of Proust's astonishing opening volume? About 15 percent of all it contained, I should guess. I recall being alternately bored, confused, and hugely impressed by the book. At the outset, I was much more taken with Charles Swann's self-torturing pursuit of the coquette Odette than I was with the little Marcel's longing for his *maman* and the older Marcel's cerebrations about time and memory. A good bit of the convolutions of poor M. Swann's exquisite masochism must have been lost on me, as was a good deal else. "The value of the work," wrote Valéry in "Homage to Marcel Proust," "is equal to the amount of life we ourselves provide." At twenty, one does not have that large a deposit of life to bring to the task. Yet, for all my not really being up to the book, I knew I was in the presence of serious stuff, the real thing, and, like Henry Miller when a coin dropped from the purse of a woman he was making love to standing up in a dank hallway in Paris, I made a mental note to pick it up later.

I was in my early thirties when I made my first full frontal assault on *Remembrance of Things Past.* I now brought a little more life to it: fatherhood, a failed marriage, a decision to live a quiet and fairly bookish life. Still, the book, like all monumental works, was a climb. One had to be up for it, and stay up to keep stride with its brilliant author. Proust's is distinctly not a bedtime, nor a beach, nor a summer holiday book. It must be read at one's most alert hours, with an intellectual receptivity that one brings to the reading of one's own will and testament. It requires scrutiny, but scrutiny enacted in a spirit of devotion.

For me this meant reading *Remembrance of Things Past* in the early morning hours. I tried to give the book an hour out of each day. In that hour I covered ten, sometimes fifteen, rarely twenty pages, depending on whether the Proust portion for the day contained more analysis than narrative, or narrative than analysis, though the two were so frequently intermixed that the distinction didn't always hold up. Seeking forward motion, I did not dally, struggling for complete lucidity and mastery over each difficult passage. Some mornings I was better than others: certain mornings, I read passages that I felt might just change my life; on other mornings, I felt myself obtuse and not at all up to my author; on all mornings, I knew I was in the presence of genius.

Proust was a genius on the same level as Henry James and, in my view, on a higher level than Sigmund Freud. I would later read Leon Edel, in the introduction to the fourth of his five-volume biography of James, make a similar though less invidious observation:

> On the level of art James was probing the same human experience — and in an analogously systematic if unconscious way — as Sigmund Freud, who was making his discoveries at this very moment in Vienna. And also at this same moment, in Paris, James's fellow artist, Marcel Proust, was engaged in examining that part of reflective experience which relates to association and memory. Proust, in the footsteps of Bergson, discovered for himself and demonstrated how a calling up of the past (which Freud was asking of his patients) establishes man in time, can give him an identity and reveal to him the realities of his being.

A work of the prodigious length of *Remembrance of Things Past* has its share of longueurs. But my tendency at the time was to assume that it was I and not Proust who was boring. ("Like many other men," Proust writes, "Swann had a naturally lazy mind and lacked imagination.") Certain characters interested me more than others: Swann, Mme. Verdurin, Saint-Loup, Vinteuil, Bergotte. Baron de Charlus in particular elicited my readerly pleasure: my attention went up when he appeared on the page; my heart sank ever so slightly when he departed.

I was always on the qui vive for snobbery, for at the top of the rap sheet on Marcel Proust is that he was a miserable snob. But by the time he came to write *Remembrance of Things Past* Proust was no longer a snob but the great chronicler of snobbery, the greatest since the Duc de Saint-Simon, who was, I believe, a true snob and who operated on the principle of it takes one to know one. Proust took the fashionable world, in which snobbery is unavoidable, for his field of study, and, as Léon Daudet remarked, "the monde mattered to him as flowers matter to a botanist, not as they do to the man who buys the bouquet." He became, in other words, both the chronicler and the anatomist of snobbery.

George Painter, who has to have given Proust and the snobbery question as much thought as anyone in the world, in an interview with Phyllis Grosskurth remarked that he didn't think Proust a snob. "He began as a snob," Painter said,

> partly because he was a Jew and a homosexual. If he could be accepted in the place where it was most difficult to get in at all, then that would make him feel better, feel more at home in the world. When he found that they [the great aristocrats of his day] had very similar failings to everybody else in his own middle classes or in the working classes of his servants, he was partly relieved, and perhaps a little disappointed. He often says how similar the bourgeois, the working classes, and the aristocracy are in their ways, except that the working classes are much kinder and more intelligent. He became an anti-snob.

Proust knew all about snobs, about upward- and downward-looking snobs, and what drove both sorts of snob. But after reading Proust, it is all but impossible to feel any regard for the modern aristocracy. "I had seen enough of fashionable society," he writes, "to know that it is there that one finds real illiteracy and not, let us say, among electricians." And then there is the great scene when poor Swann cannot get the Duchess de Guermantes to delay her departure for a party long enough to receive the news of his impending death, yet she can find time to change from black to red shoes. One does not come away from *Remembrance of Things Past* with keen admiration for the aristocracy.

My second full reading of Proust's novel took place in my middle forties. The occasion, if not the motive, for my rereading the book was the Terence Kilmartin revision of the C. Scott Moncrieff translation. I note that I had taken to sidelining, in a light pencil, passages that seemed to me significant. The number of these passages is vast. Their cast tends to be darkish. An example from *Time Regained*, Proust's final volume:

> Yes: if, owing to the work of oblivion, the returning memory can throw no bridge, form no connecting link between itself and the present minute, if it remains in the context of its own place and date, if it keeps its distance, its isolation in the hollow of a valley or upon the highest peak of a mountain summit, for this very reason it causes us suddenly to breathe a new air, an air which is new precisely because we have breathed it in the past, that purer air which the poets have vainly tried to situate in paradise and which could induce so profound a sensation of renewal only if it had been breathed before, since the true paradises are the paradises that we have lost.

With the notion of paradises lost, we are in the dense metaphysical jungle of time, Proust's larger subject. Reading him in my middle forties, now myself beginning to hear the clock tick more insistently, I was more attentive to his observations on time. These are set out most richly in *Time Regained*. Here one learns about "the incuriosity that is brought about by time"; the multifarious tricks time plays on memory, not least the contrast "between the mutability of people and the fixity of memory"; the search for those things that are extratemporal, for, as Proust writes, in a characteristic sentence:

> An hour is not merely an hour, it is a vase full of scents and sounds and projects and climates, and what we call reality is a certain connection between these immediate sensations and the

memories which envelop us simultaneously with them — a connection that is suppressed in a simple cinematographic vision, which just because it professes to confine itself to the truth of the fact departs widely from it — a unique connection which the writer has to rediscover in order to link forever in his phrase the two sets of phenomena which reality joins together.

The work of art, Proust holds, is the sole method for recapturing time, and no one gave the effort a more heroic attempt than this man whose own time would run out at the age of fifty-one.

As the chronicler of the subtle alchemistry that the passage of time wreaks, Proust understood the transitoriness of all things, and particularly of all passions. "But political passions," he writes in *The Captive,* the volume touching on the Dreyfus case, "are like all the rest, they do not last. New generations arise which no longer understand them; even the generation that experienced them changes, experiences new political passions which, not being modeled exactly upon their predecessors, rehabilitate some of the excluded, the reason for exclusion having altered."

If all is transitory, this includes happiness, the great human goal, the illusion of all illusions. "In Proust," as Howard Moss notes in his excellent *The Magic Lantern of Marcel Proust,* "the homosexuals are just as unhappy as the heterosexuals." But unhappiness is the condition toward which all tend. In good part, this is owing to the fact that, for Proust, the organizing principle of social life is snobbery, the chief emotion propelling love is jealousy. Proust can be an immensely amusing writer — his portraits of his gallery of snobs is comedy at its highest — but he is at the same time a darkly pessimistic one. Irrationality rules in his pages, kindness and generosity come to seem improbable. Selfishness, usually badly misconstrued, is pervasive. Only his artists — the painter Elstir, the writer Bergotte, the composer Vinteuil, the actress Berma, the dilettante art critic Swann — are allowed a measure of superiority, yet even they are often vaguely ridiculous. His despair, as perhaps befits a man ill all his days, is fundamental. And yet it is a despair that, conveyed through his pages, somehow doesn't depress — at least not this reader. The reason for this, I believe, is that cascading human brilliance at the height of its flow, which is how I should describe *Remembrance of Things Past,* is too grand a spectacle to allow for depression on the part of the spectator.

Perhaps more than any modern writer, Proust invites reading not merely for his story but for the power of his analysis — for, not to put too fine a point on it, his wisdom. One cannot read Proust without recognizing how, in his monumental book, he has recapitulated French literature. In the purely storytelling aspects of *Remembrance of Things Past,* one senses the great sweep of French fiction, the line that runs from Madame de Lafayette through Stendhal through Balzac through Flaubert and even through Zola to Proust. In its analytic aspect, one feels in the book the influence of Montaigne, La Rochefoucauld, La Bruyère, Pascal, Vauvenargues, Joubert, Chamfort, and the other French *moralistes.* Proust had the great French weakness — also glory — for generalization. So much is this so that Justin O'Brien, fifty years ago, extracted 428 maxims from the pages of Proust's novel, and set them out — in a small, bilingual book titled *Maxims* — under the five categories of Man, Society, Love, Art, and Time and Memory. "Proust's love of generalizing," O'Brien wrote, "has never been hampered by his material, for the maxims occur as readily in the midst of descriptive or narrative passages as they do in the more reflective sections of the work."

These maxims give Proust's work, as O'Brien points out, its justly deserved "reputation for universality," but it also gives his novel its allure as wisdom literature. Proust's maxims are not, for the most part, of the quality of La Rochefoucauld's — most are not quite so polished as perfect maxims need to be — but do have their own special power, arising as they do out of the long and elaborate story that is *Remembrance of Things Past.* Some are short and sharp: "After a certain age, the more one becomes oneself, the more obvious family traits become." Others, lengthier, such as this on neurotics, carry an equally high truth quotient:

> Who has not noticed this fact among women, and even men, gifted with exceptional intelligence but highly neurotic? When they are calm, happy, at peace with their surroundings, one cannot but admire their remarkable gifts and feel that their words are truth itself. A headache or a slight wound to their vanity is enough to change everything. The luminous intelligence — now harsh, convulsive, shriveled up — reflects only an irritated, suspicious, vain personality striving by every means to make a bad impression.

Proust is especially good, in his aphoristic mode, on literary and artistic matters. "Each artist seems to be the citizen of an unknown country, lost even from his memory and different from the country whence will come, embarking earthward, another great artist." On criticism: "Each generation of critics does nothing but take the opposite of the truth accepted by their predecessors." And on the larger subject of style: "To a writer as to a painter, style is a question not of technique but of vision. It is the revelation, which would be impossible by direct and conscious means, of the qualitative difference between our various ways of seeing the world — a difference which, but for art, would eternally remain the individual's secret."

Reading generally presents the possibility of the pleasures of plot, of style, of form, none of which need be gainsaid. But at the highest level it also holds out the prospect of wisdom, of truths previously unrevealed. Do many people still read — as I do — looking for secrets, for hitherto hidden keys that will open too-long-locked doors? It seems almost impossible to read Proust without this motive. His very style, the aphoristic shading into the philosophical, seems to invite it. Yet the trick here is not to come to him looking for answers to specific questions. ("I have an answer, I have an answer," calls out the yeshiva boy in the streets of his shtetl. "Does anybody have a question?") The trick is to have long in mind the questions for which Proust supplies the answers without himself even considering them questions.

To provide a personal example, I have long thought about the point of a literary education — the point, that is, of thoughtfully reading vast quantities of belletristic writing much of which time erases from one's memory. In part, the answer is to be found in the cultivation of sensibility; in part, I have also thought, in T. S. Eliot's lilting sentence about Henry James: "He had a mind so fine no idea could violate it." James, Eliot seems to me here to be saying, operated in the realm above ideas. Fair and true enough, but where or what is that realm, and how does one arrive there in one's own thought? The most subtle formulation I have been able to discover I found in *Remembrance of Things Past:*

> Our intellect is not the most subtle, the most powerful, the most appropriate, instrument for revealing the truth. It is life that, little by little, example by example, permits us to see that what is most important to our hearts, or to our minds, is learned not by reasoning but through other agencies. Then it is that the intellect, observing their superiority, abdicates its control to them upon reasoned grounds and agrees to become their collaborator and lackey.

Proust seems here to be taking Pascal's "the heart has its reasons that reason cannot know" and further refining it to mean that only when reason gives way, gives primacy of place, to the heart does it have a chance to learn the heart's deeper reasons — the reasons that, finally, matter most of all.

Yet one probably does best not to press Proust's pages too hard in the hope of extracting ideas from them. People who have done so seem to have come up with fistfuls of grass in their hands. Céline, for example, found Proust Talmudic, or rather the Talmud Proustian, writing: "The Talmud is constructed and designed almost like Proust's novels, tortuous, . . . a chaotic mosaic." Of course, Céline's reading wasn't helped any by his anti-Semitism. Jean-Paul Sartre viewed Proust's work as bourgeois irresponsibility in its purest form: "Proust chose to be a bourgeois, he made himself the accomplice of bourgeois propaganda, because his work spread the myth of human nature." Not smart, Sartre.

Great works of literature exist on a plane where misconceived ideas can violate them. This is to say that, while of course literature is filled with ideational content, the ideas are not so easily separated from the stories, poems, and dramas in which they are embedded without doing great violence both to the ideas and to the stories, poems, and dramas themselves. "Poetry is what is lost in translation," said Robert Frost, adding: "It is also what is lost in interpretation." Literature, one might say, is often what gets lost when ideas are extracted too cleanly from literary works.

Which makes a book such as *How Proust Can Change Your Life: Not a Novel* by Alain de Botton an odd confection indeed. De Botton, despite his altogether French name, writes in English and is the author of two previous novels of the youthful, clever, postmodern sort. He has had the extraordinary notion of turning to Proust as a guide for everyday living. What makes this extraordinary is the fact that Marcel Proust himself probably did not live a single ordinary day in his life. Great writer though he was, Proust was as neurotic as a flea. He was a man who dined at the homes of friends in his overcoat. He not infrequently left waiters tips equal to the bill. He was a man who, beyond the age of thirty, still reported on the condition of his bowels and micturition to his mother. Let us not even speak of the cork-lined room in which he spent the last fourteen years of his life. He turned night into day, day into night, working as others slept, sleeping as they worked. Proust was also smart, subtle, an authentic literary genius. But a guide to life? I don't think so.

Yet De Botton makes out, in these pages, what might be called, in the cant phrase of the day, a best-case scenario. His book has the merit of containing some charming bits. He imagines, for example, a genial meeting between Proust and James Joyce, unlike the cool and uneventful one (which De Botton recounts) that took place at a dinner at the Ritz given by Violet and Sydney Schiff for

Serge Diaghilev and his troupe of dancers and for the four geniuses of modern art the Schiffs most admired: Proust, Joyce, Stravinsky, and Picasso. Joyce arrived late, improperly dressed, and
with not a very high opinion of his great rival in the field of the
novel: "I observe a furtive attempt to run a certain M. Marcel
Proust of here [Paris] against the signatory of this letter. I have
read some pages of his. I cannot see any special talent but I am a
bad critic." Proust claimed never to have read a page of Joyce.
Alas, another of those potentially, magnificently fructifying meetings that failed to come off.

De Botton's book has other sweet bits. He informs us that
Proust, like the painter Forain, had one of the early telephones
available in France. He reports Fernand Gregh, one of Proust's
friends, recounting how the verb "to proustify" came into being:
"We created among ourselves the verb to proustify to express a
slightly too conscious attitude of geniality, together with what
would vulgarly have been called affectations, interminable and
delicious." He underscores Proust's own point that, in some fundamental way, friendship and truthfulness are incompatible, for
Proust would never tell a friend anything that might inflict the
least hurt.

De Botton puts into rather better perspective the reason why
André Gide, then a key editor at Gallimard, turned down the first
volume of *Remembrance of Things Past,* and quotes Gide, writing
to Proust, in self-extenuation for this most numbskulled of all editorial decisions: "For me, you had remained the man who fre-
quented the house of Mme X, Y, Z, the man who wrote for the
Figaro. I thought of you as — shall I confess it? — . . . a snob, a dilettante, a socialite." What Gide doesn't confess here is that, more
likely, he failed to read Proust's thick manuscript, for had he done
so all such presuppositions would have been instantly dispelled.

Only rarely does De Botton cast doubt on his bona fides as a serious *proustolâtre.* He betrays his youthfulness, and the nature of
his own undertaking, when, on page 165 of his book, he makes a
poor joke by asking: "Did Proust have any relevant thoughts on
dating? What should one talk about on a first date? And is it good

to wear black?" He also refers to "a certain Madame Sert," which shows a less than complete control over the milieu (or "maloo," as Josephine Herbst used kiddingly to pronounce it), for Misia Sert, one of the great hostesses of the belle époque and friend to Mallarmé and so many other of the modern artists of France, deserves much more than the distancing diminishment of "a certain Madame Sert."

But of course Alain de Botton's book cannot hope to embrace even a thousandth part of the richness of Proust. Any man who could write, as Proust did in *Time Regained,* that "the horror that grand people have for the snobs who move heaven and earth to make their acquaintance is felt also by the virile man for the invert, by a woman for every man who is too much in love with her," thus economically demonstrating his subtle knowledge of three different worlds, cannot be contained within so slender, however genial, a volume as *How Proust Can Change Your Life.* The best audience for Alain de Botton's book might be those who have never read Proust but long have wished to have done, for it gives several powerful glints of the glories to be found in this richest of modern literary mines. But for those who know Proust, it seems very thin soup indeed.

Phyllis Rose's *Year of Reading Proust* is a vastly different kettle of caviar. I write "caviar," not because I think the book pure caviar, but because there is something rather high-priced about the tastes of its author that plays out, in her pages, as unconscious comedy, though not everyone will find it amusing. I do, though chiefly in the way I find amusing the cast of characters around that overconfident and ignorant snob Mme. Verdurin, people so wrapped up in their own lives that they can have little or no notion that they just might be trivial.

One of the questions that one needs to ask when reading a great writer — it is often a painful but finally a pressing one — is, What would he or she think of me? How would I appear in the eyes of Tolstoy, George Eliot, Henry James, James Joyce? (Too often the answer, one fears, might well be: "Of no conceivable interest.") Of the great writers, Proust is perhaps the most tolerant, but I think nonetheless that he would have consigned Phyllis Rose to the crowd at Mme. Verdurin's, where she would have flourished among the happy, the self-satisfied, and the purblind.

Ostensibly, Rose's book is about her attempt to complete Proust's great book after many earlier failures to get past its first hundred or so pages. In fact, the book is really a memoir, a year in its author's recent life in which she recounts her family history, habits, tastes, point of view, friendships, and quotidian life. It is a year in which she awaits the death of her aged mother, long ailing from congestive heart failure, a death that, by book's end, is not accomplished. But, then, as Rose allows, at the time of writing, neither had she quite finished *Remembrance of Things Past*. As she remarks, she intends to use "Proust's masterpiece [as] my madeleine," to recall her own life, as the French biscuit dipped in tea did for Proust. But Proust offers only a frame for this book; at its center is the character of Phyllis Rose.

Phyllis Rose perhaps finds, one fears, altogether too bearable her astonishing lightness of being. Her husband — her second husband — is the son of the creator of the *Babar* books for children, who has continued to produce these books. They live in Connecticut and Key West. She and her husband collect Roman glass and prints; she finds collecting, it seems important that you and I should know, a perfectly adequate substitute for the "universal eroticization" of unmarried life. After years in psychotherapy, she concludes that "what was unique about me was that no one had ever hurt me." Hers was a happy childhood, awash in popular culture, which she still adores. "Nothing," she believes, "can cheapen the Beatles story"; a child of the sixties, she had for some years imagined herself the sole girl Beatle. E-mail, she avers, "has given me back the spontaneity I had lost to the laziness of age." A professor of literature at Wesleyan University, the author of books on Josephine Baker and on Victorian marriages, Rose offers an example of the limits of education and culture, for in her a vast overlay of both has not been able to cover up the inexhaustible shallows of a confident but unoriginal mind.

Phyllis Rose may think she is writing about Proust, but in fact she makes one wish we had a Proust around today to deal with the rich material she supplies in her memoir. Imagine what Proust might have done with her recounting the loss of her virginity after the assassination of John F. Kennedy. "It was part of the same biological response to grief, despair, and fear that led people to make love in the cattle cars on the way to Auschwitz, and I never felt guilty about it." She tells us a good deal about her dreams, confirming my own view that people who commit this exceedingly boring social act generally have more interesting dreams than actual lives. She has a deep friendship with another professor at Wesleyan who is homosexual, causing her to comment on "the sophisticated refinement of sex that homosexuality seemed to me to be." Proust could have filled her in a good bit here too, for, as the pages from *Cities of the Plain* unmistakably reveal, he thought homosexuality very far from refined.

But the great Proustian scene, which Rose simply isn't up to because she is unaware of the inherent comedy of it, occurs in the latter portion of her book, when the novelist Robert Stone, a friend in Key West, asks her to prepare an important dinner for fifteen or sixteen, telling her it is for Sonny and Gita Mehta, the chief editor at the firm of Alfred A. Knopf and his wife. But Rose soon comes to suspect that there are bigger fish to fry — or ought that to be bigger fish for whom to fry? The real reason for the dinner, the reason that its true guest could not be revealed, was because that guest was — can you bear the tension? — Salman Rushdie, whose life was still under threat of a *fatwa*. Once she learns who it is she is to entertain, Rose, without a scintilla of irony, writes: "That it would be a memorable evening for literature was true. It would be memorable for the Key West writers to meet Rushdie. And the meeting ought to be special. A great writer, a martyr to art, was owed a special evening."

The dinner for Rushdie turned out to be a bit of a fizzle. Conversations never quite meshed; the wrong subjects came up. Sonny Mehta failed to arrive. The disappointments of a snob, even an unconscious snob, can be poignant. "It kept getting away from me," Rose writes, and adds, "Of all the forms of creativity, hostessing is one of the most treacherous." Perhaps, à la Mme. Verdurin, she should have arranged to have played for the company Vinteuil's haunting sonata.

"I had flunked the test of Proust," Phyllis Rose remarks apropos of her slowness in picking up on the fact that the dinner Robert Stone asked her to give was for Salman Rushdie. "I flubbed the hard, minute work of perception. I let the insight go out of my mind so entirely that I hadn't even realized there was a 'mystery guest.'" Ah, she cannot know it, but poor Miss Rose has flunked an even graver test. In this book she demonstrates herself to be one of those people, of a kind not infrequently found in Proust, who are deprived of humor, irony, and the least measure of perspective, and hence of significant self-knowledge itself. A snob of the American educated classes, far from being possessed of Proustian insight, she is herself a contemporary version of a Proustian figure.

As for that Proustian test, it has to do not with quickness of perception, though Proust clearly must himself have been a man, as was said of Henry James, "assailed by perceptions." It has to do with something broader, something deeper. Marcel Proust, for all his neurotic tics, was a very savvy man, a man engaged with reality on the most fundamental level. Reading Proust has to do with the meshing, so impressive in Proust himself, of culture and reality. The Proustian test comes, finally, in the ability to keep in balance the contradictory notions that the world, for all its pleasures, is also a place of low deceits, vicious insensitivities, gargantuan self-deceptions, snobberies little and large, and yet, for those who cultivate awareness, it remains nonetheless a profoundly amusing place — no less profound than amusing.

In his last months, Proust told Céleste Alberet: "People will read me, yes, the whole world will read, and you'll see, Céleste. Remember this: it took a hundred years for Stendhal to become known. It will not take Marcel Proust as many as fifty." He was of course correct. He was correct because he understood, with great precision, what his own indefatigable work provided its small but hardy band of readers.

In *Time Regained*, Proust wrote: "Every reader is, in reading, a reader of himself. The writer's work is merely a kind of optical instrument, which he offers the reader so that the latter may make things out in himself that he might otherwise not have seen." If one is fortunate, if one brings to Proust a freshness of mind and the spirit of homage properly owed to a truly superior mind, one has a chance, slim but genuine, to become perhaps a little smarter about the world and about oneself. For those of us who do not make any distinction between experience and reading, but believe that reading is experience, experience acquired in tranquility, Marcel Proust is our man.

Vin Audenaire

I N AN ESSAY on the *Collected Poems of T. S. Eliot* written for the Mid-Century Book Society, W. H. Auden, never one to fear a risky generalization, remarked that "to become a poet of the first rank, great talent is not enough; one must get born at the right time and in the right place." The right time to be born, he asserted, was between 1870 and 1890, a period of great ferment in the arts. Picasso, Joyce, Stravinsky, Proust, all were born in the 1870s and 1880s, so, too, William Butler Yeats, Robert Frost, T. S. Eliot, and Wallace Stevens. And none was born in England, which was also, in Auden's view, a good place for a great poet *not* to be born, for England was still irretrievably locked into the poetic conventions of the nineteenth century—those of the Romantics, which were attenuated by the Victorians. To have been born when Auden was, in 1907, and where he was, in the city of York, later to be raised in Birmingham, left his own career short-circuited right out of the gate. The best he could hope for, or so he averred, was "the useful role of colonizer" in cultural lands already discovered by others.

Auden wrote this in 1953. Today, more than half a century later, he seems a good deal more than a mere colonizer. He seems, in fact, the last indisputably major poet to have used the English language. Although Auden put in his time as a teacher—and also as a playwright, librettist, book reviewer, anthologist, and man of all literary work—no poet since him has seemed so inevitably, so unalterably a poet, in his vocation (in the sense of calling), point of view, bearing, and very being. He wrote and said many brilliant things about literature, some lent extra authority by his accomplished poetry. Had Auden not been a poet, he would have been sad, a little ridiculous even — unthinkable, really.

Geniuses appear young only in music and mathematics; there are no Mozarts in literature. But Auden came into his gift quite early. His intellectual penetration showed itself even sooner than his poetic power: by the time he arrived at Oxford, he not only knew that he wanted to be a poet but was confident that he would be exceptionally good at it. "You don't understand," he told his Oxford tutor Nevill Coghill, who on first meeting didn't understand the seriousness of Auden's ambition. "I'm going to be a great poet."

That is of course precisely what he became, though how great remains in the flux of controversy. Philip Larkin saw a clear division between Auden's career before and after he left England for America — in 1940, at the age of thirty-three — with before, in Larkin's view and that of many others, being much better. After Auden's departure to America, Larkin thought his poetry "no longer touches our imaginations." The oddity of all this is that Larkin seems to have appreciated Auden most when, given his own views, he should have despised the ideational content of his poems most deeply.

What isn't in controversy is Auden's legendary facility. He appears to have "lisped in numbers." Christopher Isherwood has remarked that "problems of form and technique seem to have bothered him very little," and while they were in Germany together Auden took to composing poems in German such that a German writer to whom Isherwood showed them immediately detected his talent. He could apparently knock off a poem between teaching classes at Swarthmore College. He could produce birthday poems for friends on demand, and give, like the dry cleaner, same-day service. Far from being chilled, he was stimulated by a commission for a poem. "I am proud of my friends," he said, "and of my knowledge of metre." As a poet, his technical resources seem to have been without limit.

The other gift that Auden came into early was superior perspective, allowing him to see on a wide canvas. "He saw things in better proportion than most of us," a classmate from his preparatory school noted. Noteworthy for an Englishman of his generation, he sized up all the ignorance inherent in discriminations based on social class, race, and religious difference, and appeared easily to rise above them. He was able to seem a citizen of the world while remaining, even after more than thirty years in America, in some ways English to the highest power. Oliver Sacks, the neurologist and writer, who knew Auden when he, Sacks, was young, allowed that he functioned as a "reality-bearer" for him. "Wystan was," Sacks writes, "at once the most common-sensical and down-to-earth man I have known, but also the most fantastic and fanciful when he let himself go."

Auden was also the most purely intellectual of poets — the most caught up in the intellectual and political currents and movements of his time. Because many of these preoccupations found their way into his poems, his work also poses, among other questions, the question of to what extent the weight of bookishness and involvement in the realm of ideas heightens or slackens many of his poems. A serious reviser of his own work, Auden doubtless was much taken up with such matters; and perhaps all the more so as a man who, during his sixty-six years, regularly shucked off previously held ideas and thoroughly changed his politics and even his point of view.

In his own life, too, Auden poses the at first flush comical but finally serious question of how elegance of mind can live with utter squalor of quotidian life, while his poetry poses that of the real distinction between truth and beauty, since most people sensitive to poetry are in agreement that his early poems are more beautiful than his later poems, in which Auden specifically cultivated such truths as he felt available to him at the close of his life. To bring these questions into high relief, one must revert to biography, of which Auden himself would doubtless disapprove, for he made a regular habit of disparaging even as he read and wrote about every literary biography that came his way.

Auden considered himself lucky in his parents. His father was a physician with broad interests, who kept both scientific and literary books about the house. His mother was musical, churchgoing, and a stronger influence than his father—strong enough, he felt, to cause him to emphasize the feminine streak in his own nature that perhaps led to his homosexuality, with which he seems lifelong to have been on entirely comfortable terms, quite without self-pity, though at the same time he never romanticized it. In later life, writing about a poem in which C. P. Cavafy recounts a liaison with a male prostitute, which ends by Cavafy writing: "Tomorrow, the next day, years later, vigorous verses / will be composed that had their beginning here," Auden's capping remark is: "But what, one cannot help wondering, will be the future of the artist's companion?" That anchor in reality served Auden well.

Auden seems to have impressed his teachers and schoolmates by his wide knowledge and self-assurance. He took the best his early schooling had to offer, chiefly the study of Greek and Latin, which gave him a feeling for the necessity of precision in language, and made a mental note of the worst, chiefly the "very intense group life" of schoolboys, distinctly not his cup of tea. "Wystan," a public school friend remarked, "did not talk like a boy. He spoke a language which was mature, worldly, intellectually challenging." With the sang-froid that was never to desert him, he wrote: "I have never, I think, wanted to 'belong' to a group whose interests were not mine, nor have I resented exclusion. Why should they accept me? All I have ever asked is that others should go their way and let me go mine."

While he diddled around writing poems as an adolescent, what apparently turned him to thinking in earnest about becoming a poet was his stumbling upon Walter de la Mare's verse anthology *Come Hither,* which included a wide variety of poetry, all of it far from superior. Not everyone, after all, is swept away, at least at the beginning, by the sublime; sometimes the merely second rate can incite ambition, causing one to think: "Wait a minute — I can do that."

Oxford was made for Auden, and a fellow undergraduate claimed that he treated it as if it were "a convenient hotel." At first he was going to do a scientific degree, then, recognizing his commitment to poetry, did English literature instead. But what he studied didn't much matter, so intellectually finished did he already seem. His contemporaries at the university — among them Stephen Spender, C. Day Lewis, and Louis MacNiece — "saw in him," as Spender wrote in a memoir after Auden's death, "a man who, instead of being like us, romantically confused, diagnosed the condition of contemporary poetry, and of civilization, and of us — with our neuroses." ("MacSpaunday" this group of poets was known as collectively, but it is probably closer to the truth to call them Auden & Co.) Auden left Oxford with a third-class degree, a mystery to his teachers, but in fact a point of no final interest, for the deeply talented have never had need of the official approval of universities.

The young W. H. Auden had the gifts, the self-assurance, and the early mastery of the craft of poetry, at least in its technical aspects, but what would his subject be? The General Strike in England was in 1926, when Auden was nineteen, and it was followed hard upon by the Depression. The class war was the thing wherein to catch the conscience of the left wing, with which Auden (& Co.) quickly became caught up. "Private faces in public places / Are wiser and nicer / Than public faces in private places," he wrote in a poem of 1931. He put his private face into very public places fairly early in the game. His artful trick was brilliantly to limn in verse the private side of the public life, as in this sonnet of 1934, "Who's Who," partly about T. E. Lawrence:

> A shilling life will give you all the facts:
> How his father beat him, how he ran away,
> What were the struggles of his youth, what acts
> Made him the greatest figure of his day:
> Of how he fought, fished, hunted, worked all night,

Though giddy, climbed new mountains, named a sea:
Some of the last researchers even write
Love made him weep his pints like you and me.

With all his honours on, he sighed for one
Who, say astonished critics, lived at home;
Did little jobs around the house with skill
And nothing else; could whistle; would sit still
Or potter round the garden; answer some
Of his long marvelous letters but kept none.

Auden must have given the impression of greatly scattered energy. He wrote plays, much verse, reviewed books, taught at boys' schools, traveled and wrote collaboratively with Louis MacNiece and Christopher Isherwood. "He reported brilliantly," as Edward Mendelson notes in *Early Auden*, "on history and science, history and economics, people and places, and the many varieties of public and private hatred." He zipped off to Iceland, China, Spain, wanting to be where the action was. His intellectual travels were no less jaunty — or is it jumpy? — going from Marx to Freud to Kierkegaard to the twentieth-century Christian theologians, acquiring new idea systems the way other people do wardrobes.

It is to the point that W. H. Auden rarely wrote about nature, partly owing, doubtless, to his poor eyesight. Another of his biographers, Humphrey Carpenter, writes: "In fact, none of his senses seemed to be highly developed; everything had to be scanned by his intellect before he could become really aware of it." Auden himself, in "Letter to Lord Byron," wrote: "To me Art's subject is the human clay, / And the landscape but a background to the torso, / All Cézanne's apples I would give away / For one small Goya or a Daumier." Even though he wrote the best poem ever written about a painting, "Musée des Beaux Arts," on the subject of Breughel's *Icarus*, he never spent much time on visual art. (He also disliked ballet, which he called "an adolescent's art.") Cityscapes were more in the way of his specialty, as in these last six lines from "Brussels in Winter":

Ridges of rich apartments loom tonight
Where isolated windows glow like farms,
A phrase goes packed with meaning like a van,

A look contains the history of man,
And fifty francs will earn a stranger right
To take the shuddering city in his arms.

In 1928, Auden went off to Berlin with his friend, three years older, Christopher Isherwood. Weimar Republic Berlin was then a kind of Disneyland for homosexuals, and Auden made sure to go on all the rides. He and Isherwood, though they had slept together, were not actually lovers. Auden was never less than candid about his homosexuality. Always the pursuer, never the pursued — "If equal affection cannot be / Let the more loving one be me," he wrote — he felt unregenerate and unembarrassed about his sexual appetites. His various biographers speak of his having had brief affairs with women. In a *mariage blanc* of convenience (for her), he married Thomas Mann's daughter Erika, giving her instant American citizenship and thus saving her from the Nazis. Late in life, in the hope of finding domestic stability, he proposed marriage to Hannah Arendt, who didn't consider the proposal seriously. Yet he never politicized his homosexuality, never for a moment thought himself a victim because of it — though he wrote of J. R. Ackerley: "Few, if any, homosexuals can honestly boast their sex life has been happy."

The great tragicomedy of Auden's life, illustrating this last point, was his lengthy, ragged, on-again off-again relationship with Chester Kallman. Auden considered the relationship a marriage, and at one point wore a wedding ring. Kallman was fourteen years younger than Auden — he was eighteen years old when they met in 1939 at a poetry reading — Brooklyn born, Jewish, and very clever. He introduced Auden to American popular culture and, more important, to opera. (They would later collaborate on libretti, the most notable of which was for Stravinsky's *The Rake's Progress*.) He also drove him crazy with his unfaithfulness. After they had been together for a few years, Auden wrote to Kallman: "You are to me, emotionally a mother, physically a father, and intellectually a son . . . I believe in your creative gift . . . I rely absolutely on your critical judgment . . . with my body, I worship yours." The problem was that Auden, despite all his efforts to make Kallman feel his equal, was much the more talented and generally superior man. "It is through you," Auden wrote to Kallman after his own turn, or return, to Christianity, "that God has chosen to show me my beatitude." To which one can only add the commonplace thought that the Lord does indeed work in mysterious ways.

I have always thought that the material for a splendid play is to be found in the relationship between W. H. Auden and Chester Kallman, a greater and a lesser man, with the greater suffering at the hands of the lesser in good part owing to the envy of the latter for the former's gifts, position, high place in the world. The first scene for this play, a dialogue on the New York subway that actually took place, has already been written and is quoted in its entirety in Richard Davenport-Hines's *Auden:*

WYSTAN: I'm not your *father,* I'm your *mother.*

CHESTER: You're *not* my mother. I'm *your* mother.

WYSTAN: No, you've got it all wrong. I'm *your* mother!

CHESTER: You're not. You're my *father.*

WYSTAN (screaming): But you've *got* a father! I'm your bloody mother and that's that, darling! You've been looking for a mother since the age of four!

CHESTER (shouting): And you've been obsessed with your mother from the womb! You've been trying to get back ever since, so I *am* your mother! And you're my father!

WYSTAN: No, you want to replace your father for marrying women who reject you, for which you can't forgive him. But you want a mother who will accept you unconditionally, as I do . . .

CHESTER: *I'm your goddamn mother, for the same reason!* You're always sucking on me as if I were one giant tit.

WYSTAN: I must always have something to suck.
CHESTER: Not now, Wystan, not now.

Although Auden came to America before he met Chester Kallman, this relationship determined him to acquire American citizenship, lest he lose Kallman. Much speculation, some of it quite
petulant, had been proffered about Auden (and his friend Isherwood) leaving England for America just as World War II was beginning. Many people thought he skulked off to avoid the war and
was no better than a deserter. "No more Auden," Anthony Powell
wrote to Kingsley Amis. "I'm delighted that shit has gone." Cyril
Connolly called Auden and Isherwood "ambitious young men
with a strong instinct of self-preservation, and an eye on the main
chance." Evelyn Waugh referred to Auden as "a public bore," and
inserted him and Isherwood in his war trilogy as two cowardly
pansy poets.

All this was most unjust, especially in the case of Auden, who
did all he could to enlist in the war once America joined the fight.
More important, had Auden stayed on in England he might have
ended a smaller-gauge poet than he did — a John Betjeman, say, or
a Philip Larkin — more the little Englander, isolated, a touch provincial, breathing the thick smog of English irony through a thin
reed. "I knew it [that he must leave England] because if I stayed
I would inevitably become a member of the English establishment," he wrote. America opened up the world to him, though he
came to think himself less an American than a naturalized New
Yorker — New York that world city but of no known country.
America made him, I believe it can be argued, an international
poet, in a way that remaining in England would not have allowed.
It also gave him — a point of originality, this — command of two
distinct dictions, or vocabularies, English and American, which he
could alternate or mix as the poetic occasion demanded. What
Auden wanted, and found in America, was the chance to be a "minor Atlantic Goethe." He became at least that, and perhaps rather
more.

With hindsight there seems something quite as right about Auden emigrating to New York as T. S. Eliot, earlier, having emigrated to London. Eliot grew more concentrated in England as Auden widened his perspective in America. Although he remained very English — in some ways more English than the English — Auden nonetheless also seemed a most cosmopolitan poet and found himself perfectly at home in Italy and Austria, though he was staunchly Francophobe.

T. S. Eliot generally supported Auden in his poetic career, and was, while at Faber & Faber, his first publisher. Auden felt a respect bordering on reverence for Eliot: "I shall never be as great and good a man if I live to be a hundred," he told Louise Bogan. The admiration was, at first, far from reciprocal: in 1935 Eliot wrote to Virginia Woolf that Auden "was a very nice rattle brained boy." But then he also called him, when Auden was twenty-six, "about the best poet I have discovered in years," and opened up the pages of the *Criterion* to him for reviewing. Auden meanwhile, at Eliot's death in 1964, told an interviewer that "no future changes and fluctuations in taste will consign his work to oblivion."

In their personal lives, the two poets could not have been more different: Eliot, quiet, costive, beautifully organized, a careful caretaker of his career; Auden, publicatious, loquacious, voracious, living with cigarette ashes and nicotine fingers and brutally bitten-down fingernails, sleeping with overcoats, in some instances drapes, even paintings atop him, seeming to dress out of the laundry bag (not the clean laundry bag, either), finding his natural habitat in alcohol, general squalor, and relentless work. No one could have been less calculating. Although he enjoyed having money, and knew its value to the penny, Auden wrote an introduction to Dag Hammarskjöld's book *Markings* that touched on the author's delusion that he was God's servant, if not imagining he was God himself, that was certain to offend the Nobel Prize committee. Knowing this, he still refused to make any changes in it, remarking, apparently without rancor, "Well, there goes the Nobel Prize."

Whatever the disarray in Auden's life, and it was rarely less than impressive, his extraordinary intelligence always seems to have shone through. Vast imperfection of the life, near perfection of the mind seemed to be his lot. "At one or another time there must be five or six supremely intelligent people on earth," Howard Moss wrote shortly after his death. "Auden was one of them." Auden was an authentic intellectual, with all the good and bad qualities that go with the title. Not all that many superior poets have been intellectuals — I am hard pressed to name one, though Robert Lowell came close — and herein lies, I think, the source of Auden's originality and also some of his flaws.

Anthony Hecht has nicely formulated the characteristic Audenesque poem as one that "interfuses the public with the private domain," in which he "wrote of one in terms of the other." These were the poems, again to quote Hecht, in which "the outer and public world impinges, imposes upon, and endangers the personal and private realm." Perhaps the most famous among these poems of Auden are "New Year Letter," "Spain 1937," "September 1, 1939," "In Memory of W. B. Yeats," and "The Shield of Achilles" — many of them poems about which the poet had second and third thoughts, editing and shearing off parts as he grew older. He later decided that the world would not pardon Kipling and Paul Claudel for writing well and cut the passage from "In Memory of W. B. Yeats," and he deleted the famous line from "September 1, 1939" — "We must love one another or die" — concluding that, love one another till we are quite blue in the face, we shall die anyhow. As for *The Orators*, he claimed: "My name on the title-page seems a pseudonym for someone else, someone talented but near the border of sanity, who might well, in a year or two, become a Nazi."

But the single line that got Auden in the hottest of water was that of "The conscious acceptance of guilt in the necessary murder," from "Spain 1937," which seemed to justify killing for political reasons. This was the line that George Orwell jumped on in his essay "Inside the Whale," where he wrote: "The Hitlers and the Stalins find murder necessary, but they don't advertise their callousness, and they don't speak of it as murder; it is 'liquidation,' 'elimination,' or some other phrase. Mr. Auden's brand of amoralism is only possible if you are the kind of person who is always somewhere else when the trigger is pulled." Although Auden eliminated the poem from his official collected verse, he justified his position by saying that all he intended was to make the point that in any war, unless one is a pacifist, one must find it necessary to kill other human beings whose only fault is that they are fighting on the other side; and that if any war can be called just, then murder, in a just cause, becomes necessary.

Which is certainly fair enough, but it does bring up another, more complicated question: ought a poet, within his poems, to deal so directly with such opinions, ideas, issues? Everyone will remember the famous reply to Degas, who was trying to write poems, when he asked Mallarmé where he got his ideas. "But Degas," Mallarmé wisely replied, "poetry is not written with ideas but with words." This deceptively simple remark, like so many of Mallarmé's remarks, has great weight and subtlety, speaking about the dangerousness of ideas to poetry. One may end up with ideas, but one should never start out with them.

In his late poem "Thanksgiving" (1973), Auden thanks those who influenced him as a poet. His list includes Hardy, Thomas, and Frost; Yeats, Graves, and Brecht; Kierkegaard, Charles Williams, and C. S. Lewis; and ends with Horace and Goethe. But he could easily have added Marx, Freud, D. H. Lawrence, Gerald Heard, Georg Groddeck, Karl Barth, Reinhold Niebuhr, and many others. Much of Auden's experience derived from books, as opposed to observation and direct experience, and, naturally enough, the books he read most intensely were those intellectually fashionable during his time. This is what made him so very much more the intellectual than Frost, Stevens, even Eliot. Like the standard intellectual, he seemed to live completely in his time. John Bayley writes that "Auden could not get into things and people, but he got instead into the spirit and sense of the age, into its moods and dreams, its fashions and crazes, from Homer Lane to Sheldon, from the yo-yo to carbon dating."

The ideas in Auden's poetry were always what seemed to bring

Randall Jarrell up short. Jarrell, the best poetry critic of the day, could never quite come to terms with Auden. Nor could he quite leave him alone. For Jarrell, Auden always had deep flaws, but when he corrects them and goes in the right direction, he goes, for Jarrell, "a good deal too far." The best poems in the 1940 book *Another Time* are better than any poems being written, but they are accompanied by many poor poems, containing "comments that are often interesting or clever or amusing; [but] poetry is not comments." In the 1950s, Jarrell found Auden to have written better in the 1930s, though he didn't really satisfy him then, either. Auden "is the most accomplished poet alive," and "his laundry list would be worth reading—I speak as one who's read it many times, all rhymed and metered," and "even when Homer nods, it's quite a performance." Of course, "Auden was, and is potentially, one of the best poets on earth," yet when one gets down to cases, so many of his poems, for Jarrell, turn out to be, like "New York Letter," "not quite first rate."

To a long essay titled "Changes of Attitude and Rhetoric in Auden's Poetry," Jarrell appends an altered epigraph from Heraclitus: "We never step twice into the same Auden." Wherever Jarrell stepped into the long river of Auden's verse, he seemed to discover something unpleasant on his shoe. This particular essay sets out, brilliantly, all the devices—twenty-six major and many minor ones—that Auden used to get his brilliant poetic effects. The feeling one has at the end of the essay is diminishment, which Jarrell surely realized, for he closes on this note: "An essay like this may seem an ungrateful return for all the good poetry Auden has written; and I feel embarrassed at having furnished—even in so limited an article—so much Analysis and so little Appreciation. But analyses, even unkind analyses of faults, are one way of showing appreciation; and I hope at another time to try another way." Alas, Jarrell never got around to doing so.

Few people interested in the serious game of poetry would deny the enormous achievement of W. H. Auden. The poet himself surely could have had no genuine doubt about this, either. By the time he reached fifty, such was the monumentality of this achievement, he had become almost posthumous while still alive. Where complication sets in is in specifying the nature of that achievement. In the preface to the 1945 edition of his *Collected Poetry*, Auden wrote:

> In the eyes of every author, I fancy, his own past work falls into four classes. First, the pure rubbish which he regrets ever having conceived; second — for him the most painful — the good ideas which his incompetence or impatience prevented from coming to much. (*The Orators* seems to me such a case of the fair notion fatally injured); third, the pieces he has nothing against except their lack of importance; these must inevitably form the bulk of any collection since, were he to limit it to the fourth class alone, to those poems for which he is honestly grateful, his volume would be too depressingly thin.

Auden's final *Collected Poems,* edited by his executor, Edward Mendelson, comprises nearly nine hundred pages. That's a lot — a ton, really — of poems. "Though I don't think anyone doubts Auden wrote masterpieces," Howard Moss remarked soon after Auden's death, "it is not easy to say, as it is in Eliot's or Stevens's case, exactly what — which — they are." Everyone who cares about poetry will have his or her own personal Auden anthology. Mine includes "In Memory of W. B. Yeats," "In Praise of Limestone," "At the Graveside of Henry James," "Voltaire at Ferney," "Musée des Beaux Arts," "Lullaby," "Embassy," "As I Walked Out One Evening," "Their Lonely Betters," "Letter to Lord Byron," "The Shield of Achilles." Not many surprises here, I fear.

But, somehow, Auden seems more impressive than even his best poems. I know no poet who, even in quite slapdash poems, can provide more pleasant and provocative surprises. So many of Auden's rhymes have, in miniature, the same effect as a good story; they seem at once unpredictable yet inevitable: "Hunt the lion, climb the peak, / No one guesses you are weak." His juxtapositions — "Hegelian bishops" — get one's attention like those of no other poet. His diction can be ornate, arcane, colloquial, and precise. For those interested in the pure pleasure of watching language beautifully manipulated, no modern poet — make that no modern writer *tout court* — did it better than Wystan Hugh Auden.

Auden has long been regarded as "the poet's poet." This not only because poets were in the best position to appreciate what is behind his achievement, but also because of all that he did — in prosody, in opening up new realms of subject matter, in advancing the art of verse generally — to widen their own sense of possibility. "God bless this poet who took the honest chances," Karl Shapiro, in his poem "W.H.A.," wrote. "God bless the live poets whom his death enhances."

More than forty years ago, in a classroom at the University of Chicago, I heard the poet and critic Elder Olson read a long passage from *The Waste Land,* close the book, remark on its beauty, sigh, then add: "What a pity that I cannot believe a word of it!" I'm not sure that I now believe it either, but I have no doubt that T. S. Eliot did, just as he believed every semicolon in his *Four Quartets.* And, one might add, as Robert Frost believed in those "Two Tramps in Mud Time" or Wallace Stevens in the view of the world of that woman in her peignoir sitting of a Sunday morning in her sunny chair with her coffee and oranges.

The Auden problem, for me, is not only do I not believe in so many of the ideas behind his earlier poetry, but I am far from sure that he believed in them himself. His early Marxism, his Freudianism, even his Kierkegaardian existentialism leading on to his renewed Christianity — none of these seem quite convincing. (The philo-Semitic Auden once told Alan Ansen: "I've been increasingly interested in the Jews . . . I wonder what would happen if I converted to Judaism.") They feel instead more like the work of an intellectual window-shopping on the Rodeo Drive of ideas.

In his biography, Humphrey Carpenter mentions that Auden "was not especially ashamed that his poetry at this period [the early 1930s] preached ideas to which he did not really subscribe." In 1933 he wrote a friend, "I am living miserably like a hen scratching for food," which Carpenter interprets to mean that he felt "starved of an ideology," or a workable set of ideas on which to base his poetry. On this question, in *The Dyer's Hand,* Auden wrote somewhat equivocally:

> What makes it difficult for a poet not to tell lies is that, in poetry, all facts and beliefs cease to be true or false and become interesting possibilities. The reader does not have to share the beliefs expressed in the poem in order to enjoy it. Knowing this, a poet is constantly tempted to make use of an idea or a belief, not because he believes it to be true, but because he sees it has interesting poetic possibilities. It may not, perhaps, be absolutely necessary that he believes it, but it is certainly necessary that his emotions be deeply involved, and this they can never be unless, as a man, he takes it more seriously than as a mere poetic convention.

"For poetry," Auden famously told us, "makes nothing happen." Later, in confirmation of this, he would write about his own politico-poetic forays: "I know that all the verse I wrote, all the positions I took in the thirties, didn't save a single Jew. These attitudes, these writings, only help oneself. They merely make people who think like one, admire and like one — which is rather embarrassing." Did Auden ever look back on his adulatory poem about Sigmund Freud, whom he makes out to be a secular saint of science, with similar embarrassment once it began to seem that Freud's ideas may have hurt more people than they helped? Are ideas in poetry, the question is, no more than playthings, or, as the journalists have it, good copy?

Paul Valéry, the only modern French writer whom Auden unstintingly admired and who contemplated these matters all his life, felt that "philosophizing in verse was as silly as an attempt to play lotto according to the rules of chess." In his *Cahiers,* Valéry wrote: "Poetry is not obliged to expound ideas. Ideas (in the usual sense of the word) are conventional expressions or formulas. That is not the *stage* at which poetry arises. It exists at a previous point — where things themselves are as it were pregnant with ideas. So it has to shape or communicate a state which is sub-intellectual or pre-ideational and reconstitute it as a spontaneous function, using all the artifice required." Not that ideas have no place in poetry, but the purest poetry entails "the simultaneous management of syntax, harmony, and ideas" in proper register, with thought in a poem "concealed like the nutritive value in a fruit."

Auden could manage the syntax and the harmony with ease, but toward the middle of his life he began to doubt the import of his or any other ideas. At which point he turned from being the public poet so many admired — "the Court Poet of the Left," Edward Mendelson calls that incarnation of Auden — to the later, domestic one his admirers merely tolerated.

I find the domestic Auden, if not the better poet, certainly the more impressive human being. I also agree with Clive James, who wrote: "I think an appreciation of Auden's later work is the only sure test for an appreciation of Auden, just as an appreciation of Yeats's early work is the only sure test of an appreciation of Yeats." Like all highly intelligent people, Auden realized the staggering limitations of politics. His understanding of the limits of human power generally conditions much of his later thinking and writing, which takes on a more mature, hence more resigned, feeling.

He began to write more literary journalism, much of it smart and very winning. He was always in demand as a reader of his own poetry: "Though warm my welcome everywhere, / I shift so frequently, so fast, / I cannot now say where I was / The evening before last." He bought and moved into a house in Kirchstetten, half an hour outside Vienna. In New York, he lived amid the cigarette ashes, mouse droppings, and cat-piss smells in his apartment on St. Mark's Place. He lost his teeth. Christopher Isherwood said that his face belonged in the British Museum. (He apparently suffered from Touraine-Solente-Gole syndrome, causing the skin of the forehead and face to become thick and deeply furrowed.) In Manhattan he padded about the streets in house slippers, making sure to carry at least five dollars at all times so as not to disappoint muggers and turn them more violent. He continued to churn out verse — ". . . Against odds / Methods of dry farming may still produce grain" — but libretti and belletristic projects (a commonplace book, an anthology of aphorisms) began to seem his main work.

His drinking became heavier and heavier. He was certain he was living in an age of decline and, having long ago given up on saving mankind, wished only to save the language that had served him so well. (He claimed to have written poems in every meter, and he may have also written them in every form, save the epic and the chant royal.) Not much past sixty, he began to regard and carry himself as an old man, not at all displeased to be considered a back number. He ceased listening, and began telling and retelling his old anecdotes, sometimes more than once in the same evening. He became punctilious about small things — bills should be paid and returned the same day they were received — and unconcerned about large ones. He found New York, as he put it, "Hell," and arranged to move into rooms in his old Oxford college. He died one night in his sleep, in a hotel room in Vienna — where, presumably, his heart gave out — in 1973 in his sixty-sixth year.

Auden was already famous when he arrived in America in his early thirties — a reporter was waiting to interview him — and retained his fame throughout the remainder of his life. He carried himself as someone not only richly accomplished but assured of his place in literary history. But what, now, nearly thirty-five years after his death, seems likely to be that place?

Auden may have been correct about not having been born at the right time and in the right country, but I think he must also have known that his own place as a poet was below that of Eliot, Stevens, and Frost. They wrote out of direct feeling and the heart; he much more out of books and the intellect. "The work that was only *new, passionate, significant of the ideas of a period,*" wrote Valéry, "can and must perish." Not all of Auden will perish, far from it; not, I think, those poems that are not primarily ideational and proceed from the clear vision of a brilliant mind. W. H. Auden was a professional poet, an immensely talented writer, and if there is a line in Anglophone literature out of which he derives, it is, I believe, that of Alexander Pope and Lord Byron, two other professional poets, miraculously gifted, whose facility was perhaps greater than their feeling, who provided more pleasure than wisdom, and whose work will live on for as long as language beautifully handled continues to be admired.

The God-haunted Fiction of
Isaac Bashevis Singer

O N A FEW OCCASIONS I have been asked who among the writers of the past half century I thought might be read a hundred years from now. I could think of only Isaac Bashevis Singer — chiefly because he is the single writer of our time who might as easily have been read a hundred years *before* his birth. And yet most critics prefer not to delve into the reason behind Singer's literary timelessness.

Born in Poland in 1904 and coming to America only in 1935, Singer wrote all his stories in Yiddish and had translators with greater fluency in English than he. Although his knowledge of English improved greatly over the years, Singer always spoke in a greenhorn's accent. ("It is a rare mark of individuality to be a great writer in a language he speaks so badly," wrote Paul Valéry of Joseph Conrad, who never lost his strong accent, either.)

That Singer wrote in the dying language that is Yiddish makes his case all the more interesting. Three volumes of his stories have now been collected and issued by the Library of America. (The only other non-American-born writers in this canonical publishing enterprise are Vladimir Nabokov and Alexis de Tocqueville.) Singer's devotion to Yiddish — the *mama-loshen*, or mother tongue — was complete. He insisted it has "vitamins other languages haven't got" and claimed that it is "very rich in describing character and personality, though very poor in words for technology." In his Nobel Prize lecture of 1978, he remarked that the language captured "the pious joy, lust for life, longing for the Messiah, patience, and deep appreciation for humanity" of the Yiddish-speaking people among whom he came of age in Poland. Yet in the same lecture, he claimed *universality* for Yiddish, averring that "in a figurative way Yiddish is the wise and humble language of us all, a frightened and hopeful humanity."

Isaac Bashevis Singer was born in Leoncin, Poland, the son and grandson of rabbis. He grew up in an atmosphere of grinding poverty and conflicting piety. The conflict derived from the continuing argument between Singer's father's mystical tendencies and his mother's more traditional, rationalistic Judaism; the poverty, from Singer's father's refusal to take a Russian-language examination required by czarist law, so that, despite his considerable learning, he was forced to work as, in effect, a clandestine rabbi serving the poorest of Jews.

The central figure in the Singer household was his mother, Bathsheva, after whom Isaac took his middle name, Bashevis. The daughter of a distinguished line of rabbis, a woman of genuine Jewish learning in her own right, she was, from all reports, a personality of great force. Singer was said to resemble his mother physically — small-boned, blue-eyed, and red-haired — and, some say, temperamentally; and he reverenced her all his days.

The other important figure in Singer's family life was his brother Israel Joshua Singer, himself a writer and for many years one of greater renown than Isaac Bashevis. Elder by eleven years, he wrote novels famous in their day, *Yoshe Kolb* (1933) and *The Brothers Ashkenazi* (1936), and died of a heart attack when he was fifty years old. *The Brothers Ashkenazi* remains a magnificent novel, one in which the villain is no less than the country of Poland, and the first book in which I learned, a lesson often repeated, that the one thing the far left and the far right always come around to agree upon is hatred of the Jews. Although Isaac Bashevis would eventually achieve much greater fame than his brother, and although his talent was more various and fecund, he never wrote a novel as powerful as *The Brothers Ashkenazi*.

In fact, Isaac Bashevis Singer is a great writer in part because of the plentitude of his production. Here he was lucky even in his misfortune. His family's poverty caused the Singers to retreat to the backwaters to live, at one point with his mother's father in the village of Bilgoray, where the intrusions of modernity were few, and later on Krochmalna Street, in the slums of Warsaw, where a buzz of urban tumult played out on the street, which Singer later referred to as "my literary gold mine." In both the rural retreats and the intensely urban setting, the young and always observant Isaac acquired material sufficient to sustain him through a long career. His life in New York, to which he came in 1935, a life lived among the Jewish refugees from Hitler and Stalin, gave him yet more material.

Singer came by one of his major themes, the conflict between the religious and the secular life, as part of his birthright. Among Eastern European Jews, this conflict was brought to the foreground by the *Haskalah,* a period of great transition for the Jews of Eastern Europe. A delayed enlightenment, the *Haskalah* caused Western literature, philosophy, and art to impinge on traditional Jewish orthodoxy, a world hitherto contentedly self-enclosed within Torah, Talmud, and the commentaries of the sage rabbis.

As a boy and young man, Singer straddled both worlds. He was sent to a rabbinical seminary, and he spent some time teaching in a yeshiva in a Jewish village, but he did both with less than passionate enthusiasm. The distraction was his brother Israel Joshua, who was, so to say, *Haskalah* all the way. He had lived briefly in Russia, saw the Russian revolution firsthand, and had an instinctive revulsion for the lives of the shtetl Jews; in a memoir, I. J. Singer, describing these lives, refers to "the stink of religion," an unforgettable phrase. Living with the unrelenting arguments between his older brother and their parents, Singer decided, at least at the time, that "all his arguments were very strong, while the arguments of my parents seemed to me weak."

Through his brother, Singer got a job working as a proofreader for a Yiddish magazine, and fell in with the Jewish bohemian circles of 1920s Warsaw, a city that was then roughly a third Jewish. He began to publish articles and stories; he was a young man with many romantic entanglements. A relationship with a woman of revolutionary spirit produced a son, Singer's only child. The mother of the boy took him off to Russia and then to Israel. Singer himself emigrated to the United States, where his brother had arranged a job for him on the Yiddish-language *Jewish Daily Forward.*

For something like an eight-year stretch, Singer, this most productive of writers, felt himself blocked after his arrival in the United States, producing mere driblets of negligible journalism. Some claimed that the shadow of his more famous brother eclipsed him and that he began to come into his own only at his brother's death in 1943. More likely, he was stunned by the sheer force and energy of America; he found American character incomprehensible. He felt torn from his old world and his linguistic roots: he had a smattering of Hebrew, Polish, and German, but spoke only Yiddish. He was already thirty and without prospects of any kind. "In reality," as he told Richard Burgin, in *Conversations with Isaac Bashevis Singer,* "I considered myself a has-been writer, an ex-writer, a writer who lost both the power and the appetite for writing."

The writing of his family-chronicle novel *The Family Moskat* got him back on track; the fact that the novel was being serialized in the *Forward,* with the pressure of a new chapter required every week, kept him there. The book was eventually translated and published in English by Alfred A. Knopf, though originally in a much-cut version. In 1952, *Partisan Review* published his story "Gimpel the Fool," in a translation said to have been done in a few hours by Saul Bellow, and soon after the New York intellectuals took him up, though he never took them up. Not long afterward Cecil Hemley, the chief editor and publisher of the small and distinguished Noonday Press and one of those self-effacing friends of literature, arranged for a translation of Singer's first novel, *Satan in Goray,* and brought out a volume of his stories. When Farrar,

Straus & Giroux acquired Noonday Press, Hemley took Singer along. In 1967, he made a *New Yorker* connection, becoming the first writer the magazine published regularly in translation. Eleven happily productive years later, Singer won the Nobel Prize.

At first, a serious attempt was made to sell Singer as a modernist writer. Some claimed that religion formed no more than a background in his fiction, and that his novels and stories worked out only that modern trinity of the Freudian id, ego, and superego. Others claimed that "there's a religious dimension to his writing that is remarkably modern." The critic Morris Dickstein said that Singer "had a vision of life that promoted the idea that we should live all we can and live out our desires, even though it may lead us to be kind of shadows who are just dancing around in a void. Both a gloomy, grim, dark philosophy at the same time — one that had to do with a very positive view of living in the moment, and particularly about living sexually." If this reading were true, Isaac Bashevis Singer would be a much lesser writer than I believe he is.

But, then, Singer and sex is a subject unto itself. In various interviews, Singer has said that the best story is a love story. Oddly, he himself tended to write not about love but about passion, which is far from the same thing. As a character in his "The Beard" tells the story's Singer-like narrator, "You write about love, but you don't know what it is. Forgive me, but you describe passion, not love, which makes sacrifices and ripens over the years." Perhaps the best critic of Singer was Singer himself, in such squibs provided in his own stories.

Religious zeal is another realm that fascinated Singer. In his story "Passions," he describes a man who one night leaves his little house in the village of Radoszyce in Poland and walks all the way to Jerusalem; another man, a tailor, owing to a contretemps in synagogue, enters into a wager that requires him to become a serious scholar within a year; still another man decides to treat every day as if it were Yom Kippur, or the Day of Atonement: "Everything can become a passion, even serving God" is the story's final sentence.

But the main passion on display in Singer's stories and novels is usually the sexual one. His characters are inevitably swept up in the pure heat of desire, whose first consequence is to cause them to abandon duty to family, to community, above all to God. They throw away everything in the blind certainty that their pleasure in the objects of their passion will endure forever. The sheer sexiness of Singer's writing is one of the many things that infuriated his fellow refugee Yiddish writers, though not so much, one suspects, as did the envy they felt at his immense success in America.

Singer himself, a small, alopecic man with striking blue eyes who tended to dress in the greenhorn style of mismatched colors and small outrageous touches — one of my favorites was his apparent weakness for polka-dot shirts — was nonetheless, by all accounts, what used to be known as "a real ladies man" and what continues to be known as a "skirt chaser."

Everyone has a story about Singer's activities in this line. My own derives from a woman who told me that Singer came up to her, in an empty college auditorium an hour or so before a reading he was to give, to ask if she was Jewish and, if so, where her family was from. She replied that she was indeed Jewish and her family was from Bialystok. Singer told her that he knew a great deal about Bialystok and would like to know more about her family. He suggested they meet after the reading.

He had been given two rooms in the building in which he had earlier read. In the sitting room there were a couch, a few chairs, a table on which was a bowl filled with fruit. They sat on opposite ends of the couch. Singer asked the woman — she was then in her thirties, he perhaps in his late sixties — to tell him what she knew about her family history. She recounted what little knowledge she had for perhaps four or five minutes, when Singer, leaning toward her, made his move:

"Do you mind," he asked in his immigrant's accent, "if I kiss you?"

"Oh, Mr. Singer," she said, "I'm very honored you would ask, but I've just begun a second marriage and I don't want anything to go wrong. I hope you understand." (To me she said the thought of popping into bed with him "would have been like sleeping with my grandfather.")

Singer put up a hand, palm outward. "No, no, no," he said. "Don't vorry." And, pointing to the table in the center of the room, he added, "Please, take some fruit to your husband."

The point of this story is not its salaciousness, for it hasn't any. The point is to recount that Singer's knowledge of sin was not entirely theoretical. He was apparently one of those seducers who proceed on an actuarial basis, who tries all women on the statistical assumption that he might just strike fire and accepts defeat with the same equanimity as success. He was a married man, and if ever one wishes to see a face precisely describable as long-suffering, one cannot do better than gaze upon a photograph of his wife, Alma. When Alma left her husband to marry Singer, she also left her two young children, about whom, in the Singer biographies, one hears nothing further. Singer was parted from his own son for twenty years without, so far as is known, any strenuous attempts on his part to get in touch with the boy. Janet Hadda, one of Singer's biographers, and not an unsympathetic one, remarks tersely: "He was a negligent husband, an unfit father, and he knew it."

Not all the sin described in Singer's stories is sexual; sometimes it has to do with worshiping idols or following false messiahs or being too zealous in one's worship. Of his story "Pigeon Feathers," the novelist Francine Prose has remarked on "its insistence on looking beneath the surface pieties of religion to examine the unruly hungers, obsessions, rages, griefs, and mysteries that faith and culture address." I don't happen to think Singer thought religion, at least the religion of Judaism, had any pieties that he would care to call "superficial."

Isaac Bashevis Singer was a great literary artist, in the pure-storyteller division. But many critics who admire him are not quite ready to take his subjects seriously or accept his themes, preferring instead to find the modern note in him. In his story "The Briefcase," the Singer-like narrator is to give a lecture titled "Is There a Future for the Literature of the Subconscious and the Absurd?" In the story the lecture is never delivered, but elsewhere Singer has supplied the answer to the question posed in its title, and that answer is No. Insofar as modernism in literature was connected with stream of consciousness, experiments in style, or the attempt to penetrate further in the realm of depth psychology through literature, Singer eschewed the entire enterprise. He thought Joyce's *Ulysses* "almost boring," never read *The Sound and the Fury*, and thought little of Samuel Beckett. Believing literature is an art without a history of progress, he thought the best novels and short stories were, with very few exceptions, written in the nineteenth century. He was non- if not anti-modernist, above all in holding that literature and culture would never replace religion; nor did he for a moment feel they deserved to do so.

For a man who claimed to care very little for style, Singer wrote wonderfully well. His English prose is winningly rhythmical, the rhythm playing out most attractively over the length of single paragraphs. He produced strong novels — *Satan in Goray, The Magician of Lublin,* and *Enemies: A Love Story* are among the best of them — but his real mastery was in the short story. Four or five sentences into a story and he has you hooked. He knew where life's dramas lay, and he provided an endless cast of characters to work them out. He was in possession of all the perfect details required to make his stories live. No other writer could get one into a story more quickly. Here is the opening paragraph of "The Beard":

> That a Yiddish writer should become rich, and in his old age
> to boot, seemed unbelievable. But it happened to Bendit Pupko,
> a little man, sick, pock-marked, with one blind eye and a game
> leg.

And here is the opening of "Sam Palka and David Vishover":

Sam Palka sat on the sofa — stocky, a tuft of white hair on each side of his bald head, his face red, with bushy brows and blood-shot eyes that changed from pale blue to green to yellow. A cigar stuck out between his lips. His belly protruded like that of a woman in late pregnancy. He wore a navy-blue jacket, green pants, brown shoes, a shirt with purple stripes, and a silk tie on which was painted the head of a lion. Sam Palka himself looked to me like a lion which by some magic had turned into a rich man in New York, a Maecenas to Yiddish writers, a supporter of the Yiddish theater, president of an old-age home in the Bronx, the treasurer of a society that supported orphans in Israel.

Once presented with these Pupkos and Palkas, one wants to know what Singer will do with them. Extraordinary things, it turns out, but none of it would have worked if Singer hadn't understood that all good fiction is anchored in interesting character. "Something attracted me to that playful little man," he writes about a character named Liebkind Bendel in the story "The Joke." "Perhaps it was because I couldn't fathom him. Every time I thought I knew him some new whim popped up." Singer knew that character is endless in the richness of its variety, even if his characters come chiefly from the closely circumscribed world of Eastern European Jewry and those survivors of Stalin and Hitler who settled mainly in New York, though also in Buenos Aires and a few other world capitals.

To evince an interest in character is, of course, to show an interest in human nature, a subject on which, despite the best efforts of science and social science, we remain in the same centuries-long state of high ignorance. For Isaac Bashevis Singer every human being was an exception who proved no rule. That ought to be the credo of every artist. Nor was fate, the mysterious chess game of life, any more easily understood. Explanations requiring elaborate abstractions leading to clichés, a taste for which Singer found strong in Americans, only made things worse.

Philosophy did not, in Singer's view, make them much better. As a younger man, he read a great deal of philosophy. He much admired Spinoza and Schopenhauer, and called the latter "a beautiful writer, a sharp observer of human affairs." But the limits of philosophy for Singer were too strictly marked, and philosophy itself, as he told an interviewer, "a kind of learning in which you really have to believe." Nor did philosophy speak to all the mysteries of life that beset Singer and with which he besets many of his most interesting characters. One among them, Hertz Grein, in *Shadows on the Hudson*, himself a former student of philosophy, claims that he went into a "field that has been bankrupt from the start — philosophy has been dead for two hundred years . . . The riddle grows greater, not smaller, and there's absolutely no way to solve it. It's hopeless."

Many who have written about Isaac Bashevis Singer's fiction underscore the point that he writes about a world that has disappeared, by which of course they mean the world of pre-Holocaust Jewry. "They had perished in the ghettoes or concentration camps or had died in Russia of hunger, typhoid fever, and scurvy," reads a sentence from the story "The Mentor," and it could have been inserted in many another of Singer's stories with a modern setting.

In "Pigeons" Singer wrote the most beautiful story I know about the Holocaust. Not surprisingly, it does not come at the subject directly but symbolically. The story has to do with one Professor Eibeschutz, a scholar who has taken to feeding the pigeons on the street below his apartment. He tells his Polish maid, Tekla, that doing so is more important to him than going to synagogue. "God is not hungry for praise," he reasons, "but the pigeons wait each day from sunrise to be fed. There is no better way to serve the Creator than to be kind to his creatures." One recalls here that, when asked why he had turned vegetarian, Singer said that he did it not for his own but for the chicken's sake.

Like many another Singer character, the professor tends to shift into *sub specie aeternitatis*, to ponder the meaning of the universe in the light of eternity. He recalls a passage in the Talmud in which Jews are likened to pigeons. "The pigeon, like the Jew, thrives on peace, quietude, and good will." He also does not mind indulging in teleology, or the consideration of designs and ends in the universe. "It was not easy to have faith in God's benevolence," he thinks, "but God's wisdom shone in each blade of grass, each fly, each blossom and mite."

One day, while out feeding his pigeons, the elderly professor is set upon by a gang of anti-Semitic Polish thugs and struck in the head by a rock. The injury results in his taking to his bed, where he withers and soon dies. The pigeons, in flight, follow the professor's hearse to the cemetery: "their wings, alternating between sun and shadow, became red as blood and then dark as lead." The story ends on this splendid paragraph:

> The following morning broke autumn-like and drab. The skies hung low and rusty. The smoke of the chimneys dropped back, gathering on the tile roofs. A thin rain fell, prickly as needles. During the night someone had painted a swastika on the professor's door. Tekla came out with a bag of feed, but only a few pigeons flew down. They pecked at the food hesitantly, glancing around as if afraid to be caught defying some avian ban. The smell of char and rot came up from the gutter, the acrid smell of imminent destruction.

Which brings me round to the question with which I began: why I believe that Isaac Bashevis Singer is the only writer of the past fifty years likely to be read with the same interest a hundred years from now. The answer, I believe, is not that Singer is a marvelous storyteller, which he was; nor because his oeuvre presents the most complete record of *Ostjuden* life before it was obliterated by the Nazis, which it does. No, I think that Singer's fiction will continue to live because he placed his powerful talent in the service of a great theme: the continuing drama of salvation, or finding acceptance in the eyes of God based on the way that one has lived.

This drama of individual salvation was once played in the mind of nearly everyone, from kings to peasants. The Enlightenment and all that followed from it has gone a long way to muffle it. But not for everybody, not for lots of intelligent people who cannot find their answers to life's deepest puzzles in philosophy or science — and distinctly not for Isaac Bashevis Singer.

I do not profess to report on the state of Singer's soul. Apart from his literary gifts, he seems not at all godly and not exactly God-fearing. Perhaps "God-haunted" describes him best. The question of the existence of God, His design, His meaning, why He allowed suffering, such things were never far from Singer's mind. He claimed to believe in God, to have "made peace with human blindness and God's permanent silence, but they give me no rest." He also claimed to feel "a deep resentment against the Almighty," in good part owing to His permitting the Holocaust, in lesser part for being a silent God, revealing "Himself in very, very small doses, yet showing very little evidence of His mercy."

But, more important, Singer was able to revivify the old drama of finding acceptance before God. His most powerful characters do so by acting with a benevolent, wise simplicity: characters such as Gimpel in "Gimpel the Fool," Akhsa in "A Crown of Feathers," the magician in *The Magician of Lublin,* and many others. Reformed sinners, simple good souls, some who turn their backs on the world, others who struggle earnestly to understand the meaning of life, all in different ways are put to the test, are players in the drama of individual salvation.

What makes Isaac Bashevis Singer's fiction so immensely alive is that its author understood that nothing has successfully replaced this drama, with its sense that one's actions matter, that they are being judged in the highest court of all, and that the stakes couldn't be greater. No contemporary human drama has been devised that can compare or compete with the drama of salvation, including the various acquisition dramas: those of acquiring pleasure, money, power, fame, knowledge, happiness on earth in any of its forms.

Nor can the drama of progress in understanding the universe promised by science. As Hertz Grein in *Shadow on the Hudson,* a character who has fallen away from the religion of his fathers, and one of Singer's questers, reflects: "What was the universe as Einstein or Eddington conceived it? A lump of clay packed with blind atoms rushing backward and forward, hurling themselves feverishly about." In the way of personal drama, the best that science provides is that exceedingly dull, altogether predictable three-part scenario: life, death, and certain oblivion.

Meanwhile, Isaac Bashevis Singer, in a thoroughly secularized age, through the power of storytelling, can still persuade his readers that other possibilities exist and that life is not without meaning. Which is why his work will still live when that of the professionally sensitive, the socially engaged, and the literary trick-shot artists of our time is long forgot.

Truman Capote and the
Cost of Charm

CHARM WAS Truman Capote's specialty, the propellant that lifted him early off the launching pad of obscurity and sent him, for a brief while, into the stratosphere of celebrity of a luminosity given to only a few writers in the history of this country: after Mark Twain and Ernest Hemingway, no one else comes to mind. Capote could be charming on the page or in person. His prose, always rhythmically on beat, featured lilting phrases. In no other writer would Haitian ladies on the porch of a bordello "flourish paper fans that beat the air like delirious moths," or a middle-aged woman take off her rimless spectacles to reveal eyes that, "nude and moist and helpless, seemed stunned by freedom; the skimpily lashed lids fluttered like long captive birds abruptly let loose." Who but Capote could write to a friend that "there is going to be a beauty contest on Saturday to pick a Miss Taormina: if I win will send you a telegram"?

Truman Capote was of course gayer than a leap-year Mardi Gras. Small, delicately featured, with a famously high and piping voice, he would have had a tough time *passing,* to use the old-fashioned phrase. Not that it often occurred to him to do so. He appears to have been perfectly at ease with his homosexuality. He played it, too, for charm.

Charm is the desire to delight, light-handedly executed. In

most definitions of charm the word "magic" turns up, and there is, in fact, something magical about the gift of charm, for it reminds us that the world, for all its dreariness and depression, suffering and sadness, is still a highly amusing place. When he was up to it, which he was most of the time, Truman Capote could almost unfailingly provide such reminders.

The standard—and rather boring—line on Capote's charm is that it was a dodge through which he hoped to attain the love he had missed as a child. In a letter to Perry Smith, one of the two killers who are at the center of his immensely successful work of reportage *In Cold Blood,* Capote provided a quick sketch of his childhood:

> I was an only child, and very small for my age—and always the smallest boy in school. When I was three, my mother and father were divorced . . . My father (who has been married five times) was a traveling salesman, and I spent much of my childhood wandering around the South with him. He was not unkind to me, but I disliked him and still do. My mother was only sixteen when I was born and was *very* beautiful. She married a fairly rich man, a Cuban, and after I was 10 I lived with them (mostly in New York). Unfortunately, my mother, who had several miscarriages and as a result developed mental problems, became an alcoholic and made my life miserable. Subsequently she killed herself (sleeping pills).

Not enough love in the home, the verdict is, and so poor little Truman sought it everywhere else. ("Too much love in the home," I would like to have written on the papers of many of my undeservedly confident students when I was a college teacher.)

To obtain that love, the argument runs, Capote's craving for fame, his desire to produce beautiful prose, were all so much sublimation. But to hold such a view is to dishonor the complexities of human character. Life is not, after all, a Barbra Streisand song. People who need people, I have discovered, are not usually the luckiest people at all. And the world—please believe me on this one—needs a hell of a lot more than love, sweet love.

Too Brief a Treat, the title chosen by Gerald Clarke for his edition of Truman Capote's letters, comes from a phrase Capote used to complain of the shortness of a letter sent him by a friend. These letters, scrupulously edited, with exactly the right degree of annotation, are themselves too brief a treat, ending roughly in 1966, though Capote lived on to 1984. The reason they end so early in their author's life is that he no longer needed to write his friends as often, having returned to the United States after living abroad (chiefly in Switzerland, Sicily, Italy, and France). What is more, the success of *Breakfast at Tiffany's* and *In Cold Blood* made him a wealthy man and, consequently, one who wrote less and less and drank and doped himself with pills more and more. Success killed Truman Capote, who is thought to have died of a drug overdose, just short of the age of sixty.

The letters begin with young Truman living in New York, publishing stories in the popular women's magazines: "a lad of the world," as he declared himself. Like many good American writers — H. L. Mencken and Ernest Hemingway notable among them — he had taken a pass on college. The literary historian Newton Arvin, biographer of Melville, Hawthorne, and Longfellow, was an early lover, and Capote referred to Arvin, who was twenty-four years older, as his own personal Harvard. But then Capote had a quick, osmotic mind, able to pick up, sort out, and make use of everything of interest that came his way. He was smart right out of the gate and, until nearly the end, did not grow dumber.

Today one thinks of Truman Capote, if one thinks of him at all, as the gay consort to the rich women of New York's designer East Side, a party giver of high power in his own right (the party he gave for Katharine Graham, publisher of the *Washington Post*, at the Plaza Hotel in New York in 1966 was referred to at the time in the press as "the party of the decade"), and a spewer of vicious gossip on Johnny Carson's *Tonight Show* (where among other insults he said that *Valley of the Dolls* author Jacqueline Susann looked "like a truck driver in drag").

• • •

In fact, until his devastating success Capote was a writer devoted to his craft and astute in his literary judgment. Before James Jones's *From Here to Eternity* was published, he called the book a bad combination of Thomas Wolfe and Norman Mailer yet still predicted its commercial success. To his editor at Random House he knocked Bud Schulberg ("such a small sensibility") and suggested that the firm's Modern Library would do much better to reprint Sarah Orne Jewett's *The Country of the Pointed Firs*. He much admired Edith Wharton and Willa Cather. He spotted the thinness of Stephen Spender. He called James Baldwin's fiction "crudely written and of a balls-aching boredom," while remarking of Baldwin generally that "he is a mysterious mixture of real talent and real fraud," which is, by my reckoning, a perfect judgment.

A savvy man, Truman Capote, and about nothing was he more savvy than his own career. He cultivated editors and publishers with great care. Applying for a Guggenheim, he arranged for Edith Sitwell and E. M. Forster to write recommendations for him. Once his career was launched, he dropped his agent and handled all business matters — and very cleverly too — on his own. As a craftsman, a pro, he seemed able to toss off work in many modes. He wrote two excellent screenplays: *Beat the Devil,* a brilliant spoof of international gangster flicks, and *The Innocents,* a striking adaptation of Henry James's *The Turn of the Screw.* "I loathe writing for films," he later wrote to his friend Mary Louise Aswell. "I think the bit I've done so far has done me a certain amount of good, . . . but that is as far as it should go." He was offered the opportunity to write a libretto for an opera by Aaron Copland, but claimed he "couldn't work up the right kind of interest: vanity, I suppose — I kept thinking how Aaron would get all the credit." Quite right, too.

The gossip quotient in *Too Brief a Treat* is splendidly high, and the names pour out at firehose intensity. Through charm Capote insinuated himself with many of the ostensibly most elegant people of his day. If a clanging bell were to go off every time one of these names was mentioned in these letters, the book would read like a nineteenth-century fire engine. He claims to have given a party to introduce André Gide to Christian Dior, also to have had a dalliance with Montgomery Clift. He knew Humphrey Bogart and John Huston from his work on *Beat the Devil*. Audrey Hepburn, who played Holly Golightly in the movie version of *Breakfast at Tiffany's*, is a name that comes a-clanging with a fair frequency. "Jackie [Kennedy] et moi spent the whole night talking about sex" isn't a bad little specimen. The Chaplins and Orson Welles get mentioned, as do the Agnellis and Niarchoses and W. H. Auden ("such a tiresome old Aunty").

Here is a letter written from Portofino to a friend named Andrew Lyndon, as rich a plum of name-dropping, with incisive criticisms thrown in at no extra charge, as one is likely to find anywhere:

> I've liked it here and have done a lot of work, but in August [of 1953] everything became too social — and I *do* mean social — the Windsors (morons), the Luces (morons plus), Garbo (looking like death with a suntan), the Oliviers (they let her [Vivien Leigh] out [of an insane asylum]), Daisy Fellowes [heiress to the Singer Sewing Machine fortune] . . . — then Cecil [Beaton] and John Gielgud came to stay with us, and we went to Venice on Arthur Lopez's yacht — whence I've just come back. Oh, yes, I forgot Noel Coward . . .

He used to like to play a game he invented called International Daisy Chain, best attempted, he felt, when drunk. The chain was formed through the connection of people who had had affairs with people who then went on to have affairs with other people: He claimed to have been able to construct one such chain from Cab Calloway to Adolf Hitler.

Referring to a visit from John Gielgud and Cecil Beaton and Noël Coward, Capote writes, "in other words, the whole Lavender Hill mob." The Lavender Hill, or gay, element in *Too Brief a Treat* is strong and generally adds to the amusement of the proceedings. His most candid letters are written to gay friends from his early days in New York. Capote himself preferred living in a homosexual partnership, which he did for much of his life: first with Newton Arvin and then, for more than thirty years, with a novelist named Jack Dunphy. The end of his life was made even more wretched by a violent relationship with a bisexual alcoholic named John O'Shea. He was alert to the comedy, but also the horrors, of the gay cruising life.

One piece of sad news on this front comes when Capote's former lover, Newton Arvin, a longtime teacher at Smith College, was caught and exposed as a recipient of homosexual pornography through the mails. He was convicted and given a one-year suspended sentence, had a nervous breakdown, and was removed from his teaching position at Smith. As Gerald Clarke notes, Arvin was spared serving a prison sentence only because of "ratting on two younger gay faculty colleagues . . . who were untenured; both were fired by Smith in 1961."

Capote stood by his old friend, bucking him up, offering him help of every kind: "Well, what's happened has happened; and it has happened to many others — who, like Gielgud, took it in stride and did not let it be the end of the world. All your friends are with you, of that you can be sure; and among them please do not count me least: aside from my affection, which you already have, I will be glad to supply you with money should the need arise. This is a tough experience, to be met with toughness, a calm head, a good lawyer."

One might call the author of the letters in *Too Brief a Treat* Janus-faced, except that in them he wasn't merely two- but really three-faced. There was the face for gay friends, the face for non-gay friends, and the face for the friends he made in Kansas while writing *In Cold Blood*. As often as not, he is working his nongay correspondents — the Hollywood producer David O. Selznick, Bennett Cerf, the publisher of Random House, and others — for his own ends.

Especially does this apply to the Dewey family, whose head, Alvin Dewey, was the Kansas Bureau of Investigation officer assigned to the murder of the Clutter family that was the subject of *In Cold Blood*. Capote cultivated this conservative midwestern family in the most sedulous way. He warned friends not to make remarks suggesting the reality of his considerably less than bourgeois life. In an early letter to the Deweys he refers to Jack Dunphy as "a friend who is here living with me," thus disguising his homosexuality. When the Deweys go off to Los Angeles on a holiday, he arranges for David O. Selznick and his wife, the actress Jennifer Jones, to show them around Hollywood.

Whatever his motives, there cannot be much doubt that Capote came genuinely to like the Deweys of Garden City, Kansas, and they him. Psychologists of the Streisand school have argued that in the Deweys he found the solid family of which he had always been deprived. But in his many letters to them, Capote alternates charm with requests for documents and other information about the Clutter murders and the fate of the murderers. One of the Dewey sons wishes to become a writer, and Capote agrees to read his manuscripts, comments carefully on them, and gives the boy sound advice on how to go about it. Always a generous gift-giver, he sent the family pleasing presents at every opportunity. He arranged trips for them for which he paid the expenses. But they had more to give him than he could possibly repay: they put him in possession of material for the book that would be the making of him.

Without *In Cold Blood,* Capote's name would probably be forgotten today. Although his fiction is never less than skillful, with the element of charm bordering on sentimentality frequently coming into play in such stories as "The House of Flowers" and "A Christmas Memory," it often feels a touch insubstantial, derivative, fragile, and too brightly colored. When Capote published his first novel, *Other Voices, Other Rooms* (1948), George Davis, an editor of *Mademoiselle* magazine known for his lacerating remarks, said: "I suppose someone had to write the fairy *Huckleberry Finn*."

In Cold Blood took six years to finish. Capote first heard of the murder of the Clutter family when he noticed a story in the *New*

York Times of November 16, 1959, with the headline "Wealthy Farmer, 3 of Family Slain," and he contracted with William Shawn to write about it for *The New Yorker.* From the outset, Capote felt he was sitting on a masterpiece. Complications of various kinds arose, chief among them lengthy appeals that delayed the execution of the two killers for years. A striking piece of hypocrisy in this correspondence is Capote's letters of friendship with the two killers, whom he also pumped for information — set beside letters to others expressing his impatience for their execution, so that he could complete his book at last. Writers, let us make no mistake, are swine.

Several letters in *Too Brief a Treat* make plain Capote's agonizing over the composition of *In Cold Blood.* This is unusual coming from a writer who heretofore made all his writing seem so much skateboarding down a gently descending incline. With this book, though, large nails, potholes, and flaming hurdles are everywhere in his path: "No, I'm finishing the last pages of my book," he writes to Cecil Beaton, "I must get rid of it regardless of what happens . . . My sanity is at stake — and this is no mere idle phrase. Oh, the hell with it. I shouldn't write such gloomy crap — even to someone as close to me as you are."

When in the autumn of 1965 the first of four installments of *In Cold Blood* began running in *The New Yorker,* its success was greater than even its highly imaginative author could have imagined. The work was one of which no one was permitted not to have an opinion: about its accuracy, its form (which he called "a non-fiction novel"), its power. The book also showed its author's impressive range. Born into southern squalor, hanging out with the vacuous wealthy in Manhattan, Capote could also understand the lives of a strongly Protestant midwestern farm family as well as those of the two monsters who murdered them. When he was on his game, this little man with the fruity voice didn't miss much.

With book publication, the money came cascading in. Capote was forty. He acquired something close to movie-star fame. His face was on the cover of magazines. He was a great draw for the talk shows, not least the *Tonight Show* (Johnny Carson's soon to be ex-wife Joanne was a close friend), where he could be depended upon to say scandalous things about famous contemporaries. As Herbert von Karajan is once supposed to have said when a Parisian cab driver asked him where he wished to go, so now could Truman Capote say: "It doesn't matter. They want me everywhere."

With the success of *In Cold Blood*, the letters in *Too Brief a Treat* begin to peter out, though Capote had nearly twenty years to live. But nothing would ever again excite his literary passion with the same force as *In Cold Blood*. So much that he would publish afterward felt more like make-work than writing in which he was fully engaged. The decline had begun, the fall was fast approaching.

Capote planned, for a final act, to go out as the American Proust with a novel called *Answered Prayers*, about the lives of the rich Manhattan women into whose confidence, through his charm, he had insinuated himself. When he published a chapter of the novel with the title "La Côte Basque" in *Esquire* in 1975, so damaging (if perhaps also true) was it to the people who had befriended him that he was ever afterward non grata in the chic social circles upon which he had come to depend.

The final decade of Capote's life, as one learns from Gerald Clarke's excellent biography of the writer, was a shambles of drugs and booze and lawsuits and ugly gossip and betrayals perpetrated both upon him and by him. This once delicately beautiful and richly talented young man became a talk-show buffoon, a booze-bloated bag of neediness, the subject of *New York Post* gossip headlines, and one of the first victims of the celebrity culture he had helped to create. It's a sad story — made sadder by the fact that he did not retain the lucidity to write it himself. Its theme might have been that charm is a gift that, when abused, can bring a man down hard.

The Max Beerbohm Cult

L OVERS — no lesser word will do — of the prose, caricatures, and mind of Max Beerbohm constitute a cult. Membership in the cult requires a strong penchant for irony, a skeptical turn of mind, and a sharp taste for comic incongruity. Like all true cults, the Beerbohm cult is small, very small, and always in danger of guttering out — but never, I'm happy to report, quite doing so.

When Max Beerbohm died, in his eighty-fourth year, he was buried in St. Paul's Cathedral, along with a very select company of roughly three hundred other English heroes of war, politics, and culture. His family's house in Kensington, at 57 Palace Gardens Terrace, has long borne one of those periwinkle-blue plaques noting that an important figure had resided there. In his lifetime, he was knighted, praised by everyone whose praise mattered (T. S. Eliot, Virginia Woolf, Evelyn Waugh, E. M. Forster, Edmund Wilson, and W. H. Auden, among others, weighed in), and was widely respected if not revered by people of literary sensibility.

Still, he was always what Arnold Bennett called a "small-public" writer. Beerbohm, even when alive, thought he had a readership of no more than fifteen hundred in England and another thousand in America. He had no delusions about the breadth of his appeal. His "gifts were small," he felt, and he told his first biographer, a man named Bohun Lynch, that he "used them very well and discreetly, never straining them; and the result is that I've made a charming little reputation."

But reputations for charm do not usually long survive the lives of those who exhibit them, however well and discreetly. Something more than charm has kept the small if scarcely gem-like Beerbohmian flame alive. I am myself, as you will perhaps by now have gathered, a member of the Beerbohm cult. Ten or so feet behind my back, three of his caricatures (of Byron, Matthew Arnold, and Dante) hang above a bookcase. A picture of Max Beerbohm is on a wall roughly six feet from where I am now writing about him. The photograph shows an elderly man — born in 1872, he lived until 1956 — sitting on a cane chair on the terrace of his small villa in Rapallo. Ever the dandy, he is wearing a boater at a jaunty angle, a light-colored and slightly rumpled suit, a white waistcoat and dark tie with a collar pin. His left leg is crossed over his right. His head and hands seem rather large for his body. His hooded eyes peer out of deep sockets, his thick white mustache does not droop. His countenance, slightly dour like that of so many great comedians, is that of a man on whom, right up to the end of life, not much has been lost.

I first began reading Max Beerbohm the year before his death. Of all the comic reputations of that day — S. J. Perelman, James Thurber, Frank Sullivan — his is the only one, nearly fifty years later, whose comedy holds up for me. The combination of common sense and whimsy that were his special literary blend continues to work its magic. All is presented in a calm and unfaltering style of what I think of as formal intimacy; if he ever wrote a flawed sentence, I have not come across it. "To be outmoded is to be a classic," he once said of himself, "if one has written well." His economy of formulation touched on genius. Asked by the playwright S. N. Behrman what he thought of Freudianism, he replied: "A tense and peculiar family, the Oedipuses, were they not?" Ten deftly aimed words and — poof! — a large and highly fallacious school of thought crumples to dust.

I have been referring to him as Beerbohm or Max Beerbohm,

but members of the cult tend to refer to him as "Max" merely, which is how he signed his caricatures. The cult itself sometimes goes by the name "Maximilians." George Bernard Shaw, when turning over the job of drama critic on the English *Saturday Review,* said he was making way for "the incomparable Max." (Tired of the sobriquet, Beerbohm more than once implored, "Compare me, compare me.") Something of the intimacy of his style seems to make calling him "Max" rather less objectionable than, say, calling Shakespeare "Will," or Joyce "Jim." Yet I find I cannot quite bring myself to do it.

In his two books on Beerbohm, N. John Hall calls him Max, but I should say that Hall has earned the right to do so, having served him so sedulously. Hall had published a beautiful and impeccably edited collection entitled *Max Beerbohm Caricatures,* to which he supplied a fine and splendidly informative accompanying text. In that work, Professor Hall (tempted though I am, I shall refrain from calling him "N.") displayed a wide knowledge of Beerbohm and his milieu and a depth of sympathy for the large comic enterprise that are his caricatures. He produced a book in every way worthy of its subject: modest, elegant, charming, and useful — a keeper, as fishermen like to say.

Hall's second book on Beerbohm is a prose work that he has chosen to call *Max Beerbohm: A Kind of a Life.* As it happens, *A Kind of a Life* turns out to be *A Sort of a Biography* — a rare and unusual sort. There have been other Beerbohm biographies, the most complete of which is that written by the English man of letters David Cecil; and there have been various studies, none of them silly or obtuse: to be drawn to Beerbohm as a subject almost automatically insures one against pomposity, humorlessness, or academic pretentiousness. Yet for all that has been written about Max Beerbohm, no one has come close to capturing the extraordinary personality behind his small but remarkable creations both in prose and with pencil. Professor Hall comes near to suggesting that there is nothing really that needs to be captured.

Ideally, biography operates at three depths: the biographer shows how a man appears to his public, how he appears to his friends and family, and how he appears to himself. Hall's biography touches on all three, none in smothering detail, though he is stronger on the first two than the third. His book is not meant to be exhaustive or in any way definitive, and in some regards it is all the more pleasing for its modesty of intentions. "I shall keep this book relatively short," he writes, "and I shall not attempt to ferret out the inner man. The 'inner man of Max Beerbohm' sounds oxymoronic. He was very self-aware, but he was not given to introspection or soul-searching. If he did look deeply into himself—and I don't believe he did so very often—he did not tell us about it."

What this leaves Hall in his biography is a review of Max Beerbohm's career, an appreciative yet critical sorting out of his various works, and a consideration of the main unresolved questions about his remarkably quiet life. Drawing on other biographies, his book is a vade mecum of Beerbohmian information. Our biographer is immensely companionable, admitting his ignorance when it arises and deciding that many things really are not worth going into. He will provide an interpretation for, or offer a possible motive behind, a work and then blithely add, "I may be wrong," or "But these are merely biographer's fancies." For those of us who do not quite believe in biographical truth but are much more impressed by (in W. H. Auden's phrase) "the baffle of being," such casualness, far from seeming quirky, is instead rather refreshing and even admirable.

When critical, Hall often levels his criticisms in an amusingly oblique way that his subject would probably have much approved. Of the small number of fairy tales Beerbohm wrote, Hall suggests: "These three stories may be easily avoided by even the most devoted of Maximilians, if only they will try." The ironic tone of that sentence is reminiscent of Beerbohm himself once writing that, apropos of the need for historical background to write about the year 1880, "to give an accurate account of that period would need a far less brilliant pen than mine."

Hall's judgments of Beerbohm's works are quite sound. I know this is so because they agree with my own — always the best evidence for high intelligence in others. He thinks Beerbohm's single famous work, *Zuleika Dobson* — the novel about a beauty whose arrival at Oxford causes the death by suicide of all the university's undergraduates — somewhat overdone and therefore tending toward the monotonous, though even so he includes it among Beerbohm's best work. He thinks the early essays, written in the (Oscar) Wildean manner, more than a touch precious, and he believes the volumes of drama criticism suffer from having been written chiefly about second- and third-rate playwrights. He recognizes that Beerbohm tended to underrate Shaw — he had a real antipathy to geniuses, whom he thought "generally asinine" — and to overrate Lytton Strachey. The best of Beerbohm, Hall holds, includes Beerbohm's book of parodies, *A Christmas Garland;* his perfectly polished final collection of essays, *And Even Now;* and his book of short stories got up to read as if they were memoirs, *Seven Men and Two Others.*

Hall expends less space on Beerbohm's caricatures, having already devoted a lengthy book to them. He provides an excellent account of his subject's brief but brilliant performances over the BBC. But he reminds us that Beerbohm always found drawing easier than writing; and we know that, after he ceased to write for publication in his late thirties with his permanent move to Italy, he devoted himself almost wholly to the delicate and (in his hands) often devastating art of caricature. On this subject, in an early book on Beerbohm, John Felstiner, the biographer of Paul Celan (to have written books on Max Beerbohm and Paul Celan: talk about the comedy of incongruity!), rightly says that "generally Beerbohm's caricatures tend to ridicule, while his judgments in writing are less direct — the rough distinction is between satire and irony." Felstiner goes on to say that his innovation as a caricaturist was in bringing "the dynamics of parody into caricature," and it is true that the captions to Beerbohm's drawings are often as brilliant as the draftsmanship.

Max Beerbohm tended to worry about the cruelty of his caricatures and claimed not to be able to explain it, since only in rare cases — Shaw, Kipling, a now forgotten novelist named Hall Caine — did he feel a murderous impulse behind his work. (He almost never drew women.) My own feeling is that, as with so many genuine artists, he had ready recourse to detachment: "I have a power of getting out of myself," he wrote. "This is a very useful power." Writing about Aubrey Beardsley, he noted the aloofness of many artists, which allows them to see "so much" and "the power to see things, unerringly, as they are." His own detachment allowed him a serene objectivity that easily spotted the pretensions and comic self-presentations of others. He was, in the phrase of Henry James, whom he much admired, "infinitely addicted to 'noticing.'" The result, issuing from the end of his pencil, was laughter, usually, in the nature of the case, at the subject's expense. Much as I would have loved to have known Max Beerbohm, I'm not sure that personal acquaintance with him would have been worth the pain of gazing upon his drawing of me.

Some years ago, before his late-life turn to Christianity, Malcolm Muggeridge, then still an exquisite troublemaker, wrote in the pages of the *New York Review of Books* that Max Beerbohm "was in panic flight through most of his life from two things — his Jewishness and his homosexuality." Always audacious and often utterly wrong, the old Mugger this time out missed on both counts.

On the first count, David Cecil writes that of the Beerbohm family "it has often been suggested that they were Jewish . . . ; and the notion gains color in Max's case from his brains, taste for bravura, and his propensity to fall in love with Jewesses." (He finally married one, an American actress named Florence Kahn.) Although Beerbohm claimed he wished he had Jewish blood, in fact the Beerbohm family was part Dutch, German, and English in origin. Asked by Shaw if he had any Jewish ancestors, Beerbohm replied: "That my talent is rather like Jewish talent I admit readily

. . . But, being in fact a Gentile, I am, in a small way, rather re-markable, and wish to remain so."

"Jewish talent" — of what might it consist? I think for Max Beerbohm it had to do with his aloofness, his not quite fully be-longing to any groups or coteries, and with his ironic approach to life. ("I wish, Ladies and Gentlemen," he said in one of his famous BBC broadcasts during World War II, "I could cure myself of the habit of speaking ironically. I should so like to express myself in a straightforward manner.") A woman friend said he "combined an accurate appreciation of worldly values with an ultimate indiffer-ence to them." Very Jewish, this, or at least a quality that often shows up in Jews. Finally, there was his essentially comic approach to life. Believing that "only the insane take themselves quite seri-ously," Beerbohm was primarily and always an ironist, a come-dian, an amused observer standing on the sidelines with a smile and a glass of champagne in his hand. G. K. Chesterton said of him that "he does not indulge in the base idolatry of believing in himself." Rather Jewish, much of this, too.

As for Muggeridge's second count, that Max Beerbohm was at-tempting to hide his homosexuality, here the evidence appears to be purely guilt by association. As a young man, he was on the pe-riphery of the Oscar Wilde circle. (Wilde had a high opinion of Beerbohm, but it was not always returned — "he was never a real person in contact with realities," Beerbohm wrote — and some of his most brutal caricatures are of poor Wilde run to bestial fat.) Beerbohm's best friend, Reggie Turner (a novelist remembered now only for his quip that his rarest books were his second edi-tions), was also homosexual. David Cecil writes that "though he showed no moral disapproval of homosexuality, [Beerbohm] was not disposed to it himself; on the contrary he looked upon it as a great misfortune to be avoided if possible." Cecil quotes a letter from Beerbohm to Oscar Wilde's friend Robert Ross in which he asks Ross to keep Reggie Turner from the clutches of the creepy Lord Alfred Douglas: "I really think Reg is at a rather crucial point of his career — and should hate to see him fall an entire victim to the love that dare not tell its name."

David Cecil thought that Max Beerbohm was a man of "low vitality," and he was too much the gentleman to place the adjective "sexual" before the noun. The publisher Rupert Hart-Davis, an editor of Beerbohm's letters and a cataloguer of his caricatures, thought him asexual and his marriage to Florence Kahn a *mariage blanc.* Refereeing the dispute in *Max Beerbohm: A Kind of a Life,* N. John Hall says, at one point, that Beerbohm's private life doesn't matter — but then, later in the book, sides with Hart-Davis in thinking him asexual despite his marriage. A case cannot be made for Max Beerbohm as a notorious heterosexual, but I would like to weigh in with the fact that, in his essay "Laughter," he wrote that "only the emotion of love takes higher rank than the emotion of laughter." The sadness, of course, is that a case of any sort need be made at all.

Max Beerbohm was the world's greatest minor writer, with the full oxymoronic quality behind that epithet entirely intended. He claimed to be without either envy or ambition, wanting only "to make good use of such little talents as I had, to lead a pleasant life, to do no harm, to pass muster." His tact was consummate; and one has never grown less tired of a man who wrote so much in the first person, for he knew the difference, as he once told his wife, between "offering himself humbly for the inspection of others" and pushing himself forward through egotism. He felt that a goodly portion of such success as he enjoyed was owing to his not having "tired people."

Asked to give the 1941 Clark Lectures at Trinity College, Cambridge, Beerbohm responded, "I have views on a number of subjects, but no coordinated body of views on any single subject. I have been rather a lightweight; and mature years have done nothing to remedy this."

I don't think he really believed it. What he believed was that "many charming talents have been spoiled by the instilled desire to do 'important' work! Some people are born to lift heavy weights. Some are born to juggle with golden balls."

He added that the latter were very much in the minority in England then, and, of course, now. But when haven't they been? The golden jugglers are the ones with wit, the ability to pierce pretension, and the calm detachment to mock large ideas and salvationist schemes. They eschew anger and love small perfections. They go in for handsome gestures (Beerbohm refused to accept a fee for speaking about his recently dead friend Desmond MacCarthy over the BBC), have wide sympathies, and understand that a complex point of view is worth more than any number of opinions.

Nothing lightweight about any of this — quite the reverse, I'd say. Had he met Isaac Newton, Beerbohm remarked, "I would have taught him the Law of Levity." It's a powerfully useful and important law, one that Max Beerbohm helped write and that must never, not ever, be allowed to go off the books.

Lord Berners: Pink Pigeons
and Blue Mayonnaise

I HAVE A WEAKNESS for minor artists. But they must be genuinely minor, by which I mean that they mustn't lapse into minority through overreaching, want of energy, crudity, or any other kind of ineptitude. They must not be failed major artists merely. The true minor artist eschews the noble and the solemn. He fears tedium for his audience, but even more for himself. He sets out to be, and is perfectly content to remain, less than great. The minor artist knows his limits and lives comfortably within them. To delight, to charm, to entertain, such are the goals the minor artist sets himself, and, when brought off with style and verve and elegant lucidity, they are — more than sufficient — wholly admirable.

Gerald Tyrwhitt-Wilson (1883–1950), the fourteenth Lord Berners, was the very model of the minor artist, a title he would, I think, neither disclaim nor disdain. He painted, he wrote, he composed (for Diaghilev's Ballets Russes but also for the movies), and he didn't in the least mind being called an amateur or a dilettante, and on occasion declared himself both. When Max Beerbohm rendered Lord Berners at his piano in a caricature — nicely capturing his bald pate, his monocle, the careful mustache beneath his beaky nose — the caption read: "Lord Berners making more sweetness than violence." This was Berners's aim, sweetness and light, though in the correct mixture, which meant, of course, not too much of either.

Gerald Berners is a man who tends to show up in other people's memoirs, letters, and diaries. He generally does so in a somewhat oblique fashion, arriving late, leaving early, never the life of but always a guest at the party. He was part of England's smart bohemia, where society and art met — a member of that group of writers, critics, and composers who came into prominence in the 1920s and gave the prevailing tone to English culture until the early 1950s. His name pops up alongside those of John Betjeman, Duff and Diana Cooper, the Mitford girls, Cecil Beaton, Peter Quennell, Cyril Connolly, David Cecil. Thus, Evelyn Waugh to his friend Christopher Sykes: "I sought you in White's on Tuesday but found only Berners." Thus, Diana Cooper, in her autobiography: "At Augsburg we joined Emerald Cunard, Gerald Berners, Bertie Abdy, and others." Berners himself brings H. G. Wells and the Baroness Budberg to the Betjemans, and Elsa Schiaparelli to a jumble sale. Harold Nicolson mentions Berners, fleetingly, in *Some People.* Among the Sitwells, Isaiah Berlin, Siegfried Sassoon, Harold Acton, and David Cecil, there, off in a corner, ubiquitous and omnipresent, sits Lord Berners. Who was this man?

A clear answer has been made available owing to the biography of Berners by Mark Amory. Amory edited the letters of Evelyn Waugh and those of Ann Fleming, and knows well the terrain on which Berners romped. Amory's is a book written with a nice combination of sophistication, knowledge, and good sense. At 237 pages long — with fewer than twenty further pages given over to bibliography and appendices — it is also rightly, one is inclined to say just about perfectly, proportioned.

Rightly proportioned, too, is the degree of Amory's psychologizing. Lord Berners was odd — and more than a little odd, for his reputation in his own day was that of an eccentric. But he is not presented here all lashed up in psychological interpretation. As a literary psychologist, Amory uses a light hand. "The reader of his autobiography [*First Childhood*]," Amory writes, "is given no hint that Gerald himself is to be exclusively homosexual . . . All this suggests only that Gerald, who was to live openly with a man for almost twenty years, was capable of being mildly disingenuous to the end." Enough said, and Amory himself duly says very little more about it, by way of either approval or disapproval, taking his subject's homosexuality as a fact of life, worthy of neither interpretation nor speculation.

A composer, painter, and novelist, Gerald Berners was what we should, in an inflationary age, probably today call a Renaissance man. But in Berners's case you have to imagine rather a small renaissance — one in Andorra, perhaps. A shy boy who later became a shy man, he did not go up to Oxbridge but instead was removed from Eton to study for — and twice fail — the examination for the diplomatic service. No disgrace, this failure, for, with its concentration on foreign languages and history, it seems to have been much more rigorous than sitting for the standard university examination of the day. He was in any case sent as an honorary attaché to Constantinople, where Harold Nicolson was also posted.

Berners's next posting was at Rome, where he met and befriended the novelist Ronald Firbank — an instance of the shy meeting the terminally shy. "The flashes of brilliance that animated his conversation and made his company so delightful are impossible to reconstruct," Berners later wrote. "One might as well attempt to record the hovering of a humming-bird or portray the opalescence of a soap-bubble. There was an intriguing irrelevance, a delightful, fantastic silliness in all he said or did." In his own career, Berners would not be without his own Firbankian flashes.

Gerald Berners grew up, an only child, in rather stuffy late-Victorian opulence. His mother, who was, by his own account, utterly without a sense of humor, loved him; his father, who had a caustic sense of humor, did not. In *First Childhood,* he recalls his mother instructing his father to beat him for some delinquency or other, and his father saying that he was busy and couldn't be bothered. ("I remember," Berners notes, "feeling a little offended by his lack of interest.") Berners believed his father also did not care all that much for his wife, but, then, "he did not seem to be the kind of man who could ever have been seriously in love with anyone." His mother would have preferred that Gerald excel at horsemanship than anything else, and she discouraged his early passion for music. Neither parent had a clue about what interested their son, which was fine with him. At preparatory school, his headmaster warned him not to allow his music to get in the way of his studies. Such an upbringing, if one survives it, leaves one with a sense of detachment and distance that can have its artistic uses. But his upbringing also had its sadness. In *First Childhood*, Berners wrote:

> Those who say that their childhood was the happiest period in their lives must, one suspects, have been the victims of perpetual misfortune in later years. For there is no reason to suppose that the period of childhood is inevitably happier than any other. The only thing for which children are to be envied is their exuberant vitality. This is apt to be mistaken for happiness. For true happiness, however, there must be a certain degree of experience. The ordinary pleasures of childhood are similar to those of a dog when it is given its dinner or taken out for a walk, a behavioristic, tail-wagging business, and, as for childhood being carefree, I know from my own experience, that black care can sit behind us even on our rocking-horses.

Berners came into his title, money, and property in 1918, when he was thirty-five. Out of the financial wars, he would never again have to worry about earning his own income. He kept houses in Rome and London, but was most often at home — and most at home generally — in Faringdon, his estate in Berkshire. A less intellectually distinguished crew gathered there than at Lady Ottoline Morrell's, though it was a much more amusing one. Here it was that Berners earned his reputation as an eccentric. He dyed the pigeons around Faringdon bright colors (using a dye that did them no harm). He had an occasional penchant for monochromatic meals. Stravinsky recalled that "if Lord Berners's mood was pink, lunch might consist of beet soup, lobster, tomatoes, strawberries," with pink pigeons flying outside; Stravinsky's wife sent Berners a powder that allowed him to make blue mayonnaise. He built a folly, an isolated tower with no reason for being other than his desire to have it built, and to it he appended this notice: "Members of the Public committing suicide from this tower do so at their own risk." He allowed Penelope Betjeman's horse Moti into his drawing room for tea. (Amory prints a picture of the horse sipping tea out of his mistress's saucer at Faringdon.) He installed a portable piano in the back of his Rolls-Royce. As befits such behavior, Berners's outward demeanor was utterly conventional; he wore suits with vests and bow ties, even when painting.

Shy though he was, Berners said many witty things, a goodly number happily recorded by Mark Amory. Berners it was who said that T. E. Lawrence seemed "always backing into the limelight." He claimed to have gone to the House of Lords once only, because a bishop "stole my umbrella and I never went there again." When an Australian newspaper claimed that it was sad to see the once noble city of Venice full of beggars, Berners offered the corrective that it was a misprint and supposed to read "buggers." He invented frivolous riddles, of which Amory quotes the following: "if the clocks were to feel that they had no one to talk to or keep them going, what publisher would they refer to? Answer: we have no one to Chatto and Windus." Sometimes his wit could take a socially cruel (if still amusing) turn. He sent the following invitation to Sybil Colefax, who was noted for her intense social climbing:

I wonder if by any chance you are free to dine tomorrow night? It is only a tiny party for Winston and GBS. I think it important they should get together at this moment. There will be no one else except for Toscanini and myself. Do please forgive this terribly short notice.

The joke came in Berners's making both the signatory of this note and the return address on the envelope excruciatingly illegible. Poor Sybil Colefax.

Analyzing Gerald seemed to be a game Berners's friends all took a hand at playing. The best efforts were made in the fiction of his friends. Berners is Lord Merlin in Nancy Mitford's *Pursuit of Love,* where he plays a cameo role as an eccentric and a host for the world of smart bohemia (not much invention here). Of Merlin, the Nancy Mitford–like narrator remarks: "As Lord Merlin was a famous practical joker, it was sometimes difficult to know where jokes ended and culture began. I think he was not always certain himself."

Berners is at the center of Osbert Sitwell's story "The Love-Bird," where, as the character Robert Mainwroth, Sitwell subjects him to extended analysis. "To those who did not care for him, Robert Mainwroth gave an impression of being a scoffer, one who was rather eccentric and outside life. To those, on the other hand, who liked him — and, as his sensitiveness gradually evolved round itself the defensive armour of a perfect but laughing worldliness, they formed a steadily increasing band — he was a pivot of very modern, if mocking activity." The element of gentle mockery, I think, is the key one.

There is further talk of Mainwroth-Berners's "natural air of quiet, ugly distinction." Sitwell adds that "he was, in fact, a dilettante, but one in the best sense: for he aspired to be nothing but what he was." He could be happy for long periods, for he was not often bored, "and made a continual use of his continual leisure: in addition to writing and painting, he read an enormous amount." Yet "there is little doubt that he was pleased at having created this false impression of brutal lack of sentiment." He is a man, Sitwell avers, who tended to "divest himself of everything that did not appeal to him personally, either aesthetically or through humour — and his senses of aesthetics and humour were perilously akin."

Osbert Sitwell has it right when he says that it is humor that furnished Lord Berners with his aesthetic and that is behind so much of his art. As for that art, although he took immense pleasure in creative work, Berners referred to his endeavors in this line as "my little hobbies, writing, painting, and music." Although his oeuvre is small, it is, in its modest way, impressive. Stravinsky called Berners the most interesting British composer of the twentieth century; Clive Bell wrote the introduction to the catalogue of his one show of paintings; he had a ballet, *The Triumph of Neptune*, produced by Diaghilev and choreographed by Balanchine; he published poems in *Horizon;* he wrote an opera, plays, six slender novels, and two autobiographical works.

Had he not been wealthy, Berners would doubtless have turned out much more. "I don't feel very inspired at the moment," he wrote to Diaghilev. "However I bought a very pretty Renoir this morning and I hope things will now go much better." Although Berners's greatest promise was as a composer, at one point the pleasure he took from his music departed, and so he turned to painting. According to Virginia Woolf, in her diary, Berners "met a painter, asked him how you paint; bought 'hogsheads' — (meant hogs' bristles) and canvas and copied an Italian picture, brilliantly, consummately, says Clive Bell. Has the same facility there [as in his music]: but it will come to nothing he said, like the other." To walk away from something one is very good at seems a strange act, but perhaps it is less strange if one's purpose in life is, above all, to elude boredom.

Yet it is difficult not to be impressed with Berners's prowess at musical composition, especially given how little actual training he had. His attraction to music, he wrote in *A Distant Prospect*, the second of his two brief autobiographical volumes, was initially to "the sight of musical notation on the page" — he was attracted to it, that is, "pictorially." Apart from rudimentary piano lessons as a boy, his only other instruction appears to have been four sessions on counterpoint taken with Donald Tovey, the great critic and composer. He seemed to show genuine progress, at least enough to earn the support of the estimable London *Times* critic Ernest Newman, who had earlier been a detractor. Much of this was because of Berners's marvelously lucid grasp of what lay behind artistic problems. Mark Amory quotes from an unpublished Berners essay that shows how much the cerebral and highly conscious musical artist he could be:

> There are no hard and fast rules to determine the exact length a piece of music should be; nor are there canons to govern the timing of entries, the length of development or the exact amount of suspense to be inflicted on the ear before it is relieved by resolution. These are matters which depend on the tact and sensibility of the composer. If he is lacking in this sensibility, the music that he produces is apt to be unsatisfactory in that, if he errs on the side of length, it will seem to drag; if on the side of brevity, it will appear spasmodic or trivial.

Berners had a quick musical intelligence, owing in part to his general aesthetic sophistication. He has been called the English Satie, though Satie, Amory notes, was less than pleased about this, saying Berners was an amateur. I have not heard all of his music, but all that I have been able to acquire on compact disc gives pleasure. It is lively, high-spirited, often parodic, and filled with witty surprises of the kind light — but still serious — music ought to provide. It is never tedious. An important quality, the absence of tedium. In his novel *Far from the Madding War*, Berners has a character who is a composer (supposedly modeled on William Walton) and who has written a symphony that lasts an hour and a half, of which another character (one modeled on Berners himself) remarks: "Francis believed in catharsis through boredom."

I have never seen a painting by Gerald Berners. In his book Mark Amory provides rather poorly reproduced versions of a few of them, along with some of his illustrations for books and sheet music. Amory is not very high on Berners the visual artist. Nor was Evelyn Waugh, who, with his customary charity, wrote to a friend: "Gerald Berners had an exhibition of pictures and sold them all on the first day which shows what a good thing it is to be a baron." The consensus seems to have been that Berners's painting was too predictable. Christopher Wood, a younger painter, noted that he found Berners's work "just too perfect." Amory quotes a reviewer in the magazine *Apollo:* "One views his pictures with delight, only tempered by regret that being so good they are not just a little better." "Too perfect," "so good" — it sounds, Berners's condition as a visual artist does, like an incurable case of want of inspiration.

As a prose writer, Berners is more impressive. He was the product here of literary self-cultivation. David Cecil said Gerald Berners was the best-read man he had ever met. As Berners grew older, his reading narrowed. "Are you a reader of Henry James?" he asked a friend, and said, "I read practically nothing else now." Yet Berners did not at all write like James. His writing tended to be plain, traditional, a model of ironic understatement. A not untypical sentence from *First Childhood* reads: "The only real drawback to the school [his preparatory school] was the fact that the headmaster happened to be a sadist." He had, as Amory says, "a gift for being pleasurably readable."

Lord Berners's bibliography includes eight books. Two are autobiographies, the second of which, *A Distant Prospect,* takes his life only up to his departure from Eton. Six are works of fiction. All are quite brief, some under a hundred pages. Until recently, all were out of print. The most difficult to acquire remains the novel called *The Girls of Radcliffe Hall.* This is a highly campy performance intended for private circulation in which many of Berners's friends are turned into girls and Berners himself into the headmistress of a girls' school in which everyone has a crush on someone else. For people in the know, Mark Amory writes, it was a *roman* with a very clear and patently homosexual *clef.* The hero/heroine of the story, Cecil Beaton, was said to have been so angered by it, Amory reports, "that he went around acquiring copies and destroying them, in an attempt to suppress it."

A more characteristic performance is Berners's novel *Far from the Madding War.* Amory calls the plot of this delicate novella "slender, indeed inadequate." All the more interesting, therefore, that it is charming and delightfully readable, written with perfect pitch. Lend an ear, please, to this, its opening paragraph:

> Miss Emmeline Pocock sat, intently bending over a large piece of embroidery, surrounded by good taste and silence. The room she sat in was as elegantly appointed a room as anyone could wish to see, although a highly attuned connoissance of decorative subtleties might detect, here and there, a blemish: a somewhat too deliberate juxtaposition of objects; colour arrangements that envisaged artistic ideals without quite achieving them. But, on the whole, the general effect was one of harmony, discretion, lack of pretentiousness, and there was none of that absence of comfort that good taste so often entails.

Emmeline is the daughter of the Warden of All Saints College, and the novel opens as World War II has just begun. She hates the idea of war, with its great destruction, but feels that, like everyone else, she must do something for the war effort. What she decides to do is to unravel, knot by knot, stitch by stitch, a large fourteenth-century German embroidery that is in her possession. "Focussing a swivel lamp on a corner of the embroidery, she took up a small pair of scissors and, drawing up a chair, she sat down before it and began slowly, deliberately to unravel the tiny threads of silk, offering a mental prayer to God to grant her the requisite strength to persevere in her minute labour of destruction until not a single thread remained of this unique, almost monumental work of art." And, you might think, we are off.

Except we are not, for not much happens in the novel. Chiefly characters are wheeled in and out, mined for their comic content. Early among them is one Professor Trumble, a very great bore whom Emmeline wishes would undergo a reverse psychoanalysis that would give him some social inhibitions. He and his wife's "leave-takings . . . were as protracted as the finale of a Bruckner symphony."

The character Mr. Jericho appears to be based on Isaiah Berlin, and provides perhaps the last playfully disrespectful portrait of this great English social eminence. He pops up like a cuckoo out of a clock, with eyes, behind large steel-rimmed spectacles, that had "an explanation for everything," missed nothing, and "often saw a good many things that weren't there"; he suffers not from the absence but from "an excess of tact." Then there is the inevitable character based on the Oxford classicist Maurice Bowra, who prefers to talk with friends over the telephone, about Greek antiquities, moral philosophy, or local gossip, rather than in person, for over the telephone he was "unable to see his victims wince, he was less tempted to wound, and conversation was carried on in a kinder, less provocative tone."

Far from the Madding War contains a murder and a suicide, but as killings go they are as nothing next to the character analysis exhibited by the novel's author. The most analyzed character in the novel, in fact, is Berners himself, who is called Lord FitzCricket. To him is given the line: "It may well be that the proper study of mankind is man, and the study of mankind is discouraging." Certainly Berners, in this self-portrait, proffers a discouraging picture of himself. He describes himself as "completely bald," so that "when he was annoyed he looked like a diabolical egg." "He composed music, he wrote books, he painted; he did a great many things with a certain facile talent. He was astute enough to realize that, in Anglo-Saxon countries, art is more highly appreciated if accompanied by a certain measure of eccentric publicity. This fitted in well with his natural inclinations."

FitzCricket-Berners goes on to report on the way that the war "poleaxed" him. He ceased composing, writing, painting. The war, he felt, not altogether incorrectly, meant the end of people such as himself. "You see, I'm all the things that are no use in war. My character is essentially pacific and hedonistic. I like everything to be nice and jolly and I hate to think of people hating one another . . . I'm an amateur, and fundamentally superficial. I am also private spirited. I have never been able to summon up any great enthusiasm for the human race, and I am indifferent as to its future. I have also led a self-centered, sheltered life, and my little world consists of my hobbies and personal relationships."

As this passage suggests, the war sent Berners into a royal blue funk from which he never quite emerged. He went into psychoanalysis — in his excellent story "Percy Wallingford," the young diplomatist narrator based on Berners speaks of having suffered from "nervous depression" — but one imagines him too witty for it to have much helped. (People with strong humor don't often do well in therapy. One recalls George S. Kaufman firing his psychotherapist because he asked too many damn personal questions.) Berners had a relationship with a younger man that lasted twenty years, though one senses that this relationship, though important to him, was never at the center of his life. There were rumors that Berners planned to propose to Clarissa Churchill, but nothing ever came of them.

Perhaps Berners's problem was to be found in an emptiness at the core of his outwardly pleasant life. One half feels he might have wished that this emptiness could have been filled by religion, only because the subject of religious faith does come up a fair amount in his published writing. In *A Distant Prospect,* he describes the young intellectual at Eton who "did a good deal to undermine my religious faith," which, he goes on to explain, "had never been a very healthy one." He speaks in the same book of having "no aptitude for religious faith," and of the absence of "any latent talent" for religion. He also allows that he could not "understand in what way suffering fortified the soul."

In *Far from the Madding War,* Berners plays religion for laughs. When Emmeline in that book is asked if she had ever tried to find God, she replies, "I felt I wouldn't know what to do with him if I had found him." She also remarks that, when a child, she "used to think that the Day of Judgment meant that we were all going to judge God, and I still don't see why not." After Penelope Betjeman had converted to Catholicism, she tried to bring Berners into the Church, but it was no sale. "I don't mind Penelope as long as we don't have any of that God nonsense," he told a friend.

After the war, Berners's health and interest in life began to give out, though it is unclear which came first. He felt he had become distinctly a back number. And he was right. Probably always a mistake to attempt to make of one's life a work of art. A life, as opposed to art, wouldn't endure, for one thing; and, for another, old age so rarely supplies a dramatic, or even nicely understated, elegant ending.

Lord Berners, the man who so greatly feared boredom, became, in the recollection of some friends, a bit of a bore himself. He might earlier have contended that pleasure was the true end in life, yet toward the end of his own life he asserted that "the highest pleasure is creative work." As a reader and a listener, I, for one, wish he had exerted himself to have turned out more work. Did, one wonders, he wish it, too?

But life, never without its tricks, had dealt Berners too good a hand. Not needing to work, he could live in luxury and fall back on charm. Berners died, at sixty-six, a fairly easeful death, apparently not in the least fearful of what lay beyond. In the postscript to his excellent biography, Mark Amory reports that the doctor who had attended Lord Berners "during his last years refused to send a bill, saying that the pleasure of his company had been payment enough." Now there is a test of charm none of us would wish to be asked to have to pass.

The Return of Karl Shapiro?

I RECENTLY FOUND myself describing someone as a successful poet of no significance whatsoever. Karl Shapiro was just the reverse: an unsuccessful poet of considerable significance. The reasons he was unsuccessful tell a good deal about the state and condition of poetry in our time.

Karl Shapiro, who died in 2000 at the age of eighty-six, wasn't always unsuccessful. In fact, he began dazzlingly. In 1945, he emerged from World War II to win a Pulitzer Prize for his third, excellent book of poems, *V-Letter and Other Poems*. This was at a time when a Pulitzer Prize meant more than it does today. (The usual award of a guinea to anyone who can name three of the last five years' Pulitzer Prize winners in poetry.) He was thirty-two, and the world had already recognized him as a gifted poet, well up to deploying language powerfully on a major subject — in this case, that of living through a war as an enlisted soldier, a medical corpsman. An earlier book had won the praise of Louise Bogan, a poet and critic whose praise lent imprimatur to a young poet as, say, Helen Vendler's tends to do in our own day.

After Shapiro won his Pulitzer, gates opened, invitations were offered, emoluments flashed. He was made consultant in poetry at the Library of Congress in 1946. A writing professorship at Johns Hopkins, in Baltimore, the city of his birth, followed; he was the second Jew to be hired in the history of the Hopkins English department. From 1950 to 1956, he was the editor of *Poetry,* the oldest and easily most highly regarded magazine devoted to verse in America. Under its founding editor, Harriet Monroe, *Poetry* had published T. S. Eliot, Robert Frost, Wallace Stevens, Marianne Moore, all the great names in modern poetry; its European correspondent was Ezra Pound. The kingdom of poetry in the twentieth century, as in the twenty-first, was always a small one — a mountain principality, really — but Karl Shapiro, not yet forty, had a commanding place in it.

Yet today, when asked to name the key poets of Shapiro's generation, most people at the English-major level of culture would answer Robert Lowell, Elizabeth Bishop, Randall Jarrell, John Berryman, and (less likely) Delmore Schwartz and Theodore Roethke. All were poets who fell to insanity and alcoholism, or, in Wordsworth's phrasing, "in our youth begin in gladness; / But thereof come in the end despondency and madness." Karl Shapiro never cracked up. Instead he made a few crucial decisions, took a number of significant positions, that went a long way toward scuppering his career.

Before getting on to this, though, it needs to be said that John Updike's compilation of Karl Shapiro's poems — a selection of the strongest poems from the various books of poetry Shapiro published over a long career — is a splendid reminder of how good a poet Karl Shapiro could be. One of the first things to be said about Shapiro's poetry is that, various though it is, it is never gloomy. A pleasure in life, in its richness, variety, and oddity, informs many of his poems, even those that verge on the dark, such as "Auto Wreck," a poem about coming upon a car crash as a young man on his way home after leaving the bed of a lady friend. The arbitrariness of death by such a cause is what rightly strikes him:

> For death in war is done by hands;
> Suicide has cause and stillbirth, logic;
> And cancer, simple as a flower, blooms.
> But this invites the occult mind,

> Cancels our physics with a sneer,
> And spatters all we knew of denouement
> Across the expedient and wicked stones.

Similarly, in a poem called "Hospital," one of the few memorable poems not included in this collection, Shapiro begins by reminding that "Inside or out, the key is pain," but then goes on to catalogue the abundance of possibilities that lie within the walls of "This Oxford of all sicknesses: / Kings have lain here and fabulous small Jews / And actresses whose legs were always news." He could make a poem out of a fly, and in fact did, beginning: "O hideous little bat, the size of snot."

But I don't want to make Karl Shapiro seem a cheerful or relentlessly upbeat poet. ("Optimists," as Paul Valéry noted, "write badly.") He could also be angry, satirical, and smart about his contrarian nature. The prose poem "I Am an Atheist Who Says His Prayers" resounds with this last quality: "I am an anarchist and full professor at that . . . / Physically a coward, I take on all intellectuals, established poets, popes, rabbis, chiefs of staff." His sympathies tended to be wide, as a poet's should be; and his poem "Conscientious Objector," written by a man who in combat himself won several Bronze Stars, is better because subtler than E. E. Cummings's famous conscientious-objector poem "I Sing of Olaf." Shapiro's poem ends:

> You suffered not so physically but knew
> Maltreatment, hunger, ennui of the mind.
> Well might the soldier kissing the hot beach
> Erupting in his face damn all your kind.
> Yet you who saved neither yourselves nor us
> Are equally with those who shed the blood
> The heroes of our cause. Your conscience is
> What we have come back to in the armistice.

Karl Shapiro wrote no great poems — no "Sunday Morning," no "Love Song of J. Alfred Prufrock," no "Wreck of the Deutschland," no "Sailing to Byzantium," no "Stopping by Woods on a

Snowy Evening" — though in his "Elegy for a Dead Soldier" he came close. Write three or four great poems, and one is, officially, a great poet. But Shapiro wrote lots of good, even excellent poems. And he wrote few poems without a passage or phrase that grips and grabs and causes a reader to marvel. His poems all end well. He was a prosodic master, and in one of his books, *Essay on Rime,* he showed mastery of more kinds of meter than the man from Commonwealth Edison.

The chief poetic influences on Shapiro were probably William Carlos Williams and W. H. Auden. From the first he picked up confidence in his own Americanness, at a time when almost all other poets wrote with a nervous look over their shoulders to T. S. Eliot in England. He had an eye for the larger subject inhering in the small object ("no ideas but in things," Williams wrote); and he joined the campaign against a literary modernism whose program, Shapiro came to believe, meant a death of direct feeling in the composition of poetry. He rated Williams's poetry "over and above that of Pound and Eliot and Cummings and Marianne Moore."

The influence of Auden was very different. In two separate poems, "W.H.A." and "At Auden's Grave," both reprinted in Updike's selection, Shapiro lauds Auden for all he had done to open up poetry to contemporary language and thought. In the first poem, he writes: "God bless this poet who took the honest chances; / God bless the live poets whom his death enhances." And in the second he adds: "I come to bless this plot where you are lain, / Poet who made poetry whole again."

While recognizing that "Auden's great achievement . . . is the modernization of diction, the enlargement of dictional language to permit a more contemporary-sounding speech," Shapiro in the end concludes that Auden will be remembered as "a great stylist, not [as a] primary poet, the actual creator of poetry like Hopkins or Rimbaud or, among his contemporaries, Dylan Thomas." He also faults Auden for being the father of the academic poem in which, owing to his overarching irony and other arts of indirection, one finally doesn't know what the poet actually believes.

Shapiro's own beliefs are never in doubt. Nor do many of his poems require what, in the 1950s and 1960s, used pretentiously to be called *explication de texte*. Language, syntax, meaning, all are straightforward enough — all buoyed by precision and an urban comic touch. "It is California in winter and outside / Is like the interior of a florist shop," is a characteristic opening line. "How do I love you?" begins a poem of that title, and instead of attempting to count the ways, the response is "I don't even know."

One senses in many of Karl Shapiro's poems that he feels the time to go about the work of being a poet with a straight face has already passed. "We are too rich with books, our blood / Is heavy with over-thoughtful food, / Our minds are gravid — and yet to try / To backtrack to simplicity / Is fatal." Part of his admiration for William Carlos Williams was because he worked as an obstetrician and was thus able to confront life and draw from it for his writing directly in a way not available to the professional poet. "Williams wanted to be a doctor, have a family, live near New York City, and write poetry. As far as anyone knows, he did all these things admirably."

How different from the poets of Shapiro's own generation, where, as he describes the situation in one of the prose poems of *The Bourgeois Poet,* "established poets are forced to wear beards and bluejeans; they are treated kindly in bohemian zoos; mysterious stipends drift their ways." And then there is this, from "The Poetry Reading":

> But he who reads thinks as he drones his song:
> What do they think, those furrows of faces,
> Of a poet of the middle classes?
> Is he a poet at all? His face is fat.
> Can the anthologies have his birthday wrong?
> He looks more like an aging bureaucrat

Or a haberdasher than a poet of eminence.
He looks more like a Poet-in-Residence.

The job of teaching didn't, in Shapiro's case, help. "Now when I drive behind a Diesel-stinking bus / On the way to the university to teach / Stevens and Pound and Mallarmé, / I am homesick for war."

Something of this spirit also weighs on Shapiro's middle and later poems. Poetry had already lost its audience. To write poetry in America, said Henri Coulette (an American poet despite his French-sounding name), is "like making love to someone sound asleep." Unlike Auden and Coulette, though, Shapiro had an argument for why things went wrong.

He must have had the first inkling of what it was when, as one of the fellows of American literature who comprised the jury for the 1949 Bollingen Prize in Poetry, he voted against giving the prize to Ezra Pound and found himself alone with one other juror (Katherine Garrison Chapin) in doing so. In a symposium in *Partisan Review* on the subject of giving an award to Pound, who was then resident in St. Elizabeths mental hospital in Washington, D.C., Shapiro wrote: "I voted against Pound in the balloting for the Bollingen Prize. My first and more crucial reason was that I am a Jew and cannot honor anti-Semites. My second reason is as I stated in a report which circulated among the fellows: 'I voted against Pound in the belief that the poet's political and moral philosophy ultimately vitiates his poetry and lowers its standards as literary work.' This statement I would place against the official statement of the fellows, which seems to me evasive, historically untrue, and illogical."

The other members of the panel of jurors were W. H. Auden, Conrad Aiken, T. S. Eliot, Allen Tate, Robert Lowell, Louise Bogan, Robert Penn Warren, Willard Thorpe, Paul Green, Katherine Anne Porter, Theodore Spencer, and Leonie Adams, all of whom took the line that, whatever Pound's politics, his contributions to poetry outweighed them. Shapiro must have felt the loneliness of his decision — I think it was the correct one — and it not only marked him as a man distinctly not traveling with the gang, but must have encouraged the iconoclastic strain that already ran strong in him.

Iconoclasts are never more useful than when there is an abundance of false idols to tip over or smash. Shapiro soon attempted to knock over the largest of them, in what, if he were a White House speechwriter, he might have called the Pound-Eliot Axis. The first thing Shapiro noticed was the tireless logrolling that Pound and Eliot carried on in each other's behalf, with each poet regularly pumping up the other's achievements and talents. Eliot, for example, called Pound's *Hugh Selwyn Mauberley* a great poem, to which Shapiro appends the comment that "no one but T. S. Eliot would ever call it a good, much less a great poem." Together Pound and Eliot created what he called "a kingdom of Modern Poetry in which T. S. Eliot is the absolute monarch and Archbishop of Canterbury in one." He pronounced Eliot "a thoroughgoing anachronism in the modern world, a poet of genius crippled by lack of faith and want of joy."

When Ezra Pound, coming on as a revolutionary, talked about "making it new" in poetry, he meant creating a poetry that would make use of colloquial American speech, tossing standard iambic pentameter overboard, and abandoning the tradition of English verse that began in the fourteenth century with Chaucer. It hasn't worked out that way; instead, Shapiro argued, the Pound-Eliot Axis has succeeded, with the aid of the academic New Critics, in creating a poetry in which ideas and symbols replace feeling and pure love of language.

Shapiro published his attacks on Eliot and Pound in a collection of essays with the ill-chosen title *In Defense of Ignorance*. What he intended by the title was his preference for freshness and direct experience over the intellectual desiccations of Eliot and the righteous wrongness of Pound. But the title *In Defense of Ignorance*, which shows Shapiro letting his iconoclasm run away with him, was equivalent to writing a book favoring integration and enti-tling it *In Defense of Racism*. When the book first appeared in 1960, various critics and poets very much with the gang lined up to kick its author in the most tender places.

Today Shapiro's arguments seem more cogent than ever. Look-ing back on the history of twentieth-century poetry, one realizes that what Pound and Eliot accomplished, along with the building up of their own reputations, was removing poetry "from the peo-ple" and delivering it "to the classroom." They destroyed, Shapiro felt, "all emotion for poetry except for poetry arising from ideas." The joining of Eliot and Pound to the New Critics, in Shapiro's view, entailed "the voluntary withdrawal of the audience" from poetry, in which "critics have created an academic audience, that is, a captive audience." I. A. Richards, one of the leading figures among the New Critics, Shapiro called "the man who tried, and al-most succeeded, in driving the poetic mind into the test tube." The critic F. O. Matthiessen lined up for the Eliot-Pound program, even though his leftist politics couldn't have been more different from theirs. But, then, just about everyone signed on in those days, and down to the present not many have resigned.

Did poetry in America ever have a wider audience than the one provided by the classroom? Difficult to say. But there were times when men and women who liked to think themselves culti-vated felt they ought to know poetry, if only because, in Ezra Pound's definition, "great literature is simply language charged with meaning to the utmost degree," and nowhere was it more highly charged than in the best poetry. I recall Paul Freund, the Harvard Law School professor, telling me that he read and loved the poems of Wallace Stevens. My guess — though I hope I am wrong — is that no one on the Supreme Court today knows who Wallace Stevens is. Poetry receives its spurts of attention, but spurts they remain. Shapiro mentions Dylan Thomas, who, he says, "made a jump to an audience which, we have been taught to believe, does not exist." But serious poetry today is chiefly an aca-demic matter, a cult interest, presided over by teacher-priests, village explainers, to a transient audience of students, who, once out of the university, never have to deal with it again, and usually don't.

The dividing line, the point at which poetry became wholly of academic interest, was the publication and critical success of Eliot's *The Waste Land*, a poem that needed to be read under conditions laid down by the academic Sanhedrin. William Carlos Williams felt that the poem was "the great catastrophe," adding, "it wiped out our world, as if an atom bomb had been dropped upon it . . . I felt at once that it had set me back twenty years . . . Critically Eliot returned us to the classroom just at the moment when I felt that we were on the point of an escape." Shapiro writes that "had Williams been as good a theoretician as he was a poet he would probably be the most famous American poet today." But it was Eliot, an even better theoretician than poet, who was left to take on his self-appointed critic's job of, in his own phrase, "correcting taste." And correct it he did, insofar as possible, to resemble his own.

Karl Shapiro was a lively and slashing critic, and reading him one feels windows opening, clouds passing, sunlight, and a fresh breeze entering the room. Alas, he is more impressive on the attack than on the defense. What he chooses to defend is the tiresome, let 'er rip, standard team of literary romantics: Blake, Whitman, D. H. Lawrence, & Co. In this mode he wrote an essay entitled "The Greatest Living Author," who turns out to be the novelist Henry Miller, about whom Shapiro wrote: "I claim that Miller is one of the few healthy Americans alive today; further that the circulation of his books" — this was written while Henry Miller's novels were still censored in the United States — "would do more to wipe out the obscenities of Broadway, Hollywood, and Madison Avenue than a full-scale social revolution." Shapiro did not usually lapse into such mega-clichés. A pity, too, that he allowed himself to get caught in the game of choosing sides. In many fields, neither of the two contending sides is worthy of the allegiance of an intelligent person. Some kinds of ignorance are indefensible.

Shapiro himself, as he grew older, was perhaps rather too hipped on sex; he wrote a soft-porno novel called *Edsel,* which I read when it was published in 1971 and am pleased to have forgotten almost in its entirety. Of his literary enemies he wrote: "Pound is sexless, Eliot ascetic, Yeats roaring with libidinal anguish." In what he calls "the religion of modern poetry," he claimed "the Trinity is composed of Pound, Eliot, and Yeats," though he cut Yeats greater slack, writing that he "was never happy in the company of either" Eliot or Pound and, despite his confused turn to magic and mysticism, was a greater poet than both.

Intellectual courage was required for Shapiro to say the things he did, and for doing so he was, in effect, read out of the grand lodge of established poets. In 1976, John Updike notes, Karl Shapiro was dropped from the *Oxford Book of American Verse,* in which, in earlier editions, he had had a prominent place. His teaching jobs were at less than the best brand-name universities: Nebraska, then the University of California at Davis. His books of poems, although they continued to be printed, were reviewed harshly, then increasingly ignored. His sense of his own declining status is nicely caught in a poem very much in the Shapiro spirit, "My Fame's Not Feeling Well," which ends: "Sloth, acedia, ennui, otiose pride / Got it into this fix, so let it be. / I'm not one to take its history."

Publication of Karl Shapiro's poetry by the Library of America for its new "American Poets Project," well selected and gracefully introduced by John Updike, may help revive Shapiro's fame — though for how long, who can say? The hope of permanent fame may be the second-silliest motive for a career in poetry; the first is, of course, the hope for riches. Karl Shapiro wrote the best poems he could, and his best were extraordinarily good; and in prose he never wrote anything he didn't believe, a practice not many poets have been able, or appear even to try, to maintain. He plied his craft with the honor that only complete integrity brings — and next to this, fame, passing or permanent, seems a small and shriveled thing.

The Medical Keats

T HE GOOD SOLDIER, Ford Madox Ford's fine novel of 1915, sometimes known as the best French novel in the English language, was originally to be titled *The Saddest Story*. A novel about betrayal among friends and within marriages, Ford thought this the saddest story. I think he was wrong. A far sadder story is that of the death of the young: all that life unlived, all that potential unrealized, all hopes short-circuited and permanently cut off. It is not merely sad but unspeakably sad.

The only thing sadder, perhaps, is the death of a young man or woman of talent, not to speak of proven genius. Mozart (1756–1791), as everyone knows, died at the age of thirty-five, Schubert (1797–1828) at thirty-one, Mendelssohn (1809–1847) at thirty-eight. Van Gogh (1853–1890) made it only to thirty-seven. Any casualty list in science has to include the Indian mathematician Srinivasa Ramanujan (1887–1920), who pegged out at thirty-three. In literature, Shelley (1792–1822) died at thirty, by drowning; Heinrich von Kleist (1777–1811) died by his own hand at thirty-four; Aleksandr Sergeyevich Pushkin (1799–1837), at the hand of another in a duel, died at thirty-eight; and F. Scott Fitzgerald (1896–1940), with a strong assist going to the bottle, achieved only his forty-fourth birthday. Sad stories, grievous sad stories, all.

But, somehow, the saddest of all these sad stories is that of John Keats (1795–1821), who left the earth, astonishingly gifted, feeling himself deeply unfulfilled and sorely disappointed, at the age of twenty-five. Should anyone ever lapse into the belief that perfect justice is available here on earth, ten seconds' contemplation of the life of John Keats ought to suffice to put that thought permanently out of one's mind. The very cause behind Keats's death was, in any calculus of justice, all wrong: he was infected with tuberculosis — then known as consumption — while in a condition of low resistance after returning from a trip in Scotland to attend to his brother Tom, himself in an advanced consumptive state. He died, in other words, out of an act of purely selfless goodness. He also died believing that his great promise had not come to fruition. What he couldn't know, of course, was that, in substantial part, it actually had, though he may have had slight intimations of this.

Lyrical talent, and poetic talent generally, may show up earlier than other kinds of literary talent. Jack Stillinger, in his introduction to the most recent edition of Keats's poems, remarks that the great figures in the pantheon of English poetry would be unknown today if they had died as early as did John Keats. "Of the half-dozen other most highly regarded English poets," he notes, "only Spenser, who died in his later forties, did not live at least twice as long as Keats." Professor Stillinger reminds us that Chaucer and Shakespeare made it into their fifties and Milton died at sixty-five. Wordsworth and Yeats survived until, respectively, eighty and seventy-three, with Yeats's best work done in the last fifteen years of his life. What might John Keats have done had he been allotted a normal life span?

John Keats was born in 1795, the oldest of what would eventually be the four sons (one of whom died in infancy) and one daughter of Thomas and Frances Keats. Thomas Keats took over the successful livery stables owned by his in-laws, a family named Jennings. He was on his way to making them more successful still when, on the night of April 16, 1804, he was thrown from his horse, was later found on the street by a night watchman, and died a few hours thereafter. Thomas Keats was then thirty years old, his son John not yet nine, his youngest child, his daughter Fanny, less than a year old.

If Keats's father was thrown from his horse, Keats's mother was thrown by this accident from life, never really to recover. Nor did her family, which henceforth lived in permanent disarray. Frances Keats abandoned her family for an unfortunate second marriage, a mere two months after her husband's death, which, under English marital law of the day, denied her children their legal patrimony. Her second marriage ended in separation two years later. Meanwhile the Keats children, essentially orphaned, lived with their grandparents. The original plan was to send the Keats boys to Harrow, but this had to be abandoned when their maternal grandfather, with whom the children were living, died in 1805. Five years later their mother would die, of what has since been thought tuberculosis, which would eventually kill Keats's youngest brother Tom in 1819 and eventually John Keats himself, at his lodgings at 26 Piazza di Spagna in Rome, and, later still, kill his brother George, then in his early forties, in Louisville, Kentucky.

John Keats was sent to the Enfield School, which offered a liberal education for the sons of families in trade who were not expected to go on to university. Andrew Motion, Keats's biographer, refers to the school's Dissenting liberal tendency. If less scholarly in its teaching than the great English public schools, Enfield also offered less in the way of punishment and no "fagging," that cruel English public-school system of making young students essentially hostage to older students. A certain scientific underpinning accompanied much of the learning at the school, at which more science was taught than a boy was likely to encounter at Eton or Winchester. Liberal politics combined with science, and one of the principal teachers at Enfield, a man named John Rylan, was a friend to Joseph Priestley, the chemist who discovered oxygen and who was one of the best-known radical reformers of the day.

Like so many artists, Keats was not a notably good student, at least not at the outset. Small though he was — he would never grow much above five feet — he was noted for his courage, had a taste for prankishness, was known for his ready laughter. He had a masculine hardiness that made him well liked in an all-male society. A classmate, Edward Holmes, himself later to become a music critic and the author of a biography of Mozart, recalled John Keats as "a boy whom any one . . . might have fancied would have become great — *but rather in some military capacity than in literature.*"

Then, for reasons not at all clear, when he returned to Enfield School in 1810, after the death of his mother, John Keats caught intellectual fire and became a passionate reader. His taste in reading ran to Latin writers, history, travel writing, and mythology, though as another of his biographers, W. Jackson Bate, remarks, the young John Keats never became quite "bookish, in any usual sense of the word." What his reading showed, according to Bate, were his qualities of character, which made for "a union of energy, courage, and absorption in something outside himself."

Not long after the death of his mother, Keats was removed from school by his legal guardian, a skullduggerous (as he proved) tea merchant named Richard Abbey, who thought that, at fifteen, it was time for the boy to go out into the world. He and Abbey agreed on his taking up a career in medicine, and he was apprenticed to work with an apothecary-surgeon, one Thomas Hammond, a neighbor, for a period that was supposed to continue for five years and for a fee of £210, which covered board and lodgings.

What Keats's motives were in studying medicine are not known with any certainty. We do know that when his mother lay dying, he took up the exclusive nursing of her, caring for her in all ways, reading novels to her, offering what comforts he could. We know, too, that, in his last years at the Enfield School, he showed an aptitude for science, and two of the books he won as academic prizes were on scientific subjects. The boy Keats had, moreover, a winning streak of altruism; and medicine, then as now, provided every chance to do good. Finally, let us not preclude snobbery. In later years, Keats wrote, apropos of his brother George's departure for America, that there at least he wouldn't have to work "in trade." "I would sooner [my brother] should till the ground, than bow to a customer."

Trade medicine might not be, but neither was Keats able to consider the prospect of practicing medicine at what might be called its highest social level. The division of early-nineteenth-century medicine was tripart. According to Donald Goellnicht, who has written about Keats and medicine in his excellent book *The Poet-Physician,* at the upper level were the physicians, who had earned degrees at Oxford and Cambridge and Edinburgh. Wealthy themselves, the high fees they charged made their services accessible only to the well-off and privileged. The rest of the nation fell under the care of surgeons and apothecaries.

Surgeons were originally joined with barbers in the Guild of Barbers and Surgeons and only separated from them in 1745, when they formed the Corporation of Surgeons and, in 1800, the Royal College of Surgeons. The responsibilities of surgeons and apothecaries often seemed to blur — except that surgeons were formally examined and required licenses to practice. But the duties of the apothecaries, who were initially part of the Guild of Grocers, seemed quite as wide as those of surgeons in the diagnosis and treatment of disease, if not wider in that they also compounded and dispensed medicines.

By the time his medical training commenced, at the age of fifteen, John Keats's life was just about three-fifths complete. Reading Keats, in both his poems and his letters, one is always aware of a dark foreshadowing — and that dark shadow is, of course, the death that looms so near in his future. By force of the most direct experience (the early death of his parents, the death of his grandparents, the death of his brother Tom at the age of nineteen, when Keats was himself only twenty-three), he was — he could scarcely have been otherwise — deeply death-minded. Unlike most people in their early twenties, death, for Keats, was no abstraction; it did not exist, as it does for many people even well into their middle age, in that most comfortable of psychological tenses, the happily distant future. His medical training, both with Thomas Hammond and as a student at Guy's Hospital in London, where he saw death on a daily basis and in many of its most unattractive forms, could only have deepened the sense of the potential imminence of death for Keats. Although outwardly gregarious and cheerful, always the boon companion, he spoke of his own "horrid Morbidity"; and his brother George remarked on his "nervous morbid temperament."

For reasons we do not know, Keats spent four instead of five years living with Thomas Hammond before he enrolled at the medical school attached to Guy's Hospital. All indications are that Hammond was a serious and successful and highly competent medical practitioner. The training of an apprentice was heavily weighted in favor of the practical. Donald Goellnicht thinks it likely that, under Thomas Hammond's tutelage, Keats learned how to spot the symptoms of various common diseases as well as how to compound their remedies. He probably also learned how to set broken bones, pull teeth, deliver babies, and do bleedings, by either leech or venesection — that is, by opening veins.

In *Keats as Doctor and Patient,* his brief book of 1938, Sir William Hale-White, himself then a consulting physician to Guy's, reminds his readers that when Keats entered medical school, the school still trafficked with body snatchers to acquire corpses for dissection (a practice prohibited by the Anatomy Act of 1832). Anesthesiology was unknown; rum tended to be the chief anesthetic. Donald Goellnicht quotes the description of a contemporary, an uncle of William Osler, on the condition of the dissecting room at Guy's:

> On entering the room, the stink was most abominable. About 20 chaps were at work, carving limbs and bodies, in all stages of putrefaction, & of all colors; black, green, yellow, blue, while the pupils carved them, apparently, with as much pleasure as they would carve their dinners. One was pouring Ol. Terebinth on his subject, & amused himself with striking with his scalpel at the maggots, as they issued from their retreats.

Antisepsis, too, was unheard of, so that, as Dr. Hale-White reports, "almost every wound was or quickly became a foul-smell-ing, festering sore, the dressing of which had to be frequently changed, often more than once a day." This was usually done by the medical students appointed as "dressers."

Keats would probably not have gone to medical school at Guy's at all but for the passage in Parliament, in 1815, near the conclusion of his apprenticeship, of the Apothecaries Act. The act made it necessary for anyone who wished to practice medicine in England or Wales first to pass an examination before a newly organized Court of Examiners of the Society of Apothecaries. To sit for this examination, one had to have, along with the completion of a five-year apprenticeship, at least six months' study and work in a teaching hospital. Six months would earn one a licentiate; a full year's study was required for membership in the Royal College of Surgeons. Although he would end up with a licentiateship, Keats signed on for a year's study at Guy's Hospital, which was connected with the then more famous and nearby St. Thomas's Hospital. Signing on for a year suggests that, at the outset at least, Keats intended to become an apothecary-surgeon.

The men then teaching at Guy's were of generally high quality, as was, for its day, the institution itself. Guy's and St. Thomas's were thought, in the view of a French medical visitor, to be better than any hospital then in France. When Keats entered, new facilities had just been installed. More important, the practice of medicine there had shifted from the airily theoretical to the notably practical. "Nothing is known in our profession by guess," remarked Astley Cooper, then the most distinguished teacher at Guy's, "and I do not believe that from the first dawn of medical science to the present moment, a single correct idea has emanated from conjecture alone." Medical education at Guy's even had a philosophical tone, following not only the most recent developments in science but taking up, in lectures, the larger and deeper issues that these developments raised.

Three surgeons were on the staff at Guy's. First among equals was Astley Cooper, whom Hale-White describes as "a great teacher, an investigator, a bold and brilliant surgeon . . . he was always willing to help students and doctors and had a wonderful gift of remembering them and all about them even if he had not seen them for years." Cooper had an international following; and though a mere surgeon and not a physician, he was called in to treat the king, and was eventually knighted. His lectures were later published by one of his apprentices, and were used not only in England but in America and Germany long after his death. John Flint South, who was a student at Guy's at the same time that Keats was, has left a description of Astley Cooper as lecturer:

> A few moments before two Astley Cooper came briskly through the crowd, his handsome face beaming with delight and animation. He was dressed in black, with short knee-breeches and silk stockings, which well displayed his handsome legs, of which he was not a little proud. Almost to a minute he was in the theatre, where loud and continued greetings most truly declared the affectionate regard his pupils had for him. His clear silvery voice and cheery conversational manner soon exhausted the conventional hour devoted to the lecture; and all who heard him hung with silent attention on his words, the only sounds which broke the quiet being the subdued pen-scratching of the note-takers . . . as he only talked of what he really knew from his own experience, what he taught was to be implicitly trusted.

Unfortunately, Keats was assigned to the poorest surgeon in the hospital, William Lucas, Jr., a tall, awkward man, deaf and entirely misfit, by brains and aptitude, for medicine. Of Lucas, Hale-White notes: "His surgical acquirements were very small, his operations generally very badly performed and accompanied by much bungling if not worse." Astley Cooper himself remarked of Lucas as a surgeon: "He was neat-handed, but rash in the extreme, cutting amongst most important parts as though they were only skin, and making us all shudder from the apprehension of his opening arteries or committing some other error." Astley Cooper often backed up Lucas, in the hope of saving any patient from his colleague's deep and dreadful incompetence.

Keats much admired Astley Cooper, and it is tempting to speculate how his medical career — and indeed his life — might have turned out if he had come more directly under his influence instead of that of the egregious "Billy" Lucas. Yet Keats seems not to have had the instinct necessary to the surgeon. According to his friend Charles Brown, neither had he the temperament for it. "My last operation was the opening of a man's temporal artery," Keats told Brown. "I did it with the utmost nicety; but reflecting on what passed through my mind at the time, my dexterity seemed a miracle, and I never took up the lancet again."

Keats was a good if not thoroughly interested medical student. His lecture notebooks, while always grasping the main points, allowed room for the critical spirit, as when he noted: "In disease Medical Men guess, if they cannot ascertain a disease they call it nervous." Fellow students noted his growing inattention at lectures on anatomy, physiology, medicine, chemistry, and materia medica, or the botanical study then necessary to pharmacology. His lecture notes, now on display at the Keats Museum at Hampstead, are said to show much doodling of flowers and fruit and occasional squibs of verse — and a few renderings of skulls thrown in for good measure. In a fellow student's notebook he scribbled: "Give me women, wine and snuff / Until I cry out 'hold, enough!' / You may do so sans objection / Until the day of resurrection." He had begun to affect Byronic dress, wearing a soft, turned-down collar and loose kerchief at his neck and sporting a mustache. The skirmish between the poet and the doctor had begun in earnest in John Keats.

While apprenticed to Thomas Hammond, Keats kept up his connection with Enfield School by studying three afternoons a week with Charles Cowden Clarke, son of the school's headmaster. During this period, Keats's education took, for the first time, a distinctly literary turn. He completed a prose version of the *Aeneid*, began reading Spenser, read Milton and Byron, and Tasso in translation; and, through reading the journalist-poet Leigh Hunt's paper *The Examiner*, which Clarke had introduced to him, Keats became politicized, on the side of radicalism. He was eighteen and a half when he attempted his first poem, a poor imitation of Spenser.

"Medicine is my lawful wife, and literature my mistress," Chekhov, another writer-physician, once remarked, adding, "When I get tired of one, I spend the night with the other." It was apparently not in John Keats to keep these same two loves going simultaneously. (Astley Cooper told his students, contra Chekhov, that medicine was a jealous mistress, and that to succeed in it required "zeal and industry," undiverted by one's being "multi-various or vacillating in [one's] pursuits.") Keats had become very apprehensive about doing major surgery on his own — after witnessing the butcheries of William Lucas, Jr., no surprise here. But in a more general way, his mind tended to stray from medical study. "The other day, for instance," he told his friend Cowden Clarke, "during a lecture, there came a sunbeam into the room, and with it a whole troop of creatures floating in the ray; and I was off with them to Oberon and fairyland."

Ethan Canin, a novelist of our day, recounted how, though he had planned a career as a surgeon, he discovered in his third year of medical school that he could not keep his mind on the job. His first real rotation in surgery was with heart patients. "I remember leaning in close," he writes, "while the vilest thing I had ever seen — the breaking of a man's chest — was performed by two surgeons, on either side of the table. The sternum was first split with an electric saw; then a steel spreader was inserted and its gears opened like a bear trap and revealed the shining organs inside, pulsing to a steady beat. That beat was where we were going."

Enthralled and terrified though he was, where Canin's mind really wanted to go was fly-fishing. "My job," he writes, "was to hold the suction wand that pulled the blood out of the operating field. I was standing there one day, dreaming of water, of standing waist-deep in a sun-drenched pond in the woods, of arcing a frog-green popper across the cloudless New England sky . . ." It is at such moments that one learns — or one had damn well better learn — that one is not intended to be a surgeon, and probably not a physician either. Canin has since dropped medicine to write full-time.

Yet even riven in his interests, John Keats did well on his examination for an apothecary license. Because of the extra expense of obtaining a license to practice in London — and Keats had money problems throughout his brief life — he sat for a license that would allow him to practice exclusively in the country. The examination was a serious one, covering four general fields of study: the *Pharmacopoeia Officinalis Britannica* (or a translation thereof) and general prescriptions, pharmaceutical chemistry, materia medica, and the theory and practice of medicine. He passed them all.

Robert Gittings underscores, in his biography of Keats, that, "in view of a tendency to play down Keats's medical ability, what a real achievement this was." The first year the licentiate exam was given, 188 candidates applied. Ten were thought inadequately prepared even to take the examination, and another eleven were turned down on the day of the exam. During the examination itself, one of seven who took it failed. Gittings writes: "Keats had satisfied an exacting body in every way." The one catch was that, having taken his examination in 1816, at the age of twenty, he had still to wait nearly another year to begin practice, and that year would prove crucial.

And yet, for all the work he had put in, for all the financial pressure on him to begin earning a living, for all that he respected medicine as a useful pursuit and a channel for doing good, John Keats never officially practiced medicine a single day. His guardian Richard Abbey called Keats in for an account of his plans. According to Keats's friend and publisher John Taylor:

> It was Mr. Abbey's advice that John commence business at Tottenham as a Surgeon. He communicated his plans to his Ward, but his surprise was not moderate, to hear in reply that he did not intend to be a Surgeon! why what do you mean to be? I mean to rely upon my ability as a Poet — John you are either Mad or a Fool to talk in so absurd a Manner. My Mind is made up said the youngster very quickly. I know that I possess abilities greater than most men, and therefore I am determined to gain my living by exercising them. Seeing nothing could be done Abbey called him a Silly Boy and prophesied a speedy Termination to his inconsiderate enterprise.

"It is difficult to know why Keats left medicine," writes Donald Goellnicht, who then proceeds to run down the possible reasons. He refutes Dr. Hale-White's view that Keats's was too delicate a nature to face the gruesome medical conditions of the day, arguing that Keats would scarcely have put himself through a full six years of expensive training only to come to this conclusion at the end of the ordeal. True, he knew that he didn't have it in him to be a surgeon, with its requirements, in Astley Cooper's words, of "a good Eye, a steady hand, and above all a Mind which is not easily ruffled by circumstances which may occur during the Operation." It's possible that his fear of "doing evil" with a scalpel in hand, as he remarked to his friend Charles Brown, forced him to abandon his earlier plan. Yet there was still the possibility of earning his living doing apothecary work exclusively.

Medicine was in no way distasteful to Keats, and his good young mind appears to have been capacious enough to have applied himself diligently to his studies even with his mind half on poetry. But Cowden Clarke, in the autumn of 1816, had introduced Keats to Leigh Hunt and Benjamin Haydon, the painter. Through the Leigh Hunt circle he would soon meet Percy Bysshe Shelley and William Hazlitt (the only contemporary literary man of whom Keats spoke with unstinting admiration). Hunt, in a piece in his own paper, wrote in praise of the youthful poetry of Keats and Shelley and John Reynolds, allowing Keats to think himself an authentic poet. He caught the virus — caught it, one suspects, bad. I speak of the virus of art, which causes its victims to believe that nothing in the world is finally so enticing, so exhilarating, so exalting, as the creation of art. It is a virus, allow me to add, for which medicine has not discovered a cure.

But John Keats, being John Keats, apparently could not do anything out of purely selfish motive even if he wished. When he left medicine for poetry, Keats tended to regard the latter as itself a form of medicine — that is to say, of doing good by other means. Walter Jackson Bate quotes two lines from a passage that Keats had deleted from his long and uncompleted poem *Hyperion,* which run: "sure a poet is a sage; / A humanist, Physician to all men."

But then John Keats was a young man of remarkable character. He was one of the few writers of the front rank who appears not to have been flawed by selfishness, solipsism, or the least meanness. He was a sweet character, a young man of natural — I do not say preternatural — goodness, large-hearted with a fine generosity of spirit. He was the sort of young man who, living on the financial edge himself, arranges to loan money to friends. He had a highly developed sense of honor and an instinctive hatred of injustice. In one of his letters, he mentions having to stop, while running an errand, to thrash a butcher's boy whom he discovered torturing a cat.

Very much one of the boys — he smoked cigars, had a taste for claret and snuff; enjoyed jokes, not all of them, so to say, on-color; he played billiards, went to boxing matches, cockfights, bearbaitings; was a hesitant but not entirely inactive ladies' man (there is speculation that he had syphilis) — John Keats gave off that spark that seemed to convince all whom he met that they were in the presence of a young man who was much out of the ordinary. He was broad-shouldered and muscular; Leigh Hunt, in describing him, wrote that "every feature was at once strongly cut and delicately alive." His eyes were large and gave off a melancholy glow, his brown hair ended in ringlets, his mouth was at once sensitive and slightly pugnacious. This orphan would, I think, have been every life-loving man's notion of a fine son or younger brother.

Owing to the general decrease in death brought about by medicine as it entered the nineteenth century, the prestige of medical workers was beginning to rise when Keats studied medicine. But the profession had not yet risen so high that, from a more aristocratic coign of vantage, it couldn't be used against a man. When Keats's second book of poetry was published, it was laid into by the Tory press, and nowhere with greater brutality than by one John Lockhart in *Blackwood's Edinburgh Magazine,* who assigned Keats to the school of Cockney poets and used his medical training against him for comic effect. Lockhart, signing himself anonymously as Z, wrote:

His friends, we understand, destined him to the career of medicine, and he was bound apprentice some years ago to a worthy apothecary in town. But all has been undone by a sudden attack of the malady to which we have alluded [the insane belief that anyone can write poetry]. Whether Mr. John had been home with a diuretic or composing draught to some patient far gone in the poetical mania, we have not heard. This much is certain, that he has caught the infection, and that thoroughly. For some time we were in hopes that he might get off with a violent fit or two; but of late the symptoms are terrible. The phrenzy of the *Poems* was bad enough in its way; but it did not alarm us half so seriously as the calm, settled, imperturbable drivelling idiocy of *Endymion*. We hope, however, that in so young a person, and with a constitution originally so good, even now the disease is not utterly incurable.

The boys played hardball in those days. Byron, who was not a great admirer of Keats's poetry — he called it "a sort of mental masturbation" — seemed, in later years, ready to believe Shelley when he claimed that this and other harsh reviews threw Keats into such a state of agony that his "sufferings at length produced a rupture of a blood vessel in the lungs [leading to] the usual process of consumption." Shelley put roughly the same story about in "Adonais," his elegy for Keats. Bad medicine, this is even worse psychology.

Keats knew the political motivation behind *Blackwood's* and other mean-spirited reviews of his work. While he did not take pleasure in it, neither did he allow it to throw him, at least not for long. "Praise or blame," he wrote to his publisher, "has but a momentary effect on the man whose love of beauty in the abstract makes him a severe critic of his own Works." Keats was too tough to be greatly daunted by criticism, and one wonders if his training in medicine, where he saw genuine suffering, didn't contribute to this. Walking the halls of Guy's had its recompense.

John Keats is part of the tradition of writers who have studied medicine, and their numbers include, among the most famous,

Rabelais, Sir Thomas Browne, Tobias Smollett, Oliver Goldsmith, George Crabbe, Oliver Wendell Holmes, Sr., Anton Pavlovich Chekhov, Arthur Conan Doyle, Robert Bridges, W. Somerset Maugham (who, like Keats, never practiced), William Carlos Williams, and Walker Percy. A wildly disparate group they are, but what unites them is that they had all seen life in extremis, seen men and women in fear and in bravery, in selfishness and in astonishing selflessness, up close and not merely personal but indeed beneath the skin.

In some of these men, their medical training and experience is evident in their work. Rabelais's blatant comic concentration on body parts is only the most obvious example. "I don't doubt that the study of the medical sciences seriously affected my literary work," said Chekhov; "they enlarged the field of my observations, enriched me with knowledge, the true value of which for me as a writer can be understood only by one who is himself a physician."

One of the things one discovers in reading — and in reading about — John Keats is how very impressionable, both intellectually and artistically, he tended to be. Keats read intensely, passionately, as if there were no tomorrow, which in his case, alas, there scarcely was. He did not so much view visual art as devour it. When Benjamin Haydon took him to see the Elgin Marbles, those portions of the Parthenon frieze that Lord Elgin had brought to England, Keats was blown away; viewing them with a doctor's eye, he was much taken with what seemed to him the anatomical perfection of the figures. "He went again and again to see the Elgin Marbles," wrote his friend the painter Joseph Severn, "and would sit for an hour or more at a time beside them rapt in attention."

Robert Gittings, in another of his books on Keats, *John Keats: The Living Year, 1818–1819*, demonstrates how immediately and sometimes directly Keats put his reading into his writing. Gittings shows how when Keats read Spenser, he took over the nine-line Spenserian stanza for his own narrative poem "The Eve of St. Agnes." Reading Dryden's fables and his translation of Ovid, he picked up Drydenesque imagery for a sonnet he was himself working on. He used, as Gittings shows, Robert Burton's great idiosyncratic work *The Anatomy of Melancholy* as a regular fount of ideas, and took over some passages and phrases nearly word for word. But whether he is reading Milton or Shakespeare or Dante or Wordsworth or lesser writers, the results can often, with a bit of sleuthing, be found in the poetry he was writing at the time.

Any serious artist, as Henry James once pointed out, must acquire knowledge of the world well beyond his immediate experience of it. Keats acquired a vast amount of his experience from his reading. For him reading became experience itself. Where else could a man of twenty-two or -three be expected to gain it? And where better than from his education. Most of us spend a lifetime attempting, with varying degrees of success, to shed many of the ideas learned in our education. But John Keats hadn't a lifetime to spend. In his case, given his great impressionableness, this meant, to a perhaps unexampled extent, that his ideas came from his medical education. Six of his twenty-five years, after all, were spent in medical surroundings and training, and these represented more than half his intellectually conscious life.

Images from medicine suffuse Keats's poetry, and ideas learned in medical textbooks and lecture halls dominate his letters. A word here about the letters of John Keats, for Keats's reputation is based both on his poems — or perhaps on a dozen or so of his poems — and on his brilliant correspondence. Often unpunctuated, frequently misspelled, written for the most part without lengthy deliberation or revision, Keats's letters establish his claim for genius nearly as much as does his poetry. Lionel Trilling, admitting that Keats's letters, in their relation to Keats as a poet "are no more than illuminating and suggestive," goes on to write: "The fact is, however, that because of the letters it is impossible to think of Keats only as a poet — inevitably we think of him as something even more interesting than a poet, we think of him as a man, and as a certain kind of man, a hero."

The Keats letters also establish their author's intellectual bona fides. Keats's earlier reputation was that of a rather mindless poet utterly uninterested in the realm of the intellect, his work the result of pure poetic inspiration. But the letters give flight to such notions. "I feel more and more content every day to read," he wrote to Benjamin Haydon. "Books are becoming more interesting and valuable to me — I may say I could not live without them." In another of his letters, he wrote: "An extensive knowledge is needful to thinking people — it takes away the heat and fever; and helps by widening speculation to ease the Border of mystery." He found "every department of Knowledge . . . excellent and calculated toward a greater whole." This of course included medicine, for in this same letter he notes that "I am glad at not having given away my medical Books, which I shall again look over to keep alive the little I know thitherwards."

What we now know, thanks to the scholarship of Donald Goellnicht, is the debt Keats's poetry and ideas specifically owe to his medical education — and the debt is profound. Professor Goellnicht, not himself a physician, has gone back to consult the main works in chemistry, botany, anatomy, physiology, and pathology, including the lectures of Keats's teachers, and shown how central these works were to Keats's intellectual and poetic development.

Certain key words and phrases in the Keatsian vocabulary — among them "sensation," "luxuries," "sympathy," "sublimity," "fine" and "refine," "yeast" and "yeastling," "core," "essence," "ethereal" — are taken from Keats's study of chemistry and botany, anatomy and physiology. In the formation of key metaphors as well as glancing descriptive passages, Keats availed himself of concepts first learned in his medical studies. Many of his descriptions, as Professor Goellnicht writes, "are fully comprehensible only within the context of Keats's specialized knowledge of botany." The same may be said about his specialized knowledge of chemistry, anatomy, and physiology. What is more, he always used his medical knowledge with perfect precision and acute accuracy. Where he is scientifically inaccurate — as in his imputing sexuality to flowers and plants in the manner of Linnaeus — it is because such ideas were accepted in his own day.

Keats had a special interest in the brain and the nervous system, and it is tempting to think that, had he gone into academic medicine, he might have become a first-class neurologist. He not only used the then current anatomical description of the brain — which featured globes, ridges, canals, branches, arches, and vaults — in his poems, but took the way in which the brain was thought to work to form his own idea of artistic creation. Chemistry and botany — more precisely horticulture — also contributed to this idea, but it is the sensory messages sent by the brain that are crucial to Keats's notion that good poetry should produce "sensations" in its readers, sensation acting upon imagination. His own perception of the world, as he always insisted, was based on sensory experience rather than abstract ideas. "O for a life of sensations rather than thought!" he wrote to his friend Benjamin Bailey. And to John Reynolds he wrote: "Axioms in philosophy are not axioms until they are proved upon our pulses. We read fine things, but never feel them to the full until we have gone the same steps as the author."

Here, too, Keats is sounding a note he first heard played at Guy's Hospital — specifically on the fine pipes of Astley Cooper, who taught his students to distrust everything that they hadn't directly experienced, and above all to distrust systems. "I have made up my mind," Keats wrote to his brother and sister-in-law, "never to take any thing for granted." Where Keats and his medical school teachers may have parted company was in their strict adherence to experience alone. Science goes after truth piecemeal, drawing a line from one dot to another, one line at a time, confident that, at the end of its travail, all the dots will be connected, the picture filled in, the puzzle solved. Keats, with his artist's imagination — aided perhaps by a premonition of his own brief stay on earth — may not have been able to settle for that.

Negative capability, an idea first revealed in a letter of Keats's to his brother in 1817, is about the need to develop the skill of learning to live with uncertainty. It is achieved, in Keats's words, "when a man is capable of being in uncertainties, mysteries, doubts, without reaching after fact and reason." This is an idea not only temperamentally unsuited to the scientific mind — which is problem-solving and question-answering—but extremely useful to the artistic mind, which must take into account, without necessarily being fully able to explain, the mysteries of life. Not least among these mysteries are the presence of goodness and the power of evil. Beyond any doubt, Shakespeare was the writer Keats admired most, and my guess is that he did so, in large part, because Shakespeare was able directly to face and describe the many contradictions presented by life without having to pronounce doctrinally upon them. Shakespeare, the consummate artist, has the disinterest that Keats himself yearned to have, and, for a tantalizingly brief period, appears to have acquired.

"Life must be undergone," Keats wrote to Benjamin Bailey in January of 1818, "and I certainly derive a consolation from the thought of writing one or two more Poems before it ceases." Nine months later John Keats would enter upon the most creative year of his abbreviated life, and compose the poems that would ensure his permanent fame. This extraordinary year began with Keats's avowal, at a gathering in his publishers' office, that there was nothing more left to do in poetry, that it was an exhausted vein of cultural endeavor, and that he was himself done with it. In the year running from September 21, 1818, to September 21, 1819, as Robert Gittings writes, "Keats wrote, with numerous other works, practically every poem that places him among the major poets of the world." The year begins and ends with the composition of *Hyperion* and *The Fall of Hyperion,* and in between are, along with much else, the great odes to Psyche, Autumn, and a Nightingale, the odes on a Grecian Urn, Melancholy, and Indolence, along with "La Belle Dame sans Merci" and the "Sonnet to Sleep." A synthesizing maturity dominates these poems; in them, as the critic F. R. Leavis writes, "poet and letter-writer are at last one." These poems, again to quote Leavis, are "clearly the expression of a rare maturity; the attitude is the product of tragic experience, met by discipline, in a very uncommonly strong, sincere and sensitive spirit." In short, Keats was now writing poems built—and utterly deserving—to last.

Those twelve months were for John Keats, as we now say

about athletes, a career year. In literature it was the career year to end all career years. "The year . . . may be soberly described," W. Jackson Bate writes, "as the most productive in the life of any poet of the past three centuries. The mere variety in style is difficult to parallel within the same limit of time." Without the work of 1818–19, John Keats would today be an unknown figure, as obscure a poet as his friend John Reynolds, except that, unlike Reynolds, it could not even have been said of him that he was a friend to John Keats.

How this year came about is one of those unexplained but endlessly fascinating phenomena. Matthew Arnold, writing about the French poet Maurice de Guérin, notes: "In him, as in Keats . . . the temperament, the talent itself, is deeply influenced by their mysterious malady: the temperament is *devouring;* it uses vital power too hard and too fast, paying the penalty in long hours of unutterable exhaustion and premature death." Highly suggestive though that is, I myself much prefer the less mystical concluding view of Aileen Ward, yet another of Keats's biographers, which holds that "Keats earned his place in the tradition of English poetry by his courage to take the great dare of self-creation, his willingness to accept failure and move beyond it, his patience in learning his craft from those who could teach him." The sadness is that John Keats didn't have long to enjoy what he had achieved, for seventeen months after this astonishing creative outburst, he was dead.

For better or worse, Keats's own medical training had placed him in the position of being the first to know how grave was his illness. Throughout his letters, Keats reports contracting colds and sore throats, but in February of 1820 he began to undergo serious bleeding from his lungs. On the night of February 3, he returned home to Hampstead, telling his friend Charles Brown, with whom he was sharing quarters, that he had felt a severe chill. "But now I don't feel it. Fevered! of course a little." He took to his bed, where he coughed slightly, but in examining the stain his cough had left on the sheets, he asked Brown to bring him a candle so that he could examine it more closely. Brown recalled Keats looking at him with great — I like to think with physicianly — calm and saying: "I know the colour of that blood; — it is arterial blood; I cannot be deceived in that colour; that drop of blood is my death-warrant. I must die."

Medicine had never entirely departed Keats's mind. After he left it for poetry, he continued to diagnose and prescribe for the maladies of his friends. Cowden Clarke, afflicted with what he called "stomachic derangement," recalled Keats treating him with "a remarkable decision of opinion, describing the functions and actions of the organ with the clearness and, as I presume, technical precision of an adult practitioner." Down on his financial luck and certain it wasn't likely to change, Keats at one time thought of going to sea as a ship's doctor on a vessel bound for India. During periods of discouragement, he thought of setting up as an apothecary. At another time, he contemplated returning to medical school — specifically, at the University of Edinburgh.

But Keats's medical training was finally to serve him most pertinently — if not efficaciously — in his own final, fatal disease. Dr. Hale-White believes that Keats "knew in his own mind . . . that his disease was mortal." Which was more than could be said for the doctors who were called in to treat him. The first to see him said that there was no "pulmonary affection" at all, and that the disease was all in his mind. The second, as Keats reported to his sister, believed that "there is nothing the matter with me except nervous irritability and a general weakness of the whole system which has proceeded from my anxiety of mind of late years and the too great excitement of poetry."

Yet someone must have known something serious was up, for Keats was advised not to attempt to endure the harsh English winter and to sail to Italy, which he did, on September 17, 1820, in the company of the painter Joseph Severn, who was to prove the most steadfast of friends. The trip was arduous. Bad weather and quarantines caused it to be extended to fully two and a half months. A fellow passenger, a Miss Cottrell, was also suffering from tuberculosis, which Keats, with his medical eye, quickly spotted, causing him, as Aileen Ward writes, "to be faced with a living image of his own disease for the whole voyage." In fact, from his bunk, Keats, the doctor in him emerging yet again, gave Severn instructions on treating the poor woman when her condition worsened.

In Rome, Keats was put into the care of a Dr. James Clark, a good and kindly man, who also misdiagnosed Keats, believing that his trouble was in his stomach. In the approved method of the day, he had him bled, put him on a near-starvation diet, allowing him a single anchovy and piece of toast a day. (Hale-White makes plain that doctors knew so little about the diagnosis and treatment of tuberculosis in the early decades of the nineteenth century that he likens them to "extremely near-sighted people trying to grope around without glasses.") Soon Keats's hemorrhaging increased, his fever soared, he could not sleep. At one point, he reached for the laudanum he had had Severn purchase, hoping to do away with himself. Severn stopped him from doing so.

Weeks went by of increased weakening before Keats would die. He tried but could find no comfort in thoughts of an afterlife. Severn read to him, from, among other works, *Don Quixote.* Sick as he was, he characteristically worried about his friend Severn's health, prescribing medicines and exercise for him. "He is my doctor," Severn would write to John Taylor, Keats's publisher.

When the end came, Keats attempted to steel Joseph Severn for it. When he asked Severn if he had ever witnessed a death, and Severn said no, Keats replied: "Well then I pity you — poor Severn, what trouble and danger you have got into for me." When death came at last, Keats, still the doctor, alerted Severn: "Don't be frightened — I shall die easy — be firm, and thank God it has come." One is here put in mind of the sixth stanza from "Ode to a Nightingale":

> Darkling I listen; and, for many a time
> I have been half in love with easeful Death,
> Call'd him soft names in many a mused rhyme,
> To take into the air my quiet breath;
> Now more than ever seems it rich to die,

To cease upon the midnight with no pain,
  While thou art pouring forth my soul abroad
    In such an ecstasy!
  Still wouldst thou sing, and I have ears in vain —
    To thy high requiem become a sod.

Some seven hours later, finally having lost the fight against drowning being waged in his own lungs, John Keats died on February 23, 1821, apparently, at the very last at least, without pain.

A few days before his death, Keats, weary of the long struggle, asked Dr. Clark, "How long will this posthumous life of mine continue?" He could not know, of course, but in another sense his posthumous life would go on forever. "I think I shall be among the English poets after my death," he wrote in 1818 to his brother and sister-in-law in America. And so today John Keats is, not merely among the English poets, but after only Shakespeare and Milton, perhaps the very greatest of them. Not at all bad, really, for a fellow who didn't quite make it through medical school.

III

Attacks

Mortimer Adler: The Great Bookie

O N JUNE 28, 2001, Mortimer J. Adler, propagandist for the reading of great books, indexer extraordinaire, and the world's highest-salaried philosopher, died at the age of ninety-eight. I worked for Mortimer, as we all called him, in the late 1960s. After a yearlong stint as the director of an anti-poverty program in Little Rock, Arkansas, I had acquired, through the good offices of Harry Ashmore, a job as something called "senior editor" at Encyclopaedia Britannica, Inc., in Chicago. As with every other job I have ever had, I was not so much eager for this job as I was to escape the job I then held. (White flags were shooting up everywhere in what was unhappily called the War on Poverty.) So I was hired, along with ten or twelve others, to design a vast, genuinely radical revision of the *Encyclopaedia Britannica*. The pay was high, the comedy turned out to be wild, and the job put me back in Chicago, city of my birth.

Apologies to Diderot, D'Alembert, & Co., but the making of encyclopedias has never seemed to me of much interest. I felt no more affinity for cross-referencing than I did for cross-dressing. Etymologically buried within the word "encyclopedia" is the notion that all knowledge is a great, linked circle. Not at all my idea of a good time: altogether too intertwined, vast, grandiose. But it was something to do until I felt the need to escape this job, too, which four years later I did.

I was hired not by Mortimer Adler but by a man named Warren Preece, a former journalist who had been executive secretary at the Center for the Study of Democratic Institutions, then a very slow-moving and luxuriously run think tank in Santa Barbara, California, which was paid handsomely to illustrate nothing so much as the Leisure of the Theory Class. Things at Britannica, Inc., at the outset certainly couldn't have been more leisurely or theoretical. We were asked to write papers suggesting themes around which the new *Encyclopaedia Britannica* might best be organized. I wrote one on "struggle" as a possible theme — a paper that, if I have any luck at all, will long ago have been shredded, lost, or disintegrated. An entire week, sometimes two, would go by without having anything to do. Meanwhile, the *unterwerkers,* the subject editors and the picture editors, toiling in the hard gravel of fact on which any good reference book depends, kept things going on *Britannica,* doing the real work of running an encyclopedia.

After a year or so of this high-level dithering, Mortimer Adler was brought in to organize the new set. His energy and stamina were greater than those of anyone I have ever known. I have seen him lecture — browbeat is closer to it — a room of specialists on each of their own subjects for ten hours, do a two-hour call-in radio show interview afterward, return home to work on a book (he liked to turn out one a year), and, I should not have been in the least shocked to learn, end the day by making vigorous love to his thirty-odd-years-younger wife, and at last fall asleep, doubtless while attempting to draw a bead on some tangled epistemological problem.

After a tumultuous career as a teacher at the University of Chicago, where he had offended everyone but the janitorial staff, Adler departed to form Great Books clubs and to publish, under the auspices of Encyclopaedia Britannica, Inc., a set of fifty-four volumes called, collectively, *The Great Books of the Western World,* with two thick index volumes he christened the "Syntopicon," which must constitute the world's largest and most difficult to use index of ideas.

· · ·

Through lucubrations too elaborate and boring to go into here, Adler decided that there were 102 great ideas—running alphabetically from Angel to World—and was able to hire a staff of unemployed intellectual workers to plow through the fifty-four volumes, constituting roughly 32,000 pages, to discover 163,000 referents in them to the 102 great ideas. The project took eight years and roughly a million dollars, back in the 1950s, when a million dollars really was a million dollars.

Nobody, apparently, was around within Encyclopaedia Britannica, Inc., with sufficient authority to tell Adler that, far from being a great idea, the Syntopicon didn't even qualify as a dopey notion. After the books' publication, the intellectual journalist Dwight Macdonald didn't mind doing so, and in a fine devastation he amusingly dubbed the entire project "the Book of the Millennium Club." After making the crucial point that the Syntopicon failed to distinguish between major and minor references, Macdonald called it "one of the most expensive toy railroads any philosopher was ever given to play with."

Mortimer was sixty-five when I first encountered him, and looked more like fifty. Stocky, perhaps five foot six, rosy rather than ruddy of complexion, jowly, broad-chested, short-legged, expensively dressed, he was built, as they used to say of a certain kind of automobile of the era, to hold the road. He had a slight lisp, notable when saying the word "perspicacious," which he said a lot. A racing mind caused him to stammer, especially in argument, where he preferred to kill off opponents quickly. A broadsword not a rapier man, he once debated Bertrand Russell on the subject of the right ends of education, and after Adler spoke, Russell began his rejoinder by saying, "I greatly admire Dr. Adler's rough-hewn simplicity." People who heard the debate judged that Mortimer won but had sustained so many rhetorical lacerations that the victory wasn't worth it.

Sitting in a room around an immense conference table, we senior editors, now that Mortimer was in charge, were put to the task of designing what our chief called a "topical" table of contents, a device that, once up and running, would organize the subject matter of the new *Britannica* with a logic and efficiency of extraordinary . . . well, perspicacity. World knowledge was neatly divided up into ten parts, and each of the editors was to design outlines for these parts, or parts of the parts, that would form Adler's table of contents. From these extended outlines, the design of the articles in *Britannica* would be dictated. The larger aim was to supply readers of the new encyclopedia with no mere source of information but the means to a liberal education.

Two members of Mortimer's old Columbia University connection, Charlie Van Doren and Clifton Fadiman, joined the group. Fadiman easily won the prize for the most pretentious outlines. (Seeing Fadiman and Adler together, I used to think: two Sancho Panzas and no Don Quixote in sight.) I seem to remember Fadiman's composing for his outline on popular culture a rubric about the origin of the movies that ran, "The beginning of cinema: the curious confluence of an emerging technology and a surgent entrepreneurial ethnic group." After reading this, I passed along a note to the editor sitting next to me that read, "I think he means that the Jews got there first."

Mortimer claimed to be a proponent of arriving at positions through reasoned discussion — he was on record approving "intellectually well-mannered disputation" — but things didn't quite work out that way. The combination of deadlines and his impatience soon forced him into intellectual bullying. He did not suffer subtlety gladly. To hold his brief attention, one had to develop to a high power the art of quick blunt statement. He also erected a number of distinctions — "first-intentional and second-intentional knowledge" was a notorious one — that served as barbed wire to keep everyone at bay. "I know nothing more stupid and indeed vulgar than wanting to be right," wrote Paul Valéry, who wouldn't have done at all well in our meetings, and to whom Adler wouldn't have listened in any case.

I recall a scruffy subeditor who was invited in on the day we discussed psychology, his specialty. Tieless, he put his feet up on the table and announced, "The main thing here is that you don't want to pigeonhole this material." But pigeonholing, feathers and guano all over the joint, was of course the whole intent and meaning of our job. At the break, Mortimer said that he never wanted to see this man at another of our meetings, and he was banished from the project.

Never big on civility, Mortimer was an imperialist of the ego. The best, often the only, way to keep his interest was to talk to him about himself. Even then he would abandon you in midsentence if a more important person entered the room. He would tromp over people who disagreed with him, especially if they were employees, while lavishing sycophantic attention on the very rich or on people he needed at the moment.

Mortimer often enraged me, until I came to view him, I believe rightly, as an essentially comic character—not an idiot but a clown-savant. The comedy, as old as Aristophanes, was that of the inept philosopher: the man with his eyes on the heavens who, missing everything in front of him, falls into the mud. His physical ineptitude was considerable. All mechanical objects deranged him. He was famous as a nonswimmer, failing to get his bachelor's degree at Columbia because he couldn't pass the then compulsory swimming requirement; he also dropped out of gym classes, and was excused, owing to a want of coordination, from the student army training corps. You have to imagine a Diogenes whose lamp is unlit not to make a philosophical point but because he doesn't know how to light it.

Mortimer's ineptitude carried on well into his adulthood. In one story, his wife wished to hang a small painting, and, there being no hammer in their Chicago Gold Coast apartment near the Drake Hotel, she sent him out to buy one. Since there were no hardware stores on posh Michigan Avenue nearby, he went directly to Dunhill's where, *mirabile dictu,* no hammers being available, he brought back a gold-plated showerhead, which he used to hammer in the nail.

A friend of mine who worked for him recalls a love letter Mortimer wrote that contained the sentence "I love you with all the passions attendant thereto." Mortimer didn't have much luck with women. In the first volume of his autobiography, *Philosopher at Large* (1977), he claims to have married his first wife because both had had their hearts broken by earlier relationships, and he provides no other reason for what he portrays as a loveless marriage beyond his avowed immaturity. The marriage dragged on for thirty-three years, at the end of which Adler called in, from a hotel in San Francisco, that he wasn't coming home again. In the middle of this marriage, he fell in love with a secretary at the University of Chicago, and his ardent pursuit of her nearly caused his dismissal from the university for behavior regarded, as he puts it, as "intolerable."

Between his first and second marriage, Adler became engaged to a woman who, with her boyfriend, had been hatching a plot that called for insuring him into the stratosphere and then, with the aid of her boyfriend, shaking him down and possibly bumping him off. Adler's friends had her followed by a detective, and when the plot was revealed, Adler didn't at first want to believe it, then spent months of depression trying to get over it. The world was not too much with our philosopher, but frequently too much for him.

Adler apparently didn't care all that much about money, as long as he had enough of it to go first class, which he always did. "I must confess I have the propensities of a sybarite," he wrote in *Philosopher at Large*, adding in his second volume of autobiography, *A Second Look in the Rearview Mirror*, "Get over the folly of thinking that there is any conflict between high living and high thinking: Asceticism is for the birds." Impossible to imagine him traveling coach. In Chicago he lunched at the Tavern Club, bought his cigars — along with his hardware — at Dunhill's. At Britannica, he hired roomfuls of people for jobs that later turned out to be quite unnecessary. He resembled that Hollywood director who was given an unlimited budget and exceeded it, and he came close to sinking Britannica, Inc. He and Robert Hutchins were America's first six-figure intellectuals.

Hutchins and Adler were, in fact, an intellectual Abbott and Costello act, the one tall, elegant, and suave, the other short, nervous, bumptious without peer. I once saw Adler present no fewer than eleven reasons to "Bob," as he called him, for adapting a certain policy for the new *Britannica,* at the end of which Hutchins, removing his pipe from his sensuous lips, replied, "I do not consider that an adequate statement of the alternatives," promptly reinserting the pipe in his mouth, leaving Adler in a condition of pure speechless stammer.

Adler referred to his meeting in 1927 with Hutchins, who was then, at twenty-eight, acting dean of the Yale Law School, as changing "the whole course of my life." It changed Hutchins's quite as much. When Hutchins became president of the University of Chicago in 1929, at the age of thirty, he took Adler along with him. From the outset Adler practiced a form of intellectual tactlessness that made him enemies throughout the university. He let it be known that he thought the philosophy department a bunch of clucks. He wrote papers demeaning social science's pretensions to being legitimate learning, when social science was what the University of Chicago was most famous for. "I continued to challenge my colleagues instead of trying to persuade them," he wrote. Confident of his possession of the truth, he always took out his trusty blunderbuss and fired away. "I can see that you are the kind of young man who is accustomed to winning arguments," Gertrude Stein said to him one night during a visit to Chicago.

Winning arguments but, Miss Stein might have added, losing battles. Hutchins allowed that Adler did much to educate him, chiefly through introducing him to the great-books curriculum that he had acquired in John Erskine's General Honors Seminar at Columbia in the early 1920s. But Adler also did much to complicate Hutchins's life as president of the University of Chicago by alienating large segments of the faculty. Adler could get an argument to the shouting stage quicker than anyone I've ever known.

The fight at the University of Chicago over what constitutes the right curriculum for undergraduates — which Adler, even forty years later, falsely characterized as the "controversy over facts and ideas, and intellectualism and anti-intellectualism" — need never have reached the level of furor it did had Hutchins conducted it on his own and not allowed Mortimer to serve as his point man. One of Hutchins's great weaknesses was absolute loyalty to the wrong people. Edward Shils, who was on the scene at the University of Chicago during these years, described the relation of Robert Hutchins and Mortimer Adler by saying that "at least Prince Hal had the good sense, once he became king, to get rid of Falstaff."

I do not know of any genuine contribution that Mortimer Adler made to serious philosophy, though before he went into big-time indexing he was thought a serious Thomist. He also in several of his books insisted on the continuing relevance of ancient philosophers to modern problems, questions, and issues, chief among them Aristotle and Saint Thomas. ("Should auld Aquinas be forgot," Hutchins used to joke.) Like a gila monster, which is said never to let go, he was a persistent attacker of pragmatism, from his days in John Dewey's lectures to the end of his life. Sidney Hook once told me that it was proof of Dewey's honorableness that not even Mortimer Adler could drive him into anti-Semitism.

Perhaps Adler's major contribution has been in spreading the gospel of the great books. Hutchins and Adler, along with Scott Buchanan and Stringfellow Barr, took over the dying St. John's College in Annapolis, Maryland, where in 1937 they established an undergraduate program based exclusively on great books, with works on ancient and modern mathematics and science added; less intensive programs went into operation for a limited portion of the student body at the University of Notre Dame and at St. Mary's College in California.

I was myself the recipient of a partial great-books education at the University of Chicago, which Hutchins was able to install after the smog of controversy had cleared. Mine was assuredly better than a bad-books education, such as is nowadays offered at almost every school in the land, but education, I have come to conclude, is mostly luck in finding good teachers. I myself never found any at Chicago. (They were there in the persons of Frank Knight, Edward Shils, Joseph Schwab, and a few others, but I didn't search them out.) What I did discover at Chicago was an atmosphere where erudition was taken seriously. Because all the books taught were first class — no textbooks were allowed, no concessions were made to the second rate for political reasons, and one was graded not by one's teachers but by a college examiner — I gradually learned on my own the important writers and eternal issues, and where to go if one wished to stay with that unending work in progress called one's education.

Adler remained a lifelong advocate for the great books. Through an outfit called the Great Books Foundation, he helped set up seminars in many of the major cities of America, and himself taught in certain such seminars for decades — particularly the Aspen Institute, where, as I like to think, he ruined the holidays of many a corporation executive by forcing him to read John Locke. I have met a few people who have sat in these seminars for several years; they seem greatly to have enjoyed it. What is less clear is what they got out of it. After years of reading Plato, they seem no closer to escaping the cave than the rest of us. "Participants in the Aspen experience," Adler wrote, "were awakened to a realization that, in the scale of values, the Platonic triad of the true, the good, and the beautiful takes precedence over the Machiavellian triad of money, fame, and power." The least cynical of men, Adler probably actually believed this.

In a self-congratulatory mode, Adler spoke of himself getting more and more out of repeated rereadings of his great books, finding, as he put it, "a growth of understanding and insight" within himself. Yet insight and understanding are precisely the two qualities most absent from Mortimer Adler's character. Throughout

Philosopher at Large, Adler abjures any interest in human personality or behavior. "If I had as much interest in human beings as I do in human thought, this [his autobiography] would be a different story . . . Throughout my life it has been human thought to which I have reacted with the kind of concern that others have for human beings. I have given hurt sometimes because of this, and sometimes I have suffered it."

Adler is asking here not to be judged by his life but by his works. "An interest in human beings is one thing; an interest in thought another; and one should not be allowed to get in the way of the other," he wrote as a young man in an attack on Will Durant's *Story of Philosophy.* Yet despite Adler's admonitions, would anyone doubt it matters that Nietzsche went mad or that Socrates accepted his unjust death with serenity? In Adler's case, his own lack of interest in human beings and their idiosyncrasies destroys much of what passes for his philosophy, especially his educational philosophy.

Adler's ignorance of human psychology — of human nature *tout court* — led him to believe that everyone is educable. In his extreme egotism, he believed that, in his work on the Syntopicon and in revising the *Encyclopaedia Britannica,* he had supplied the tools for the perfection of humanity. "The two sets of books together," he wrote in *A Second Look in the Rearview Mirror,* "covered the waterfront; neither alone sufficed." He apparently went to his death with no notion that in the Syntopicon he merely created something useless — and with no idea that in his work on the *Encyclopaedia Britannica,* ripping it up every which way, allowing a maniacal Lego-set structure to distort content and make information more difficult to find, he had a major hand in helping to destroy something excellent.

When I was working for Britannica, he called me one morning and in much perturbation asked if I thought novels could contain ideas. An amazing question, really, from the great impresario of *The Great Books of the Western World.* Style was simply unavailable to him; he had an active dislike of it, believing that in a thinker such as Santayana it covered up a lack of substance. His own writing has a deep dryness — there, I believe, by deliberation. The last time we spoke, he told me that his newest book contained ten typos, and he sent me a copy with a note asking if I could find them. But to do that I would, of course, have had to read the book, which was not something I felt could be done.

Mortimer's was a powerful and lucid yet coarse and deeply vulgar mind. His must have been an astonishingly high IQ, but his brain functioned in him like a biceps: a large and showy thing with which one cannot finally do all that much but menace and beat down other people. He took logic, upon which he prided himself, all the way out. When he gave the lectures that resulted in the book he called *The Difference of Man and the Difference It Makes*, he argued that it was the power of "propositional speech" and conceptual thought that distinguished human beings from all other animals. If dolphins could utter coherent sentences, I asked him after one of these lectures, would this make them human? "Yes, absolutely," he replied, without a trace of irony. I don't know where Mortimer Adler might be just now, but I like to think he is being lectured to interminably by a very severe and humorless dolphin with an IQ much higher than his own.

Curious George Steiner

I N T H E W O R L D of intellectual journalism, George Steiner has always been a figure of controversy. No one who reads him seems to be neutral about him, with opinion divided between those who think his range of learning and power of dramatizing ideas astonishingly brilliant, and those who think him a fake of astounding portentousness and pomposity. Judgments about him are made even more complicated by the fact that he has been the victim of English academic anti-Semitism, colder and more disdainful than which civilized Jew-hating does not get.

Steiner is a writer who has always come on high, toweringly high. His first book, *Tolstoy or Dostoyevsky* (1959), set the tone for his unremitting highbrowism. For many years he moved the heavy mental lumber for *The New Yorker,* reviewing works on Walter Benjamin, Franz Kafka, and Paul Celan, bringing his taste for the abyss to that otherwise lighthearted journal. *Men in Dark Times,* the title of a collection of Hannah Arendt essays, is a phrase that provides a rubric for Steiner's own intellectual proclivities. If one is looking for a fifth horseman of the Apocalypse, Steiner is your man. I once, in print, referred to Harold Bloom as George Steiner without the sense of humor, which was, as Senator Claghorn used to say, "A joke, Ah say, that's a joke, son," because more humorless than Steiner human beings do not come.

I find myself unable to resist reading George Steiner, these days more often than not in the London *Times Literary Supplement,* where he is still doing his men-in-dark-times number. His is one of the tightest acts of our day. My friend Edward Shils once gave me a useful clue to the best way to read Steiner. He claimed that many years ago he read a splendid parody of Steiner's of the way a Soviet *apparatchik* thought. Steiner, he felt, was a genius mimic. And so, I have come to see, he is. What George Steiner has been doing, over the past forty or so years, is an incomparable impression of the world's most learned man.

The performance is near flawless. If you don't take him too seriously, it's great fun to watch his by now patented moves, feints, operatic touches. Rounding off paragraphs in *Lessons of the Masters,* his recently published Charles Eliot Norton Lectures on the relation between teachers and students, Steiner writes, "Here, too, the finale of the *Tractatus* is pertinent," or "Are there in this model ironized versions of Orphic or Pythagorean doctrines?" or, after a reference to Plotinus, "The phenomenon will recur in Wittgenstein's coven." Adumbrations like that one does not run into every day.

Steiner's pretensions are to polymathy. He claims just about all knowledge as his province. His reading is three stages beyond omnivorous—although he might admit, on the rare occasion, to a bad conscience over not reading an eight-volume history of the French Revolution (by Albert Sorel) that you had not hitherto known existed. He is multi-, he sometimes suggests omni-, lingual. He'll talk Boolean algebra with you, fourth-level composers, and even Knute Rockne, the great Notre Dame football coach, a high proportion of whose players, he informs readers of *Lessons of the Masters,* went on to become major coaches at Notre Dame and elsewhere. Whether he knows all he claims to know in any genuine depth, or is instead a high-level kibitzer, is difficult to say.

That Steiner is not a more powerful or highly valued critic has to do with his want of originality. He generally deals with material at second or third hand, writing most frequently about what this writer said about that writer. He enjoys tracing literary and philosophical influences—always a dubious enterprise—making connections across centuries, sometimes millennia. "Is it likely that," Steiner writes, in a sentence only he could have cobbled together, "Henry Adams was unacquainted with Julius Langbehn's immensely influential identification of artistic eminence and national destiny in *Rembrandt als Erzieher (Rembrandt as Educator)*, a tract which focuses also on the 'teutonic, titanic' role of Beethoven?"

At one point in his text Steiner refers to "mandarin ostentation" and at another he remarks upon using an "orotund flourish" deliberately. But without mandarin ostentation and orotund flourishes, Steiner's prose would not exist and he himself would be out of business. Nearly every sentence he indites contains the title of a book, the name of the author, an -ism or an -ology, foreign phrases, and plenty of quotation marks to go round. "Relations with Taoism and Confucianism will be those of rivalry and reciprocal insemination," is a fairly standard Steinerian sentence. Dramatic, slightly surprising juxtapositions are another specialty chez Steiner, so that we get "penetrative tenderness," "ironized topography," "incandescent intellectuality," and more, lots more. Things that are not iconic tend to canonic, and a vast number of things are "seminal." Steiner, one begins to feel after reading him for many years, greatly underrates the power of semen.

The *Lessons of the Masters* is a book about the teaching transaction, the dissemination (there's that damn fluid again) of knowledge as it is passed from generation to generation through teacher to student. Why do some teachers so captivate their students that what they convey leaves a lifelong impression? The standard explanations hold that the great teachers know their subject, have boundless passion for learning, widen and deepen consciousness, provide in their persons a model of how a great-souled person ought to live. This only leaves out the key element of magic — which is to say, the unexplainable reason why some teachers can radically change lives.

Over the course of 185 dense pages George Steiner does not really explain the magic in teaching. Instead he provides partial portraits of some famously great teachers — Socrates (of course), Jesus, the Hasidic masters, Heidegger, Alain, Nadia Boulanger, and others — and takes up a number of issues, questions, and problems surrounding teaching. Among these are the responsibility of teachers for disciples, the tensions (erotic, rivalrous, etc.) between teacher and student, the differing nature of humanistic and scientific teaching, the blights of sexual harassment and political correctness on contemporary teaching, and the increasingly large role of masterly female teachers.

Steiner, who reports that he has former students on five continents, claims to have loved teaching, and now feels himself orphaned and bereft in retirement from the classroom. He is said to have been a mesmerizing lecturer. My guess is that his revved-up language comes across better orally than on the cold page, where it can be scrutinized more carefully for emptiness and laughs. Of the experience of teaching a doctoral seminar in Geneva for twenty-five years, Steiner, with characteristic overstatement, remarks that this was "as near as an ordinary, secular spirit can come to Pentecost." He then pulls out one of the two great clichés of false humility used by teachers to describe their experience: "By what oversight or vulgarization should I have been paid to become what I am? When, and I have felt this with sharpening malaise, it might have been altogether more appropriate for me to pay those who invited me to teach?" In other words, he would have done it for nothing. (The other standard teaching cliché has to do with how much a teacher has learned from his students.)

Having not long ago closed down a university teaching career of thirty years, I would like to go on record as saying that I wouldn't have done it for a penny less. Teaching is arduous work, entailing much grinding detail and boring repetition, interrupted only occasionally by moments of always surprising exultation. And I should like to add that I don't think I learned a thing from my students, God love 'em.

So high does Steiner come at things, so greatly does he dramatize (and self-dramatize) ideas and all experience, that one may lose sight of the fact that he is himself a very considerable cliché-meister. Most of his clichés, of course, come from books. One finds little evidence in Steiner's writing that he knows either man or life, only "ideas."

One in particular that plays through *Lessons of the Masters* is the ample "homoerotic" element in the teacher-student relationship. (Steiner doesn't neglect to emphasize that the relationship can also be Oedipal, but let's let that go, for it is probably best to take up only one cliché at a time.) "In the Platonic Academy or Athenian gymnasium, in the Papuan long house, in British public schools, in religious seminaries of every hue, homoeroticism has not only flourished but been regarded as educative." (Hope you picked up on and enjoyed that lilting reference to the Papuan long house.) The homoerotic element in teaching derives from the statements and conduct in the *Symposium* of Alcibiades, who attempts (with no luck) to seduce Socrates, illustrating the attraction of the beautiful student to the physically unattractive teacher.

Plato tended to eroticize a great deal, but I wonder if the sexual component in teaching isn't vastly overstated. As a student I felt admiration for a small number of my teachers, and as a teacher I found my heart going out to certain of my students, but on neither side of the transaction, as student or as teacher — that is, in the role of beauty or of beast — did it occur to me to hop in the sack with anyone. Hannah Arendt may have slept with her teacher Heidegger, and then returned to his bed much later, but Arendt, however brilliant she may have seemed as a writer, was a woman of consistently poor judgment outside of books.

Steiner touches on the question of discipleship but does not go deeply into why some teachers want disciples and some are uninterested in them. He makes only a single mention of F. R. Leavis, the Cambridge don who cultivated followers such that, from the 1950s through the 1970s, one spoke of "Leavisites" with supreme confidence that everyone in lit biz knew what one meant. Steiner touches on Leo Strauss, by way of a mention of Saul Bellow's novel *Ravelstein,* but does not go into the phenomenon of the Straussians, a school of political philosophy now in its fourth generation of disciples. An investigation of the school of Strauss, as Steiner himself might put it, is a work eagerly awaited.

The question of writing and teaching is treated in the same glancing fashion. Socrates and Jesus, the world's two greatest teachers, chose not to publish. One used regularly to hear about great teachers—Jacob Klein at St. John's in Annapolis, Frank O'Malley at Notre Dame, and others—who published little or nothing. In some ways, their being above the coarse appetite for print added to their allure.

The question of publishing and teaching seems to me a central one in modern higher education. A professor at Washington University in St. Louis, which is enjoying a vogue just now as a popular school, told me that the genius of the place is in its convincing the parents of its students that it is a great teaching college while making plain to its faculty that it remains a research university: publish, in other words, or perish.

The split is one that is probably in the end reconcilable. In my own teaching experience, I felt that my being a widely published writer gave me a good deal of such authority as I had with my students. Against George Bernard Shaw's famous apothegm—"He who can, does. He who cannot, teaches"—I did, and it seemed to help. At the same time, because I always thought of myself primarily as a writer, I felt myself scamping on the full-time duties of teaching. Most of the great modern teachers have not been active writers. One might go further to say that, as Nietzsche claimed a married philosopher was a joke, so a married teacher is at the disadvantage of not being at the full-time service of his students, as was, for a notable recent example, Allan Bloom, a seldom-published bachelor who was, I am told, at the complete disposal of his students.

No honest person can teach other than a scientific subject, music, or a foreign language in a contemporary university without feeling at least a bit of a fraud. As a teacher of English and American literature and of prose writing, I know I felt a complex but genuine inadequacy. Sydney Smith, one of the few writers whom

Steiner does not quote, once said that if the culinary arts had advanced no further than those of teaching, we should still be eating soup with our hands. Certainly, no other institution is as inefficient in delivering the goods as so-called (always "so-called") higher education, especially in the humanities, where one teaches, say, to a room of thirty students and perhaps nine students really grasp one's meaning.

Anyone who has taught the humanities or history must have longed, at one point or another, as I know I did, to have taught science, or mathematics, or music—subjects where talent and ability show up early and can be tested soundly. Literary talent and skill at humanistic subjects, more often than not, don't come into play until well into one's twenties and sometimes later.

Teaching would-be writers, which I have also done, is an especially complicated enterprise. I used to tell students all that I could not do for them: give them a love of language, make them more observant, imbue them with a dramatic sense, reveal the mechanics of wit, and much more. All I could hope to do for them was point out the possibilities in prose style, many of which they were unlikely to be aware of, and where their own mistakes might lie. This is not, when you think about it, all that much. I used to end with a little Zen koan of my own devising: "Writing cannot be taught, but it can be learned."

In teaching literature, there is the question of whether one ought to be teaching what one does in the first place. Lionel Trilling made this point in his essay "On the Teaching of Modern Literature," in which he quite appropriately asked if it is right to inculcate the dark visions in the young of such standard-curriculum writers as Kierkegaard, Nietzsche, Dostoyevsky, and Freud. I felt much the same teaching the perhaps less dark but still difficult Henry James, Joseph Conrad, and Willa Cather to people at the end of their adolescence, who already had enough on their minds, and in their hormones, without having to worry about, say, Conrad's essential message that we come into the world, live, and die absolutely alone. Does one really need to know this at nineteen?

• • •

One of Steiner's best portraits in *Lessons of the Masters* is of the philosopher and teacher Alain, an original thinker long dear to me for telling a friend of his recovering from surgery that he should give way to his depression, which was only natural after surgery, an insult to the body, but that he mustn't let this depression get him down. Alain felt, as do I, that the real teaching was done not in universities but at the secondary school level, and he spent all his teaching years at the lycée. Yet Alain's most famous student was Simone Weil, who ended up starving herself to death for political reasons. So much for the far-reaching influence of great teachers.

Not long ago I appeared on a panel in which two women, in a slightly scornful-of-America way, talked about the glories of their educations in France and in Austria. "At *Gymnasium*," one of them reported, "we studied Goethe and Schiller in a most careful manner." I had to report that I myself went to a high school taught by mentally disturbed teachers. I added that in education America was the land of the second chance. One could be an uninterested student at the grammar, secondary, even university level and still have the opportunity to acquire a decent education. My own recollection as a student is that when a professor was remarking that there were eight reasons for the Renaissance, I was wondering why he, or anyone else, would ever have bought so dreary a necktie and then stained it with soup.

Perhaps because I was so mediocre a student I have an abiding interest in famous men who, when young, were in the same condition. Henry James was one: inept at engineering school, a flop at Harvard Law School. Having established his incompetence in two fields, he found all that was left for him was to write brilliantly. Paul Valéry was another. He was thought especially poor at mathematics, which kept him from a naval career; later in life mathematics became one of his intellectual passions.

As a teacher, I noted many students whom I came to think of as "good at school." The phrase, as I use it, is nonapprobative and carries no more weight than, say, "good at soccer." These students have been trained to take tests, to write the A paper, to score high on their SATs. They understand that the first question confronting the college student is what the hell does the professor want. Once they discover this, they deliver it. They may or may not be genuinely interested in books, ideas, culture. But culture isn't their goal — getting into business or law or medical school is.

Among the topics that Steiner touches on is, inevitably, the Internet. "Fascinatingly," he writes, "the interactive, correctable, interruptible, media of word processors, of electronic textualities on the Internet and the web, may amount to a return, to which Vico would call a *ricorso,* to orality." He continues: "The screen can teach, examine, demonstrate, interact with a precision, a clarity, and a patience exceeding that of the human instructor. Its resources can be disseminated at will. It knows neither prejudice nor fatigue. In turn, the apprentice can question, answer back in a dialectic whose pedagogic value may come to surpass that of spoken discourse."

Something about this suggests that Steiner, once again nicely removed from reality, doesn't himself spend a lot of time at a computer. As an instrument of learning, the computer is at best a source of quick information — information, surely he would agree, isn't education — and even here it is often incomplete and frustratingly untrustworthy. The most interesting thing I had heard about education on the Internet comes from a man I know who taught a business-education course through computers. He remarked that he thought it possible to learn on the Internet, but that it is hell to teach on it: answering endless e-mails from students, feeling the inflexibility of programs that could not be easily altered, having no real human contact whatsoever — all this made, on the part of the teacher, for an excruciating boredom.

Almost all that is interesting in education is lost on George Steiner, owing to his relentless profundity. Always the deep-sea diver, he prefers to become entangled in the weeds found at the depths, while the treasures of common sense, floating high above on the water's surface, inevitably elude him.

Bloomin' Genius

HAROLD BLOOM, the Yale professor and literary critic, has been on a roll. Two of his major books, *The Western Canon: The Books and School of the Ages* and *Shakespeare: The Invention of the Human,* were both bestsellers — unusual in itself for works of such high intellectual pretension. When the latter came out in paperback, its U.S. publisher sent out a vast number of copies with their own special floor display, à la John Grisham. Bloom has won a MacArthur fellowship, better known as a genius grant or a Big Mac; been chosen to deliver the Charles Eliot Norton Lectures at Harvard; and been awarded the gold medal for criticism by the American Academy of Arts and Letters, of which he is also a member. The *Washington Post* called Bloom one of the three most important literary critics writing in English in the twentieth century — the other two being F. R. Leavis and Edmund Wilson.

Bloom's success is of a peculiarly American kind and yet not easily fathomed. As a critic, he is not that accessible and is capable of producing strikingly pretentious prose. ("Like Thoreau, Whitman has a touch of the Bhagavad-Gita, but the Hindu vision is mediated by western hermeticism, with its Neoplatonic and Gnostic elements.") He claims to be of the school of aesthetic critics, saying that "I feel quite alone these days in defending the autonomy of the aesthetic." Yet he himself doesn't produce anything approaching the aesthetically pleasing in his own writing. In an interview in the *Paris Review,* he declared that he never revises his prose, and nothing in his work refutes this impressive claim. Any critic ready to avail himself of such gargoylesque words as "psychokabbalistic" and "pneumognostic," or who can write about the cosmos's having been "reperspectivized by Tolstoy," may be many things, but he ain't no aesthete.

Nor does Bloom project an attractive, let alone a seductive, character. He is not the charmingly nutty, but rather the exhaustingly garrulous professor. Such is Bloom's loquacity that he discovered, in the midst of his psychoanalysis, that he was paying to give his analyst lectures "several times a week on the proper way to read Freud." Bloom writes like a man accustomed to speaking to his inferiors — to students, that is, a captive audience. To them he may lay down the law, take great pleasure in his own performance, be utterly unworried about someone coughing politely and saying, "Excuse me, pal, but what you just said seems to me a bunch of bullshit!"

Harold Bloom resembles no one so much as Zero Mostel, with something of the same physique and verbal mania but none of the amusing punch lines. Such laughs as are to be found in Bloom are all unconsciously created on his part. In *The Western Canon,* he reports that every time he rereads *Bleak House* he cries whenever Esther Summerson does, "and I don't think I'm being sentimental." In the same book, he also reports that he uses the poems of Walt Whitman to assuage grief. "I remember one summer, in crisis, being at Nantucket with a friend who was absorbed in fishing, while I read aloud to both of us from Whitman and recovered myself again." Poor friend, one feels, poor fish.

Critics come in varying styles: from subtle, self-effacing, and sardonic to oracular, vatic, apocalyptic, and plain intelligent. The one quality indispensable to the critic, however, is authoritativeness.

Bloom has had no problem mastering the tone of authoritativeness. If he came off any more ex cathedra in his judgments, he'd be pope. He is all assertion and no proof. Samuel Johnson is, for Bloom, "unmatched by any critic in any nation before or after him." Oscar Wilde "was right about everything." Tolstoy's story "Hadji Murád" is his "touchstone for the sublime of prose fiction, to me the best story in the world." And then there is Emily Dickinson, who, "at the height of her powers," is "the best mind to appear among western poets in nearly four centuries." What's that qualificatory "nearly" doing there, one wonders. Why not round it off and make it an even half millennium?

Bloom presents himself as a genius battling his way through the dark forces of the ignorant. He ranges across literatures, absorbs religious ideas, swallows whole cultures, happily making pronunciamentos upon them as he passes. His pretension rate is outside the solar system. In *The Book of J*, for example, he argued that the real author of the Hebrew Bible was a woman who belonged to the Solomonic elite and wrote during the reign of Rehoboam. Every serious scholar on the subject shot holes in this notion. Yet, to this day, Bloom placidly refers to the "J writer" as if his speculation is the unshakable truth.

Born in 1930, Bloom began his professional life as a critic of Romantic poetry, and quite a good one, as his book *The Visionary Company* shows. But his ambition grew and he soon became the intellectual equivalent of the character in P. G. Wodehouse who looked as if he were poured into his clothes and forgot to say when. The sensible Bloom still occasionally peeks through. "You cannot teach someone to love great poetry if they come to you without that love," he writes in *The Western Canon*. "How can you teach solitude?" But for many years now bombast and confident obscurity have been his reigning notes.

"The personality of the critic is much deprecated in our time," Bloom wrote in *The Western Canon*. Sad, because the great critic — that would be Professor Bloom — is engaged in a dramatic struggle at a depth and with an accompanying danger beyond our imagining. In *Kabbalah and Criticism*, Bloom writes that "reading is defensive warfare, however generously or joyously we read." If you are what Bloom calls a "strong reader," it gets even worse, as he notes in his *Map of Misreading*: "Such a reader . . . self-deconstructed yet fully knowing the pain of his separation both from text and from nature, doubtless will be more than equal to the revisionary labors of contraction and destruction, but hardly to the antithetical restoration that increasingly becomes part of the burden and function of whatever valid poetry we have left or may yet receive." It's enough to make you turn in your library card.

Writing, for Bloom, isn't much easier. "One writes to keep going, to keep oneself from going mad," he told his *Paris Review* interviewer. "Maybe it's an apotropaic gesture, maybe one writes to ward off death." As with writing criticism, so with teaching literature: "The various times I have taught [Emily Dickinson's] poems have left me with fierce headaches, since the difficulties force me past my limits."

Bloom is that most comic of unconscious comic figures: the academic Dionysian, calling for higher fires, more dancing girls, music, and wine, all from an endowed chair. His literary taste runs to the hot-blooded, long-winded, and apocalyptic: Blake, Whitman, Nietzsche, D. H. Lawrence, Norman Mailer are among the writers who light our aging professor's fire. Apart from Shakespeare, Bloom's great culture heroes are Emerson and Freud, who, in combination, yield a gasbag with a dirty mind. "Why criticism has not addressed itself to the image of masturbation in Whitman," Bloom writes, "I scarcely know." A critic's work, as you can see, is never done.

"Criticism," Bloom has said, "is either a genre of literature or it is nothing." But criticism becomes literature only when it satisfies one of two standards. The first is that it be so well written that it gives some of the same pleasure that literature itself does. William Hazlitt and V. S. Pritchett qualify here. Bloom, whose writing is charitably described as "difficult" by his Yale colleague John Hollander, does not. The second way criticism can qualify as literature is through the elucidating power of its ideas. Samuel Johnson, Matthew Arnold, T. S. Eliot, F. R. Leavis, and, perhaps, Northrop Frye qualify. It is here that Bloom would no doubt wish to stake his claim.

Bloom has been known as a man with a "big idea." The idea is named in the first of three books he devoted to it, *The Anxiety of Influence* (the others are *A Map of Misreading* and *Kabbalah and Criticism*). Written in prose with the translucency of isinglass, these books, as the Germans say, *sie lassen sich nicht lesen* — do not permit themselves to be read. Still, one can make out their broader lineaments. The big idea, which was more modestly and lucidly put forth first by W. Jackson Bate, the biographer of Dr. Johnson and Coleridge, is that writers feel haunted by their predecessors, causing them to feel sorely belated, as if everything they wish to do has already been done before them. Weaker writers are crushed by this, the idea holds, but strong writers go on to challenge and sometimes surpass their precursors.

As a theory of literary influence, based on the psychology of authorship, Bloom's idea has not been widely taken up either by his fellow academics or by practicing critics. So far as one can determine, *The Anxiety of Influence* has had very little influence and appears to have caused anxiety chiefly in Harold Bloom, who claims that few people really understand it. A characteristic passage from the book may indicate why not:

> What is the primal scene, for a poet as poet? It is his poetic father's coitus with the muse. There he was begotten? No — there they failed to beget him. He must be self-begotten, he must engender himself upon the muse his mother. But the muse is as pernicious as the sphinx or covering cherub, and may identify herself with either, though more usually with the sphinx. The strong poet fails to beget himself — he must wait for his son, who will define him even when he has defined his own poetic father. To beget here means to usurp, and is the dialectical labour of the cherub.

Bloom sees literary influence everywhere, and his claims have the clarity that only freedom from evidence or consecutive argument give. In *The Western Canon*, Bloom tells us that "Shakespeare is everywhere in Freud, far more present when unmentioned than when he is cited." Then the plot quickens, thickens, and sickens: "Freud, as prose-poet of the post-Shakespearean, sails in Shakespeare's wake; and the anxiety of influence has no more distinguished sufferer in our time than the founder of psychoanalysis, who always discovered that Shakespeare had been there long before him, and all too frequently could not bear to confront this humiliating truth." How do we know? We know because Professor Bloom tells us so.

Finding the anxiety of influence in your favorite writer may work better as an after-dinner game than it does in actual criticism, though Bloom thought his idea would change poetic history and provide "a wholly different practical criticism." As with most of what Bloom has written, the anxiety-of-influence theory has a nice arbitrariness about it. Tennyson, Arnold, Hopkins, and Rossetti, he tells us, felt anxiety over the influence of Keats, though among them, according to him, only Tennyson triumphed. Dostoevsky, like Freud, had to struggle free of the influence of Shakespeare (though this notion seems to have eluded Dostoevsky's biographer Joseph Frank, who makes no mention of it in five volumes of biography). T. S. Eliot and Wallace Stevens felt anxious about the influence of Whitman. Ezra Pound had to square off against Browning.

No one denies that literary influence exists, but it almost always does in ways too subtle for precise tracing. Does influence always necessitate anxiety, an *agon* (a favorite Bloom word), a misreading of a writer's precursors? Nobody but Bloom seems to think so. As an idea, the anxiety of influence chiefly gets in the way; so that, for example, in his biography of Balzac, Graham Robb feels compelled to note: "The anxiety of influence is not much in evidence in Balzac's early writings. Rather, he seems to be cheered on by his predecessors . . . If anything, Balzac was underwhelmed by the intellectual achievements of humanity."

Bloom seems happiest viewing the world locked in endless struggle. He sees himself in battle with the younger generation of American professors, among them feminists, new historicists, deconstructionists, Marxists — the rather pathetic motley that Bloom calls the "school of resentment." He also sees fundamentalist religion and the spread of computers and television combined "into one rough beast," presaging a future that would cancel out the literary canon. Something like a school of resentment does exist, and, true enough, it is destroying literature as an academic subject. But in attacking these academics, Bloom portrays himself as the heroic outsider, single-handedly taking on the barbarian hordes. Not quite so.

Bloom is an establishment man. He is the consummate literary politician, riding to hounds with those literary personages who have themselves already been declared winners. In contemporary literature, eschewing heterodoxy, he takes few chances, and none that are likely to cost him future emoluments or useful friends. Thus he attacks Alice Walker but lays off Toni Morrison. He everywhere pretends to condemn the stridently political in literature, yet in *The Western Canon,* in the section called "A Canonical Prophecy," he lists Tony Kushner's *Angels in America* — a play that is all politics and little else — as a likely canonical work of the future. If one runs down the names of contemporary poets he admires in this same appendix, these turn out for the most part to be the usual suspects, who each year award one another Pulitzer, Lannan, and other jolly prizes.

The mystery is that Bloom, for all his nearly perfect unreadability, today finds himself in that small but lucky elite of writers whose books sell without being actually read. I spent a week plowing through *Shakespeare: The Invention of the Human,* and I can only report that it is difficult to imagine anyone completing it who has not been paid to write about it. The Shakespeare book, too, has a large, useless idea at its center — namely, that Shakespeare invented our feelings and way of feeling and so, through his plays, invented (or, as Bloom sometimes says, "reinvented") human personality. Reading Bloom on this point is, as John Carey put it, "like chatting with an acquaintance and gradually realising he believes death rays are issuing from his television screen."

Bloom's book on Shakespeare is a great ramble, play by play, in which he piles opinionation upon opinionation, agreeing with this critic, arguing with that, inserting bits of uninteresting academic autobiography, establishing his own superiority, providing as heavy-breathing a solipsistic performance as one is likely to find off a Beverly Hills psychoanalytic couch. Choice selections of Bloomian prose are the raisins in this indigestible pudding of a book: "Shakespeare's uniqueness, his greatest originality, can be described either as a charismatic cognition, which comes from an individual before it enters group thinking, or as a cognitive charisma, which cannot be routinized." As a work of bardolatry, it succeeds in giving even Shakespeare a bad name.

Genius, a more recent Bloom book, is a thick compendium of what appears to be a collection of old prefaces cleaned up and recycled to look like fresh goods. Bloom loves to roll around in his rich pollution of -isms — gnosticism, hermetism, et alia — and to substitute the religion of art for that of God. The book is organized, he informs the reader, along the lines of the Kabbalah, the body of Jewish mystical thought, yet here, be assured, no tables levitate, no wine pours from the walls. For Bloom, great literature is not merely next to godliness, but a sign of godliness itself.

All the usual tics are in place — the bardolatry, the "anxiety" chatter, the old grudges against his fellow English teachers. A reader who had never read anything else Bloom has written could have no notion of what, much of the time, he is talking about. He is so allusive as to border on the incomprehensible. ("The Hermetists were Platonists who had absorbed the allegorical techniques of Alexandrian Jewry, and who developed the Jewish speculation concerning the first Adam, the Anthropos or Primal Man, called the Adam Kadmon in Kabbalah, and 'a mortal god' by the Hermetists.") In a profile of Bloom in *The New Yorker,* he is quoted as remarking, apropos of lecturing at Oxford, "I watched the faces of my audience . . . and I saw blank incomprehension. I had a vision of an airplane flying over cows in a meadow." A vision of reading Harold Bloom — my own — is of standing in an airfield and watching a cow fly over.

The first of the two tasks Bloom has set himself in this large book is to defend the notion of genius in literature from what he takes to be its many detractors in university departments. Genius is "fiercely original," he tells us; it "invokes the transcendental and the extraordinary, because it is fully conscious of them." Genius, he argues, augments our consciousness: "However I have been entertained by a writer, has my awareness been intensified, my consciousness widened and clarified? If not, then I have encountered talent, not genius." Much that is true here is not new, and the little bit that is new doesn't feel very true.

Bloom's other task is "to activate the appreciation of genius in my readers." I must confess to not having read every page of *Genius* — from the quality of its prose, my guess is that Bloom hasn't either — but where I have kitchen-tested Bloom's "appreciations" of his one hundred geniuses, they do not add much to my appreciation. Paul Valéry qualifies as one of Bloom's geniuses, but Bloom manages to evade much of the brilliant complexity of the Frenchman's thought. On the other hand, I have never read the Portuguese novelist Eça de Queirós, but reading about him in *Genius,* where only a tedious plot summary of his novel *The Relic* studded with lavish quotation is on offer, I am not eager to do so now. Bloom is altogether too self-regarding to be among the successful critical appreciators of literature. Most of the time one can't get around Bloom himself to a clear view of his subject. Reading him is like watching a man pirouetting in front of a steamy bathroom mirror with a much too small towel around him.

If every writer has an ideal reader, so must he have an antipathetic one. For Bloom this reader would, I believe, be Max Beerbohm, with his dislike of theory and distrust of genius. "Very exquisite literary artists seldom are men of genius," Beerbohm wrote. "Genius tends to be careless of its strength. Genius is, by the nature of it, always in rather of a hurry. Genius can't be bothered about perfection." As a critic, Bloom has all these qualities, except, alas, the actual genius.

T. S. Eliot once said that the best method for being a critic is to be very intelligent. Bloom is merely learned, in a wildly idiosyncratic way. He has staked out his claim for being a great critic through portentousness and extravagant pretension, and seems to have achieved it.

This comes about, in part, through a lack of competition. What Randall Jarrell, half in rue, once called the Age of Criticism — the cavalcade of whose names include Eliot, Edmund Wilson, F. R. Leavis, Lionel Trilling, Erich Auerbach, and René Wellek — seems to have been over for more than two decades, to be replaced by . . . well, by not much. In Europe there is George Steiner, who has all Bloom's pomposity and pretension but none of what a wag — me, actually — once referred to as the latter's modesty and lighthearted humor. Christopher Ricks and Denis Donoghue write careful and serious literary criticism, but neither seems to want to set up shop as omniscient in the way Bloom does. Frank Kermode, though very learned, writes with a modesty that is almost the reverse of Bloom's assertiveness.

Proust says that in art, medicine, and fashion there have to be new names, by which he meant that new names will arise whether they are worthy or not of being known. The same principle operates in literary criticism, where the name that has now popped up is Harold Bloom's. But his is a reputation much in need of puncturing if literary criticism is once again to be taken — and is to take itself — seriously.

Thank You, No

HERE ARE SOME JOBS I believe are distinctly not worth having. Urologist, proctologist, seismologist come immediately to mind. In a more general line, I would add any job that requires sucking up to the rich. (Oops: eight university presidents, five museum directors, and the business managers of three opera companies just left the room.) Or any job that puts you in charge of vast sums of money, which entails other people feeling the need to suck up to you. (When a man I know took a job as a foundation executive, a wise friend told him that he would probably never eat another bad lunch and no one would ever again tell him the truth.) Or any job that, because of the relentless social obligations, makes it impossible to find the time to read a book. Or any job that forces you to make life worse for other people. Or any job that causes you to lie to yourself a lot more than you now do. And finally, to close out this depressing list, there is one job instead of having which I'd rather be the last (possibly also the first) Jewish coal miner in West Virginia, or a veterinary cosmetic surgeon in Malibu, or the man wielding the wide broom who follows the elephants in the great Ringling Bros. and Barnum & Bailey circus parade — and that job is poet laureate of the United States.

Poet laureate of the United States — something there is exceedingly pompous, not to say a little preposterous, about the very title. Poet laureate of England does not sound quite so hollow —

though closer inspection reveals it isn't all that full, either — perhaps because poetry has so much longer a history and solider a tradition in England than in America. The first truly great American poets, Emily Dickinson and Walt Whitman, after all, didn't emerge until after the Civil War. Then we had to wait for the work of that remarkable generation of poets born between 1870 and 1890, the roster of whose names includes Wallace Stevens, T. S. Eliot, Robert Frost, and Marianne Moore, for the United States to stake anything like a serious claim to having a poetic tradition at all.

W. H. Auden was poet laureate neither in England nor in America, though on skill and achievement and by citizenship he qualified for both. Auden was professor of poetry at Oxford, in some ways a more prestige-laden job than that of poet laureate and one for which he was pleased to have been voted, since it gave him free rent at Oxford. Auden once said that the time for major poets was past, for something had happened to poetry to change its nature, its practitioners, and its audience. One cannot know for certain, of course, but one has a strong hunch that Auden would have viewed the job of poet laureate of the United States as, at best, highly amusing, if not outright hilarious. One likes to think of him taking the money — an annual salary of $35,000 — and laughing all the way to the bank.

As a man who has published a single poem, my own position is that I would like to be asked to be poet laureate of the United States so that I could refuse it, for this seems to me a job that would bring much greater glory to turn down than to take up. True, I am not in danger of being asked to become poet laureate of the United States — or even of Illinois, the state in which I live, if it, like several other states, has a poet laureate (I've made a note someday — though not too soon — to check). But I have been a more than thirty-year subscriber to *Poetry* magazine; I am someone who came of age with Oscar Williams's splendid *A Little Treasury of Modern Verse;* and I continue to believe that, though the calling and craft of poetry have been debased every which way and in most others is in trouble, some of the best writing done in

America continues to be written by poets and to show up in verse. Because I have great respect, affection, and love for poetry, I find the creation of the poet laureateship of the United States a comical insult to a serious enterprise, and one that ought properly to be mocked every chance one gets.

Poets have long been supplied with laurels — from which the word "laureate" of course derives — most famously beginning with Emperor Augustus's taking up Virgil as, in effect, his house or palace poet. In the Middle Ages, kings great and minor kept court poets (also, it is well to remember, court jesters). In England, Ben Jonson received a salary from King Charles I, though he was assigned the writing of plays, not verse. The first official poet laureate in England was John Dryden, appointed by Charles II in 1668. Dryden was given a salary of £200 for the combined jobs of poet laureate and historiographer royal, with a butt (or 126-gallon cask) of good wine thrown in. Since Dryden, a professional writer and craftsman of the highest order, things for the poet laureateship in England have, I think it fair to say, tended for the most part to go downhill.

Wordsworth held the office briefly, having been given it when he was seventy-three years old, and was never called upon to write an official poem while in office, if office is what a poet laureateship is. Tennyson held the job for fully forty-two years, from 1850 until his death in 1892. Much speculation about who would take up the laureateship followed his death. The interesting candidatures of Algernon Swinburne and Thomas Hardy were passed over for Robert Bridges. Bridges was succeeded not by A. E. Housman or Kipling, as some had hoped, but by John Masefield.

In between John Dryden and today lots of middling men have been appointed poet laureate, such as Thomas Shadwell (1642?–1692), Laurence Eusden (1688–1730), and Robert Southey (1774–1843). Poets laureate have not been universally admired by their contemporaries. Byron, for example, regarded Southey as an arch prince of cant, and a wit of the day said that Southey's reputation would live long after Homer's had expired, but not until. In England, with a few exceptions, the preference for the job of poet laureate has generally been for the rugged middlebrow over the original or difficult talent. Andrew Motion, the current poet laureate, whose biography of Philip Larkin fingered the best poet of his time for being politically incorrect, is a perfect man for the job. What is wanted in a poet laureate is a rather solemn and high-toned mediocrity, someone whose work, though found perfectly acceptable in its time, is unlikely to divert the attention of posterity.

Interesting, is it not, that T. S. Eliot was never chosen as poet laureate, for he was a man who, one would think, might have luxuriated in the job. His being poet laureate would certainly have completed his transformation from American to Englishman. And yet Eliot was perhaps too fine, too deep, too original a poet to be laureate. He was also an extremely careful caretaker of his career, and might have supposed — correctly, in my view — that being the poet laureate of England would have been a comedown for the man who was the only internationally famous poet of his day, a poet who found audiences in the thousands attending his readings. He was really the unofficial poet laureate of the world, and in the realm of literature, "unofficial" is always better.

T. S. Eliot was dead more than twenty years before the creation of the poet laureateship in the United States in 1986. Before that, beginning in 1937, there was a consultant in poetry to the Library of Congress, first held by a now forgotten man named Joseph Auslander. Robert Penn Warren, the first poet laureate, was also, in 1944–45, a consultant in poetry. Other people who held consultantships were Allen Tate, Robert Lowell, Elizabeth Bishop, Robert Frost, and Maxine Kumin, the usual suspects. I was surprised to discover that Archibald MacLeish was never consultant. He would have been nearly perfect, though not as perfect as Carl Sandburg, in whose person and poetry clichés ran as thickly as calories run through cheesecake, who also, somehow, missed out.

The poet laureate of the United States is chosen by the librarian of Congress, who consults previous poets laureate and other poets, which means that the fix is probably in. Poets tend to be clubbier than Chicago aldermen, and quite as artful at awarding one another patronage. Whereas the English poet laureate serves for life, the American laureateship lasts a year, but is sometimes extended to two years. The $35,000 salary for the poet laureate — whose exact title is Poet Laureate Consultant in Poetry — is put up by the foundation of Archer M. Huntington, son of one of the four men who laid down the Central Pacific Railroad.

I think it fair to say that one of the first qualifications of an American poet laureate is that he not in any way be dangerous. Amiri Baraka, the former LeRoi Jones, was canned as poet laureate of New Jersey for writing some fairly insane anti-Semitic verse — rightly canned, in my view. Let Mr. Baraka write all the anti-Semitic verse he wishes — may he find joy in his Jew-hating, as my people say — but he ought not to be permitted to do so while on the payroll of the great state of New Jersey.

Allen Ginsberg is a stellar example of someone who could never have been poet laureate. Some years ago I was told about an award given to Ginsberg at which time the master of ceremonies thanked Ginsberg for his courage in coming out so early and so openly as a homosexual when it took real courage to do so, making the way easier for men like him, the master of ceremonies, who wished on this occasion to thank him for all he had done for the cause of gay liberation. Ginsberg, in dinner clothes for this grand occasion, rose to the podium and said, "Thank you, but after that introduction, I'm not sure whether I am getting this award for my poetry or my cocksucking." I don't much like that word, and there isn't all that much of Ginsberg's poetry that lights my fire either, but I like this story, because it points up the emptiness of conjoining politics and art.

Somehow poetry and politics are never rightly conjoined. Those of us who have reached a certain age will remember Robert Frost, having agreed to read a poem at the inauguration of John F. Kennedy, white hair flapping in the breeze, fighting strong winds to get his less than considerable *vers d'occasion* read; because of the weather, it was certainly not heard. A great flop is what it was. One felt that the gods had sent the weather in detestation of this forced alignment of poetry with power.

The current American poet laureateship is marked — marred, is more precise — not only by the kiss of death of being an official job but also by political correctness. As one runs down the list of American poets laureate, the only explanation for certain names appearing there is that they are women or black or otherwise "with the show," as they say on the carnival grounds. Make the ostensibly sweet bow in the direction of political correctness, and art, like reality in the face of a social science concept, leaves the room. The list of American poets laureate has included the good, the mediocre, and the merely acceptable. But nobody who has uttered any truly heterodox views is asked to play at laureate. Heterodoxy is one of the things serious poetry is, or at least ought to be, about. The poet laureate of the United States should also be the best poet in the country; if he isn't, then the job is meaningless.

I keep falling back on the word "job," but does the poet laureate of the United States do any actual work? In England, the poet laureate used to be asked to write poems for official occasions: coronations, deaths of monarchs, and the rest. (Pity that Ted Hughes, who was then poet laureate, wasn't asked to write about the death of Princess Diana; that would have been a poem of genuine interest.)

The official literature has it that "the [American] laureate gives an annual lecture and reading of his or her poetry and usually introduces poets in the Library's annual poetry series, the oldest in the Washington area, and among the oldest in the United States." The poets laureate are pretty much left alone, "in order [this again from the official literature] to afford incumbents maximum freedom to work on their own projects while at the Library."

The laureates' "projects" have been varied, though most have had to do with efforts to widen the readership of poetry, which is always thought to be in need of as much widening by way of promotion as it can get. Every laureate his own Gideon Society. Joseph Brodsky, when he had the job, attempted to place poetry in airports, supermarkets, and hotel rooms; Gwendolyn Brooks visited lots of elementary schools to talk up the wonders of poetry;

Rita Dove did a more exclusively black turn, by bringing together writers to "explore the African diaspora through the eyes of its artists"; and so on. If I were poet laureate I would put a poem in every pair of pajamas, fortune cookie, and National Hockey League game program published during my tenure. Which is my coarse, jokey-jakey way of saying that poetry cannot really be promoted, only appreciated.

Poetry is caviar — an acquired taste, and not for most people, not even for some highly intelligent people — and I happen to believe that selling poetry as if it were hot dogs demeans it. Many of the poets laureate have, I fear, seen the job as calling for slapping on the mustard while moving the dogs along. Even bringing poetry into grammar and high schools is probably a mistake. I am reminded here that Willa Cather, while she was alive, insisted that no school editions of her novels or stories be printed, lest kids be forced to read her under so-called educational conditions and never read her again as adults, when they were really ready for her. Sounds smart to me.

Easy to understand the desire to widen the audience for poetry, a warrant for which seems to be written into the job of poet laureate. Every scribbler in every genre longs for a large audience. At some point, a writer, if he is lucky, is faced with the decision whether or not to seek that larger audience through the small compromises often required to obtain it. Poets are rarely offered the chance to make such a decision. If one is nutty enough to expect a large audience for one's poetry, certain demoralization awaits. Besides, at these prices, a poet ought to write and say exactly what he thinks and in precisely the way he thinks best to say it.

Contemporary poets, alas, have prizes instead of readers. The number of poetry prizes in the land is astonishing. The *Times Literary Supplement* once ran a brief piece on these prizes under the title "Shock Absorbers for Poets." Such is their plentitude that one is almost inclined to think contemporary poetry less an art than a charity in need of constant donations. Nor are many of the sums offered trivial: the Wallace Stevens Award ($150,000), the Lilly

Prize ($100,000), the Lannan Award ($120,000), and the Griffin ($40,000 Canadian). The last named reminds me that an old joke has it that the one thing you never ask a prostitute is if she'll accept Canadian money, but this obviously isn't a problem for poets.

A funny time for poetry, ours, no doubt about it. While fewer and fewer people seem to be reading poetry, more and more people seem to be teaching both it and the writing of it. Most nonprofessionals who do read it do so chiefly while in college, and then more or less slowly drop away from it. Many otherwise quite literary people find they cannot — or do not wish to — make time in their reading budget for it. With so much poetry around, Gresham's relentlessly vicious law kicks in, the bad driving out the good. What's a poet to do?

What the good poets have always done, I believe, which is to take care of business. Business for the poet is to write as well as possible and leave alone the job of promoting poetry in a manner sure to vulgarize it, if not utterly trivialize it. The least one can do in this regard is, if offered the job of poet laureate of the United States, to turn it down, preferably in a wittily obstreperous way. More money and self-respect is to be earned selling ladies' handkerchiefs.

Forgetting Edmund Wilson

"Mommy, you mean my father is a great critic?" — and he
smiled — "I always thought he was just a two-bit book reviewer."

— MARY MCCARTHY, recalling a postdivorce conversation
with her then nine-year-old son Reuel Wilson

Y OU WROTE *Finlandia*, didn't you?" the wife of the Aspen
Institute's president asked Edmund Wilson at a dinner in
New York at which the Institute awarded him a $30,000
prize. If Wilson were alive today at a similar event, he might be
less likely to be confused with the composer Jan Sibelius than with
the sociobiologist and entomologist Edward O. Wilson. Twenty
years from now, perhaps ten, the question might be, "Edmund
who?"

Through the last decades of his life (he died in 1972), the label
tediously affixed to Edmund Wilson was "our last great man of
letters." Over a long career, he had tried his hand at every literary form — fiction, poetry, drama, intellectual and literary history,
travel-anthropology, journal-keeping. But in the end, a critic is
what Wilson primarily was, and such reputation as he still enjoys
is based on his literary criticism. The body of this criticism is one
of the main emphases of an exhaustive biography of Wilson by
Lewis Dabney, a work decades in preparation and altogether admiring of its subject.

Born in 1895, Wilson lived through what the poet Randall
Jarrell, in a famous essay of the 1950s, called the Age of Criticism.

But when one thinks of the names of the other critics of the time — Van Wyck Brooks, John Crowe Ransom, F. R. Leavis, Northrop Frye, Yvor Winters, Newton Arvin, Philip Rahv, Lionel Trilling, Irving Howe, Alfred Kazin — names first fading from prominence and now beginning to fade from memory, one realizes that literary criticism is not an easy path to immortality.

Does Edmund Wilson's literary criticism figure to endure any longer than that of these others? One thing going for him was that, unlike the critics mentioned above, Wilson never had a permanent academic appointment. He worked at editorial jobs, beginning in the 1920s at *Vanity Fair* and then moving on to the *New Republic;* from the 1940s until the end of his life, he was under contract to *The New Yorker.* Late in life he also inherited money, but not enough to maintain him and the children produced by his four marriages. Chiefly he lived off his voluminous writing, and this independence was part of his cachet.

Apart from *Memoirs of Hecate County* (1967), a collection of short stories whose commercial success was aided by its having been censored for pornographic content, none of Wilson's books sold particularly well. But the readers who cared for him cared a very great deal. His admirers formed a club, of which, I ought to delay no longer in saying, I was once a member in good standing. Wilson introduced us to a vast number of important writers — he was something of a walking version of the Modern Library — in prose that seemed virile, informed by a long literary tradition, and wonderfully free of academic jargon. To young men and women with literary aspirations, there was also something more: as early as 1929, Lionel Trilling remarked of Wilson that "he seemed, in his own person, and young as he was, to propose and to realize the idea of the literary life." That was it, exactly.

Metropolitan in his manner, his sweep, the breadth of his interests — he wrote about burlesque and about the Dead Sea Scrolls — Wilson was the contemporary and friend of F. Scott Fitzgerald and John Dos Passos. He had been the first critic to spot and praise the writing of Ernest Hemingway, who once told Wilson that his opinion was the only one "in the States that I have any respect for." All this conduced to make Wilson himself seem a key figure of the 1920s, the last unequivocally rich, even glamorous, period in our national literature. Nor did it hurt that Wilson had family connections going back in American history to the seventeenth century, giving him something like patrician standing in a field increasingly occupied by Jewish sons of immigrants eager to find jobs in formerly anti-Semitic university English departments.

A major part of Wilson's modus operandi was his sheer authoritativeness. Since in literature no one can finally prove anything, except perhaps the technical defects of prosody in a poem, criticism lives or dies by the persuasiveness of the critic, a persuasiveness based largely on his confidence and the strength of his assertions. No one was more aware of this than Wilson, who put the case perhaps as well (and as baldly) as it can be put:

> The implied position of the people who know about literature (as is also the case in every other art) is simply that they know what they know, and that they are determined to impose their opinions by main force of eloquence or assertion on the people who do not know.

Adding to this authoritativeness was that Wilson, who from late adolescence seemed to have the gift of perpetual middle age, became, when middle-aged, precociously old. Crankiness, of opinion and of manner, became part of his armament. By the 1950s he had bowed out of contemporary literary life, ceasing to comment on current work: "If I now play at being old," he wrote in *The Sixties*, one of the collected volumes of his journals, "I never played at being young." From then on he responded to requests from editors and readers with a postcard listing all the things he refused to do, and the list was impressive in its inclusiveness.

Until the 1950s, though, Wilson was very much a man of his time. In the 1920s he was a powerful advocate of literary modernism (a term he grew to dislike), and in his book *Axel's Castle: A Study of the Imaginative Literature of 1870–1930* (1935), he explained to the uninitiated the meaning and mechanics of the work of James

Joyce, W. B. Yeats, Gertrude Stein, T. S. Eliot, and other avant-garde writers. In the 1930s, he became politicized, reporting on union strikes and on unemployment and poverty in America. This writing was later collected in *The American Earthquake* (1951).

Anti-Americanism had long since become a strong strain in Wilson's intellectual makeup; the country was always letting him down. His politics had begun in pacifism, brought on by a stint as an ambulance driver in World War I, where he witnessed at close quarters the chewed-up bodies of the war's wounded and dead. High on the camaraderie he felt with his fellow enlisted men, he then also declared himself a socialist. By the thirties, with the Depression, he added the anti-capitalist component, and in 1932, along with a large number of other intellectuals, he voted for William Z. Foster, the Communist candidate for president.

Exuberant about the prospects of socialism, Wilson wrote a long book about it, *To the Finland Station: A Study in the Writing and Acting of History* (1940). The story told in this book culminates in the arrival in Petrograd of its hero, Vladimir Ilich Lenin, to take control of the Russian Revolution. Wilson could never quite bring himself to say flat out that Lenin was no hero but one of the great barbarians of history, and that it would have been much better for the Russian people had his train never arrived.

By the fifties, a broad touch of snobbery, of the I'm-well-out-of-it variety, was brought on board; in a book called *A Piece of My Mind* (1956), Wilson remarked that he did not recognize the country depicted in the pages of *Life* magazine. All of this came together in *The Cold War and the Income Tax: A Protest* (1963). Wilson, who owed taxes for several years running, purported to be outraged at the realization that some of his (as yet unpaid) tax money would go for weapons that might be used in war.

Those unpaid taxes were emblematic of another facet of Edmund Wilson's life. One of the unintended consequences of Lewis Dabney's biography, which fully endorses Wilson's politics and general point of view, is to establish the grave disorder of that life in its every phase and aspect.

It is no secret that Wilson was what is euphemistically called a functioning alcoholic; the euphemism lies in the suggestion that one can drink a lot and still function. Function, true enough, Wilson did, at least as a writer: his literary production never slackened. I used to think of him awakening in the morning after a hard night's boozing, shaking himself like a dog coming in out of the rain, then repairing to his desk to take notes and write out a summary of some dreary southern Civil War diary for another of his thick literary-historical books. But Wilson's drinking also left his life in almost perpetual disarray and, until his final marriage, bohemian squalor.

Much is made by Dabney, as by commentators before him, of Wilson's following in the tradition of his father. Edmund Wilson, Sr., had been the Republican attorney general of New Jersey, from which office he prosecuted important corruption cases with such success that President Woodrow Wilson, a Democrat, offered him various jobs in his administration, none of which he accepted. A man of great probity, the elder Wilson believed that investing in the stock market was a species of gambling, and therefore steered clear of it; he gave popular lectures with a note of moral uplift; he provided for the family of his ill younger brother.

Edmund Wilson, Sr., also suffered from hypochondria, to the point of undergoing what Dabney describes as lengthy "eclipses." This tightly strung, neurotic element is something that Dabney speculates may have been inherited by his son. Little else was. Upon his death, the elder Wilson put his wife in charge of his estate, under the assumption that his son was incapable of managing his own finances. This was not a foolish assumption: Edmund Wilson was the sort of person who could get into a cab in Manhattan and tell the driver to take him to Cape Cod.

Ineptitude in the details of life is a motif playing throughout Dabney's lengthy biography. Not only was Wilson incapable of driving a car, he could not type, could not handle money, and had no sense of practical politics. He also had no notion of how to be affectionate with his own children. With women, his method of seduction was often the fatal one of proposing marriage. Sexually, he was ardent; physically, repellent. "If you were just prose," a woman named Elizabeth Waugh wrote to him, "I'd be mad about you."

But he wasn't just prose, and he certainly wasn't poetry. He was instead a bald, pudgy little man with a drinking problem, a nearly perpetual erection, and a mean streak.

Wilson at his meanest shows up in Dabney's account of his marriage to the novelist and critic Mary McCarthy — a marriage made in 1937 when he was forty-two and she was twenty-five. "I was too young," McCarthy would later claim, and "I was too old," Wilson would counter. It would be closer to the truth to say that both were too selfish and wanting in the least human insight. McCarthy always mistook her snobbery for morality; Wilson mistook life for literature. Dabney, summing up this wretched partnership, writes: "American letters has not seen another alliance so flawed and so distinguished." So flawed and so distinguished — what a way to characterize the union of a true bitch and a genuine bully.

The Wilson-McCarthy marriage does supply Dabney with the most interesting chapter of his book. As recorded in Dabney's deadpan prose, this nightmare had everything: abortion, cuckoldry, beatings, the exchange of insults meant to maim, desertion, unhelpful psychotherapeutic counseling, and lots of drunken rage and hysteria to go around. My favorite moment occurs during the testimony, in court, of Nathalie Rahv, the wife of Philip Rahv, the coeditor of *Partisan Review* and Mary McCarthy's lover before she left him for Wilson. According to Mrs. Rahv, Wilson humiliated McCarthy by accusing her of poor housekeeping in front of friends. Mary McCarthy a poor homemaker — shocking!

After the breakup of Wilson's marriage to McCarthy in 1945, Dabney's biography begins to lose its interest. Much of Wilson's literary criticism required the elaborate summary of the works he was commenting on, so Dabney is left with the dreary task of summarizing summaries, interspersed with the recital of trips on and off the wagon. Dabney neglects to mention that Wilson's books and journals can be longueur-laden well beyond the legal limit; one of his specialties in his journals was great boring descriptions of landscape. In his later life Wilson spent a good deal of time in the half-ruined old house at Talcottville, in upstate New York, that he had inherited and that his last wife hated. There he drank and scribbled away, living a role resembling nothing so much as a character out of Tennessee Williams, but in a northern setting and with a Calvinist work ethic added.

Wilson, Dabney reports, "was the only well-known literary alcoholic of his generation whose work was not compromised by his drinking." That begs the question of why he drank so much. Among the reasons one can think of is that he did not really set out to be a literary critic. He wanted instead to be a literary artist: as Dabney puts it, "a writer of poetry, drama, or fiction who also writes criticism, or someone whose literary criticism feeds a larger historical project." It took him a long time — and the production of a fair amount of drab fiction — to admit that such strengths as he possessed lay in writing not about life directly but about literary and historical figures.

Lionel Trilling, the only American critic who rivaled Wilson for renown during their lifetimes, was also less than content in his career. Trilling was a larger, more philosophical, more finely meshed thinker than Wilson, yet, as published portions of his diaries make plain, he wished he had had the courage to devote himself to fiction instead of settling for a life of teaching and criticism.

The sad fact is that, for a capacious and lively mind, literary criticism, the job of regularly registering opinions of other people's work, is for the most part an insufficient activity. "You know Plato's contempt for the image of an image," George Santayana replied to a correspondent who once suggested that he give up metaphysics to devote himself to literary criticism, "but as a man's view of things is an image in the first place, and his work is an image of that, and the critic's feelings are an image of that work, and his writings an image of his feelings, and your idea of what the critic means only an image of his writings, please consider that you are steeping your poor original tea leaves in their fifth wash of hot water, and are drinking slops."

Thanks all the same, Santayana summed up, but he would stick to philosophy.

In the history of literary criticism written in English, very few names have survived, or probably deserve to survive. Samuel Johnson is one, perhaps the only true genius who put his mind chiefly to criticism; and Johnson also happens to have been a great man, which gives his writing all the more authority. Matthew Arnold is another, not so much for his particular pronouncements, which could be very smart and sharp, as for their cultural sweep and continuing relevance.

Some might include William Hazlitt in this company, though he was a better writer than critic, and what he thought of the actors, poets, and painters of his day is less important than that he understood the spirit of his age and wrote brilliantly and courageously about it. Others might claim a place for T. S. Eliot, but much of Eliot's best criticism is rather narrowly confined to adjusting the canon of English poetry — metaphysical poets up, John Milton down — and to the principles behind literary creation.

Does Edmund Wilson belong on this short list of critics of enduring interest? I certainly thought so once — and I was hardly alone. To his many admirers, Wilson — courageous in his opinions, deep in his culture, broad in his point of view, unassailable in his integrity — seemed to exist in the closest possible relationship with literature itself. Versatile, productive, cosmopolitan, he was a being organized for writing. To judge by the reverential reviews written about Dabney's biography, this is still the received opinion.

In *Axel's Castle,* Wilson observed that W. B. Yeats, whose poetry in this respect he likened to Dante's, could "sustain a grand manner through sheer intensity without rhetorical heightening." Citing this remark, Dabney tells us that the writer Clive James has singled it out as an example of "permanent criticism." How permanent it is cannot be known; but it does strike the characteristic Wilson note.

As a critic, Edmund Wilson was at his best explaining *how* literature worked; what seemed to interest him most was the mechanics of creation. He was able to demonstrate why the modernist writers were important by showing precisely how they went about doing things not hitherto done. He was less good, I think, at what Henri Bergson defined as the center of the critic's task—namely, "developing in thought what artists wanted to suggest emotionally."

As a young critic, Wilson fancied himself a director of traffic in literary reputations. T. S. Matthews, who worked as Wilson's assistant on the cultural pages of the *New Republic,* recalled in his autobiography how Wilson "aimed" him, giving marching orders on which authors to praise and which to deflate. The poet E. E. Cummings neatly captured this generalissimo aspect of Wilson when he called him "the man in the iron necktie."

As a literary cop, however, Wilson did not always get his man. He failed to recognize the importance of Robert Frost and of Wallace Stevens, the two most lasting poets writing during his lifetime. Although on to Hemingway from the start, he underrated Willa Cather, and allowed himself to be so put off by Theodore Dreiser's clumsy style as to miss his power. Later he much overrated James Baldwin, probably for political reasons. Aloof patrician though Wilson wished to seem, he was also a bit of a *bienpensant,* and broadcast no opinions likely to give offense in the academic and editorial quarters of the literary establishment that had come to dominate culture in the United States during the last decades of his life.

Saddest of all, Wilson could not bring himself to get full-out behind his friend and Princeton classmate F. Scott Fitzgerald. (T. S. Eliot, in a letter to Fitzgerald, called *The Great Gatsby* the first major step forward for the American novel since Henry James.) After Fitzgerald's death, Wilson edited his notebooks, published under the title of *The Crack-Up* (1945), and completed (not very successfully) Fitzgerald's unfinished novel *The Last Tycoon* (1960). Yet, as Dabney writes, Wilson "would never be free of the need to measure himself against his wonderfully talented friend"—and, as Dabney might have added, would always come up short. Wilson must have found it galling that Fitzgerald, an Irish *arriviste* with

pathetic social aspirations who could not spell, had magical gifts —
of storytelling, of phrasing, of human understanding—that he
himself would never come close to attaining.

Wilson's stately, confidently cadenced prose is another of the
items that come up for commendation in the standard praise for
his work. And yet it is difficult to think of memorable phrases or
powerful formulations in Wilson's criticism. (An exception is his
remarking that "the cruelest thing that has happened to Lincoln
since he was shot by Booth has been to fall into the hands of Carl
Sandburg.") He was a man, as I have indicated, for the long summary, heavily burdened with extensive quotation. He was perhaps
at his best at literary portraiture. The flashiest single piece of criticism he wrote is his interpretation of *The Turn of the Screw*, Henry
James's novella about household ghosts corrupting young children. In Wilson's reading of this tale, every word of which shim-
mers with James's deliberate ambiguity, the solution to the problem of whether the ghosts really exist lies in realizing that the
story itself is the delusory neurotic invention of the governess
who tells it.

This interpretation, whatever its persuasiveness, happens to be
in some ways characteristic not only of Wilson's critical method
but of his intellectual spirit. In rereading him, one realizes how
unoriginal he could be: a Marxist in a time of Marxists, a Freudian in a time of Freudians, he did not strike out much on his own.
Another of his famous essays, "Philoctetes, the Wound and the
Bow," holds that artistic creation is bound up with psychic wounds.
In a collection of essays entitled *The Wound and the Bow: Seven
Studies in Literature* (1947), Wilson accordingly marched Dickens,
Kipling, A. E. Housman, John Jay Chapman, and Hemingway
through the same gauntlet, showing that all of them labored un-
der the burden of serious wounds acquired in childhood, the sub-
limation of which resulted in significant art.

If such heavy psychologizing seems less compelling today than
it did fifty or so years ago, that may be partly owing to the fact
that, as Proust wrote, "each generation of critics takes the opposite of the truth accepted by their predecessors." But partly, too, it

is because Freudianism itself is no longer so compelling as an explanation of human behavior, let alone of artistic creation.

Wilson was impressed by the two idea systems of Freudianism and Marxism, my own view is, because he was insufficiently impressed by life's mysteries; as a professional explainer, he preferred problems that had solutions, questions for which there were answers, and in Freudianism and Marxism he found no shortage of both. I suspect his difficulty with Joseph Conrad and Franz Kafka, two major writers whose power he could never quite comprehend, stemmed from the fact that each took as his subject, precisely, the complex mystery of life: Conrad on the cosmic level, asking why we are put on earth; Kafka on the level of human nature, asking why we are as sadly and comically limited as we are.

One sees this weakness most glaringly in Wilson's essay on Abraham Lincoln in *Patriotic Gore* (1962), his collection of studies of American Civil War figures. What troubles Wilson most is Lincoln's belief in God. That Lincoln felt there was a design in the universe (he referred to God as "the Almighty Architect"), that he called on God's help in attempting to keep the Union together, is interpreted by Wilson as either self-delusion or political convenience, or both. He concludes his thoughts on Lincoln's assassination by suggesting that "it was morally and dramatically inevitable that this prophet who had crushed opposition and sent thousands of men to their deaths should finally attest his good faith by laying down his own life with theirs."

This poor attempt at irony is further evidence that Edmund Wilson had decided morality was beside the point in political life generally and in dealings among nations specifically. In his preface to *Patriotic Gore,* he concluded that an appropriate metaphor for the behavior of nations was that of sea slugs, each trying to engorge itself on the next. This instinctive animalist behavior, he claimed, is what also characterized our dealings with the Soviet Union, and it "prevents us from recognizing today, in our relation to our cold-war opponent, that our panicky pugnacity as we challenge him is not virtue but at bottom the irrational instinct of an

active power organism in the presence of another such organism."
The Civil War, the cold war, probably World War II, and every
other conflict among men were merely thin disguises behind
which lay more or less hidden imperialist appetites — especially
American ones.

In his own final summation, Dabney suggests that, like Samuel
Johnson, Wilson may one day be viewed as the central figure of
his time. "In the meantime," Dabney concludes, "he and his writing, in a word that he took over from Emerson, are fortifying."
Samuel Johnson was indeed central to the second half of the
eighteenth century, but Edmund Wilson hadn't anything approaching Johnson's gravity, his conviction, his scholarship, his subtle insight into everyday life, or his irradiating moral force. As for
whether Wilson's writings are fortifying, just whom they fortify is
less than clear. On rereading, I find they no longer fortify me.

One of the advantages artists have over critics is that they can
be nearly complete damn fools and still produce interesting and
important, even lasting, art. Critics are not permitted such large
margins of stupidity. It matters that they get things right; their
opinions, which is all they chiefly have, are crucial. Wisdom, in a
critic, is never excess baggage. Edmund Wilson, it begins to be
clear, traveled light.

IV

The Intellectual Life

Intellectuals, Public and Otherwise

I CANNOT RECALL when I first heard or read the ornate term "public intellectual," but I do recall disliking it straightaway. I felt like a man who has been used to buying the same solid shirt for years — white oxford cloth, button-down collar — and one day enters his favorite store only to discover that someone has gone and added epaulets to it. When I noted the people who were being identified as public intellectuals, I knew that to superfluity had been added gross imprecision. "Public intellectual" was a phrase, in short, that absorbed no truth whatsoever.

Yet "public intellectual" seems to have taken stronger and stronger hold, popping up in print with little or no explanation of what it means. The late Lionel Trilling, one reads, "was the public intellectual and mainstay of *Partisan Review.*" Edward Said, one learns, "is an American by default and a public intellectual by virtue of the mean accidents of political history." Richard A. Posner and Ronald Dworkin are "two of the nation's most admired public intellectuals," while the late Noel Annan was "as pure an example of the public intellectual as [one] could summon up." Best of all, I recently came across the news that at Florida Atlantic University in Boca Raton there is a full course of study designed to prepare you to become a public intellectual, providing a Ph.D. in whatever it is public intellectuals are supposed to do.

In Russell Jacoby's *The Last Intellectuals* (1987), the term gets a fairly good workout, and it may be that Jacoby first put it into circulation. In his own usage, a public intellectual "contributes to public discussion" and is also "an incorrigibly independent soul answering to no one," committed "not simply to a professional or private domain but to a public world—and a public language, the vernacular." This definition supplies a pair of pants baggy enough for Walter Cronkite and Jackie Mason to fit into together. In the usage of others, a public intellectual emerges as an academic specialist who can write the op-ed piece or do the political talk show. For still others, the public intellectual is someone vaguely intelligent who happens to appear before the public: Ted Koppel, say, or Frank Rich.

As for intellectual, plain and simple, that is, or was, something else altogether. I cannot recall when I first heard this term, either, but I do vividly recall my first experience of the phenomenon itself. In my third year as an undergraduate at the University of Chicago, I discovered the periodical room at Harper Library and what were then called little magazines. ("Our intellectual marines," wrote W. H. Auden, "landing in little magazines.") The year was 1957, and these magazines were still at high tide. I read as many as I could find, but particularly *Partisan Review* (now often described as, in those days, the house organ of American intellectuals), *Commentary,* and *Encounter.* The last of these, which came out in England, was coedited by the poet Stephen Spender and Irving Kristol (who had formerly been on the editorial staff of *Commentary*), and had only recently begun publication.

I find it difficult to do justice to the deep pleasure I took in these magazines. Education, as everyone knows, is a disorderly business. It is chiefly available through four different means: schools, new- and used-book stores, conversation with intelligent friends, and good magazines. For me, coming to them pretty much tabula rasa, these intellectual magazines were easily the key element in my own education. Although the University of Chicago had taught me who were the essential writers and which were the perennially important questions—no small thing, granted—I had had no great teachers or important educational experiences in its classrooms and lecture halls. Serious learning commenced in the periodical room at Harper Library and continued for a great many years afterward as I searched out back issues of the intellectual magazines and fell upon them with the combined ardor of a collector and a glutton. They made me want to be an intellectual, a term I then took as an unqualified honorific.

I was not wholly unprepared for the call. Max Weber's *The Protestant Ethic and the Spirit of Capitalism,* which I had recently read, had dazzled me by the brilliance of Weber's historical connections and the power of his formulations. But what the intellectual magazines showed me was that not all brilliance was in the past — that some very interesting minds were still at work.

Some of the names I came across in the pages of these magazines were European and already known to me from my general reading: André Malraux, Ignazio Silone, Bertrand Russell. (These were the days when Americans still existed in a condition of cultural inferiority vis-à-vis Europe.) Others I discovered there for the first time: Lionel Trilling, Isaiah Berlin, Philip Rahv, Sidney Hook, Hugh Trevor-Roper, Richard Crossman, George Lichtheim, Harold Rosenberg, Hannah Arendt, Saul Bellow, Mary McCarthy, Goronwy Rees, Gertrude Himmelfarb, Leslie Fiedler, Clement Greenberg, Delmore Schwartz, James Baldwin, Irving Howe, William Barrett, Hilton Kramer, Robert Lowell, Randall Jarrell, John Berryman. These writers introduced me to still others — Aleksandr Herzen, François Mauriac, Paul Valéry, Max Beerbohm — and to scores of subjects of which I was still ignorant; and so the net of my intellectual acquaintance grew wider and wider.

Although *Commentary, Partisan Review,* and *Encounter* published fiction and poetry, some of it quite distinguished, at their heart was the discursive essay: ambitious in choice of subject, sometimes aggressively polemical in spirit, unhesitant in authority, often brilliant in execution. Looking back at representative American exemplars of the form, I would single out Robert Warshow and Dwight Macdonald. Warshow, an editor at *Commentary,* died in 1955 at the age of thirty-seven, and I read him only later, when I began rummaging through back issues. Macdonald had been an editor of *Partisan Review* and then, after breaking with his colleagues over World War II, to which he claimed moral objections, veered off to edit his own magazine, called *politics.*

In his brief career, Warshow wrote more about the movies than about any other subject, but neither he nor Macdonald — who also wrote about the movies — can be said to have had an intellectual specialty. Nor was either of them a scholar, though Macdonald's best book, an anthology titled *Parodies,* contains much genuine scholarship. Neither man was remotely academic in either style or spirit; both were genuine freelances, writing about subjects they found interesting and attempting to draw out their widest implications.

Warshow's "The Gangster as Tragic Hero" (1948) provides a perfect illustration of what I have in mind. In this essay, Warshow sets out to discover both the real meaning of American gangster movies and the source of their attraction. The distillation is highly concentrated; it takes him fewer than three thousand words to make his case.

Inherent to our pleasure in gangster movies, Warshow asserts in "The Gangster as Tragic Hero," is the element of sadism: in watching them, "we gain the double satisfaction of participating vicariously in the gangster's sadism and then seeing it turned against the gangster himself." But the deeper significance of these movies lies in the way they encapsulate "the intolerable dilemma" we all feel about success. The gangster, in brief, is "what we want to be and what we are afraid we may become." And so the effect of the gangster movie "is to embody this dilemma in the person of the gangster and resolve it by his death. The dilemma is resolved because it is his death, not ours. We are safe; for the moment, we can acquiesce in our failure, we can choose to fail."

Warshow's essay is the act of an intellectual at its most characteristic. Here is an author who possesses no specialized knowledge, or even any extraordinary fund of personal experience. He does what he does with no other aid but the power of his mind. He has seen the same movies we have all seen. But he happens to have seen more in them than the rest of us recognized was there.

"This interior need to penetrate beyond the screen of immediate concrete experience," wrote my friend Edward Shils, "marks the existence of the intellectuals in every society." A precise description, that, of Robert Warshow at work.

Very different from Warshow, Dwight Macdonald was dashing and slashing in his prose, more amusing than penetrating in his thought. In both culture and politics he assumed the stance of the immitigable highbrow. Whenever capitalism played a large part in any work of art or cultural production, he tended to attack it. He was death on middlebrow culture, writing rollicking blasts at Encyclopaedia Britannica's *Great Books of the Western World* and the New English Bible. He could ambush a bestseller, and in the case of James Gould Cozzens ("By Cozzens Possessed") dealt so devastating a blow to the novelist that, even now, fifty years later, his literary reputation has yet to recover.

Macdonald's opinions were, however, less than original; they were those of the herd of independent minds, in Harold Rosenberg's withering phrase. Although Macdonald attempted a systematic formulation of his theory of culture in a lengthy essay, "Masscult and Midcult" (1960), it was riddled with contradictions and, theoretically, a mess. Late in life, at a symposium at Skidmore College, he acknowledged that he was at his best as a counterpuncher, writing against some work or idea. "Every time I say 'Yes,'" he remarked, "I get in trouble." His last big yes was on behalf of the student rebellion at Columbia University in 1968, where yes was once again the wrong answer.

It was from Dwight Macdonald — whom I can hardly read today but who once gave me so much pleasure — as well as from Robert Warshow and a few other marines in little magazines (including Irving Howe and Paul Goodman) that I took much of my own notion of what constituted an intellectual. This exotic creature, they taught me, was a species of grand amateur — an amateur of the mind. He was distinguished from other mind workers, or intelligentsia, by his want of specialization. He knew not one but many things.

Unlike the scholar, for example, the intellectual did not work with primary sources, did not feel himself responsible for presenting the most accurate and detailed knowledge of his subjects, did not feel the need to back up his assertions with footnotes, did not seek out new factual material that might change the shape of a subject. True, there were scholars, scientists, occasionally artists, jurists, and even politicians who had wide intellectual interests, but when they were functioning in their specialties they were not, strictly speaking, intellectuals.

The natural penchant of the intellectual was not to go deeper but wider — to turn the criticism of literature or art or the movies or politics into broader statements about culture. His lucubrations might have all sorts of consequences, but insofar as he was operating purely as an intellectual, he was less concerned with influencing policy, effecting change, or doing anything other than seeing where his ideas — and the boldness of his formulations — took him.

The intellectual, in the standard if unwritten job description, functioned best as a critic — be it stressed, an *alienated* critic — of his society. Guardian and gatekeeper, the intellectual had to be wary above all of the amorphous yet pervasive influence of Wall Street, Madison Avenue, the middle class, the middlebrow, the mainstream, the bourgeoisie, the big interests. In Dwight Macdonald's worldview, writers and intellectuals were always in danger of selling out to the devil, with the devil usually envisioned as Henry Luce and hell as Time Inc. — where Macdonald once worked.

Where politics was concerned — and politics was always concerned — anti-communism was permitted as an ideological component in the intellectual's makeup, or at least it was at the time my own intellectual aspirations took hold. (With the war in Vietnam, this, too, would become a contentious position.) But what was also assumed was a high reverence, theoretical and sentimental, for socialism. In those days — the late 1950s, the early 1960s — it did not seem possible to be an intellectual and not to be of the left. This reverence for socialism was never entirely absent even in so otherwise independent-minded a figure as George Orwell.

• • •

If Warshow and Macdonald were representative intellectuals, Orwell was in many ways the perfect type of the intellectual, both in his strengths and in his limitations. He wrote well about politics, literature, and popular culture. He was devoted to truth-telling, even when that meant, as in the case of the truths he told about Communist totalitarianism, being cut off from the *bien-pensant* crowd of his day and from the journals that provided much of his income. He was also large-minded enough to be hospitable to ideas that went against his own, writing favorably, for example, about Friedrich Hayek's *The Road to Serfdom*. Although neither right about everything nor entirely able to evade self-deception, Orwell probably had a higher truth quotient — especially when it came to difficult truths — than any other intellectual of the past century.

But if George Orwell represented the type of the intellectual at his best, he also manifested a number of its limitations. He was clever, he was penetrating, he was even prophetic — and that is a lot — but no one could claim that he was deep. Like most modern intellectuals, he was insufficiently impressed with the mysteries of life, which is why his fiction so often seems stillborn. Except at odd moments, Orwell never quite progressed beyond ideas: their stranglehold suffocates not only *1984* and *Animal Farm* but even his less directly political fiction.

Still, better to be in the grip of ideas that happen to be true — as Orwell, for the most part, was — than of ideas that are false and trivial, or odious and brutal. If the social and political speculations of intellectuals can lend charm to life — risky generalizations, especially those that sound cogent, are among the best stimulants to thought — the claim of the intellectual to be more than a high-order kibitzer often remains fairly thin. Like the kibitzer, the intellectual stands at the rim of the game, risking nothing by his assertions. An American intellectual once announced to Edward Shils that, when it came to the politics of the state of Israel, he was of the war party. "Yes," Shils said in reporting this conversation to me, "Israel will go to war, and he'll go to the party."

· · ·

But, then, intellectuals have never been known for their deep loyalty. This is a point underscored by Noel Annan in his book *The Dons*, in which he notes that intellectuals "vacillate and move gingerly to judgments about people, slide away at first hint of trouble, . . . and then decamp when their friend is in trouble, or worse, when he is in disgrace." Herman Wouk made essentially this point, a long while ago, in *The Caine Mutiny*, whose one really shameless character is the intellectual—played perfectly by Fred MacMurray in the movie—who goads the executive officer into wrongful action and then backs away when the going gets tough. The larger point is that you probably do not want an intellectual in your foxhole.

The historian Richard Hofstadter, noting the "passion for justice" of intellectuals, wrote that "one thinks here of Voltaire defending the Calas family, of Zola speaking out for Dreyfus, of the American intellectuals outraged at the trial of Sacco and Vanzetti." Yet such can be the fecklessness of many intellectuals that this same passion for justice has also surfaced as a penchant for mischief-making, and on a monumental scale. Next to alienation, one of the most enticing ideas to intellectuals has been revolution. This is no doubt partly because a number of actual intellectuals—Leon Trotsky, Zhou Enlai, Che Guevara—have played prominent (and in no way salubrious) roles in actual revolutions. As a young intellectual-in-training, I knew more about the Russian than about the American Revolution; after all, intellectuals had been much more conspicuous in the run-up to the former. Most intellectuals have felt that when the revolution arrives, not the least of its results will be a general recognition of the importance of you'll never guess who.

Even when they have not lent their energies to promoting schemes for human betterment that depend on the mass coercion of real human beings, the intellectuals' overdependence on ideas, and their consequent detachment from reality, have often turned them into little demons of ignorant subtlety. During World War II, a number of left-wing British intellectuals were convinced that what really lay behind America's entry into the war was the hope of stopping the spread of socialism in England — prompting George Orwell's acid remark: "Only an intellectual could be so stupid." When Barry Goldwater ran for president of the United States in 1964, Hannah Arendt, certain that America was on the edge of being taken over by fascists, sought an apartment in Switzerland. Susan Sontag, in 1982, announced to a New York audience her belated conclusion that communism should no longer be the name of any thinking person's desire but was rather to be regarded as "fascism with a human face." To those who had troubled over the years to follow Sontag's own public imprecations against Western democracy or against the "white race" as the "cancer of human history," or her earnest championing of Communist North Vietnam as "a place which, in many respects, *deserves* to be idealized," her public change of mind, however carefully qualified, must have offered a moment of grim amusement. But her audience — in 1982! — was nevertheless shocked by even so cautious a defection, and she herself never again ventured to say anything remotely so out of line.

Wrong or not, alienated or not, until the 1960s American intellectuals seemed to live easily if not prosperously enough, enjoying some of the comforts of a coterie existence. Not least among those comforts was the feeling of being vastly superior to their countrymen, of being among Stendhal's happy few. Unlike today's so-called public intellectuals, they were not invited to offer their opinions on radio and television, and their names were not much known outside the readership of the intellectual magazines.

Yet even in the forties and fifties, their influence was not negligible — though it might take a while to be felt. Edmund Wilson, perhaps the literary intellectual par excellence, had been a crucial figure in importing and explaining modernism in literature to an American audience, especially in his book *Axel's Castle*, and in introducing readers to a vast international array of writers, living and dead. In the forties and fifties, Clement Greenberg had done something similar for Abstract Expressionism and the New York school in painting. Meanwhile, a number of men who wrote for the intellectual magazines — including James Agee, Irving Howe, and Louis Kronenberger — were also putting in time working for the devil himself at *Time* and *Fortune;* and so, in the sociological phrase, there was transmission of knowledge on this front, too. If one read both the intellectual magazines and that portion of the popular press that had intellectual pretensions, one saw how the ideas from the former began to percolate down to the latter.

By the early 1960s, "percolate" would no longer accurately describe the quickness of this transaction. In those years Harold Rosenberg became the art critic of *The New Yorker,* and Hannah Arendt, James Baldwin, and Mary McCarthy also published there. Dwight Macdonald not only became a *New Yorker* writer but signed on to write about movies for *Esquire.* In 1963 and 1964, respectively, McCarthy's *The Group* and Saul Bellow's *Herzog* were bestsellers. In 1964, Susan Sontag wrote an essay in *Partisan Review,* "Notes on Camp," that resulted within what seemed a matter of weeks in the spread of the word "camp" to just about everywhere, including *Vogue.* Intellectuals had suddenly gone public; they, or at any rate some of them, were on the Big Board.

At least as significant for the new integration of intellectuals into American life was another development, an early sign of which was the appointment of Philip Rahv, one of the founding editors of *Partisan Review,* and Irving Howe, then the editor of *Dissent,* to professorships at the newly founded Brandeis University. Neither Rahv nor Howe had a doctorate or anything resembling an academic specialty; what they had was intellectual authority, and that, apparently, was now deemed enough. The postwar expansion of the universities would soon siphon away a larger number of such people — until, in the end, American intellectual life was itself all but siphoned away by the universities.

Sometimes this was literally so, as when first Rutgers and then Boston University took over *Partisan Review,* with Rutgers installing a full-time academic, Richard Poirier, as one of the magazine's editors. More generally, the acceptance of intellectuals into the American university dealt a serious blow to the freelance spirit. The successors to the older generation of American intellectuals — among them Richard Sennett, Marshall Berman, Morris Dickstein, and Louis Menand — now tended to operate with a net under them, the net known as academic tenure; and, though their pretensions might be intellectual, their style tended to be highly academic.

Still, apart from the absorption of intellectuals by the universities, it was really the decade of the 1960s that finished off the old intellectual life. Before the sixties, the issue that had most divided intellectuals was Stalinism. That rancorous and deadly quarrel was much on the minds of some participants in the political disputes that arose during the 1960s over the war in Vietnam, the Black Power movement, the meaning of urban riots, and the nature of America itself. The effect was momentous. As Midge Decter noted: "The 'partisan' community would become unstuck in the 60s, with several defections from among its ranks to the camp of the radical students, and would blow up even further in the 70s with the onset of neoconservatism."

In two of his memoirs, *Breaking Ranks* (1979) and *Ex-Friends* (1999), Norman Podhoretz has chronicled this sundering of the community of intellectuals he once dubbed the Family, as well as his own emergence as a neoconservative. Behind much of the anger that greeted at least the first of these books was the implicit charge that Podhoretz had betrayed the very essence of the intellectual vocation as it had come to be defined — that is, he had refused to consider it his first duty to be unrelentingly critical of his own country, to maintain his alienation, and to assert his disdain for middle-class life.

But Podhoretz was not entirely alone. Owing to the sixties, others were coming to regard the so-called intellectual vocation, at least as now construed, as outmoded if not downright dangerous, both to the life of the mind and to the life of society. The word "intellectual" no longer seemed such a clear honorific, and the baggage that went with the job — the pose of alienation, the contempt for the social class of one's origin, the pretense of distaste for the culture of one's country — seemed false to the experience of life. When it came to the breakdown of the universities, the racial bullying of the Black Power movement, and the general destruction of standards in society, the intellectuals had by and large run with the pack. Later, having long deserted such convictions as they might once have had, most intellectuals chose to stand aside when culture itself came under attack by the philistine forces of political correctness and radical feminism.

Other factors were at work in this decline. For one thing, recent decades have not exactly provided a hardy diet of ideas of the kind once on the intellectual's table. Consider Marxism in politics and modernism in the arts, the staples of the old *Partisan Review.* The former, with its prediction of ultimate revolution, is now a dead letter; party politics, once considered beneath the interest of an American intellectual, is now all that is left to him. Modernism, now more than a century old with many great discrete works to its credit, was always connected to an interest in the avant-garde; but the contemporary avant-garde, for the most part a mélange of political yahooism, in-your-face nastiness, and sexual liberationism, can hardly hold the interest of anyone seriously devoted to art. As for other big-system ideas once the meat and drink of intellectuals — including Freudianism — they have taken a ferocious drubbing over the past quarter century, while structuralism, deconstructionism, and the rest of the theory stew have proved digestible only by academics.

Then, too, the very notion of the sellout, once so dear to intellectual thought, has become murky in the extreme. Nowadays, if one is sufficiently antinomian, one is likely to find one's art sponsored by Mobil Oil, one's novel receiving a six-figure advance from a major publisher, or oneself put on the faculty at Princeton. The problem for the talented is no longer selling out, but deciding where — and when — to buy in.

Another factor working against the idea of the traditional intellectual is the greater degree of specialization that infects the social sciences, literary studies, and philosophy. As recently as the 1960s, Lewis Mumford and Edmund Wilson, nonacademics both, could mount full-scale attacks on the heavily pedantic Modern

Language Association editions of Emerson, Twain, and other American writers, inspiring sufficient discomfort among the officials in charge to make them feel the attacks had to be answered. I am not sure there is an intellectual alive today who commands the authority to do anything similar.

And so the traditional intellectual has been replaced by a new type, the public intellectual, a figure who, as likely as not, retains all or most of the political attitudes of the sixties, suitably updated for the moment, and who has become adept at packaging them in academic dress. These are the Edward Saids and Ronald Dworkins of our time, the Richard Rortys and Cornel Wests, the Martha Nussbaums and Stanley Fishes, the Catharine MacKinnons and Peter Singers. Unlike the unattached intellectuals of earlier days, such people usually have university careers and arrangements at influential publications. Columnists, professors writing on subjects of putative contemporary relevance, soon, if Florida Atlantic University has its way, full-fledged Ph.D.s in public intellectuality itself—they are the inheritors of a mantle for which one now qualifies not by any particular mental power but by going public with one's intelligibility and one's mere opinions.

Words change for a reason, generally to fit changes in the world. We thus now have the empty term "public intellectual," because the real thing, the traditional intellectual, is on his way out. As for me, harshly though I have written about the traditional intellectual, I now find myself rather sorrowful at his departure from the scene. What once distinguished him was a certain cast of mind, a style of thought, wide-ranging, curious, playful, genuinely excited by ideas for ideas' sake. Unlike so many of today's public intellectuals, he was not primarily a celebrity hound, a false philosopher-king with tenure, or a single-issue publicist. An elegantly plumed, often irritating bird, the traditional intellectual was always a minuscule minority, and now he is on the list of endangered species. Anyone who was around in his heyday to see him soar is unlikely to forget the spectacle.

C'mon, Reiny, Let's Do the Twist

THE FIRST and probably ineradicable cliché about editors is that they are frustrated writers. There's something to it, but only in the sense that T. S. Eliot — himself both a writer and an editor — put it: "Most editors are failed writers — but so are most writers." As someone who has worked most of his life simultaneously as editor and writer, and who has also put in his time as an Anglophile, I can only add, "Just so. Spot on."

A writing career of any length is, in essence, a series of relationships with various editors. One may talk about an audience for one's writing as long as one wishes, but the primary audience for just about everything I have ever written has been one or another of the editors I have dealt with over the years — those who have edited my articles for magazines and those who have edited my books. These men and women have run the gamut from old sweet softies to cold sardonic swine. Some have praised my work extravagantly; others have criticized it strongly even when accepting it. Some have shown the most elegant manners; others clearly feel the least show of consideration to be an act of abject weakness. I just wrote a piece for a small-circulation magazine from whose editor I have yet to hear anything; but then perhaps I shouldn't have expected to hear, since I wrote the piece without fee.

No one sets out in life to become an editor; it is a job one falls, or slides, or lapses into. In my own case, I knew from a fairly early age I wanted to write; my only problem was that I hadn't anything in particular to write about, which didn't stop me from beginning to publish at the age of twenty-two. While awaiting content, I worked on style, and thought perhaps the best place to do this was on a magazine as an editor. I was lucky, I now think, to get a job on a magazine called the *New Leader*, which in those days, the early 1960s, required lots of editing.

Most of the pieces in the magazine were about politics, many about politics in foreign countries. Those written by Englishmen, some of which came in longhand, needed the least work. We ran lots of material by Kremlinologists, who were dedicated to discerning, usually on the most amazingly slender evidence, what went on behind the thick walls of the Kremlin. Many of these men were themselves Russians, and their English prose tended to be Pninish, but without the laughs. A number of refugees from World War II, whose first language was German, also wrote for us. They could produce some fairly gnarled copy. I regularly rewrote the single-page column of an elderly socialist named William Bohn. He never complained. If I am still scribbling away at his age — I would estimate early nineties — and some kid in his twenties does that to me, I shall threaten legal action.

Although I thought of myself as a back-of-the-book man, interested in books and the arts, the staff on the *New Leader* wasn't large enough to allow for such specialization. We were a threesome, a principal editor and two associate editors. The copy would come in, and we would have a go at it. The metaphor of butchery comes to mind. ("Yours, sir, is the butcher's trade," wrote Henry James to Bruce Richmond, his editor at the *Times Literary Supplement,* when Richmond wanted to cut a small portion of a lengthy James essay.) Each manuscript laid on my desk was a carcass, to be stripped of its fat and gristle and made sufficiently presentable for the somewhat less than lustrous showcase in which it would eventually appear.

For prose that took on the complexity but none of the style of late rococo, the prize went to the theologian Reinhold Niebuhr, who used the *New Leader* as a forum to comment on world affairs. Niebuhr was a genuinely great man, but sometime in the early

1960s he had had a stroke, which deprived him of the use of I don't know what parts of his body but of the space bar on his typewriter certainly. Every sentence seemed a multiple-choice question to which the answer, inevitably, was none of the above.

I remember sentences that ran along something like the following lines:

> Whether the Kennedy administration wishes to stage a three-pronged attack on the double revolution of poverty and underdevelopment or instead place the weight of its focus on arms control, with especial attention to underground testing and the attendant so-called "nth-country problem," or take a strong stance on the bifurcation inherent in the Commonwealth or Common Market question, all the while refraining from direct confrontation with the civil rights movement in its more militant aspect, remains to be seen.

Now imagine this sentence with no space between every second or third word.

As the youngest editor in the office, I was regularly assigned the Niebuhr pieces. It was an initiation ritual. At the *New Republic* of those days, I am told, they would give the newest editor the task of calling up a journalist named Gerald Johnson to go over his galley proof, neglecting to tell the young fellow that Johnson was very nearly deaf. Everyone else in the office would sit around suppressing laughter as the poor guy soon found himself screaming proof changes into the phone. It might take me the better part of a day to unravel and then restitch Niebuhr's words. The best part of the assignment was at the very beginning, when I would stand at my desk over his copy, remove my suit jacket, loosen my tie, and sing, à la Chubby Checker, "C'mon, Reiny, let's do the twist."

On this job I learned that I had a small knack for bullying other people's sentences into presentable shape. I edited the copy of the literary critic Stanley Edgar Hyman and the social critic Irving Kristol, neither of whom, to my mild resentment, had the least need for my ministrations. But in pulling apart and reassembling lesser articles and reviews, I think I discovered a thing or two about how brief compositions — "pieces," to use the trade term — work, or, more often, don't.

I discovered all the crutches that limping prose needs to get from paragraph to paragraph. While doing so I longed to write a composition that never had recourse to the words "yet," "but," "still," "however," and "moreover"; also the phrases "to be sure," "what is more," and "in any event." Thirty years later, I haven't written it yet.

I took most pleasure in editing Albert Goldman, who then wrote about jazz and classical music for the *New Leader*. In the strange detours life provides, Goldman went from teaching the Romantics at the School of General Studies at Columbia — "working the lounge at Columbia," he used to call it — to writing thick books about such popular-culture figures as Lenny Bruce, Elvis Presley, and John Lennon, that last tome causing him to be called "human vermin" by Elton John, an amusing if not entirely enviable accolade.

Al was a very psychoanalytic character, and at that time he viewed editing as therapy by other (much less expensive) means. I edited a book for him that he wrote about De Quincey and plagiarism. Sometimes I would meet him at his apartment to talk him through a piece on which he felt blocked (in those days, editors made house calls). One Saturday morning, he phoned to ask me what kind of typewriter I used. When I told him, he wanted more details, until it became clear that what he really wanted was for me to take him to buy a new typewriter. "Al," I said, "I think this may be a bit sicker than we want to let things get."

"Isn't it, though," he said, loosing his fine cackly laugh.

Toward the end of my days at the *New Leader*, I wrote my first review for the *New Republic*. It was about a small-press edition of the verse of Max Beerbohm, written at the request of the journal's literary editor, Robert Evett. It was not a long review, but Beerbohm, himself so meticulous a craftsman, is a writer I love, and so I took great pains with it. Prying open the thickly packed *New Republic* envelope in which I expected to find galley proofs, I

found instead my own typescript, with large sections contemptu-
ously rubbed out with a thick and smudge-making pencil. Long
wavy lines connected sentences that, logically, resisted juxtaposi-
tion. Transitions were eliminated. The notion of a paragraph as
both rhythmically and intellectually coherent was completely undone. Any gracefulness, elegance, wit that the original review
might have contained was brutally eliminated. I felt quite as devas-
tated as my review.

"Mr. Evett," I said, "I'm afraid that I can't let this piece appear
in print as it has been edited. It doesn't make any sense."

"Don't worry about it," he said. "Gilbert [Harrison, the editor
in chief at the time] edited it. His wife died not long ago, so he
drinks his lunch, comes back, and edits copy, with the results
you've just seen. All you have to do is tell me you want everything
restored, and I'll do it."

"I want everything restored," I said.

"I just did it," he said.

This happened once more, with the same second act: "I want
everything restored." "I just did it."

I came to like Robert Evett, whom I called Bobby. He was a
convert to Catholicism, a homosexual, a man with drinking and
pill problems, and, withal, a sweetheart. He gave me all sorts of
books to review, at a time when I needed the money; his telephone conversations were filled with rich gossip and lots of shared
laughter; and once, when he heard from someone else that I was
onto financially lean days, he offered to loan me money, which I
didn't take, though I was much touched by the offer.

Bobby's true vocation was that of a composer of serious music, for which he received a great many commissions. He mentioned this part—the main part, really—of his career to me only
in passing. Sometimes the shakiness of his life, when it was going
badly, was unmistakable: too much drink, trouble with his gentleman friend, difficulties at the office, medical worries, the full catastrophe.

I was going to say that I awaited Bobby's calls with pleasure,
but the pleasure was usually admixed, however slightly, with anxi-

ety. For a call from Bobby meant, above all, a judgment on the piece I had recently sent him. He never rejected anything that I wrote for him, at least not that I can recall, nor did he go in for much in the way of making changes in my copy, but neither of these facts stood in the way of my being nervous about his acceptance. After having published my writing for more than forty years, I regret to have to confess that I am still nervous about acceptance. "Perhaps worry is always tapping on the door of the true artist," wrote Gerald Moore. I would only add that it's there for the working writer, too.

The other side of being nervous about acceptance is that of being excessively susceptible to praise, or vitamin P, as Thomas Mann referred to it. I have had many handsome injections of vitamin P and have never come close to overdosing, but the man who used to lay it on most thickly for me, not with a trowel but a bulldozer, was an editor for whom I used to write articles on American writers for the United States Information Agency. So heavy was his praise that even I, with my swollen writer's vanity, felt embarrassed by it — which isn't, please note, quite the same as saying I couldn't believe it. One day I told him that I had come up with a way to eliminate his having to praise my work any further. All he had to do was write me a letter, on USIA stationery, in which he thanked me for my writing and told me that he thought it was a force for change in Latin America. Since at that time — 1969 — nothing was a force for change in Latin America, I thought this was sufficient praise. He wrote the letter, but alas, I have lost it.

Some magazines edit more heavily than others. As an editor, I have gone in for some heavy editing myself, even performing what, in the precomputer age, used to be called a "typewriter job," which meant putting a fresh piece of paper in one's typewriter and simply rewriting an entire article. Eliot Cohen, the founding editor of *Commentary,* is said to have gone in for heavy editing in a big way, and the tradition of serious editing has continued at that magazine to the present.

Sometimes the results of this heavy editing can lead to odd deceptions. One cannot be certain if one is reading the writer or the editor. I remember, in the late sixties, reading brilliant articles in *Commentary* on the civil rights movement by Bayard Rustin and thinking how extraordinary it was that this man could organize impressive marches on Washington and still find the time to write so beautifully. In fact, as I subsequently learned, the ideas in the articles were Rustin's but the sentences in which they were set afloat were those of Norman Podhoretz, the magazine's editor. On the other hand, Daniel Patrick Moynihan, as I can vouch from having edited him, was both an important U.S. senator and an impressive prose writer.

I have received some splendid editing in my day, from *The New Yorker*, from the *Hudson Review*, from the *New Criterion*, but above all from *Commentary*, where Neal Kozodoy has been my editor. Kozodoy has a nice sense for the flow of argument in a piece, and he has, in many instances, untwisted my own logic. He is also excellent at sniffing out inconsistencies, overwriting, small but key flaws in short stories. He has saved me the embarrassment of many solecisms, factual faux pas, grand blunders of my own devising.

Neal Kozodoy is a big cut-man, a founding member of the less-is-more school, known to many of his clients as "the Butcher of 56th Street," though I prefer to think of him as "Cleaver," as in "Leave It to Cleaver," which I seem frequently to have done by sending him manuscripts longer than he wished them. On one piece I wrote for him, I sent him, via e-mail, the following communication: "Dear Neal, Wrote five fine paragraphs of Solzhenitsyn piece yesterday, four of which you should be able to remove easily."

One of the saddest lessons any writer has to learn is that anything he writes can be cut and that, worse news, the writing is often — not always but more often than not — better for being briefer. The Gettysburg Address is 272 words long; with an editor's help, I'm sure Lincoln could have brought it in at under 200. I have never counted the number of words in the Lord's Prayer, but it, too, could, I'm sure, be readily cut; its second phrase, "who art in heaven," is pretty clearly tautological; I mean, where else would the Lord be, in Passaic, New Jersey?

Kozodoy's cuts can be more than editorial. In a short story I once wrote for *Commentary*, my narrator has written a *New Yorker* profile of a writer that runs to sixty thousand words; Neal cut that down to forty thousand. In an essay I sent him about the days I lived in Little Rock, I mentioned that someone had sent me a letter saying I was still considered a small legend in that city, to which I responded, "At 5′7″, I suppose I am a small legend"; he made it *at under 5′7″*, so he has cut not only my manuscripts but my actual height. Now that's editing.

I have neglected to add that I think Neal Kozodoy one of the very best editors going, and the one whom, because of my regard for his acumen and his strong anti-crapola radar, it gives me the greatest delight to please. He, of course, would have cut this entire paragraph.

Of all the invitations to write for magazines I have ever received, the most amusing, in connection with editing, came from a man, now dead, named Ronald Sanders, who was then the editor of *Midstream*. He suggested a piece he wanted me to write, then added: "I don't know whether you get a lot of editing at *Commentary, Harper's,* and other places that you write, but I can promise you that you won't have to worry about any editing at *Midstream*. It's not that we don't believe in the value of editing — it's just that we're too tired to do any."

Editors can also function usefully as goad and conscience, especially to those of us who are used to writing for deadlines — that is to say, for those of us used to missing deadlines. As a magazine writer and editor, I have been given and myself gave any number of false deadlines. I think of deadlines as coming in three kinds: the first deadline, the adult deadline, and the *real* deadline. I generally make the *real* deadline and half feel I ought to be paid a bonus for making the first deadline.

The advent of fax, overnight delivery, and e-mail has made the deadline-making aspect of writing even goofier. Now one can wait for the very last moment — and still miss the deadline. As a writer, I have not missed many, but enough to diminish my own moral authority as an editor able to chastise other writers for missing theirs. I am not sure that I need deadlines, but I do think that they have made me more productive, since I am the sort of writer who functions best under those delightful twins of self-laceration, guilt and shame.

I once had a piece owed to me at a magazine I edited, *The American Scholar*, for fully seventeen years. When it finally came in, it was not, truth to tell, all that great. But I was not about to send it back to its author for revisions. The wildest excuse by a writer for missing a deadline that I have ever heard was made by the late Anatole Broyard, and was told to me by Hilton Kramer, who was then briefly working as the cultural-news editor of the *New York Times* and was the editor to whom the excuse was given. Broyard called in one day to tell Kramer that he wouldn't be able to have his regular book review in on time because his wife was having her period. Kramer was so flabbergasted by the non-sequiturial quality of this excuse that he said okay and hung up, neglecting to ask what the hell Broyard's wife's menstrual cycle had to do with it.

In my experience, many of the best manuscript editors are not themselves writers; or, if they do write, they do so only occasionally and probably do not think of themselves primarily as writers. William Shawn of *The New Yorker* was consummately such an editor. Nonwriting editors tend to be more selfless. You never sense any rivalrousness in them, or the feeling that they are like frustrated actors, waiting tables and hanging around until they are cast in a good part. As a former writing editor myself, I know whereof I speak.

The same is true in book publishing, where the steadiest editors — Maxwell Perkins, Robert Giroux, Elizabeth Sifton — do not generally produce books of their own. From a writer's standpoint, steadiness is much valued, and not all that often found, in a book editor. Hemingway left three wives but never left Maxwell Perkins, his editor at Scribners.

Nowadays the powerful editors have their own imprints, a sign of the editor's growing importance to the world of publishing. But how exactly did book editors come into being at all? Initially, an author wrote for his bookseller; and as every less-than-best-selling present-day writer will be only too eager to tell you, no contemporary writer would confuse his publisher with a bookseller. In the eighteenth century, a bookseller would decide how much to pay a writer, he would decide how many copies to print, and he might have to decide whether to bowdlerize material. But my sense is that the notion of an editor getting in there and making serious alterations in books belongs to a much more recent time. William C. Brownell, the principal editor at Scribners before Maxwell Perkins, noted: "I don't believe much in tinkering, and I am not *suffisant* enough to think the publisher can contribute much by modifications." The editor was still nothing like the fellow worker, companion in creation, combination buddy-shrink-critic-tough-father-kindly-mother that is implied in the following dedication, in *Of Time and the River*, from Thomas Wolfe to Perkins:

> [To] a great editor and a brave and honest man, who stuck to the writer of this book through times of bitter hopelessness and doubt and would not let him give in to his own despair, a work to be known as "Of Time and the River" is dedicated with the hope that all of it may be in some way worthy of the loyal devotion and the patient care which a dauntless and unshaken friend has given to each part of it, and without which none of it could have been done.

If this seems a bit fulsome, perhaps you should know that Perkins felt, rightly, he had to cut the dedication back from its original length of three pages.

I worked for roughly a year as an editor of books and found I had neither the temperament nor the taste for it. I didn't have the patience to await the fruition of long-term projects, and I didn't have the appetite for simultaneously stroking the egos of writers and stoking the greed of publishers. The job felt altogether too much that of a middleman between writer and publisher, and I quickly grew tired of lying to each about the admirable intentions of the other.

Apart from collections of essays and stories, I have written only six full-blown books, and in every case the help of an editor would have been appreciated, at least at that midway point where one is certain that the whole project has been a very big mistake. I had as an editor for one and a half of these books — the reason for the fraction will become clear presently — an extraordinary man named Hal Scharlatt. He was one of the hot young editors of the day, a likable, talented, wildly undependable man who died on a tennis court at the age of thirty-eight, in the middle of a set and — the nerve! — in the middle of my second book.

Hal Scharlatt was one of those editors who answered neither letters nor most phone calls. If you sent him a chunk of manuscript, he might deign to comment on it, but then again he might not. Once I was to meet him in Chicago for lunch, for which he showed up forty-five minutes late, just five minutes before I was set to walk out, tear up my contract, look for another editor, publisher, book idea. It took him a minute to calm me down, and only two more to charm the socks and shin hair off me.

None of this would have worked, of course, if Hal Scharlatt hadn't been very good at what he did. What he did was two things. The first was to create a certain amount of excitement for a book even before it was written. Not long after I signed up to write my first book for him, I got a call from a producer at NBC, telling me that he heard I was writing this fascinating book and would I like to come on a prime-time show to discuss my subject? Where could he have gotten this idea? Only, somehow, from a grapevine Hal Scharlatt had planted.

The other thing Scharlatt was good at was judging the pace of a book-length manuscript. I don't think he touched a sentence in the one complete book I wrote for him, but he was able, at various places, to point out that "things seemed to slow down badly at this point — I'd cut the next twenty pages by roughly a third." His instinct in these matters was excellent, and I found myself following his suggestions to good effect.

Yet having these genius editors can be very trying. Given a choice, I'd rather have an editor who catches me using a dash badly on page 279 and feels that I have not used the word "egoist" with quite the precision it requires.

But if book editors are a relatively new phenomenon, the notion of an editor fiddling with magazine copy is older than one may have thought. Francis Jeffrey, the editor of the *Edinburgh Review*, not only chose the topics and contributors for his distinguished journal but got in there to muck around with their pieces when it pleased him to do so. Jeffrey was not above laying about with his blue pencil, cleaning up the extravagances and what he felt were the barbarities in the prose of William Hazlitt, writing in paragraphs, even entire pages, he felt were wanting in other contributors. Jeffrey was a great editor and able to get away with it. Yet I'm glad he didn't get his hands on everyone. One of the appropriate criticisms of an over-edited magazine is that nearly everything in it reads alike.

What would he, or another Jeffrey-like editor, have done, two and a half centuries earlier, with Montaigne, who wrote: "I go out of my way, but rather by license than carelessness. My ideas follow one another, but sometimes it is from a distance, and look back at each other, but with a sidelong glance . . . It is the inattentive reader who loses my subject, not I."

I tend to prefer the idiosyncratic in style to survive and flourish, even at the cost of irregularity and even, on occasion, barbarity. Yet in practice, I tended to be an editor of the hands-on sort. I found I couldn't bear to have certain words, phrases, even syntax in any magazine I edited. I would go prowling around other people's prose, unsplitting those split infinitives, sweeping prepositions from the ends of sentences, removing certain over- and ignorantly used words. I have conducted search-and-destroy campaigns against "lifestyle," "impact," "process," the pretentious "intriguing." Just now I am quite nuts on the matter of "focus," a word that shows up in journalism more frequently than Jesse Jackson at the funerals of the famous. I also didn't permit ideas, movements, or anything except people in a car to be "driven," nor anything other than large physical objects to be "massive." I have scores of other tics, quirks, and downright prejudices. I can't help myself; I have to clean it all up. Anality, you may say. "Anality," I respond, in the words of a character in a Kingsley Amis novel, "my ass."

I once thought that a magazine is all the power an intellectual needs; today I would say it is all the power he deserves. The power derives from the opportunity to influence public opinion. Examples of its having been done, and on a monumental scale, are not wanting. The great nineteenth-century Russian exile Aleksandr Herzen's *The Bell*, published in London, is said to have had a strong hand in the breakup of serfdom. Solzhenitsyn's dealings with Aleksandr Tvardovsky, the editor of *Novy Mir* who determined to print *One Day in the Life of Ivan Denisovich*, was filled with even greater historical implications — namely, the beginning of the end of the Soviet Union. Dwight Macdonald used to claim that his review in *The New Yorker* of Michael Harrington's book on poverty helped start the anti-poverty program in the United States. Jeane Kirkpatrick got her job as ambassador to the United Nations owing to an essay in *Commentary*.

The great editors have had in common, I believe, their own odd, individual aesthetic, the notion of this elegant, this glittering, this lovely thing, a magazine, with every word written as one would like to write oneself: pellucidly, powerfully, penetratingly. It's a splendid dream, and as a former editor I continue to have it myself, usually only to wake, pencil in my hand, ready once more, without Reinhold Niebuhr as my partner, to do perhaps my ten thousandth version of the editorial twist.

The Torture of Writer's Block

RALPH ELLISON and Joseph Mitchell, two of America's most remarkable writers — one a novelist, the other a journalist, each thought by many people to be the best at his respective trade — had in common the nightmare of decades-long writer's block.

Invisible Man, published in 1952, may well be the most solidly made and most intelligent novel produced by an American in the past sixty years. Wildly comic, philosophically deep, socially significant, it is a book of a kind that, if one had written nothing else, would be enough to give one a strong reputation for the rest of one's life, and perhaps beyond. And in the case of Ralph Ellison, who wrote no further novels, it did just that.

As for Joseph Mitchell, he represented the urban tradition at *The New Yorker*, the tradition of John McNulty and A. J. Liebling, as opposed to the small-town tradition of James Thurber and E. B. White. Mitchell was fortunate to live long enough to see his own reputation revived in 1992, when *Up in the Old Hotel*, a compendium of all his earlier books, appeared with heavy jeroboams of praise.

But both Ellison and Mitchell became at least as famous for writer's block. Block is the supreme torture for a writer. When a writer is blocked, he cannot write; his craft and talent and energy suddenly flee him. The condition can last a week, a month, a year, a lifetime. And like inspiration, writer's block can show up utterly without warning. It is a condition that seems inexplicable, and is painful in the extreme.

I believe most cases of writer's block do have an explanation, and one not necessarily to be found down in that dark psychic disco where the superego is doing the tango with the id. Sometimes a writer may be blocked because he really isn't prepared to write what he has promised to write; he just doesn't have the knowledge, experience, or wit to carry out the job. Or sometimes, midway through a lengthy piece of writing, he discerns the falsity of all that he has written up to now and hasn't the stomach or stamina to return and begin again. Sometimes he simply cannot bring the introspection and honesty to the job that it requires, and sometimes contemplating the serious consequences of what he is writing — in loss of friendships, status, or future earnings — may be more than he can bear.

The great fear of a writer is that he will find himself locked into the kind of writer's block that afflicted both Ellison and Mitchell. The one question you didn't ask Ralph Ellison was "Hey, kiddo, how's the new novel going?" For after the splendid success of *Invisible Man*, Ellison was never able to produce that novel. There were stories about his having lost nearly an entire manuscript to a fire. After *Invisible Man*, forty years passed, during which Ellison produced two books of essays, collected a vast number of honorary degrees, served on endless editorial and other boards, and kept his cool and courage at a time when it was easy for a black writer to make a serious jerk of himself. But the thing he was put on earth to do, write more beautiful novels, was precisely what he was unable to do.

Joseph Mitchell's block was of a different order, though it lasted thirty years. Mitchell's final book, *Joe Gould's Secret*, was published in 1965, and its first sentence shows his deft touch: "Joe Gould was an odd and penniless and unemployable little man who came to the city in 1916 and ducked and dodged and held on as hard as he could for over thirty-five years." Many of his admirers, myself among them, longed for more such sentences, though they were never to come.

Mitchell once described to me, in his deep North Carolinian accent, the book he said he was working on. It was about "double exile," which, he went on to explain, was the peculiar condition of feeling a stranger wherever he was: in New York he felt himself a southerner, while in the South he felt himself a pure New Yorker. The book seemed one of those "enchanted cigarettes," the term Balzac gave to those books one dreams about but almost are certain never to get written.

Another of the things Ellison and Mitchell had in common is that each treated me to a single memorable afternoon, the better part of both of which I spent in the same chair on the second floor in the ample room facing onto 43rd Street at the Century Club in New York. I met each man once, felt I had made a friend, and afterward never had another contact with either of them.

I spent the afternoon of January 26, 1978, with Ellison. He had earlier published a fine essay in *The American Scholar*, the magazine I edited, called "The Little Man from Chehaw Station," which I had read in its first-draft form as a commencement address and which he added on to and greatly improved for publication. My journal entry for the day notes: "He is a smaller man than I had imagined him to be, though, as I had imagined, well turned out sartorially (the only flaw here being too large a wristwatch) and with the manner of a courtly gent." He nicely broke through this formal manner by using the phrase, ten or so minutes into our lunch, "fucking distinguished," to refer to a pompous figure in publishing who came up to our table. Our conversation was desultory—we told jokes, he told Depression stories, we discussed literature, personalities, politics—and unrelievedly wonderful. I arrived at twelve-thirty and left, in the dark of a Manhattan winter evening, at five.

I thought I had a friend for life. When I returned to Chicago, I wrote Ellison a brief note, thanking him for the lunch and for the fine afternoon. No answer. A month or so later, I wrote again, this time proposing an essay for him to write for *The American Scholar*. Again no answer. Perhaps a year later, I wrote yet again, and again no response. All very strange. It was as if you had gone out with a very attractive woman, and thought you had both had a swell time, except that she refused afterward to take any of your calls. What was going on?

Five or six years later, I corresponded with a man who, in the course of one of his letters, asked me if I knew Ralph Ellison. The reason he asked was that he and his wife once attended a jazz festival with Ellison and his wife, during which they were nearly inseparable. The four of them seemed to have a splendid time. Yet when they returned home, Ellison failed to answer any of this man's letters. Did I have any idea what was going on?

The only reason I can come up with to explain Ralph Ellison's odd behavior is his writer's block. He was a naturally friendly, happily gregarious man, I think, and yet he must have worried about the cost of his sweet openness of spirit. With that uncompleted second novel hanging always before him, like surgery that he knew he couldn't postpone forever, though he somehow did, what he least needed was lots of new friends: insistent, responsibility-exacting, time-consuming friends. Friends may have been fine things, but it was the consequences of friendship that he couldn't afford, the consequence of time above all — time that would have to be taken from that damn unfinished novel to be a friend. That the novel wasn't getting written anyhow still didn't mean that one could take time from it. Such is the nightmare of a writer's block — one can't for more than a moment take pleasure in the leisure it imposes or think of anything except the writing one cannot do.

My one meeting with Joe Mitchell was less lengthy but no less enjoyable. We had corresponded years before, and had even spoken over the telephone a time or two. From his few letters to me, I was surprised to learn that Mitchell, whose specialty as a writer was observation of the common life, was a regular reader of intellectual journals and knew all about "the boys on the quarterlies," as his old friend A. J. Liebling used to say. He wrote to me, who was nobody if not one of the boys on the quarterlies, and said that he had read me over the years in *Encounter, Commentary,* the *New Criterion,* the *Times Literary Supplement,* and elsewhere.

In print, Mitchell was all cool objectivity, without opinionation, self-effacing, benevolent in his views of human nature. In private he was sly, opinionated, witty in a way that his writing didn't usually reveal. He turned out to be greatly interested in visual art and apparently spent much time going to exhibitions and galleries. When I told him that the art critic Hilton Kramer was a dear friend, he expressed admiration for him, especially for the courageousness of his views. Straightforward expression of views was never part of Mitchell's own modus operandi, at least not as a writer. That didn't mean he didn't have views, quite strong ones. He talked a good deal about missing his friend Liebling. He was critical of E. B. White, the preachiness of whose writing he couldn't abide.

Much in the current scene put him off, not least its liberationist tendencies. "You know, Joe," he said, "I am of a generation that can never consider sex a trivial act. When I was a young man, growing up in the South, if you did ugly to a girl, his brother would shoot you." "Did ugly to a girl" is a phrase I am not soon likely to forget.

I had no sense that Mitchell suffered greatly from not writing. My best explanation for his writer's block is that his subject matter had disappeared on him, and my guess is that he knew it. Mitchell had made his reputation writing about characters in New York, but characters, interesting idiosyncratic men and women, had long since been replaced by cases, some of them dangerous. Joe Gould today would be viewed as a slightly menacing homeless person; the amiable drunks at McSorley's, the "wonderful saloon" that is still there on East 6th Street owing in good part to the fame Mitchell gave it in various *New Yorker* essays, would now seem hopelessly lost. Mitchell was as bereft of a subject as Hogarth might have been under communism.

Writers who have written something substantial and then are blocked are one thing; writers who are blocked long before they hit their peak quite another. The toughest trick, and one of the greatest causes of writer's block, may be that of following one's own strong opening act. Writing a good or financially successful book the first time out can be filled with peril. This appears to have been not only Ellison's problem. It was also, at a lower level of literary creation, the problem of Thomas Heggen and Ross Lockridge, the authors, respectively, of *Mr. Roberts* and *Raintree County*. Both men had enormous commercial successes and each killed himself before producing a second work.

Frank Conroy took nearly twenty years between *Stop-Time*, his fine autobiographical book, and his next work, a collection of stories not many people remember. When I knew him, Conroy seemed in no hurry to produce a second book; having gotten it right the first time, perhaps he felt there was no rush. As the author of nineteen books, with a twentieth in press, I often wonder if I would have written less if I had got it right on the first try — or, for that matter, on the nineteenth.

Sometimes quite good writers, usually highly productive ones, will suddenly go silent. When inquiries are made of people who know them, one learns that they are blocked. This apparently is the case with Michael J. Arlen, who wrote some excellent television criticism for *The New Yorker* and a fine book about his Armenian forebears and who hasn't been in print for a number of years. Renata Adler, a key writer at *The New Yorker* and at the *New York Review of Books*, also had a block that caused her to close up shop for the better part of a decade.

The saddest case of writer's block I know was that of my late friend Marion Magid, for many years the managing editor of *Commentary*. Marion began brilliantly in her twenties, writing winningly about such varied subjects as Tennessee Williams for *Commentary* and hippie life in Amsterdam for *Esquire*. She straightaway had a style and a point of view — perhaps they are the same thing — and could, as they say about the best infielders, really pick it. You have to imagine a young Joan Didion, but smarter, more amusing, without the overlay of depression.

And then, for no good explanation I ever heard, the flame went out. Through her thirties, forties, fifties, up to her death at the age of sixty, Marion never really broke out of her block. All that I can remember her publishing those many years was a single review, in *Commentary*, of a book about American communism by Vivian

Gornick. I made the mistake of complimenting her by calling that piece "a nice little review"; she rejoined by telling me that if I knew what effort went into it, I would never call it "little." On another occasion, when a letter she sent to me failed to arrive, she all but groaned and said, "God, talk about being blocked—now even my letters aren't getting through."

I don't think I can hope to understand the suffering Marion Magid went through. She was the real thing, a true writer and, as the early evidence shows, a brilliant one, but unable to work at the trade she loved above all others. How immensely frustrating! She could hear the music but never find the words.

One of the signs of a real writer is the need to write almost all the time, and along with this need goes the feeling of self-loathing when one isn't writing. To what can one compare the pain of the blocked writer? Perhaps to a fine athlete, still in his prime, banned from playing the game he most loves. Hellacious!

When I lived in New York in the early 1960s, a time when psychotherapy was a dominant force among artists and intellectuals, lots of writers seemed, if not altogether blocked, then highly costive. If in the course of a year these people wrote a single book review, or an essay, or a short story, or two or three poems, it seemed production enough. Wallace Markfield, in his novel *To an Early Grave*, captures the spirit of the blocked writer in a character, a literary critic named Holly Levine, whom he shows moving around the word "certainly" in about six or seven recastings of the same sentence, until he is saved by a phone call that allows him to abandon the effort. Another day of nothing accomplished.

So endemic was writer's block in New York in the fifties and early sixties that there was a shrink, Edmund Bergler, one of whose specialties was unblocking writers. In a Teutonic accent, or so I have been told, he all but yelled at his patients, telling them that they were immature, they must knock off this nonsense, return to their typewriters, pay his fee. It may well be that some blocked writers derive a perverse pleasure from their blocks. But I doubt that pleasure had much to do with it.

Perfectionism is yet another important reason for writer's block.

For a writer stuck with perfectionism, writer's block just about comes with the territory, and such a writer figures to be blocked fully half the time. When a one-book novelist named Hannah Green — her one book is a novel that she finished at the age of forty-six and that I have never read titled *The Dead of the House* — died a number of years ago, her obituary in the *New York Times* noted "her almost obsessive pursuit of a perfection that always seemed just one rewrite away." The real wonder, her husband tossed in, was that she finished a book at all. "She never wanted to let go," he said. (One never truly finishes a poem, Paul Valéry said, one merely abandons it.) Miss Green had been working on a second book for the last twenty-five years of her life.

I write all this in trepidation, lest I incur the wrath of the furies and they strike me with a block of my own. Forty years in the business, say I with merely a grin and a great thumping knock on wood, and I have had the good luck to write pretty much what I have wanted without any hint of block. Perhaps a few people who have felt themselves unkindly treated by me are even now sticking pins in my books and ringing their own ever-so-slight change on the old football chant, "Block that kick."

I suppose that every writer for whom writing is not the painful drama it is often made out to be, but is instead an intense delight, worries a little about exhibiting this delight too frequently in public. Edith Wharton coined the term "magazine bore" for those writers who appear too often in too many magazines. You pick up a magazine and there they are, like the fellow in the orange fright wig and the "Jesus Saves" T-shirt who used to show up at all major sporting events.

It is probably a mistake to make writing look too easy. Anthony Trollope's having done so by recounting his writing regimen in his autobiography — he averaged 10,000 words a week, and some weeks wrote as many as 28,000 words — caused his reputation to suffer. He made writing seem altogether too mechanical an activity. A writer, Trollope believed, must approach his task as if he were working at the post office, which Trollope, in fact, for many years did: "He should sit down at his desk at a certain hour." He should eliminate the *Sturm und Drang* aspect of writing: "He need tie no wet towels round his brow, nor sit for thirty hours at his desk without moving, — as men have sat, or said that they have sat." Writing cannot be done in one's sleep, but for Trollope it could be done on the edge of sleep: "A man to whom writing well has become a habit may write well though he be fatigued." Trollope prided himself on having published twice as much as Carlyle and even more than Voltaire, and having accomplished this while holding a second job much of the time.

Writing quickly does have its own odd satisfactions, among them the delusion that one has mastered one's craft. Usually, one hasn't. More likely one has only had a lucky good day. I once had an essay reprinted in a college reader, and the editor offered me an additional $600 if I would write a thousand or so words explaining any difficulty encountered along the way of composing the original essay. I told myself I would do it if I could complete the job in less than an hour. And — yippee ti yo! — I did. Not only was this gratifying in itself, but I could now tell myself that I was a $600-an-hour writer. Unfortunately, the next thing I wrote, a long essay on the Austrian writer Robert Musil, took me so long to write that it returned me to thinking of myself as a minimum-wage man.

I once asked the critic F. W. Dupee, at that time freshly retired from the English department at Columbia and a finely polished prose writer, to write for *The American Scholar.* He wrote back to thank me for my invitation, but told me, in a sentence that sent a little chill through me, "I have stopped writing."

"I have stopped writing." That is the admission that Ellison could not make, nor Mitchell, who went into his office at *The New Yorker* every day for thirty years before his death without ever submitting a word to his editors. I cannot imagine myself, short of a knockout stroke or severe illness, ever saying that. My guess is that Dupee, good as he was, didn't really *have* to write. He must have been among those perhaps fortunate people who can write, and write extremely well, but can get through life quite nicely without having to write. A true writer, for better *and* worse, needs to write.

Needs to — and, despite all the widely advertised agonies, loves to. Writing has given me pleasure like nothing else I have ever done, and I mean the very act of writing. Raymond Chandler, when he learned that the detective-story writer John Dickson Carr disliked writing, speaks for me when he writes "A writer who hates the actual writing, who gets no joy out of the creation of magic by words, to me is simply not a writer at all. The actual writing is what you live for. The rest is something you have to get through in order to arrive at that point. How can you hate the actual writing . . . How can you hate the magic which makes of a paragraph or a sentence or a line of dialogue or a description something in the nature of a new creation?"

The only argument I would have with that passage is the use of the word "creation." Best, when thinking about writing, to keep the pretension level as low as possible. The first rule in avoiding writer's block is never to think of writing as in any way a creative activity, with its own dramas and tensions. For as soon as one does think about writing as creative — a bogus word in any case — one thinks about all that can go wrong with it. Much better, I have always found, to demystify writing as completely as possible. I frequently remind myself that formulating sentences remains one of the most amusing of all pastimes — and, besides (though I shouldn't want this to get around), it beats working all to hell.

Is Reading Really at Risk?

EADING AT RISK" is one of those hardy perennials, a government survey telling us that in some vital area — obesity, pollution, fuel depletion, quality of education, domestic relations — things are even worse than we thought. In the category of literacy, the old surveys seemed always to be some variant of "Why Johnny Can't Read." "Reading at Risk" — the most recent survey, carried out under the auspices of the National Endowment for the Arts as part of its larger Survey of Public Participation in the Arts, the whole conducted by the U.S. Census Bureau — doesn't for a moment suggest that Johnny Can't Read. The problem is that, now grown, Johnny (though a little less Jane) doesn't much care to read a lot in the way of imaginative writing — fiction, poems, plays — also known to the survey as literature. For the first time in our history, apparently, less than half the population bothers to read any literature (so defined) at all.

Such surveys are as meat and drink — perhaps pot and coke might be more precise — to editorialists, who can usually be counted on to discover their findings anywhere from worrying to alarming to frightening. They haul out their best solemn tone; words such as "distressing" and "grave concern" and "dire" are brought into play; look for "threat to democratic society" to pop up with some frequency; nor will "crisis" be in short supply; "serious action," one need scarcely add, is called for. Nothing remains, really, but to ring up the livery service and order the handbasket in which we, along with the culture, shall all presently ride off to hell.

"Reading at Risk" reports that there has been a decline in the reading of novels, poems, and plays of roughly ten percentage points for all age cohorts between 1982 and 2002, with actual numbers of readers having gained only slightly despite a large growth (of 40 million people) in the overall population. More women than men continue to participate in what the survey also calls literary reading — in his trip to the United States in 1905, based on attendance at his lectures, Henry James noted that culture in America belonged chiefly to women — though even among women the rate is slipping. Nor are things better among the so-called educated; while they do read more than the less educated, the decline in literary reading is also found among them. But the rate of decline is greatest among young adults eighteen to twenty-four years old, and the survey quotes yet another study, this one made by the National Institute for Literacy, showing that things are not looking any better for kids between thirteen and seventeen, but are even a little worse.

Although the general decline in literary reading is not attributed to any single cause in "Reading at Risk," the problem, it is hinted, may be the distractions of electronic culture. To quote an item from the survey's executive summary: "A 1999 study showed that the average American child lives in a household with 2.9 televisions, 1.8 VCRs, 3.1 radios, 2.1 CD players, 1.4 video game players, and 1 computer." By 2002, to quote from the same summary, "electronic spending had soared to 24 percent [of total recreational spending by Americans], while spending on books declined . . . to 5.6 percent." Up against all this easily accessible and endlessly varied fare — from BlackBerrys to iPods — the reading of stories, poems, and plays is having a tough time competing.

Many of the facts set out in "Reading at Risk" are less than shocking. Whites do more literary reading than blacks, who do more than Hispanic Americans, though the rate of reading in all three groups goes up with family income. Concomitantly, the rich and the college educated do more literary reading than people less well-off or less trained to read through advanced schooling. People who do such reading also tend to go to a lot more — roughly three times more — art museums, plays, concerts, operas, and other performing-arts events; they also participate more in civic affairs generally. Among the divisions of literary reading, fiction is read by roughly 96 million people (or 45 percent of the population), some form of poetry by 25 million people (or 12 percent of the population), while plays are read by 7 million people (or 4 percent of the population). The results of the "2002 Survey of Public Participation in the Arts" show that literary reading, then, is still a popular but declining leisure activity.

"Reading at Risk" does provide a few not exactly surprises but slight jars to one's expectations. For me, one is that "people in managerial, professional, and technical occupations are more likely to read literature than those in other occupation groups." I would myself have expected that these were all jobs in which one worked more than an eight-hour day and then took work home, which, consequently, would allow a good deal less time for reading things not in some way related to one's work. The survey also claims that readers are "highly social people," more active in their communities and participating more in sports. I should have thought that lots of reading might make one introspective, slightly detached, a touch reclusive even, but, according to the survey, not so. "People who live in the suburbs," the survey states, "are more likely to be readers than either those who live in the city or the country." Perhaps this is owing in good part to suburbs' being generally more affluent than cities; and, too, to book clubs, in which neighbors meet to discuss recent bestsellers and sometimes classics, and which tend to be suburban institutions.

The one area in which "Reading at Risk" is (honorably) shaky is in its conclusions on the subject of television, which is the standard fall guy in almost all surveys having to do with education. Only among people who watch more than four hours of television daily does the extent of reading drop off, according to the survey, while watching no television whatsoever makes it more likely one will be a more frequent reader. On the other hand, the presence of writers on television — on C-SPAN and talk shows — may, the survey concedes, encourage people to buy books. No mention is made of those people, myself among them, who are able to read with a television set, usually playing a sports event, humming away in the background.

In the end, "Reading at Risk" concludes that "it is not clear from [its] data how much influence TV watching has on literary reading." The survey does suggest that surfing the Internet may have made a dent in reading: "During the time period when the literature participation rates declined, home Internet use soared." But it does not take things further than that.

One mildly depressing finding of the survey is that the only increase in putatively literary activity is in the realm of creative writing. "In 1982, about 11 million people did some form of creative writing. By 2002, this number had risen to almost 15 million people (18 or older), an increase of about 30 percent." This is owing in part to the increase of creative-writing courses in universities and community colleges ("creative writing is most common among those under 25"), and perhaps, regrettably, to the increase of falsely inflated personal self-esteem, in which altogether too many people feel, quite wrongly, that they are artistic. (An earlier survey, run by a vanity-press company, claimed that 80 percent of Americans felt they had a book in them, which is also, in my view, bad news, for the vast majority of them don't.) In any case, the rise in creative writing set alongside the decrease in the reading of literature suggests that there is some truth to the old quip that holds one can either read or write books, but one can't really do both.

Two points of great importance about "Reading at Risk," and which cripple its significance, need to be underscored: first, that in its findings the *quality* of the reading being done is not taken into consideration; and, second, neither has serious nonfiction been tabulated. As for the quality of reading, the survey presumably counted mysteries, science fiction, bodice-ripping romances, and sentimental poetry as literature. The literature being read, in the reckoning of the survey, is, then, fairly likely not to be of a serious nature: more Tom Clancy than Ivan Turgenev is doubtless being registered, more Maya Angelou than Marianne Moore. The thought that 96 million people in our happily philistine country are regularly reading literature, even though it might represent a decline over twenty years earlier, would still be impressive, except for the fact that we don't know how many of them are reading, not to put too fine a point on it, crap.

The surveyors probably had no choice here, for setting a standard of what constitutes reading of genuine literary merit would entail vast complication. One can see a committee of literary panjandrums arguing into the night about whether to include, say, the novels of Alice Walker or John Galsworthy or Gore Vidal. But excluding serious nonfiction is perhaps a more radical problem. One could be reading a steady diet of Saint Augustine, Samuel Johnson, and John Ruskin and fall outside the boundaries of what the report calls "literary" readers. Given this exclusion, who can be certain that, for example, George Kennan, Jacques Barzun, or J. Robert Oppenheimer would have qualified as among the survey's readers of literature?

A great many people, of course, do a vast amount of reading, chiefly in newspapers, magazines, and on the Internet, but little of it in books and none of it in the realm of imaginative literature. For people who want merely information — just, or mainly, the facts, ma'am — there is no reason to presume that it is best available in the form of books. People bring so many motives to their reading — the need for consolation, the search for pleasure, a quest for the reinforcement of one's prejudices, the hunt for truth and wisdom — and no one can say with any certainty what they take away from it.

Still, skewed though "Reading at Risk" may be by these two items, the demographic fact remains that the audience for the reading of novels, poems, and plays, even junky ones, fell over the past twenty years from 56 percent to 47 percent of the nation's population. The decline, moreover, was across the board: "In fact," the survey has it, "literary reading rates decreased for men, women, all ethnic and racial groups, all education groups, and all age groups."

My own speculation is that our speeded-up culture — with its FedEx, fax, e-mail, channel surfing, cell-phoning, fast-action movies, and other elements in its relentless race against boredom — has ended in a shortened national attention span. The quickened rhythms of new technology are not rhythms congenial to the slow and time-consuming and solitary act of reading. Sustained reading, sitting quietly and enjoying the aesthetic pleasure that words elegantly deployed on the page can give, contemplating careful formulations of complex thoughts — these do not seem likely to be acts strongly characteristic of an already jumpy new century.

For all its shortcomings, "Reading at Risk" has set off some wild responses. The most extreme reaction to the survey I have seen was in an op-ed piece by Andrew Solomon in the *New York Times*. Under the ominous title "The Closing of the American Book," playing off Allan Bloom's *The Closing of the American Mind*, Solomon sets out what he feels are the frightening implications for a nation in which the reading of literature is radically in decline. The author of an autobiographical book on depression, Solomon believes that the passive activity of watching television, and not reading, is a serious factor in the spread of depression in our day. Escalating levels of Alzheimer's, too, he feels, can be ascribed to the lack of engagement of adult minds of the kind that reading is supposed to provide. What the decline in the reading of literature really means, according to Andrew Solomon, is that "the crisis in reading is a crisis in national health." Not reading, I believe he is saying, is bad for your health.

If that sounds a bit loony, don't be surprised, for reading is one of those subjects that, like religion, quickly get people worked up, their virtue glands pumping. Perhaps it is not going too far to say that for some people, reading is their religion. In the July 19, 2004, *Chicago Tribune*, W. Ralph Eubanks used the occasion of the publication of "Reading at Risk" to blame the Patriot Act, through its implication that reading is dangerous, for its potential for further discouraging reading. "These two events are completely unrelated," writes Eubanks, the director of publishing for the Library of Congress, who then proceeds to attempt to relate them. Eubanks reports that "at the heart of the NEA survey is the belief that our democratic system depends on leaders who can think critically, analyze texts, and write clearly." If this were true, the United States would have been done for around the time of Andrew Jackson.

W. Ralph Eubanks's statement reminds me of the time I sat on a panel on government and the arts with the playwright Edward Albee, who opened the proceeding by blithely announcing that, until such time as every member of Congress had a solid education in the arts, the country was in danger of lapsing into fascism. Eubanks himself lapses into mere self-congratulation, writing: "I learned to think clearly by reading great literature, even books that contained ideas I disagreed with or that disturbed me."

People who openly declare themselves passionate readers are, like Eubanks, usually chiefly stating their own virtue, and hence superiority, and hence, though they are unaware of it, snobbery. "So many books and so little time," reads a T-shirt that shows up occasionally at the farmers' market to which I go. "I adore reading," I have had people tell me, and then go from there to reveal that much of what they read is schlock, and of a fairly low order even for schlock. Young parents who read to their infant children are always delighted to report that the kids are mad for books; they take it as a sign, a premonition, of brilliance and success ahead.

The assumption — and it is also the assumption behind "Reading at Risk" — is that reading is, per se, good. But is it, immitigably and always? Surely everything depends upon what is being read and the degree of intelligence brought to the task. Even so powerful a reader as Samuel Johnson claimed that his indulgent reading of romances deepened his plunge into depression.

The unspoken assumption of Oprah's Book Club is that reading, like broccoli or sound dental hygiene, is intrinsically good for you. Something, albeit of minimal significance, to it, I suppose, but very minimal. When you are reading, after all, you are, ipso facto, not raping or pillaging. But might you as easily be wasting your time?

So what? It's still reading, Roscoe. And reading is good, even reading books that aren't themselves all that good. The reading of less than good books, after all, can lead to the reading of superior books, right? The argument that reading even junk is intrinsically a fine thing is a reverse on the old slippery-slope argument. Instead of slipping downward, the reverse-slippery-slope argument here holds that the reading of junky books is likely to lead in time to the reading of good ones. But literary culture has no supply side; it trickles neither down nor up.

Add the general dumbing down in the culture at large, and access to the good or great book becomes more improbable. As part of this dumbing down, popular culture cuts a wider and wider swath through higher education. Outside universities, the *New York Times Book Review* has long run what it calls "chronicles" of mystery and science fiction books, and has now added comics (or graphic novels) to its chronicles. If one ever wishes to retain one's fantasies about the good sense of the people in the realm of literary taste, one does best never to consult the bestseller lists.

As someone permitted the luxury of reading books during what for other people are working hours, I have long been surprised at the amount of reading that does get done in America, even though I believe, contra "Reading at Risk," that nowhere near 96 million Americans read serious books. So many other things nowadays demand time. The job, including getting to and returning from it; one's family, especially in our day when the rearing of children has become a full-time, full-court-press affair; friendships and community life; the various pleasing distractions that modern life affords the even mildly affluent in the form of sports, travel, entertainment, and much else. To me the shock isn't the discovery that Americans are reading less; it is the knowledge that we read as much as we do, though no one can say with any precision how much of this reading is really serious.

One of the statistical reportings of "Reading at Risk" that surprised me is the very low rate of reading among people over sixty-five. Among the middle classes, at any rate, adult education, which features much reading, would appear to be a highly attended activity. No doubt many older people attend such classes out of boredom or loneliness, but many more, I suspect, are trying to fill in some of the larger blank spots in their knowledge — to do, as a former student of my own once put it to me, a "second draft" of their own education.

If some people are too secure in their own virtuousness because of their reading, many more feel vastly insecure, sure they haven't read enough books, or the right books. They are even more certain that they will never catch up, and one day arrive at that august condition known as being "well read." The bad news is that, while some people are better read than others, nobody is well read enough, ever. Well read is a condition that, like perpetual happiness, cannot be achieved in this life. Anyone who has been bedeviled by feeling inadequate about his reading will take comfort, I hope, in Gertrude Stein's remark that the happiest day of her life was the day on which she realized she could not read even all the world's good books.

More and more books are published every year, which further complicates things, with bad books Greshamly helping to drive out good. According to one source, the number of books published in the United States in 2005 was a shelf-groaning 172,000, despite the decline in reading generally and the reported flatness of book sales.

"Reading at Risk" breaks down its readers into light (reading 1–5 books a year), moderate (6–11 books a year), frequent (12–49 books a year), and avid (50 or more books). Alexander Gerschenkron, the economic historian, who in his day passed for the most erudite man at Harvard, claimed to have read two books a week, outside of reading required by his profession. That meant that, over a fifty-year career of adult reading, he would have been able to read only five thousand or so books, a pathetic figure when one considers how many books there are in the world.

Like all surveys, "Reading at Risk" is an example of the style of statistical thinking dominant in our time. It's far from sure that statistics are very helpful in capturing so idiosyncratic an act as reading, except in a bulky and coarse way. That the Swedes read more novels, poems, and plays than Americans, and the Portuguese read fewer than we do, are statistical facts, but I'm not sure what to do with them, especially when you don't know the quality of the material being read in the three countries. The statistical style of thinking has currently taken over medicine, where it may have some role to play: I am, for example, taking a pill because a study has shown that 68 percent of the people who take this pill and have a certain condition live 33 percent longer than those who don't. Dopey though this is, I play the odds — the pill costs $1 a day — and go along. But I'm not sure that statistics have much to tell us about a cultural activity so private as reading books.

Serious reading has always been a minority matter. By "serious reading" I mean the reading of those novels, plays, and poems — also philosophies, histories, and other belletristic writing — that make the most exacting efforts to honor their subjects by treating them with the rich complexity they deserve. Serious readers at some point make a usually accidental connection with literature, sometimes through a teacher but quite as often on their own; when young they come upon a book that blows them away by the aesthetic pleasure they derive from it, the wisdom they find in it, the point of view it provides them.

Nor do the serious often come from places one might think. No one social class has a monopoly of them. Nor were they necessarily good students. When I was the editor of *The American Scholar,* the intellectual quarterly sponsored by Phi Beta Kappa, many people assumed the magazine was read by the 400,000-odd Phi Beta Kappas roaming around the world. Not so. When the magazine attempted an intensive direct-mail campaign to get Phi

Beta Kappas to subscribe, the results were dismal. What became plain was that merely being good at school didn't mean that these people had the least interest in things artistic or intellectual. More often than not they did as well as they did at school because they were by nature obedient or because they hoped to get into other (medical, law) schools, thence to earn a good living.

The final question that "Reading at Risk" avoids is the point of reading fiction, poems, and plays. It does send its readers, in its "Summary and Conclusions" section, to a perfectly sound classical statement of the case for reading, "What Use Is Literature?" by Myron Magnet, that originally appeared in *City Journal* and a key paragraph from which reads:

> Literature is a conversation across the ages about our experience and our nature, a conversation in which, while there isn't unanimity, there is a surprising breadth of agreement. Literature amounts, in these matters, to the accumulated wisdom of the race, the sum of our reflections on our own existence. It begins with observation, with reporting, rendering the facts of our inner and outer reality with acuity sharpened by imagination. At its greatest, it goes on to show how these facts have coherence and, finally, meaning. As it dramatizes what actually happens to concrete individuals trying to shape their lives at the confluence of so many imperatives, it presents us with concrete and particular manifestations of universal truths. For as the greatest authors know, the universal has to be embodied in the particular — where, as it is enmeshed in the complexity and contradictoriness of real experience, it loses the clarity and lucidity that only abstractions can possess.

That is a grand statement of the case, perhaps a little too thumpingly elevated for the taste and temper of our day, but I was struck in reading it by the penetrating ending of its final sentence, where the unusual and highly interesting claim is made that reading great imaginative literature helps us to lose "the clarity and lucidity that only abstractions can possess."

Ours is an age of abstractions. "Create a concept," Ortega y

Gasset said, "and reality leaves the room." Careful reading of great imaginative writing brings reality back into the room, by reminding us how much more varied, complicated, and rich it is than any social or political concept devised by human beings can hope to capture. Read Balzac and the belief in, say, reining in corporate greed through political reform becomes a joke; read Dickens and you'll know that no social class has any monopoly on noble behavior; read Henry James and you'll find the midlife crisis and other pop psychological constructs don't even qualify as stupid; read Dreiser and you'll be aware that the pleasures of power are rarely trumped by the advertised desire to do good.

Read any amount of serious imaginative literature with care and you will be highly skeptical of the statistical style of thinking. You will quickly grasp that, in a standard statistical report such as "Reading at Risk," serious reading, always a minority interest, isn't at stake here. Nothing more is going on, really, than the *crise du jour,* soon to be replaced by the report on eating disorders, the harmfulness of aspirin, or the drop in high school math scores.

The Perpetual Adolescent

WHENEVER ANYONE under the age of fifty sees an old newsreel film of Joe DiMaggio's fifty-six-game hitting streak of 1941, he is almost certain to be brought up by the fact that nearly everyone in the male-dominated crowds — in New York, Boston, Chicago, Detroit, Cleveland — seems to be wearing a suit and a fedora or other serious adult hat. The people in those earlier baseball crowds, though watching a boyish game, nonetheless had a radically different conception of themselves than most Americans do now. A major economic depression was ending, a world war was on. Even though they were watching an entertainment that took most of them back to their boyhoods, they thought of themselves as no longer kids but grown-ups, adults, men.

How different from today, when a good part of the crowd at any ball game, no matter what the age, is wearing jeans and team caps and T-shirts; and let us not neglect those (one hopes) benign maniacs who paint their faces in home-team colors or spell out, on their bare chests, the letters of the names of star players: S-O-S-A.

Part of the explanation for the suits at the ballpark in DiMaggio's day is that in the 1940s and even 1950s there weren't a lot of sport, or leisure, or casual clothes around. Unless one lived at what H. L. Mencken called "the country-club stage of culture" — unless, that is, one golfed, played tennis, or sailed — one was likely to own only the clothes one worked in or better. Far from casual Fridays, in those years there weren't even casual Sundays. Wearing one's "Sunday best," a cliché of the time, meant wearing the good clothes one reserved for church.

Dressing down may first have set in on the West Coast, where a certain informality was thought to be a new way of life. In the 1960s, in universities casual dress became *de rigueur* among younger faculty, who, in their ardor to destroy any evidence of their being implicated in evil hierarchy, wished not merely to seem in no wise different from their students but, more important, to seem always young; and the quickest path to youthfulness was teaching in jeans, T-shirts, and the rest of it.

This informality has now been institutionalized. Few are the restaurants that could any longer hope to stay in business if they required men to wear a jacket and tie. Today one sees men wearing baseball caps — some worn backward — while eating indoors in quite good restaurants. In an episode of *The Sopranos*, Tony Soprano, the boss of a Mafia family, representing life of a different day, finds this so outrages his sense of decorum that, in a restaurant he frequents, he asks a man, in a quiet but menacing way, to remove his goddamn hat.

Life in that different day was felt to observe the human equivalent of the Aristotelian unities: to have, like a good drama, a beginning, middle, and end. Each part, it was understood, had its own advantages and detractions, but the middle — adulthood — was the lengthiest and most earnest part, where everything serious happened and much was at stake. To violate the boundaries of any of the three divisions of life was to go against what was natural and thereby to appear unseemly, to put one's world somehow out of joint, to be, let us face it, a touch, and perhaps more than a touch, grotesque.

Today, of course, all this has been shattered. The ideal almost everywhere is to seem young for as long as possible. The health clubs and endemic workout clothes, the enormous increase in cosmetic surgery (for women and men), the youth-oriented television programming and moviemaking, all these are merely the more obvious signs of the triumph of youth culture. When I say "youth culture," I do not mean merely that the young today are transcendent, the group most admired among the various age groups in American society, but that youth is no longer viewed as a transitory state, through which one passes on the way from childhood to adulthood, but an aspiration, a vaunted condition in which, if one can only arrange it, to settle in perpetuity.

This phenomenon is not something that happened just last night; it has been under way for decades. Nor is it something that can be changed even by an event as cataclysmic as that of the September 11 terrorist attacks, which at first were thought to be so sobering as to tear away all shreds of American innocence. As a generalization, it allows for a wide variety of exceptions. There still are adults in America; if names are wanted, I would set out those of Alan Greenspan, Robert Rubin, Warren Buffett, and many more. But such men and women, actual grown-ups, now begin to appear a bit anomalous; they no longer seem representative of the larger culture.

The shift into youth culture began in earnest, I suspect, during the ten or so years following 1951, the year of the publication of *The Catcher in the Rye.* Salinger's novel exalts the purity of youth and locates the enemy — a clear case of Us versus Them — in those who committed the sin of having grown older, which includes Holden Caulfield's pain-in-the-neck parents, his brother (the sell-out screenwriter), and just about everyone else who has passed beyond adolescence and had the rather poor taste to remain alive.

The case for the exaltation of the young is made in Wordsworth's "Intimation of Immortality," with its idea that human beings are born with great wisdom from which life in society weans them slowly but inexorably. Plato promulgated this same idea long before: for him we all had wisdom in the womb, but it was torn from us at the exact point that we came into the world. Rousseau gave it a French twist, arguing that human beings are splendid all-round specimens — noble savages, really — with life out in society turning us mean and loutish, which is another way of saying that the older we are, the worse we get. We are talking about romanticism here, which never favors the mature, let alone the aged.

The triumph of youth culture has conquered perhaps nowhere more completely than in the United States. The John F. Kennedy administration, with its emphasis on youthfulness, beginning with its young president — the first president routinely not to wear a serious hat — gave it its first public prominence. Soon after the assassination of Kennedy, the Free Speech Movement, which spearheaded the student revolution, positively enshrined the young. Like Yeats's Byzantium, the sixties utopia posited by the student radicals was "no country for old men" or women. One of the many tenets in its credo — soon to become a cliché, but no less significant for that — was that no one over thirty was to be trusted. (If you were part of that movement and twenty-one years old in 1965, you are sixty-two today. Good morning, Sunshine.)

Music was a key element in the advance of youth culture. The dividing moment here is the advent of Elvis Presley. On one side were those who thought Elvis an amusing and largely freakish phenomenon — a bit of a joke, really — and on the other, those who took him dead seriously as a figure of youthful rebellion, the musical equivalent of James Dean in the movie *Rebel Without a Cause*, another early winning entry in the glorification-of-youth sweepstakes then forming. Rock 'n' roll presented a vinyl curtain, with those committed to retaining their youth on one side, those wanting to claim adulthood on the other. The Beatles, despite the very real charms of their non-druggie music, solidified things. So much of hard rock 'n' roll came down to nothing more than a way of saying bugger off to adult culture.

Reinforcement for these notions — they were not yet so coherent as to qualify as ideas — was to be found in the movies. Movies for some years now have been made not only increasingly for the young but by the young. I once worked on a movie script with a producer who one day announced to me that it was his birthday. When I wished him happy returns of the day, he replied that it wasn't so happy for him; he was turning forty-one, an uncomfort-

ably old age in Hollywood for someone who hadn't many big suc-
cess-scalps on his belt.

Robert Redford, though now seventy, remains essentially a guy
in jeans, a handsome graduate student with wrinkles. Paul Newman, now eighty, seems uncomfortable in a suit. Hugh Grant, the
English actor, may be said to be professionally boyish, and in one
role, in the movie *About a Boy,* is described in the *New York Times* as
a character who "surrounds himself with gadgets, videos, CDs,
and other toys" and who "is doing everything in his power to
avoid growing up." The actor Jim Carrey, who is in his mid-forties,
not long ago said of the movie *The Majestic,* in which he stars, "It's
about manhood. It's about adulthood," as if italicizing the rarity
of such movies. He then went on to speak about himself in standard self-absorbed adolescent fashion: "You've got that hole you're
left with by whatever your parents couldn't give you." Poor baby.

Jim Carrey's roles in movies resemble nothing so much as
comic-book characters come to life. And why, just now, does so
much of contemporary entertainment come in the form of animation or comic-book cartooning? Such television shows as *The
Simpsons* and *King of the Hill,* the occasional back page in the *New
York Times Book Review* or *The New Yorker* and the comic-book
novel, all seem to suggest that the animated cartoon and comic-
book formats are very much of the moment. They are of course
right, at least if you think of your audience as adolescents, or,
more precisely, as being unwilling quite to detach themselves from
their adolescence.

Recent history has seemed to be on the side of keeping people
from growing up by supplying only a paucity of stern tests of the
kind out of which adulthood is usually formed. We shall never
have another presidential candidate tested by the Depression or by
his experience in World War II. These were events that proved
crucibles for the formation of adult character, not to say manli-
ness. Henceforth all future presidential — and congressional — candidates will come with a shortage of what used to pass for significant experience. Crises for future politicians will doubtless be

about having to rethink their lives when they didn't get into Brown or found themselves unequipped emotionally for Stanford's business school.

Corporate talent these days feels no weightier. Pictures of heads of corporations in polo shirts with designer logos in the business section of the *New York Times,* fresh from yet another ephemeral merger, or news of a young honcho's acquiring an enormous raise after his company has recorded another losing year, do not inspire confidence. "The trouble with Enron," said an employee of the company in the aftermath of that corporation's appalling debacle, "is that there weren't any grown-ups."

The increasing affluence the United States enjoyed after World War II, extending into the current day, also contributed heavily to forming the character I've come to think of as the perpetual American adolescent. Earlier, with less money around, people were forced to get serious, to grow up — and fast. How quickly the Depression generation was required to mature! How many stories one used to hear about older brothers going to work at eighteen or earlier so that a younger brother might be allowed to go to college, or simply to help keep the family afloat! With lots of money around, certain kinds of pressure were removed. More and more people nowadays are working, as earlier generations were not, with a strong safety net of money under them. All options opened, they now swim in what Kierkegaard called "a sea of possibilities," and one of these possibilities in America is to refuse to grow up for a longer period than has been permitted any other people in history.

All this is reinforced by the play of market forces, which strongly encourage the mythical dream of perpetual youthfulness. The promise behind 95 percent of all advertising is that of recaptured youth, whose deeper promise is lots more sex yet to go. The ads for the $5,000 wristwatch, the $80,000 car, the khakis, the vodka, the pharmaceuticals to regrow hair and recapture ardor, all whisper, Display me, drive me, wear me, drink me, swallow me — and you stop the clock. Youth, baby, is yours.

The whole sweep of advertising, which is to say of market, culture since soon after World War II has been continually to lower the criteria of youthfulness while extending the possibility for seeming youthful to older and older people. To make the very young seem older—all those ten- and twelve-year-old Britney Spears and Jennifer Lopez imitators, who already know more about brand-name logos than I do about English literature—is another part of the job. It's not a conspiracy, mind you, not six or eight international ad agencies meeting in secret to call the shots, but the dynamics of marketing itself, finding a way to make it more profitable all around by convincing the young that they can seem older, and the old that they can seem a lot younger. Never before has it been more difficult to obey the injunction to act one's age.

Two of the great television sitcom successes of recent years, *Seinfeld* and *Friends,* though each is different in its comic tone, are united by the theme of the permanent adolescent loose in the big city. One takes the characters in *Seinfeld* to be in their middle to late thirties, those in *Friends* in their late twenties to early thirties. Charming though they may be, both sets of characters are oddly stunted. They aren't quite anywhere and don't seem to be headed anywhere, either. Time is suspended for them. Aimless and shameless, they are in the grip of the everyday *Sturm und Drang* of adolescent self-absorption. Outside their rather temporary-looking apartments, they scarcely exist. Personal relations provide the full drama of their lives. Growth and development aren't part of the deal. They are still, in spirit, locked in a high school of the mind, eating dry cereal, watching a vast quantity of television, hoping to make ecstatic sexual scores. Apart from the high sheen of the writing and the comic skill of the casts, I wonder if what really attracts people to these shows—*Friends* and *Seinfeld* still in their everlasting reruns—isn't the underlying identification with the characters because of the audience's own longing for a perpetual adolescence, cut loose, free of responsibility, without the real pressures that life, that messy business, always exerts.

For perpetual adolescents, time is curiously static. They are in no great hurry—to succeed, to get work, to lay down achievements. Perhaps this is partly because longevity has increased in recent decades — if one doesn't make it to ninety nowadays, one feels slightly cheated — but more likely it is that time doesn't seem to the perpetual adolescent the excruciatingly finite matter, the precious commodity, it indubitably is. For the perpetual adolescent, time is almost endlessly expandable. Why not go to law school in one's late thirties, or take the premed requirements in one's early forties, or wait even later than that to have children? Time enough to toss away one's twenties, maybe even one's thirties; forty is soon enough to get serious about life; maybe fifty, when you think about it, is the best time really to get going in earnest.

The old hunger for life, the eagerness to get into the fray, has been replaced by an odd patience that often looks more like passivity. In the 1950s, people commonly married in their twenties, which may or may not have been a good thing, but marriage did prove a forcing house into adulthood, especially where children issued from the marriage, which they usually did fairly quickly. I had two sons by the time I was twenty-six, which, among other things, made it impossible, either physically or spiritually, for me to join the youth movement of the 1960s, even though I still qualified by age. It also required me to find a vocation. By thirty, one was supposed to be settled in life: wife, children, house, job — "the full catastrophe," as Zorba the Greek liked to say. But it was also a useful catastrophe. Today most people feel that they can wait to get serious about life. Until then one is feeling one's way, still deciding, shopping around, contributing to the formation of a new psychological type: the passive-nonaggressive.

Not everywhere is nonaggression the psychological mode of choice. One hears about the young men and women working the fourteen-hour days at low-six-figure jobs in frontline law firms, others sacrificing to get into MBA programs for the single purpose of an early financial score. But even here one senses an adolescent spirit to the proceedings. The old model for ambition was solid hard work that paid off over time. One began at a low wage, worked one's way up through genuine accomplishment, grew wealthier as one grew older, and, with luck, retired with a sense of financial security and pleasure in one's achievement. But the new American ambition model features the kid multimillionaire — the young man or woman who breaks the bank not long out of college. An element of adolescent impatience enters in here — I want it, *now!* — and also an element of continued youthfulness.

The model of the type may be the professional athlete. "The growth of professional basketball over the past twenty-odd years, from a relatively minor spectator sport to a mass-cultural phenomenon," notes Rebecca Mead in *The New Yorker,* "is an example of the way in which all of American culture is increasingly geared to the tastes of teenage boys." Mead writes this in an article about Shaquille O'Neal, the center for the Miami Heat, who earns, not counting endorsements, $20 million a year and lives the life of the most privileged possible junior high school boy: enjoying food fights, go-carts, motorcycles, the run of high rides at amusement parks. It may be a wonderful, but it's also a strange, life.

And yet what is so wrong about any of this? If one wants to dress like a kid, spin around the office on a scooter, not make up one's mind about what work one wants to do until one is forty, be noncommittal in one's relationships — what, really, are the consequences? I happen to think that the consequences are genuine, and fairly serious.

"Obviously it is normal to think of oneself as younger than one is," W. H. Auden, a younger son, told Robert Craft, "but fatal to want to be younger." I'm not sure about fatal, but it is at a minimum degrading for a culture at large to want to be younger. The tone of national life is lowered, made less rich. The first thing lowered is expectations, intellectual and otherwise. To begin with education, one wonders if the dumbing down of culture one used to hear so much about and which continues isn't connected to the rise of the perpetual adolescent.

Consider contemporary journalism, which tends to play everything to lower and lower common denominators. Why does the *New York Times,* with its pretensions to being our national newspaper, choose to put on its front pages stories about Gennifer Flowers's career as a chanteuse in New Orleans, the firing of NFL coaches, the retirement of Yves Saint-Laurent, the canceling of the singer Mariah Carey's recording contract? Slow news days is a charitable guess; a lowered standard of the significant is a more realistic one. Since the advent of its new publisher, a man of the baby-boom generation, an aura of juvenilia clings to the paper. Frank Rich and Maureen Dowd, two of the paper's most-read columnists, seem not so much the type of the bright college student but of the sassy high school student—the clever, provocative editor of the school paper out to shock the principal—even though both are in their fifties.

Television comes closer and closer to being a wholly adolescent form of communication. Clicking the remote from major-network news shows, one slides smoothly from superficiality to triviality. When Brian Williams announces that some subject will be covered "in depth," what he really means is that roughly ninety seconds, perhaps two minutes, will be devoted to it. It's scarcely original to note that much of contemporary journalism, print and electronic, is pitched to the short attention span, the sound bite, photo op, quickie take, the deep distaste for complexity—in short, so much is pitched to the adolescent temperament.

Political correctness and so many of the political fashions of our day, from academic feminism to cultural studies to queer theory, could be perpetrated only on adolescent minds—minds, that is, that are trained to search out one thing and one thing only: is my teacher, or this politician, or that public spokesman, saying something that is likely to be offensive to me or members of any other victim group? Only an adolescent would find it worthwhile to devote his or her attention chiefly to the hunting of offenses, the possibility of slights, real and imagined.

Self-esteem, of which one currently hears so much, is at bottom another essentially adolescent notion. The great psychological sin of our day is to violate the self-esteem of adolescents of all ages. One might have thought that such self-esteem as any of us is likely to command would be in place by the age of eighteen. (And what is the point of having all that much self-esteem anyhow, since its logical culminating point can only be smug complacence?) Even in nursing homes, apparently, patients must be guarded against a feeling of their lowered consequence in the world. Self-esteem has become a womb-to-tomb matter, so that in contemporary America the inner and the outer child can finally be made one in the form of the perpetual adolescent.

The coarsening of American culture seems part of the adolescent phenomenon. Television commercials have gotten grosser and grosser. The level of profanity on prime-time television shows has risen greatly over the years. Flicks known to their audiences as "gross-out movies," featuring the slimy and hideous, are part of the regular film menu. Florence King, writing about this phenomenon in her column in the *National Review*, noted: "Since arrested development is as American as apple pie, it is easy to identify the subconscious motivation of the adult male Ughs who produce all these revolting movies and commercials." What makes these things possible is what is known as "niche programming," or the aiming of entertainment at quite specific segments of the audience — African Americans, or teenagers, or the upper middle class, or the beer brutes. But increasingly, apparently, we are all being forced into that largest of niches, the American adolescent mentality.

Consider now what must be taken as the most consequential adolescent act in American history during the past half century, the Bill Clinton–Monica Lewinsky relationship. I hesitate to call it an affair, because an affair implies a certain adult style: the good hotel room, the bottle of excellent wine, the peignoir, the Sulka pajamas. With Bill and Monica, you had instead the pizza, the canoodling under the desk, the cigar business, even the whole thing going without consummation. No matter what one's politics, one has to admit that our great national scandal was pure high school.

In a 1959 review of Iona and Peter Opie's *The Lore and Language of School Children*, the poet Philip Larkin revealed first sensing a sharp waning of his interest in Christianity when he read the Bible verse that promises one will return to one's childish state upon entry into heaven. Larkin wanted nothing more to do with being a child or with the company of children. He looked forward to "money, keys, wallets, letters, books, long-playing records, drinks, the opposite sex, and other solaces of adulthood."

I wanted these things, too, and as soon as possible. From roughly the age of fourteen, I wanted to stay out all night, to dress like Fred Astaire, to drink and smoke cigarettes with the elegance of William Powell, to have the company of serious women like Susan Hayward and Ingrid Bergman. As I grew older, I sadly began to realize it wasn't going to happen, at least not in the way I had hoped. What happened instead was the triumph of youth culture, with its adoration of youth, in and for itself, and as a time in one's life of purity and goodness always in danger of being despoiled by the corruption of growing older, which is also to say, of "growing up."

At a certain point in American life, the young ceased to be viewed as a transient class and youth as a phase of life through which everyone soon passed. Instead, youthfulness was vaunted and carried a special moral status. Adolescence triumphed, becoming a permanent condition. As one grew older, one was presented with two choices: to seem an old fogey for attempting to live according to one's own standard of adulthood, or to go with the flow and adapt some variant of pulling one's long gray hair back into a ponytail, struggling into the spandex shorts, working on those abs, and ending one's days among the Rip Van With-Its. Not, I think, a handsome set of alternatives.

The greatest sins, Santayana thought, are those that set out to strangle human nature. This is of course what is being done in cultivating perpetual adolescence, while putting off maturity for as long as possible. Maturity provides a more articulated sense of the ebb and flow, the ups and downs, of life, a more subtly reticulated graph of human possibility. Above all, it values a clear and fit conception of reality. Maturity is ever cognizant that the clock is running, life is finite, and among the greatest mistakes is to believe otherwise. Maturity doesn't exclude playfulness or high humor. Far from it. The mature understand that the bitterest joke of all is that the quickest way to grow old lies in the hopeless attempt to stay forever young.

The Culture of Celebrity

C ELEBRITY at this moment in America is epidemic, and it's spreading fast, sometimes seeming as if nearly everyone has got it. Television provides celebrity dance contests, celebrities take part in reality shows, perfumes carry the names not merely of designers but of actors and singers. Without celebrities, whole sections of the *New York Times* and the *Washington Post* would have to close down. So pervasive has celebrity become in contemporary American life that one now begins to hear a good deal about a phenomenon known as the Culture of Celebrity.

The word "culture" no longer, I suspect, stands in most people's minds for that whole congeries of institutions, relations, kinship patterns, linguistic forms, and the rest for which the early anthropologists meant it to stand. Words, unlike disciplined soldiers, refuse to remain in place and take orders. They insist on being unruly, and slither and slide around, picking up all sorts of slippery and even strange meanings. An icon doesn't stay a small picture of a religious personage but usually turns out currently to be someone with spectacular grosses. "The language," as Flaubert once protested in his attempt to tell his mistress Louise Colet how much he loved her, "is inept."

Today, when people glibly refer to "the corporate culture," "the culture of poverty," "the culture of journalism," "the culture of the intelligence community" — and "community" has, of course, itself become another of those hopelessly baggy-pants words, so that one hears talk even of "the homeless community" — what I think is meant by "culture" is the general emotional atmosphere and institutional character surrounding the word to which "culture" is attached. Thus, corporate culture is thought to breed selfishness practiced at the Machiavellian level; the culture of poverty, hopelessness and despair; the culture of journalism, a taste for the sensational combined with a short attention span; the culture of the intelligence community, covering-one's-own-behind viperishness; and so on. Culture used in this way is also brought in to explain unpleasant or at least dreary behavior. "The culture of NASA has to be changed" is a sample of its current usage. The comedian Flip Wilson, after saying something outrageous, would revert to the refrain line "The debbil made me do it." So, today, when admitting to unethical or otherwise wretched behavior, people often say, "The culture made me do it."

As for "celebrity," the standard definition is no longer the dictionary one but rather closer to the one that Daniel Boorstin gave in his book *The Image; or, What Happened to the American Dream:* "The celebrity," Boorstin wrote, "is a person who is well-known for his well-knownness," which is improved in its frequently misquoted form as "A celebrity is someone famous for being famous." The other standard quotation on this subject is Andy Warhol's "In the future everyone will be world-famous for fifteen minutes," which also frequently turns up in an improved misquotation as "Everyone will have his fifteen minutes of fame."

But to say that a celebrity is someone well known for being well known, though clever enough, doesn't quite cover it. Not that there is a shortage of such people who seem to be known only for their well-knownness. What do a couple named Sid and Mercedes Bass do except appear in boldface in the *New York Times* Sunday Styles section and other such venues (as we now call them) of equally shimmering insignificance, often standing next to Ahmet and Mica Ertegun, also well known for being well known? Many moons ago, journalists used to refer to royalty as "face cards"; today celebrities are perhaps best thought of as bold faces, for as such do their names often appear in the press (and in a *New York Times* column with that very name, "Bold Face").

The distinction between celebrity and fame is one most dictionaries tend to fudge. I suspect everyone has, or prefers to make, his own. The one I like derives not from Aristotle, who didn't have to trouble with celebrities, but from the career of Ted Williams. A sportswriter once said that Williams wished to be famous but had no interest in being a celebrity. What Ted Williams wanted to be famous for was his hitting. He wanted everyone who cared about baseball to know that he was — as he believed and may well have been — the greatest pure hitter who ever lived. What he didn't want to do was to take on any of the effort off the baseball field involved in making this known. As an active player, Williams gave no interviews, signed no baseballs or photographs, chose not to be obliging in any way to journalists or fans. A rebarbative character, not to mention often a slightly menacing s.o.b., Williams, if you had asked him, would have said that it was enough that he was the last man to hit .400; he did it on the field, and therefore didn't have to sell himself off the field. As for his duty to his fans, he didn't see that he had any.

Whether Ted Williams was right or wrong to feel as he did is of less interest than the distinction his example provides, which suggests that fame is something one earns — through talent or achievement of one kind or another — while celebrity is something one cultivates or, possibly, has thrust upon one. The two are not, of course, entirely exclusive. One can be immensely talented and full of achievement and yet wish to broadcast one's fame further through the careful cultivation of celebrity; and one can have the thinnest of achievements and be talentless and yet be made to seem otherwise through the mechanics and dynamics of celebrity-creation, in our day a whole mini- (or maybe not so mini) industry of its own.

Or, another possibility, one can become a celebrity with scarcely any pretense to talent or achievement whatsoever. Much modern celebrity seems the result of careful promotion or great good luck or something besides talent and achievement: Mr. Donald Trump,

Ms. Paris Hilton, Mr. Regis Philbin, take a bow. The ultimate celebrity of our time may have been John F. Kennedy, Jr., notable only for being his parents' very handsome son—both his birth and good looks factors beyond his control—and, alas, known for nothing else whatsoever now except for the sad, dying-young-Adonis end to his life.

Fame, then, at least as I prefer to think of it, is based on true achievement; celebrity on the broadcasting of that achievement, or the inventing of something that, if not scrutinized too closely, might pass for achievement. Celebrity suggests ephemerality, while fame has a chance of lasting, a shot at reaching the happy shores of posterity.

Oliver Goldsmith, in his poem "The Deserted Village," refers to "good fame," which implies that there is also a bad or false fame. Bad fame is sometimes thought to be fame in the present, or fame on earth, while good fame is that bestowed by posterity — those happy shores again. (Which doesn't eliminate the desire of most of us, at least nowadays, to have our fame here and hereafter, too.) Not false but wretched fame is covered by the word "infamy" — "Infamy, infamy, infamy," remarked the English wit Frank Muir, "they all have it in for me" — while the lower, or pejorative, order of celebrity is covered by the word "notoriety," also frequently misused to mean noteworthiness.

Leo Braudy's magnificent book on the history of fame, *The Frenzy of Renown*, illustrates how the means of broadcasting fame have changed over the centuries: from having one's head engraved on coins, to purchasing statuary of oneself, to (for the really high rollers—Alexander the Great, the Caesar boys) naming cities or even months after oneself, to commissioning painted portraits, to writing books or having books written about one, and so on into our day of the publicity or press agent, the media blitz, the public-relations expert, and the egomaniacal blogger. One of the most successful of public-relations experts, Ben Sonnenberg, Sr., used to say that he saw it as his job to construct very high pedestals for very small men.

Which leads one to a very proper suspicion of celebrity. As

George Orwell said about saints, so it seems only sensible to say about celebrities: they should all be judged guilty until proven innocent. Guilty of what, precisely? I'd say of the fraudulence (however minor) of inflating their brilliance, accomplishments, worth, of passing themselves off as something they aren't, or at least are not quite. If fraudulence is the crime, publicity is the means by which the caper is brought off.

Is the current heightened interest in the celebrated sufficient to form a culture — a culture of a kind worthy of study? The anthropologist Alfred Kroeber defined culture, in part, as embodying "values which may be formulated (overtly as mores) or felt (implicitly as in folkways) by the society carrying the culture, and which it is part of the business of the anthropologist to characterize and define." What are the values of celebrity culture? They are the values, almost exclusively, of publicity. Did they spell one's name right? What was the size and composition of the audience? Did you check the receipts? Was the timing right? Publicity is concerned solely with effects and does not investigate causes or intrinsic value too closely. For example, a few years ago a book of mine called *Snobbery: The American Version* received what I thought was a too greatly mixed review in the *New York Times Book Review.* I remarked on my disappointment to the publicity man at my publisher's, who promptly told me not to worry: it was a full-page review, on page 11, right-hand side. That, he said, "is very good real estate," which was quite as important as, perhaps more important than, the reviewer's actual words and final judgment. Better to be tepidly considered on page 11 than extravagantly praised on page 27, left-hand side. Real estate, man, it's the name of the game.

We must have new names, Marcel Proust presciently noted — in fashion, in medicine, in art, there must always be new names. It's a very smart remark, and the fields Proust chose seem smart, too, at least for his time. (Now there must also be new names, at a minimum, among movie stars and athletes and politicians.) Implicit in Proust's remark is the notion that if the names don't really exist, if the quality isn't there to sustain them, it doesn't matter;

new names we shall have in any case. And every sophisticated society somehow, more or less implicitly, contrives to supply them.

I happen to think that we haven't had a major poet writing in English since perhaps the death of W. H. Auden or, to lower the bar a little, Philip Larkin. But new names are put forth nevertheless — high among them in recent years has been that of Seamus Heaney — because, after all, what kind of a time could we be living in if we didn't have a major poet? And besides, there are all those prizes that, year after year, must be given out, even if so many of the recipients don't seem quite worthy of them.

Considered as a culture, celebrity does have its institutions. We now have an elaborate celebrity-creating machinery well in place — all those short-attention-span television shows (*Entertainment Tonight, Access Hollywood*); all those magazines (beginning with *People* and far from ending with the *National Enquirer*). We have high-priced celebrity-mongers — Barbara Walters, Diane Sawyer, Jay Leno, David Letterman, Oprah — who not only live off others' celebrity but also, through their publicity-making power, confer it and have in time become very considerable celebrities each in his or her own right.

Without the taste for celebrity, they would have to close down the whole Style section of every newspaper in the country. Then there is the celebrity profile (in *Vanity Fair, Esquire, Gentlemen's Quarterly*; these are nowadays usually orchestrated by a press agent, with all touchy questions declared out-of-bounds), or the television talk-show interview with a star, which is beyond parody. Well, *almost* beyond: Martin Short in his parody of a talk-show host remarked to the actor Kiefer Sutherland, "You're Canadian, aren't you? What's that all about?"

Yet we still seem never to have enough celebrities, so we drag in so-called It Girls (Paris Hilton, Cindy Crawford, other supermodels), tired television hacks (Regis Philbin, Ed McMahon), back-achingly boring but somehow sacrosanct retired news anchors (Walter Cronkite, Tom Brokaw). Toss in what I think of as the lower-class punditi, who await calls from various television news and chat shows to demonstrate their locked-in political views and meager expertise on network and cable stations alike: Pat Buchanan, Eleanor Clift, Mark Shields, Robert Novak, Michael Beschloss, and the rest. Ah, if only Lenny Bruce were alive today, he could do a scorchingly cruel bit about Dr. Joyce Brothers sitting by the phone wondering why Jerry Springer never calls.

Many of our current-day celebrities float upon hype, which is really a publicist's gas used to pump up and set aloft something that doesn't quite exist. Hype has also given us a new breakdown, or hierarchical categorization, of celebrities. Until twenty-five or so years ago great celebrities were called "stars," a term first used in the movies and entertainment and then taken up by sports, politics, and other fields. Stars proving a bit drab, "superstars" were called in to play, this term beginning in sports but fairly quickly branching outward. Apparently too many superstars were about, so the trope was switched from astronomy to religion, and we now have "icons." All this takes Proust's original observation a step further: the need for new names to call the new names.

This new ranking—stars, superstars, icons—helps us believe that we live in interesting times. One of the things celebrities do for us is suggest that in their lives they are fulfilling our fantasies. Modern celebrities, along with their fame, tend to be wealthy or, if not themselves beautiful, able to acquire beautiful lovers. Their celebrity makes them, in the view of many, worthy of worship. "So long as man remains free," Dostoyevsky writes in the Grand Inquisitor section of *The Brothers Karamazov*, "he strives for nothing so incessantly and painfully as to find someone to worship." If contemporary celebrities are the best thing on offer as living gods for us to worship, this is not good news.

But the worshiping of celebrities by the public tends to be thin, and not uncommonly it is nicely mixed with loathing. We also, after all, at least partially, like to see our celebrities as frail, ready at all times to crash and burn. Cary Grant once warned the then young director Peter Bogdanovich, who was then living with Cybill Shepherd, to stop telling people he was in love. "And above all," Grant warned, "stop telling them you're happy." When

Bogdanovich asked why, Cary Grant answered, "Because they're not in love and they're not happy . . . Just remember, Peter, people do not like beautiful people."

Grant's assertion is borne out by our grocery press — the *National Enquirer,* the *Star,* the *Globe,* and other variants of the English gutter press. All these tabloids could as easily travel under the generic title of the *National Schadenfreude,* for more than half the stories they contain fall under the category of "See How the Mighty Have Fallen": Oh, my, I see where that bright young television sitcom star, on a drug binge again, had to be taken to a hospital in an ambulance! To think that the handsome movie star has been cheating on his wife all these years — snakes loose in the Garden of Eden, evidently! Did you note that the powerful senator's drinking has caused him to embarrass himself yet again in public? I see where that immensely successful Hollywood couple turn out to have had a child who died of anorexia! Who'd've thought?

How pleasing to learn that our own simpler, less moneyed, unglamorous lives are, in the end, much to be preferred to those of these beautiful, rich, and powerful people, whose vast publicity has diverted us for so long and whose fall proves even more diverting now. "As would become a lifelong habit for most of us," Thomas McGuane writes in his short story "Ice," "we longed to witness spectacular achievement and mortifying failure. Neither of these things, we were discreetly certain, would ever come to us; we would instead be granted the frictionless lives of the meek."

Along with trying to avoid falling victim to schadenfreude, celebrities, if they are clever, do well to regulate the amount of publicity they allow to cluster around them. Celebrities are in danger of becoming publicity bores, though few among them seem to sense it. Because of improperly rationed publicity, along with a substantial helping of self-importance, the comedian Bill Cosby will never again be funny. The actress Elizabeth McGovern said of Sean Penn that he "is brilliant, *brilliant* at being the kind of reluctant celebrity." Saul Bellow used to work this bit quite well on the literary front, making every interview (and there have been hundreds of them) feel as if given only with the greatest reluctance, if not under actual duress. Others are brilliant at regulating their publicity. Johnny Carson was very intelligent about husbanding his celebrity, choosing not to come out of retirement, except at exactly the right time or when the perfect occasion presented itself. Apparently it never did. Given the universally generous obituary tributes he received, dying now looks, for him, to have been an excellent career move.

Careful readers will have noticed that I referred above to "the actress Elizabeth McGovern" and felt no need to write anything before or after the name Sean Penn. True celebrities need nothing said of them in apposition, fore or aft. The greatest celebrities are those who don't even require their full names mentioned: Marilyn, Johnny, Liz, Liza, Oprah, Michael (could be Jordan or Jackson — context usually clears this up fairly quickly), Kobe, Martha (Stewart, not Washington), Britney, Shaq, J-Lo, Frank (Sinatra, not Perdue), O.J., and, with the fastest recognition and shortest name of all — trumpets here, please — W.

One has the impression that being a celebrity was easier at any earlier time than it is now, when celebrity-creating institutions, from paparazzi to gutter-press exposés to television talk shows, weren't as intense, as full-court press, as they are today. In the *Times Literary Supplement,* a reviewer of a biography of Margot Fonteyn noted that Miss Fonteyn "was a star from a more respectful age of celebrity, when keeping one's distance was still possible." My own candidate for the perfect celebrity in the twentieth century would be Noël Coward, a man in whom talent combined with elegance to give off the glow of glamour — and also a man who would have known how to fend off anyone wishing to investigate his private life. Today, instead of elegant celebrities, we have celebrity criminal trials: Michael Jackson, Kobe Bryant, Martha Stewart, Robert Blake, Winona Ryder, and O. J. Simpson. Schadenfreude is in the saddle again.

American society in the twenty-first century, received opinion has it, values only two things: money and celebrity. Whether or not this is true, vast quantities of money, we know, will buy celebrity. The very rich—John D. Rockefeller and powerful people of his era—used to hire press agents to keep their names out of the papers. But today one of the things money buys is a place at the table beside the celebrated, with the celebrities generally delighted to accommodate, there to share some of the glaring light. An example is Mort Zuckerman, who made an early fortune in real estate, has bought magazines and newspapers, and is now himself among the punditi, offering his largely unexceptional political views on *The McLaughlin Group* and other television chat shows. Which is merely another way of saying that, whether or not celebrity in and of itself constitutes a culture, it has certainly penetrated and permeated much of American culture.

Such has been the reach of celebrity culture in our time that it has long ago entered into academic life. The celebrity professor has been on the scene for more than three decades. As long ago as 1962, in fact, I recall hearing that Oscar Cargill, in those days a name of some note in the English department of New York University, had tried to lure the then young Robert Brustein, a professor of theater and the drama critic for the *New Republic,* away from Columbia. Cargill had said to Brustein, "I'm not going to bullshit you, Bob, we're looking for a star, and you're it." Brustein apparently wasn't looking to be placed in a new constellation, and remained at Columbia, at least for a while longer, before moving on to Yale and thence to Harvard.

The academic star, who is really the academic celebrity, is now a fairly common figure in what the world, that ignorant ninny, reckons the Great American Universities. Richard Rorty is such a star, so is Henry Louis Gates, Jr. (who as "Skip" even has some celebrity nickname recognition), and, at a slightly lower level, there are Marjorie Garber, Eve Sedgwick, Stanley Fish, and perhaps now Stephen Greenblatt. Stanley Fish doesn't even seem to mind that much of his celebrity is owed to his being portrayed in novels by David Lodge as an indefatigable, grubby little operator (though Lodge claims to admire Fish's happy vulgarity). Professors Garber and Sedgwick seem to have acquired their celebrity through the outrageousness of the topics they've chosen to write about.

By measure of pure celebrity, Cornel West is, at the moment, the star of all academic stars, a man called by *Newsweek* "an eloquent prophet with attitude." (A bit difficult, I think, to imagine *Newsweek* or any other publication writing something similar of Lionel Trilling, Walter Jackson Bate, Marjorie Hope Nicolson, or John Hope Franklin.) He records rap CDs and appears at benefits with movie stars and famous athletes. When the president of Harvard spoke critically to West about his work not constituting serious scholarship (as if that had anything to do with anything), it made front-page news in the *New York Times*. When West left Harvard in indignation, he was instantly welcomed by Princeton. If West had been a few kilowatts more the celebrity than he is, he might have been able to arrange for the firing of the president of the university, the way certain superstars in the National Basketball Association — Magic Johnson, Isiah Thomas, Larry Bird, Michael Jordan — were able, if it pleased them, to have their coaches fired.

Genuine scholarship, the power of ratiocination glowing brightly in the classroom, is distinctly not what makes an academic celebrity or, if you prefer, superstar. What makes an academic celebrity, for the most part, is exposure, which is ultimately publicity. Exposure can mean appearing in the right extra-academic magazines or journals: the *New York Review of Books,* the *London Review of Books,* the *Atlantic Monthly; Harper's Magazine* and the *New Republic* possibly qualify, as do occasional cameo performances on the op-ed pages of the *New York Times* or the *Washington Post.* Having one's face pop up on the right television and radio programs — PBS and NPR certainly, and enough of the right kinds of appearances on C-SPAN — does not hurt. A commercially successful, much-discussed book helps hugely.

So does strong public alignment with the correct political causes. Harvey Mansfield, the political philosopher at Harvard, is a secondary academic celebrity of sorts, but not much in demand, owing to his conservatism; Shelby Steele, a black professor of English who has been critical of various aspects of African-American politics, was always overlooked during the days when universities knocked themselves out to get black professors. Both men have been judged politically incorrect. The underlying and overarching point is, to become an academic celebrity, you have to promote yourself outside the academy, but in careful and subtle ways.

One might once have assumed that the culture of celebrity was chiefly about show business and the outer edges of the arts, occasionally touching on the academy (there cannot be more than twenty or so academic superstars). But it has also much altered intellectual life generally. The past ten years or so have seen the advent of the public intellectual. There are good reasons to feel uncomfortable with that adjective "public," which drains away much of the traditional meaning of "intellectual." An intellectual is someone who is excited by and lives off and in ideas. An intellectual has traditionally been a person unaffiliated, which is to say someone unbeholden to anything but the power of his or her ideas. Intellectuals used to be freelance, until fifty or so years ago, when jobs in the universities and in journalism began to open up to some among them.

Far from being devoted to ideas for their own sake, the intellectual equivalent of art for art's sake, the so-called public intellectual of our day is usually someone who comments on what is in the news, in the hope of affecting policy, or events, or opinion in line with his own political position or orientation. He isn't necessarily an intellectual at all, but merely someone who has read a few books, mastered a style, a jargon, and a maven's authoritative tone, and has a clearly demarcated political line.

But even when the public intellectual isn't purely tied to the news or isn't thoroughly political, what he or she really is, or ought to be called, is a publicity intellectual. In Richard A. Posner's interesting book *Public Intellectuals,* intellectuals are in one place ranked by the number of media mentions they and their work have garnered, which, if I am correct about publicity being at the heart of the enterprise of the public intellectual, may be crude but is not foolish. Not knowledge, it turns out, but publicity is power.

The most celebrated intellectuals of our day have been those most skillful at gaining publicity for their writing and their pronouncements. Take, as a case very much in point, Susan Sontag. When Susan Sontag died in December 2004, her obituary was front-page news in the *New York Times,* and in the inside of the paper it ran to a full page with five photographs, most of them carefully posed — a variety, it does not seem unfair to call it, of intellectual cheesecake. Will the current prime ministers of England and France when they peg out receive equal space or pictorial coverage? Unlikely, I think. Why did Sontag, who was, let it be said, in many ways the pure type of the old intellectual — unattached to any institution, earning her living (apart from MacArthur Foundation and other grants) entirely from her ideas as she put them in writing — why did she attract the attention she did?

I don't believe Susan Sontag's celebrity finally had much to do with the power or cogency of her ideas. Her most noteworthy idea was not so much an idea at all but a description of a style, a kind of reverse or anti-style, that went by the name of Camp and that was gay in its impulse. Might it have been her politics? Yes, politics had a lot to do with it, even though when she expressed herself on political subjects, she frequently got things mightily askew. To cheer up the besieged people of Sarajevo, she brought them a production of Samuel Beckett's *Waiting for Godot.* She announced in *The New Yorker* that the killing of three thousand innocent people on 9/11 was an act that America had brought on itself. As for the writing that originally brought her celebrity, she later came to apologize for *Against Interpretation,* her most influential single book. I do not know any people who claim to have derived keen pleasure from her fiction. If all this is roughly so, why, then, do you suppose that Susan Sontag was easily the single most celebrated — the greatest celebrity — intellectual of our time?

With the ordinary female professor's face and body, I don't think Ms. Sontag would quite have achieved the same celebrity. Her attractiveness as a young woman had a great deal to do with the extent of her celebrity, and she and her publisher took that (early) physical attractiveness all the way out. From reading Carl

Rollyson and Lisa Paddock's biography *Susan Sontag: The Making of an Icon,* one gets a sense of how relentlessly she was promoted by her publisher, Roger Straus. I do not mean to say that Sontag was unintelligent or talentless, but Straus, through having her always dramatically photographed, by sending angry letters to the editors of journals where she was ill reviewed, by bringing out her books with the most careful accompanying orchestration, promoted this often difficult and unrewarding writer into something close to a household name with a face that was ready, so to say, to be Warholed. That Sontag spent her last years with Annie Leibovitz, herself the most successful magazine photographer of our day, seems somehow the most natural thing in the world. Even in the realm of the intellect, celebrities are not born but made, usually very carefully made — as was, indubitably, the celebrity of Susan Sontag.

One of the major themes in Leo Braudy's *The Frenzy of Renown* is the fame and celebrity of artists, and above all writers. To sketch in a few bare strokes the richly complex story Braudy tells, writers went from serving power (in Rome) to serving God (in early Christendom), to serving patrons (in the eighteenth century), to serving themselves, with an eye cocked toward both the contemporary public and posterity (under romanticism), to serving mammon, to a state of interesting confusion, which is where we are today, with celebrity affecting literature in more and more significant ways.

Writers are supposed to be aristocrats of the spirit, not promoters, hustlers, salesmen for their own work. Securing a larger audience for their work was not thought to be their problem. "Fit audience, though few," in John Milton's phrase, was all right, so long as the few were artistically alert or aesthetically fit. Picture Lord Byron, Count Tolstoy, or Charles Baudelaire at a lectern at Barnes & Noble, C-SPAN camera turned on, flogging (wonderful word!) his own most recent book. Not possible!

Some superior writers have been very careful caretakers of their careers. In a letter to one of his philosophy professors at Harvard, T. S. Eliot wrote that there were two ways to achieve literary celebrity in London: one was to appear often in a variety of publications, the other to appear seldom but always to make certain to dazzle when one did. Eliot chose the latter, and it worked smashingly. But he was still counting on gaining his reputation through his actual writing. Now good work alone doesn't quite seem to make it; the publicity catapults need to be hauled into place, the walls of indifference stormed. Some writers have decided to steer shy from publicity altogether: Thomas Pynchon for one, J. D. Salinger for another (if he is actually still writing or yet considers himself a writer). But actively seeking publicity was thought, for a writer, vulgar — at least it was until the last few decades.

Edmund Wilson, the famous American literary critic, used to answer requests with a postcard that read:

> Edmund Wilson regrets that it is impossible for him to: Read manuscripts, Write articles or books to order, Make statements for publicity purposes, Do any kind of editorial work, Judge literary contests, Conduct educational courses, Deliver lectures, Give talks or make speeches, Broadcast or appear on television, Take part in writers' congresses, Answer questionnaires, Contribute to or take part in symposiums or "panels" of any kind, Contribute manuscripts for sales, Donate copies of his books to libraries, Autograph books for strangers, Allow his name to be used on letterheads, Supply personal information about himself, Supply photographs of himself, Supply opinions on literary or other subjects.

A fairly impressive list, I'd say. When I was young, Edmund Wilson supplied for me the model of how a literary man ought to carry himself. One of the things I personally found most impressive about his list is that everything Edmund Wilson clearly states he will not do, Joseph Epstein has now done, and more than once, and, like the young woman in the Häagen-Dazs commercial sitting on her couch with an empty carton of ice cream, is likely to do again and again.

I tell myself that I do these various things in the effort to acquire more readers. After all, one of the reasons I write, apart from pleasure in working out the aesthetic problems and moral questions presented by my subjects and in my stories, is to find the best readers. I also want to sell books, to make a few shekels, to please my publisher, to continue to be published in the future in a proper way. Having a high threshold for praise, I also don't in the least mind meeting strangers who tell me that they take some delight in my writing. But, more than all this, I have now come to think that writing away quietly, producing (the hope is) good work, isn't any longer quite sufficient in a culture dominated by the boisterous spirit of celebrity. In an increasingly noisy cultural scene, with many voices and media competing for attention, one feels — perhaps incorrectly but nonetheless insistently — the need to make one's own small stir, however pathetic. So, on occasion, I have gone about tooting my own little paper horn, doing book tours, submitting to the comically pompous self-importance of interviews, and doing so many of the other things that Edmund Wilson didn't think twice about refusing to do.

"You're slightly famous, aren't you, Grandpa?" my then eight-year-old granddaughter once said to me. "I am slightly famous, Annabelle," I replied, "except no one quite knows who I am." This hasn't changed much over the years. But of course seeking celebrity in our culture is a mug's game, one you cannot finally hope to win. The only large, lumpy kind of big-time celebrity available, outside movie celebrity, is to be had through appearing fairly regularly on television. I had the merest inkling of this fame when I was walking along one sunny morning in downtown Baltimore, and a red Mazda convertible screeched to a halt, the driver lowered his window, pointed a long index finger at me, hesitated, and finally, the shock of recognition lighting up his face, yelled, "C-SPAN!"

I was recently asked, through e-mail, to write a short piece for a high price for a book about the city of Chicago. When I agreed to do it, the editor, who is young, told me how pleased she was to have someone as distinguished as I among the volume's contributors. But she did have just one request. Before making things final, she wondered if she might see a sample of my writing. More than forty years in the business, I thought, echoing the character played by Zero Mostel in *The Producers,* and I'm still wearing the celebrity equivalent of a cardboard belt.

"Every time I think I'm famous," Virgil Thomson said, "I have only to go out into the world." So it is, and so ought it probably to remain for writers, musicians, and visual artists who prefer to consider themselves serious. The comedian Richard Pryor once said that he would deem himself famous when people recognized him, as they recognized Bob Hope and Muhammad Ali, by his captionless caricature. That is certainly one clear criterion for celebrity. But the best criterion I've yet come across holds that you are celebrated, indeed famous, only when a crazy person imagines he is you. It's especially pleasing that the penetrating and prolific author of this remark happens to go by the name of Anonymous.

Why Are Academics So Unhappy?

I HAD A FRIEND, now long dead, named Walter B. Scott, a professor at Northwestern University whose specialty was theatrical literature, who never referred to university teaching as other than a — or sometimes *the* — "racket." What Walter, a notably unambitious man, meant was that it was an unconscionably easy way to make a living — a soft touch, as they used to say. Working under conditions of complete freedom, having to show up in the classroom an impressively small number of hours each week, with the remainder of one's time chiefly left to cultivate one's own intellectual garden, at a job from which one could never be fired and which (if one adds up the capacious vacation time) amounted to less than six months' work a year for pay that is far from miserable — yes, I'd say "a racket" just about gets it.

And yet, as someone who came late to university teaching, I used to wonder why so many people in the racket were so obviously disappointed, depressed, and generally demoralized. Granted, until one achieves that Valhalla for scholars known as tenure — which really means lifetime security, obtainable on no other job that I know — an element of tension is entailed, but then so is it in every other job. As a young instructor, one is often assigned dogsbody work, teaching what is thought to be dull fare: surveys, composition courses, and the rest. But the unhappier academics, in my experience, are not those still struggling to gain a seat at the table, but those who have already grown dour from having been there for a long while.

So far as I know, no one has ever done a study of the unhappiness of academics. Who might be assigned to the job? Business school professors specializing in industrial psychology and employer-employee relations would botch it. Disaffected sociologists would blame it all on society and knock off for the rest of the semester. My own preference would be anthropologists, using methods long ago devised for investigating a culture from the outside in. The closest thing we have to these ideal anthropologists have been novelists writing academic novels, and their lucubrations, while not as precise as one would like on the reasons for the unhappiness of academics, do show a strong and continuing propensity on the part of academics intrepidly to make the worst of what ought to be a delightful situation.

Faculty Towers is a report on the findings of those novelists who have worked the genre long known as the academic novel. The book is written by an insider, for Professor Elaine Showalter, now in her late sixties, is, as they used to say on the carnival grounds, "with the show." At various places in her slight book, she inserts her own experience as a graduate student and professor, though not to very interesting effect. An early entry in the feminist sweepstakes, she is currently the Avalon Foundation Professor of the Humanities at Princeton, a past president of the Modern Language Association, and a founder of "gynocriticism" (or the study of women writers) — in other words, guilty until proven innocent. She has been described (readers retaining a strong sense of decorum are advised to skip this sentence) as "Camille Paglia with balls" by PrincetonInfo.com.

Professor Showalter's book is chiefly a chronological account of Anglophone academic novels written during the past sixty or so years, beginning with C. P. Snow's *The Masters* (1951) and running through examples of the genre produced in the twenty-first century. *Faculty Towers* is, for the most part, given over to plot summaries of these novels, usually accompanied by judgments about their quality, with extra bits of feminism (mild scorn is applied where the plight of women in academic life is ignored) thrown in at no extra charge.

The book's title, playing off the John Cleese television comedy *Fawlty Towers,* suggests the book's larger theme: that the university, as reflected in the academic novels Showalter examines, has increasingly become like a badly run hotel, with plenty of nuttiness to go round. The difficulty here is that Showalter believes that things are not all that nutty. *Mirabile dictu:* she finds them looking up. "The university," she writes, "is no longer a sanctuary or a refuge; it is fully caught up in the churning community and the changing society; but it is a fragile institution rather than a fortress."

The feminism in *Faculty Towers* is often no more than a tic, which the book's author by now probably cannot really control, and after a while one gets used to it, without missing it when it fails to show up. The only place Showalter's feminism seriously gets in the way, in my view, is in her judgments of Mary McCarthy's *The Groves of Academe* (a forgettable, and now quite properly forgotten, novel that she rates too highly) and Randall Jarrell's wickedly amusing *Pictures from an Institution* (which she attempts, intemperately, to squash). The two misjudgments happen to be nicely connected: the most menacing character in Jarrell's novel, Gertrude Johnson, is based on Mary McCarthy, who may well be one of Showalter's personal heroines, of whom Jarrell has one of his characters remark: "She may be a mediocre novelist but you've got to admit that she's a wonderful liar."

Being with the show has doubtless clouded Showalter's judgment of *Pictures from an Institution,* which contains, among several withering criticisms of university life, a marvelously prophetic description of the kind of characterless man who will eventually — that is to say, now, in our day — rise to the presidencies of universities all over the country. Cozening, smarmy, confidently boring, appeasers of all and offenders of none, "idiot savants of success" (Jarrell's perfect phrase), not really human but, like President Dwight Robbins of the novel's Benton College, men (and some women) with a gift for "seeming human."

C. P. Snow's *The Masters* is a novel about the intramural political alignments involved in finding the right man to replace the dying master of a Cambridge college. In the book, the worthiness of the university and the significance of the scholars and scientists contending for the job are not questioned; the conflict is between contending but serious points of view: scientific and humanistic, the school of cool progress versus that of warm tradition. In 1951, the university still seemed an altogether admirable place, professors serious and significant. Or so it seemed in the 1950s to those of us for whom going to college was not yet an automatic but still felt to be a privileged choice.

One might think that the late 1960s blew such notions completely out of the water. It did, but not before Kingsley Amis, in *Lucky Jim* (1954), which Showalter rightly calls "the funniest academic satire of the century," first loosed the torpedoes. In *Lucky Jim,* the setting is a provincial English university and the dominant spirit is one of pomposity, nicely reinforced by cheap-shot one-upmanship and intellectual fraudulence. Jim Dixon, the novel's eponymous hero, striving to become a regular member of the history faculty, is at work on an article titled "The Economic Influence of Developments in Shipbuilding Techniques, 1450 to 1485," a perfect example of fake scholarship in which, as he recognizes, "pseudo light" is cast upon "false problems." Amis puts Dixon through every hell of social embarrassment and comic awkwardness, but the reason Jim is lucky, one might tend to forget in all the laughter, is that in the end he escapes the university and thus a life of intellectual fraudulence and spiritual aridity.

Amis's hero is a medieval historian, but the preponderance of academic novels are set in English departments. The reason for this can be found in universities choosing to ignore a remark made by the linguist Roman Jakobson, who, when it was proposed to the Harvard faculty to hire Vladimir Nabokov, said that the zoology department does not hire an elephant, one of the objects of its study, so why should an English department hire a contemporary writer, also best left as an object of study? Jakobson is usually mocked for having made that remark, but he was probably correct: better to study writers than hire them. To hire a novelist for a university teaching job is turning the fox loose in the hen house. The result — no surprise here — has been feathers everywhere.

Showalter makes only brief mention of one of my favorite academic novels, *The Mind-Body Problem* by Rebecca Goldstein. Goldstein is quoted on the interesting point that at Princeton Jews become Gentilized, while at Columbia Gentiles become Judaized, which is not only amusing but true. Goldstein's novel is also brilliant on the snobbery of university life. She makes the nice observation that the poorest dressers in academic life (there are no good ones) are the mathematicians, followed hard upon by the physicists. The reason they care so little about clothes — also about wine and the accoutrements of culture — is that, Goldstein rightly notes, they feel that in their work they are dealing with the higher truths and need not be bothered with such *kakapitze* as cooking young vegetables, decanting wine correctly, and knowing where to stay in Paris.

Where the accoutrements of culture count for most are in the humanities departments, where truth, as the physical scientists understand it, simply isn't part of the deal. "What do you guys in the English department do," a scientist at Northwestern once asked me, quite in earnest, "just keep reading Shakespeare over and over, like Talmud?"

"Nothing that grand," I found myself replying.

Professor Showalter does not go in much for discussing the sex that is at the center of so many academic novels. Which reminds me that the first time I met Edward Shils, he asked me what I was reading. When I said *The War Between the Tates* by Alison Lurie, he replied, "Academic screwing, I presume." He presumed rightly. How could it be otherwise with academic novels? Apart from the rather pathetic power struggles over department chairmanships or professorial appointments, love affairs, usually adulterous or officially outlawed ones, provide the only thing resembling drama on offer on the contemporary university campus.

Early academic novels confined love affairs to adults on both sides. But by the 1970s, after the student troubles of the late 1960s, students — first graduate students, then undergraduates — became the lovers of (often married) professors. If men were writing these novels, the experience was supposed to result in spiritual refreshment; if women wrote them, the male professors were merely damned fools. The women novelists, of course, were correct.

The drama of love needs an element of impossibility: think *Romeo and Juliet,* think *Anna Karenina,* think *Lolita.* But in the academic novel, this element seems to have disappeared, especially in regard to the professor-student love affair, where the (usually female) student could no longer be considered very (if at all) innocent. The drama needed to derive elsewhere. That elsewhere hasn't yet been found, unless one counts sexual harassment suits, which are not yet the subject of an academic novel but have been that of *Oleanna,* a play by David Mamet, who is not an academic but grasped the dramatic element in such dreary proceedings.

Sexual harassment touches on political correctness, which is itself the product of affirmative action, usually traveling under the code name of diversity. Many people outside universities may think that diversity has been imposed on universities from without by ignorant administrators. But professors themselves rather like it; it makes them feel they are doing the right thing and, hence, allows them, however briefly, to feel good about themselves.

Nor is diversity the special preserve of prestige-laden or large state-run universities. In the 1970s, I was invited to give a talk at Denison University in Granville, Ohio. I arrived to find all the pieces in place: on the English faculty was a black woman (very nice, by the way), an appropriately snarky feminist, a gay man (not teaching the thing called queer theory, which hadn't yet been devised), a Jew, and a woman named Ruthie, who drove about in an aged and messy Volkswagen bug, whose place in this otherwise unpuzzling puzzle I couldn't quite figure out. When I asked, I was told, "Oh, Ruthie's from the sixties." From "the sixties," I thought then and still think, sounds like a country, and perhaps it is, but assuredly, to steal a bit of Yeats, no country for old men.

By the time I began teaching in the early 1970s, everyone already seemed to be in business for himself, looking for the best deal, which meant the least teaching for the most money at the most snobbishly well-regarded schools. The spirit of capitalism, for all that might be said on its behalf, wreaks havoc when applied to culture and education. The English novelist David Lodge neatly caught this spirit at work when he created, in two of his academic novels, the character Morris Zapp. A scholar-operator, Zapp, as described by Lodge, "is well-primed to enter a profession as steeped in free enterprise as Wall Street, in which each scholar-teacher makes an individual contract with his employer, and is free to sell his services to the highest bidder." Said to be based on the Milton man Stanley Fish, an identification that Fish apparently has never disavowed but instead glories in, Morris Zapp is the ultimate freebooter turned loose in academic settings: always attempting to strengthen his own position, usually delighted to be of disservice to the old ideal of academic dignity and integrity. Fish himself was for a spell a dean at the University of Illinois in Chicago, with a salary said to be $250,000, much less than a utility infielder in the major leagues makes but, for an academic, a big number.

By the time the 1990s rolled around, all that was really left to the academic novel was to mock the mission of the university. With the onset of so-called theory in English and foreign-language departments, this became easier and easier to do. Professor Showalter does not approve of these goings-on: "The tone of [1990s academic novels]," she writes, "is much more vituperative, vengeful, and cruel than in earlier decades."

The crueler blows are required, I should say, to capture the general atmosphere of goofiness, which has become pervasive. Theory, and the hodgepodge of feminism, Marxism, and queer theory that resides comfortably alongside it, has now been in the saddle for roughly a quarter century in American English and Romance-language departments, while also making incursions into history, philosophy, and other once humanistic subjects. There has been very little to show for it — no great books, no splendid articles or essays, no towering figures who signify outside the acad-

emy itself—except declining enrollments in English and other department courses featuring such fare.

All that is left to such university teachers is the notion that they
are, in a much-strained academic sense, avant-garde, which means
that they continue to dig deeper and deeper for lower and lower
forms of popular culture—graffiti on Elizabethan chamber pots—
and human oddity. The best standard in the old days would have
university scholars in literature and history departments publish
books that could also be read with enjoyment and intellectual
profit by nonscholars. (Such was said to be the aim of Ph.D. dis-
sertations at Columbia University.) Nothing of this kind is being
produced today. In an academic thriller (a subdivision of the academic novel) cited by Showalter called *Murder at the MLA,* the
head of the Wellesley English department is found "dead as her
prose." But almost all prose written in English departments these
days is quite as dead as that English teacher.

For Professor Showalter, the old days were almost exclusively
the bad old days. A good radical matron, she recounts answering
the phones for the support group protesting, at the 1968 Modern
Language Association meeting, "the organization's conservatism
and old-boy governance." Now it almost seems as if the annual
MLA meetings exist primarily for journalists to write comic pieces
featuring the zany subjects of the papers given at each year's conference. At these meetings, in and out the room the women come
and go, speaking of fellatio, which, deep readers that they are,
they can doubtless find in Jane Austen.

Such has been the politicization of the MLA that a counter-or-
ganization has been formed, called the Association of Literary
Scholars and Critics, whose raison d'être is to get English studies
back on track. I am myself a dues-paying ($35 annually) member
of that organization. I do not go to its meetings, but I am sent the
organization's newsletter and magazine, and they are a useful reminder of how dull English studies have traditionally been. But it
is good to recall that dull is not preposterous, dull is not always ir-
relevant, dull is not intellectual manure cast into the void.

The bad old days in English departments were mainly the dull old days, with more than enough pedants and dry-as-dusts to go round. But they did also produce a number of teachers whose work reached beyond university walls and helped elevate the overall culture: Jacques Barzun, Lionel Trilling, Ellen Moers, Clifford Geertz, Aileen Ward, Robert Penn Warren. The names from the bad new days seem to end with the entirely political Cornel West and the late Edward Said.

What we have today in universities is an extreme reaction to the dullness of that time, and also to the sheer exhaustion of subject matter for English department scholarship. No further articles and books about Byron, Shelley, Keats, or Kafka, Joyce, and the two Eliots seemed possible (which didn't of course stop them from coming). The pendulum has swung, but with a thrust so violent as to have gone through the cabinet in which the clock is stored.

From an academic novel I've not read called *The Death of a Constant Lover* (1999), by Lev Raphael, Professor Showalter quotes a passage that ends the novel on the following threnodic note:

> Whenever I'm chatting at conferences with faculty members from other universities, the truth comes out after a drink or two: Hardly any academics are happy where they are, no matter how apt the students, how generous the salary or perks, how beautiful the setting, how light the teaching load, how lavish the research budget. I don't know if it's academia itself that attracts misfits and malcontents, or if the overwhelming hypocrisy of that world would have turned even the von Trapp family sullen.

My best guess is that it's a good bit of both. Universities attract people who are good at school. Being good at school takes a real enough but very small talent. As the philosopher Robert Nozick once pointed out, all those A's earned through their young lives encourage such people to persist in school: to stick around, get more A's and more degrees, sign on for teaching jobs. When young, the life ahead seems glorious. They imagine themselves inspiring the young, writing important books, living out their days in cultivated leisure.

But something inevitably goes awry, something disagreeable turns up in the punch bowl. Usually by the time they turn forty, they discover the students aren't sufficiently appreciative; the books don't get written; the teaching begins to feel repetitive; the collegiality is seldom anywhere near what one hoped for it; there isn't any good use for the leisure. Meanwhile, people who got lots of B's in school seem to be driving around in Mercedes-Benzes, buying million-dollar apartments, enjoying freedom and prosperity in a manner that strikes the former good students, now professors, as not only unseemly but of a kind a just society surely would never permit.

Now that politics has trumped literature in English departments the situation is even worse. Beset by political correctness, self-imposed diversity, without leadership from above, university teachers, at least on the humanities and social science sides, knowing the work they produce couldn't be of the least possible interest to anyone but the hacks of the MLA and similar academic organizations, have more reason than ever to be unhappy. How, they wonder, did "academic" become synonymous with "ridiculous"?

And so let us leave them, overpaid and underworked, surly with alienation and unable to find any way out of the sweet racket into which they once so ardently longed to get.

What Happened to the Movies?

I WROTE A MOVIE ONCE. A man from a television production firm connected with Warner Brothers called one day to say that he wished to take an option on two stories of mine, and wondered if I would like to write a screenplay uniting the two. He did not have much money to offer, he said. At the time, the minimum fee for a screenplay by a member of the Writers Guild of America was $57,500, and he could pay me that, along with my option money.

I told him I'd like the weekend to think about it, hung up the phone, and on the spot did an elaborate and extended touchdown dance. A week later, I wrote a check for $1,000, taking out a membership in the screenwriters' guild. In another few weeks, thick contracts arrived from Warner Brothers. I was a screenwriter.

I would like to be able to report now on the monstrous vulgarity of the producer who contacted me: how he wanted me to write into the script all manner of fancy fornication, to make the family dog a lesbian, and to add more touches along the same lines. None of this occurred. He was a bright and earnest man, helpful in every way. I, truth to tell, was less than a dab hand at screenwriting. When, without realizing it, I set three scenes in a row over lunch in different restaurants, my producer said to me, very gently, "It's called a *movie*, Joe, so couldn't we have the characters move around a little?"

One day he asked if I knew how lucky I was. "You write something," he said. "You make it as good as you can. You send it to a publisher or a magazine editor. Either they take it or they don't — and in your case they mostly do — and that's the end of it. I, on the other hand, have to go through endless committees, deal with countless fools and con artists, and little of what I want to do ever gets done."

As I sent him bits of my screenplay, my producer would say encouraging things like, "This could be a splendid little movie"; "I see a really fine little movie emerging here"; "Great little movie you're turning out." Always that word "little" popped up.

"You know," he said one day, "this could be a major movie."

"What happened to 'little'?" I asked. "How did we suddenly become 'major'? I don't recall writing in a part for Buddha or Moses."

"Oh," he said, "as the script is developing I can now see a part for Dustin Hoffman." What would that mean? I asked in my naiveté. "As things stand," he explained, "we have here maybe a twenty-million-dollar movie. If Dustin Hoffman is in it, it becomes at least a sixty- or seventy-million-dollar movie. For example, you now have a scene set in 1960 in the Pump Room at the Ambassador East Hotel. If we're talking about a twenty-million-dollar movie, we'll duplicate the livery of the waiters, we'll find the same banquettes and menus, and we'll get a neon sign that reads 'Pump Room.' But if it's a seventy-million-dollar movie, we'll rebuild the goddamn Pump Room."

With this, Irving Berlin's line about no business like show business took on newly vivid meaning.

I finished my screenplay and got my money, but before anything further happened my producer was fired and the project died. If the movie had been made, I would have received another $100,000 and a share of any net profits — also known among screenwriters, I was told, as *nyet* profits, since, thanks to creative Hollywood accounting, a net profit has yet to be shown on *Gone With the Wind.*

I didn't feel much bothered that the project died. In his novel *The Red White and Blue,* John Gregory Dunne has a Hollywood producer dividing all the scripts sent to him into two categories:

"piece of shit" and "not a piece of shit." I'm not sure into which category mine would have fallen; I've never gone back to reread it, and have no interest in doing so now.

The best deal of all for a writer, it has been said, is to sell his book to the movies for $1 million, and then they never make the movie. Sounds right to me. Somehow I never felt the screenplay I'd written was quite mine, even though I had written every word of it and it drew loosely on my stories. I wrote it but did not sense that I really owned it, and I had put up no fight at all when asked to make extensive changes. I once heard David Mamet say, about the screenplay he had written for the movie *The Untouchables,* that he felt toward it like an aunt toward a nephew: "I love it, but it's not really my child."

The role of ownership plays a large part in David Thomson's *The Whole Equation,* a remarkable book by the English-born movie historian and critic best known for his *Biographical Dictionary of Film.* Thomson believes you cannot control and finally perhaps not even love what you do not own, and very few screenwriters — or directors — own the movies they make. Nor, significantly, are they ready to put up their own money to see them made. While he blames the awfulness of most contemporary movies on the ignorance and cynicism of producers and Hollywood studio executives, he sweeps much wider in his search for the reasons why movies in general seem so much less good than they ought to be — and for the key to the mystery of his own and everyone else's enchantment with them.

Impressive in its comprehensiveness, *The Whole Equation* includes just about everything known about the movies, except the color of the dishes (periwinkle blue) my mother brought home from the 400 Theater during World War II and the name of the Greek family (I don't know it, either) who ran the candy shop next door, from which I bought popcorn for a nickel cheaper and with more butter than was available at the Nortown Theater, where small light bulbs simulating stars flickered on and off in the blue ceiling.

Eschewing chronology, Thomson proceeds more or less thematically. In *The Whole Equation* you will find chapters or extended passages on the changes in movie distribution; on the effects of technological change (Thomson thinks sound a great advance, paradoxically allowing actors to be silent, but is less charitable toward color, which destroyed the interesting effects of the play of light made possible by black-and-white film); on the role of fantasy and the voyeuristic impulse in audiences; on the trajectory of movie careers, complete with numerous examples; on the issue of censorship and politics in the movie industry ("Actors," Thomson writes, "are not trained to take responsibility for what they say. That's why politics eats them up"); on the significance of the industry's being located in southern California, with its sunshine and lack of urban tradition; on studio dealings with unions and gangsters; on how the old studio system was born and flourished, and the role of talent agents in killing it; and on much else besides.

Throughout, Thomson is digressive, idiosyncratic, cranky, quirky, heterodox, gossipy (did you know that Humphrey Bogart wore a toupee?). He does go on, but over the course of this book's nearly four hundred pages one rarely wants to say, with John Wayne–like impatience, "Okay, kid, let's get the cows to Abilene." Reading *The Whole Equation* resembles nothing so much as being talked to nonstop by a breathless, slightly overdramatizing, but extremely intelligent man who really does know what he's talking about. "You can take Hollywood for granted like I did," Cecelia Brady, a character in F. Scott Fitzgerald's *The Last Tycoon*, says on that novel's first page, "or you can dismiss it with the contempt we reserve for what we don't understand. It can be understood too, but only dimly and in flashes. Not half a dozen men have ever been able to keep the whole equation of pictures in their heads."

Borrowing her thought for his title, David Thomson clearly wrote *The Whole Equation* in the hope of becoming one of the half dozen. Even if in the end he does not quite bring it all off, along the way he has produced a work of vast information and considerable brilliance.

• • •

Of all the issues Thomson deals with, perhaps the most interesting is the connection between art and profit, or between what he describes dryly as "the urge to tell . . . stories" and "the wish to make money," adding that the "passion in the [whole] equation is to convince you that the two are one." Thomson understands that for all their power the movies cannot compete with literature as an art. When literature is operating at a high level as, in Lionel Trilling's words, "the human activity that takes the fullest and most precise account of variousness, possibility, complexity, and difficulty," they cannot even come close.

Comparing, for example, the 2002 movie made from Michael Cunningham's novel *The Hours* to Virginia Woolf's *Mrs. Dalloway*, on which both the movie and the Cunningham novel are partly based, Thomson "cannot hold back the realization that the movies have never been good enough." As a form, he writes, movies are "most acute when fixed on what happens next; whereas literature, sooner or later, is about the meaning behind events." This explains better than anything else I know why it is that the finest movies seem to have been made not from first- but from second-rate fiction: *The Maltese Falcon* (Dashiell Hammett), *The Postman Always Rings Twice* (James M. Cain), *Farewell, My Lovely* (Raymond Chandler), *The Treasure of the Sierra Madre* (B. Traven). In all these books, plot takes primacy over style and penetrating observation.

Which brings us to screenwriters. "Product," the old Hollywood moguls used to call the movies they made. Most of them were main-chance Jewish operator types who ran their studios on the factory model. They were aware that the right actors and actresses were crucial and were what people paid their money to see. Directors who knew how to get the best out of these actors were also important, as were producers with a talent for organization and for keeping all these temperamental characters in line. But without writers there was nothing; the game could not even begin until writers had put the ball in play.

And yet writers, as everyone knows, have always been thought the most dispensable element in the Hollywood equation. "You heard about the ambitious Polish starlet who, hoping to advance her movie career, slept with a screenwriter?" An old joke, but one that nicely describes the powerless state of the Hollywood writer. Powerless, perhaps, with good reason.

F. Scott Fitzgerald, broke, out of print, and out of luck, with a wife in an insane asylum and a drinking problem as big as the Ritz, came to Hollywood as a screenwriter in 1927 in the hope that its money might bail him out. It did not. In 1940, at the age of forty-four, he died of a heart attack, perhaps partially brought on by a broken heart, in an apartment on Hayworth Avenue off Sunset Boulevard.

From all reports, Fitzgerald was treated respectfully in Hollywood — and paid decently, too. But he could not give them quite what they wanted, and he never succeeded there. In *The Last Tycoon*, Fitzgerald gives ample evidence not only that he thoroughly understood the Hollywood system as it then operated — the magnificence of it, and the nightmare, too — but why he himself failed in it.

The novel, unfinished at Fitzgerald's death, is a *roman à clef* about the career of the legendary producer Irving Thalberg. David Thomson agrees with Fitzgerald's high estimate of Thalberg, writing that he was "inspired by an urge to lift the picture business from its grubby origins and to bring it closer to the standard of the legitimate theater." But it was Thalberg who installed the system under which writers were employed in the old Hollywood. In the words of Fitzgerald's Thalberg character, Monroe Stahr, "Writers are children — even in normal times they can't keep their minds on their work"; they "poop out and get all mixed up and someone has to come and straighten them out." Thalberg invented the notion of putting several different writers on a project, sometimes simultaneously and occasionally even unbeknownst to one another. Necessary though they were, writers were also replaceable, rather like supremely well-paid office temps.

"I never thought," Fitzgerald has his Thalberg character say, "that I had more brains than a writer has. But I always thought that his brains belonged to me — because I knew how to use them." It is far from clear that Fitzgerald disagreed with this. (I don't believe I do, either.) He was probably also in agreement with this sentiment of Stahr/Thalberg: "We don't have good writers out here . . . Oh, we hire them but when they get out here they're not good writers — so we have to work with the material we have."

Would Daniel Fuchs, a professional screenwriter, have disagreed? The author of a trilogy of New York novels that flopped commercially when first published in the mid-1930s (but were republished to great acclaim in 1961, and yet again in 2006), Fuchs left a job as a $6-a-day substitute teacher in Brooklyn to write for the movies. Arriving in Hollywood in 1937, he remained there until his death in 1993, during which time he acquired only twelve screen credits. One among them, *Love Me or Leave Me* (1955), won an Oscar, though Fuchs, a modest man, believed this owed as much to James Cagney's performance as to the words he had provided for him.

Fuchs's thoughts on the movie can be consulted in a collection of his work, *The Golden West: Hollywood Stories.* Never an astronomically well-paid writer, he claims that at the height of his career he did not make much more than $60,000 a year. In an interesting anecdote, he tells about being assigned to a picture and finally figuring out the problems of its complicated story, only to be replaced because the producer thought him too low-priced for the job. This struck a chord with me. Asked once by a famous producer to work on someone else's screenplay, I said that I could arrange to do it, that it would take three or so weeks of my time, and that I would charge $25,000. Nothing ever came of it. When I told this story to Frederic Raphael, who wrote the screenplays for, among other movies, *Darling, Two for the Road, Far from the Madding Crowd,* and *Eyes Wide Shut,* he responded that the producer probably thought me a peon; I should have asked for $25,000 per week.

Having chosen a Hollywood life, Daniel Fuchs seems to have had few regrets. He raised his sons safely and lived comfortably among beautiful landscapes. *"Nothing is given freely,"* he writes, supplying his own emphasis; *"payment is exacted."* In his case, in exchange "for the boon of work; for the joy of leisure, the happy, lazy days; for the castles and the drowsy back lots; for the stalwarts I've come to know; . . . [for] the flowers, the sycamores, the blessings of the sun," he gave up such art as was at his command. Did he make a terrible deal, a pact with the devil? He appears never to have thought so.

Edmund Wilson used to say that the two great enemies of literary talent in the United States were Hollywood and Henry Luce. Today this rings rather hollow. My guess is that the people who cashed in their chips for better money in movies or journalism were not holding very high artistic cards to begin with. Few must be the great works that never appeared because someone was turning out journalism or movies for a mass audience.

By contrast, the ever-modest Fuchs offers a generally high assessment of Hollywood itself. In "Writing for the Movies," an essay first published in 1962, he asked if it was really fitting, in the name of highbrow snobbery, "to pass by so indifferently the work of [Hollywood directors and producers like] Ford, Stevens, Wilder, Mankiewicz, Huston, Zinneman, William Wellman, Howard Hawks, Sam Wood, Clarence Brown, Victor Fleming, William Van Dyke, King Vidor, Raoul Walsh, Henry Hathaway, Henry King, Chaplin, Lubitsch, Goldwyn, Selznick, Milestone, Capra, Wyler, Cukor, Kazan?" The accomplishments of these men, he argued, had had a worldwide effect, and their achievement was of a magnitude equal to that of the best American architects and inventors. "Generations to come, looking back over the years, are bound to find that the best, most solid creative effort of our decades was spent in the movies, and it's time someone came clean and said so."

David Thomson is not that someone. Thomson does not hesitate to give the names of movies he admires — and he likes a lot of them — but he nonetheless sees in the world of movies a moral drama between art and profit in which art generally goes down to defeat. If, for him, people in Hollywood have not quite sold out, the giant infusions of money to actors and big-name directors, who currently share in a movie's gross profits, mean at least that they have been bought out. Jack Nicholson, for example, now probably a $20-million-a-movie man, is unlikely to make the better sorts of movies on which he acquired his reputation: *Five Easy Pieces, The King of Marvin Gardens,* and others. The worse Marlon Brando's acting became, Thomson notes, the higher the salary he could command: $5 million, late in life, for ten minutes on film in *Christopher Columbus — The Discovery.*

Thomson does not like the direction in which contemporary movies are going. "I regret," he writes, "the way America has elected to make films for its bluntest section of society and in ways that flatter them, and we have to recognize how much of that is being done for money." He adds that "much in American films supports the worst views held of us in other parts of the world: that we are combat-ready, aggressive, adolescent, greedy, sensationalist, without humor, depth, or imagination, rampant devotees of technology (as opposed to enlightenment)."

As this suggests, Thomson's politics are fairly standard liberal. But that is not the same thing as standard Hollywood liberal — if only because his critical sense often rises above his politics. (He says flat-out, for example, that *Easy Rider,* that quintessential hippie movie so much admired by the counterculture, is drivel.) Although he is especially partial to noir films, what Thomson longs for above all is a return to movies for adults. Good movies do still get made, but for Thomson we are long past the point (which he places in the 1970s) when a good movie was the exception that proved the rule.

"That's All Folks," the tag line at the end of the old Looney Tunes and Merrie Melodies cartoons, is the sad and pessimistic title of Thomson's final chapter. Although he is not quite announcing the death of the medium, he does sense its deadening, its loss of the magic that the best movies of his (and my) youth had in such seemingly ample supply. And although he allows that he does not know where movies are headed, he suspects "technology will lead the way."

In *The Big Picture,* Edward Jay Epstein corroborates Thomson's suspicions. A journalist with a strong taste for the inside story, Epstein takes up marketing trends and other financial questions that affect the movie industry in the twenty-first century. In clear prose, he fills in much of the story that David Thomson sketches but may not have had the heart to complete. *The Big Picture* might as easily have been titled *The Dark Picture.*

As both Thomson and Epstein relate, the latter in careful and elaborate detail, the production of movies has grown more and more expensive. Thanks to complex deal-making, the better directors and higher-priced actors now work less often but for much more money. Whereas under the studio system Hollywood turned out between 500 and 700 movies a year, the number currently is closer to 200. Agents have played a large role here: of Lew Wasserman, who came near to controlling Hollywood movie production by forcing up salaries for actors and directors and getting them share-in-the-gross deals, it was said that he took the show out of show business.

With the biggest-named actors earning between $20 and $30 million a movie, the average price for turning out a film today is said to be $63.8 million — a rise in cost proportionally greater even than the rise over the years in ticket prices. No wonder, then, that going to the movies is being supplanted by watching movies at home, now my own passive pleasure of choice. And hardly mine alone: during the second half of the 1940s, when the population of the United States was 151 million, more than 90 million people went to the movies every week; today the population of the country is 300 million, but only roughly 25 million people attend weekly, and the chief income from movies no longer derives from ticket sales at the box office.

Epstein shows how the giant corporations — Viacom, Disney, News Corporation, Time Warner, General Electric — now own what remains of the old Hollywood studios. Running them with an eye toward a global audience, they concentrate on objectives that supersede the idea of making entertaining flicks that can both turn a profit and every so often aspire to quasi art. Their main production model was discovered long ago by Walt Disney: find a niche audience (children, in Disney's case) and be astute about licensing the rights to toys, books, cartoons, and other products that spin off the original movie. George Lucas's *Star Wars* has acted on that model, and created an empire that has struck back again and again — struck the cash register, that is — through lucrative licensing agreements.

Globalism, whatever else may be said for it, also means lowest-common-denominatorism, and technology plays right into it. "With the geometric increases in computer power that will be available to Hollywood in the near future," writes Epstein, "much, if not all, of conventional moviemaking [will be] increasingly replaced by digital animation." Besides, the global market turns out to be largely the youth, or adolescent, market, and that market, brought up on cartoons, comic books, television, and Nintendo games, is much more interested in spectacle than story, in car crashes than catharsis.

For those of us brought up instead on the movies, who in our childhood went to Saturday-afternoon double features without even inquiring into what was playing, and rarely came away disappointed, movies have been an entertainment, a mass medium, a purveyor of ideology, a part of our education, sometimes an art, but above all a habit. That habit is now becoming more and more difficult to feed. True, thanks to DVD, a person can live off older movies while hoping against hope that the odd new one, domestic or foreign, will somehow slip through the mesh — as still occasionally happens. But I, for one, await the sad day when some evil genius finds a way to turn *The Treasure of the Sierra Madre, Double Indemnity, Lawrence of Arabia,* and other beloved old movies into so many animated cartoons.

I'm History

T HIS IS, I believe, my ninety-second essay for *The American
Scholar* written under the name Aristides, and my final
one. I should have liked to have rounded the number off
at an even hundred, but it was not to be. The first such essay, titled
"A Literary Mafia?," ran in the spring 1975 issue. It was the only
Aristides essay to carry a biographical note, which read: "Aristides
will comment from time to time in this column on matters of cultural and intellectual interest. He is not, nor is he in any way related to, that same Aristides whom the citizens of Athens were
supposed to have ostracized because they grew tired of always
hearing him called The Just."

When I instituted this column under the rubric "Life and Letters," my plan was to let other, often distinguished, members of
the magazine's editorial board fire off essays under names of their
own choosing. But no one stepped forth to write the second essay,
so I wrote it, and the same was true of the third, which I also
wrote. By the sixth or seventh, I would not have relinquished the
"Life and Letters" column to anyone, so fond had I become of
writing it, and so I just wrote the next eighty-five or so essays
myself.

No writing, I have to report, has come as easily to me. I never
wanted for a subject, and—capacious gasbag that I am—I always
had the 6,500 words needed to cover that subject. By rough count,
I have written nearly 600,000 words in this space. I have produced

six books of essays from the Aristides column. Aristides the Just? A lot closer to Aristides the Loquacious, I'd say.

Soon after beginning these Aristides pieces, I heard it bruited about that I had reinvented the familiar essay, the form begun in England by Addison and Steele and brought to a high sheen by Charles Lamb and William Hazlitt. Closer to our day, it continued in the vastly different work of Max Beerbohm and George Orwell. It was nice to hear this; I love being thought in the line of succession of such writers, but reinventing anything was very far from what I had set out to do. As I saw it, my task was to fill up eight pages of each quarter's *American Scholar*.

I usually had a three-month lead on these essays. During this time notions, quotations, and occasionally something that felt suspiciously like an idea would occur to me, and I would write them down and place them in a manila folder. Sometimes I found apposite quotations in a series of commonplace books I keep. Many people thought that I pulled these quotations out of my sleeve and that I possessed one of the great memories of the age. Not quite so. Nor did I have much of a sense of structure. I never began one of these essays with more than a general feeling about where I wanted it to go. I decided to let interest dictate structure: if I could manage to write one interesting paragraph after another, I believed, structure would take care of itself. My motto became Yogi Berra's wise saying, "When you come to a fork in the road, take it." The trick with these essays is to take what seems a small or mildly amusing subject and open it up, allow it to exfoliate, so that by the end something arises that might be larger and more intricate than anyone — including the author — had expected.

I have had the most generous response imaginable to these essays. I don't know how many letters I have had from readers who appreciated them, or wished to argue with points made in them, found errors in them, or even hated them, but the number must be in the thousands. What made these letters all the more pleasurable is that I never wrote any of the essays with particular readers in mind. If one tends to write for anyone, it is, in my experience, an editor; and in this case, I was the editor (though I was often saved the embarrassment of being caught out in egregious errors by my two friends and coeditors Jean Stipicevic and Sandra Costich). In fact, I wrote the Aristides essays and I edited *The American Scholar* for myself and for strangers who might happen to share my interests.

The question of what I might do for readers of this magazine came up only once, when I was being interviewed for the job of editor. The year was 1974, and the smoke from the years of "student unrest" — still my favorite of all euphemisms — had not yet cleared. One of the members of Phi Beta Kappa's search committee, who was then president of the University of Virginia, in an earnest voice with a southern accent, asked me: "Mr. Epstein, what would you do, if you were editor of *The American Scholar*, for the young among your readers?" I thought for perhaps two seconds, then replied: "I would let them grow older."

The sang-froid of that reply was based on two things: first, I genuinely didn't care much about the young, that transient class that wasn't, after all, an ethnic group; and, second, I didn't in any event really think I would get the job, which made candor all the easier. A few months before, my friend Hilton Kramer told me that he had put me up for the job in answer to a letter from Robert Heilman, the literary critic, asking for candidates. Not long after, I received a call from Professor Heilman telling me that I was on the shortlist of candidates and asking if I would agree to come to New York to be interviewed. I said yes, sure, why not?

When the date of the interview was announced, I suggested to the woman who has long since become my wife that she join me for a day in New York. She could go to Bloomingdale's for sunglasses, which she needed, while I was interviewed, and then we could have a good early dinner and fly back to Chicago. It would be a larky day in old New York, and half the expenses would be paid by Phi Beta Kappa, a society whose qualifications I never came close to meeting as a student.

She found a fine pair of sunglasses, we had a swell dinner at a restaurant on 63rd Street called the Running Footman, and the interview apparently must have come off well, for I got the job. I did, however, tell one rather large lie during the interview, though I wasn't aware that it was a lie at the time. I said that I would attempt to edit a magazine marked by disinterestedness in the political conflicts of the day — which at that time were still between intellectuals gathered around such magazines as *Commentary* and the *New York Review of Books*. As it turned out, though I do not think of myself as a passionately political person, I could not stay disinterested forever.

I was pleased to have gotten the job as editor of *The American Scholar*. When I told my friend Edward Shils about it, he said, "Oh, Joseph, this will be very good for the country." Edward would sometimes say such grandiose things, and in this case I thought he was vastly overstating things, but I believe he meant it.

I was thirty-seven at the time. I was early addicted to magazines, beginning with *Sport* and *Life* and the *Saturday Evening Post* in the 1940s. Magazines, chiefly intellectual magazines — the early *Partisan Review, Commentary, Kenyon Review, Hudson Review, Sewanee Review,* and *Encounter* (in England) — but also *The New Yorker* and *Harper's Magazine* and the *Atlantic Monthly*, had contributed more to my largely autodidactic education than any university or educational institution. I was delighted to have control of such a magazine.

My wife, who is a Phi Beta Kappa, had a subscription to *The American Scholar*, and I would always have a look at it but rarely found all that much to read in it. The magazine edited by my predecessor, an extraordinary man named Hiram Haydn, was a great hotchpotch. Haydn, whom I never met, was a large man who wrote large novels (a thick novel of his titled *The Hands of Esau* was in all the used-book shops I haunted in the mid-seventies). He was a teacher, a novelist, the author of a book on the Renaissance, a psychoanalysand, and a publisher whose specialty was young novelists (William Styron was his most famous discovery) and who was one of the founders of Atheneum Books. He was also a high roller, a sport. In the summer he used to fly the staff of the magazine up to his place at Martha's Vineyard to read page proofs.

The way he ran his magazine was, as near as I can make out,

not all that carefully. Occasionally good things appeared in it. In 1960, his publishing firm brought out *The American Scholar Reader*, which has many distinguished contributors, but one had the sense that they tended to send the magazine their less-than-best efforts. The most famous piece to have run in the magazine was a spoof by Richard Rovere, then *The New Yorker's* Washington correspondent, on the American Establishment, which caused an amusing stir in its day.

But one didn't have a sense of a strong hand at the helm. If anything, *The American Scholar* of those years seemed a bit small-town, a touch corny. Its book review section carried the rubric "The Revolving Bookstand." Biographical notes on contributors tended to be folksy, informing readers that this or that poet liked to water-ski with her four children and cocker spaniel at the family summer home on Lake Tippicanoe. One of its regular columns, devoted to biological and ecological subjects and written by a Nobel Prize–winning biologist, carried the rubric "The Despairing Optimist," causing a friend of mine to wonder why its author didn't get off the damn fence.

The title of the magazine came, of course, from Ralph Waldo Emerson's essay, originally delivered as a Phi Beta Kappa address at Harvard, and the magazine then carried under its title the rather self-congratulatory tag line, in caps, A QUARTERLY FOR THE INDEPENDENT THINKER, followed by an Emerson quotation: "In the right state the scholar is Man Thinking." I soon removed both the tag line and the quotation, though for a long period after I became editor of the magazine, it seemed that anyone who wrote an essay or gave a speech on Emerson sent it to me. Poor fellows, did they ever miss hitting the mark.

If *The American Scholar* was truly a quarterly for the independent thinker, its circulation ought to have been somewhere between thirty and forty, for I doubt that the country has ever had more than that number of independent thinkers (I'm not sure I quite qualify as one myself, though I still hope to get there). Instead, when I became the editor of the magazine, it had a circulation of roughly thirty thousand, small change in the world of

mass-magazine publishing but impressive for a quarterly intellectual journal.

The job of editor had, for reasons a bit cloudy to me, immense
prestige. "Do you know Joseph Epstein?" people would say when
introducing me when I first began the job, adding, "He's the editor of *The American Scholar.*" Or: "You know Joe Epstein, the
editor of *The American Scholar.*" For a while I began to think
"the editor of *The American Scholar*" was part of my name, rather
like "the wily" seemed to be part of Ho Chi Minh's name in the
American press. I also began to feel a bit like "Johnson of the
OPA" in one of the first off-color jokes I heard as a boy. In the joke,
Johnson was a man who felt that his affiliation with an important
institution — the Office of Price Administration during World War
II — allowed him to help himself to sexual favors from hitherto
strange women: "It's all right," he'd say, "I'm Johnson of the
OPA." "I'm Epstein of *The American Scholar,*" I used to joke with
my wife, "and I do believe I'll have another piece of cake."

Part of the prestige of *The American Scholar* derived from its
connection with Phi Beta Kappa, which Edward Shils used to describe as an organization set up to confirm neurotic Jewish mothers in the rightness of their persistent nagging of their children to
study harder. Its prestige derived, too, from its editorial board,
which could, as the English used to say, be very "namey," or at
least seemed so to me at the time. When I came on the job, members of the editorial board included Jacques Barzun, Lillian Hellman, Robert Motherwell, William Styron, Diana Trilling, Ken-
neth B. Clark, J. Bronowski, and John Archibald Wheeler. The
board then met thrice a year, twice in New York, once in Washington. At its meetings, board members discussed magazine policy
and recommended writers and subjects for the editor to pursue
for future issues.

Although I have never been able to sustain awe for very long, I
approached my early meetings with the editorial board with what
I would describe as mild trepidation. I soon learned that most
board members were barely interested, a number to the point of
not even having read the magazine. Some — I think in particular

of Jacques Barzun — were extremely helpful, both in board meetings and in writing for the magazine. Some said little. John Archibald Wheeler, an important physicist, never spoke, but at the end of the meetings he always handed me a small piece of paper with the names of scientists from whom I might get interesting material.

A number of the board members clearly disliked one another. They were, after all, intellectuals, and intellectuals are nothing if not disputatious. Diana Trilling and Lillian Hellman were nearly in litigation with each other. But in the editorial board meetings they never argued. I thought this an impressive show of decorum. A friend of mine said that what I failed to understand was that each of these women was more temperamental than a diva, but each, Diana and Lillian, sang different roles.

I liked Lillian Hellman and thought her very smart, except when the initials CIA or FBI appeared in her sentences. (Unfortunately, they appeared in a great many of them.) One evening in Washington, I walked from our business meeting to dinner at a nearby French restaurant with Lillian and Paul Freund, the legal scholar and a board member who didn't say much but whose sweet seriousness lent an air of agreeable gravity to any room he inhabited. Lillian asked Paul what plans he had for the summer. He said that he was going to be attending the Salzburg Seminar. "Oh, Paul," Lillian asked, "are they still run by the CIA?" Without skipping a beat, he replied: "I don't think so, Lillian. The food is quite poor."

Diana Trilling was something else. A friend had tipped me off that she had ceased any serious reading in 1965, and I came to believe it. She would not uncommonly suggest we get an article on a particular subject when such an article was in the current issue. Once she filled an entire ninety-minute meeting with complaints about a quite neutral article in the *Scholar* about her deceased husband, Lionel, whom she referred to as L. T. (putting one in mind of Leo Tolstoy). At the end of the meeting, she resigned her membership on the board. Edward Shils tried to mollify her, but no one could have. He afterward told me that he regretted attempting to do so and wished he had said to her instead, "Madam, leave the public bath."

At its best, the editorial board resembled a fine little club of exceptional scholars: Arnaldo Momigliano, Glen Bowersock, Peter Brown, and Mary Lefkowitz, for example, handsomely represented the field of ancient history; S. Chandrasekhar, Freeman Dyson, and Jeremy Bernstein represented science. But easily the most valuable member was Edward Shils. Through his suggestions — sometimes made in meetings, more often in private — the scope of material in the magazine was widened, first to include many Oxbridge scholars, then many Continental ones. In some ways, Edward was my silent coeditor; and, though I would often seek the articles he thought might be of interest, I rarely showed them to him before they were in print. Sometimes, after they did go into print, he would zing me on their not really being as good as they could have been. He functioned, Edward did, as an editorial conscience, all without emolument.

Soon after becoming editor, I was presented with a recently completed readers' survey, which I found comically baffling. Some readers thought there wasn't enough science in the magazine, others thought there was too much; some thought there was too much literary criticism, others felt that literary criticism should be at the heart of the magazine; some wanted more about movies and popular culture, others hoped we would dispense with popular culture altogether. It was at this point that I said the devil with these readers — and the devil with surveys. I decided that in editing the magazine my own motto would be "I interest myself." My view was that I was not a dull boy, and therefore what interested me would interest other intellectually lively people. If I was mistaken about this, it would be better to find it out early, be fired, and seek work in plumbing, where there was at least a chance to make a serious buck.

I decided not to print any movie criticism, almost no art criticism, and very little literary criticism that wasn't larger in its range than that produced by highly specialized English departments. If any article, in any discipline, seemed to me of possible interest only to specialists, I determined that it wasn't for us. I wasn't much interested in contemporary politics, or at least in reading about the subject in a quarterly, and it secretly pleased me that entire political administrations — Carter, Reagan, Bush the First — passed without the names of any of these presidents appearing in our pages.

During the course of my editorship, I became more and more interested in music, so I published a fair amount on that subject. I ran lots of memoirs. I loved to run offbeat pieces: an essay by a lawyer in Denver about his singing in an opera chorus; a consideration of the puppeteer Señor Wences; a visit to the Pittsburgh Pirates' spring training camp; an account of the comedy of being a professional lecturer. I had a longstanding interest in historiography — and a belief in Lewis Namier's maxim to the effect that long study of history teaches us how things do not happen — and I ran pieces on it and on historians whenever I could procure them. I had begun to teach at Northwestern University the year before I began my editorship, and my interest in teaching techniques and the influence of teachers led me to run a series of profiles of putatively great teachers, written by their students.

It pleased me to run the work of younger writers — I think I may have been the first to print Richard Rodriguez, and I published Shelby Steele very early in his career — but I also solicited manuscripts from a number of older writers from what I now think of as the strong generation: Oscar Handlin, Arnaldo Momigliano, Jacques Barzun, Paul Horgan, Sir William Haley, Paul Kristeller, Alexander Gerschenkron. I would occasionally get a letter from a freshly minted feminist telling me that she was canceling her subscription because I didn't run enough women writers. I generally answered such letters by remarking that I thought myself without prejudice in this matter, that I was interested only in getting the best possible copy into the magazine, and that I would run good writing produced by a hermaphroditic zebra.

When I began editing it, *The American Scholar* paid $250 for an article and $50 for a book review. During my editorship, the fees were raised to $500 for an article and between $100 and $200 for a book review — an improvement, but still not enough to set anyone up for that long weekend at the Ritz. The practical consequences of these low fees were that I couldn't pursue as contributors writers who earned their living through writing and I couldn't ask anyone to write an article that entailed travel or elaborate research. Consequently, many of our contributors turned out to be academics, or younger writers, or talented people for whom writing was not their first job. I wrote a great many letters soliciting material when I began editing the magazine. I wrote to all the still extant writers that I admired. Some responded generously, some not at all.

Once the magazine under my editorship got under way — after, say, three years — several excellent writers started sending things to me without my soliciting them. I took this to mean that the magazine had begun to hit its stride, to take on character, to represent something that attracted them. These writers either thought the magazine simpatico with their own views and interests or liked the company of its contributors. Sometimes they felt they had, somehow or other, written an *American Scholar* piece. H. L. Mencken, praised for discovering so much talent when editing the *American Mercury,* replied that all he did was open the mail. I began to understand what he meant.

Without planning many issues, I always had enough copy in the house to run what seemed to me a decent — and sometimes a bit better than decent — issue. Cyril Connolly used to say, of his years editing *Horizon,* that he was disappointed by each issue, "being given once a month the opportunity to produce a perfect number and every month failing, and just when despair sets in, being presented with one more chance." I was always surprised that an issue of our magazine had turned out as decently as it had, and I was not at all sure I would be able to do it again. I don't mean to imply that I am a better editor than Cyril Connolly was during his ten-year editorship of *Horizon,* but only that, perhaps having lower standards than he, I took a mildly amazed view of the proceedings passing under my hand.

Connolly edited a monthly, I a quarterly. I came to like the distance from current events that a quarterly provides. One couldn't possibly keep up with the news in a quarterly, so why bother? A quarterly, too, allowed one to vary one's contributors and not, as in a weekly or even a monthly, to have to rely on the same small cadre of dependable but in time just slightly boring contributors. Although I used a small number of writers on several occasions, I don't think there was anything like a regular group of *American Scholar* contributors, and I found this variety pleasing.

I also came to like the magazine's being thought a little out of it. Edmund Wilson, in "A Literary Worker's Polonius," suggests that, on the matter of redesign, "the most that can be done with a magazine is to subject it to a sort of face-lifting process, which, though it may improve its look at long distance, only exposes it, on closer examination, in a more hideous state of senility." Soon after I became editor of *The American Scholar*, I had its cover redesigned, though not its type or interior. I remember, when I showed the cover design I most liked to my editorial board, that William Styron, in criticism, remarked: "It looks like a Dutch philological journal." Ah, thought I, a Dutch philological journal, perfecto — just what is wanted.

Some magazines pride themselves on running the new and exciting, others on their eclecticism; I decided that the magazine I edited would attempt to sustain itself intellectually by invocation of the tradition of liberal arts learning — a tradition just then under serious attack in the universities. Through the choice of subjects and authors, I would try to reanimate the tradition, remind people of its strength and beauty, its charm and wit.

The American Scholar, it delighted me to learn, soon acquired a reputation for being well written. I'm not sure how much this had to do with editing. In the beginning, I did rather more heavy editing than I later did; sometimes I even rewrote entire pieces. E. H. Gombrich once withdrew a lecture he had offered me because I asked him to change the few small lecture-like gestures at the beginning of the composition. I once took large hunks of Freudian material out of a manuscript, causing its author to accuse me, good-naturedly, of performing a "sigmundectomy" on him — quite right, too. But I soon lost either the interest or the energy to rework everything I ran in the magazine. Better, I felt, to acquire writers who were themselves attracted to careful prose style. The only editing standard I applied — to poems as well as to prose — was intelligibility. We would publish nothing we didn't understand ourselves.

The magazine's reputation for being well written may have had something to do with my strict proscription, if not outright purge, of certain words and phrases — quite a few words and phrases — from its pages. One of the first words I refused to permit was "lifestyle," which, by 1974, was already well on its way to being a meaningless word. I recall attempting to remove it from an essay by Max Delbrück, the Nobel Prize–winning biologist, where Delbrück referred to "the lifestyle of a cell." "Professor Delbrück," I said to him over the phone, "I have been carrying on a little campaign against the word 'lifestyle' and wonder if I can't persuade you to remove it from your excellent essay." "Aach," he said, in a strong Teutonic accent, "I hate it, too, but zis is how ze idiots in ze field refer to it."

I didn't allow "impact" in my pristine pages either, unless it referred to automobile crashes or dentistry. "Arguably" was excised; no flying "whatevers" were allowed, and most "indeeds" at the beginning of sentences were lopped away. "Experienced" as a verb didn't make the cut, and neither did "intriguing," except when it referred to plotting and spying. Anything that smacked of the psychobabblous was out, which included "special," "caring," and "sharing." Academic locutions took a beating: very few "in terms of" got by, fewer "as it weres," and no "if you wills" whatsoever; the Latin abbreviations "i.e." and "etc." were sent to the showers.

More recently, nothing in our pages was "driven by" anything else; we also didn't cotton to "community" to describe all those groups — ethnic, artistic, sexual, and economic — that obviously were not in the least community-like. I removed scores of "incredibles." Hocus-pocus! . . . and gone was "focus." I closed out "closure." Words and phrases of the journalistic moment — "values," "chilling effects," "process" — were similarly drummed out. Just for the sport of it, I put back the hyphens in many words and

phrases for the lovely tyrannous reason that I much preferred the look of "anti-democratic" to "antidemocratic" and "trance-like" to "trancelike." Now that I no longer edit a magazine, I shall have a sign made for my desk that reads: "Responsible for My Prose Only."

I decided not to let any serious profanity, and no obscenity whatsoever, into the magazine, even though I myself might hold the record for using the ubiquitous F-word a greater number of times in the *Times Literary Supplement* than any other writer in that paper's history. (The occasion was a review of the first volume of the *Historical Dictionary of American Slang*.) Since profanity was becoming an increasing part of contemporary life — on television, in drama, in literature, in magazines — I felt it would be nice to declare our magazine a profanity-free zone. When I would occasionally cut profane words from a manuscript — it wasn't required all that often — I would comfort the author by telling him that he may count himself among the last writers censored in America and that there was real distinction in that.

In my twenty-three years as editor of *The American Scholar*, the title "Ms." never appeared in its pages. "Chair" or "chairperson" didn't make it, either. I thought the first unpronounceable, the second patently silly. In choosing between the pronoun-clogging prose that political correctness requires — "He and she know that his and her values are unlikely to affect him and her" — and a confidently cadenced prose, I went for the latter every time, let the pronoun police complain as they may. I moved slowly, allowing plenty of time for bandwagons to pass, on changing from "Negro" to "black" to "African American." I was not big on "gay," either, and herein hangs a tale, and also a tail — nearly my own, actually.

One day a review came in over the transom — as unsolicited material has been called from the day when doors had transoms — concerning the scientific findings about the origins of homosexuality. It was written by two young men at MIT. It was no great shakes, but it was informative on a subject of endless complexity, and I accepted it. For some reason — good instincts, perhaps — I did not run the review right away. I finally held it so long that I wrote to its authors apologizing, saying that I could no longer run it. One of the authors wrote back, begging me to run the review, arguing that it was too late to find another place for it. I gave in, edited the review, among other things changing the word "gay" to "homosexual" throughout the manuscript. The other author wrote to tell me that I couldn't do that—that in certain phrases in the scientific literature on the subject (like my old friend the cell with his lifestyle) "gay" was the word that was used. We exchanged a few of what I thought were polite letters on the subject, agreed on a compromise arrangement—"homosexual" would be used sometimes, "gay" other times—and the review was published.

Not long afterward, the *Gay Community News* ran two articles about "homophobia in publishing"; in one of the articles, I turned out to be one of the prominent homophobes. The man I had corresponded with reported that I had given him a very rough time, first delaying publication of his review, then editing his manuscript in an unacceptable way. His article ended with the suggestion that readers of *Gay Community News* send in letters of protest of my behavior to Phi Beta Kappa, and more than a hundred people, some of them Phi Beta Kappa members, did.

This left an opening for those people in the Phi Beta Kappa Senate who did not approve of the magazine under my editorship to seek my dismissal. These were, for the most part, academics who had an investment in feminism, black history, and gay and lesbian studies. I had mostly treated these subjects in *The American Scholar* by ignoring them. I had asked a prominent feminist in the Phi Beta Kappa Senate to write for the magazine, adding only that I hoped she would be able to transcend feminist platitudes in doing so, but she never came forth with a contribution. We ran nothing about gay and lesbian studies and almost no black history. I did run a critical piece on multiculturalism and a strong denunciation of academic Marxism; occasionally, I ran a piece about some strangely off-center interpretation of an American literary classic. The truth was, I found much in current academic life either boring or crazy, and I didn't want to devote much space to things in which I could not take any serious interest. I tended to view the occasional article that we ran on these strictly academic subjects as, in effect, opening the blinds to reveal the baboons at play, as if to say, "Betcha didn't think their behinds were quite so purple as that." I myself wrote an essay for the *Hudson Review* titled "The Academic Zoo." My condescension had to have left an unpleasant taste.

One day I received a letter, written on the stationery of a New York financial firm, informing me that my correspondent was a trustee of a private foundation. He wished me to know that the late founder of the foundation was a devoted reader of *The American Scholar* and that he gave thirty or so gift subscriptions to the magazine every year. Since he had cared so much for our magazine, the trustees thought that perhaps *The American Scholar* should be the recipient of a grant, possibly to establish a prize in the founder's name. When I spoke with the man who had written to me about how much money the foundation had it in mind to give, he said rather casually, "Oh, something in the low seven figures." It took great control on my part not to invoke the names of the Lord in the world's three major religions.

In my discussions with the foundation, I mentioned that another prize was not what the world needed. There was, I said, no shortage of prizes, merely a shortage of worthy recipients for those now being awarded. What I proposed instead was that younger writers be paid decent fees ($10,000 or so) to do assignments that would require considerable research, and possibly extensive travel, on such subjects as contemporary medical education or the training of diplomats. I hoped also to use part of the grant to find new readers. Were there more *American Scholar* readers in the country—perhaps another twenty or thirty thousand? It would have been splendid to try to find out without the fear of crushing our normal budget, and the foundation didn't object.

But it was never to happen. The generosity of the foundation was viewed by the magazine's enemies in the Phi Beta Kappa Senate as a right-wing plot to save the job of the editor of *The American Scholar*. The annual interest on the $2 million, which the foundation genuinely wished us to have, dangled temptingly for more than three years unused. A pity, a shame, a deep sadness, at least in my view. It might have been put to extremely happy uses.

Although the magazine seemed to gain in prestige, although readers registered regular pleasure in it through correspondence and occasional surveys, I felt my time as editor running out. The small clique of people who despised *The American Scholar* under my editorship were winning the day within the Senate of Phi Beta Kappa, which is, in the final analysis, the publisher of the magazine. Phi Beta Kappa's Senate, far from being representative of the organization at large, is almost wholly made up of academics, and in academic argument, I have noticed, the radicals almost always win, even though they rarely constitute a majority. Conservatives, dependably a minority, usually don't care enough to take a strong stand against them. Liberals, though generally the majority, are terrified about seeming to be on the wrong side of things and so seek compromises that inevitably favor the radicals. The model here is the Russian Duma, with the minority of Bolsheviks cracking the moderation and ultimately the backs of the Mensheviks.

One of the liberal Phi Beta Kappa senators, sensing that my days as editor were running out, asked me how much longer I thought I might like to continue editing the magazine. I said that four more years, which would give me an even quarter of a century, would be sufficient. The Senate voted me two. I was fired, but, in a way characteristic of academic life, very slowly; I had two years to clean out my desk.

I ought to be depressed about all this, but I'm not. I had a long and fine roll of the dice. I edited an intellectual quarterly without financial worry or intellectual interference for twenty-three years. I have missed the many readers in whom I have always professed not to be all that interested. I have missed the regular rhythm of writing my quarterly Aristides essays, and the challenge of coming up with a memorable closing for these essays. Perhaps I can be excused here for borrowing certain endings that, in my youth, always pleased me:

Good night, Mrs. Calabash, wherever you are. How sweet it is! Say good night, Gracie. Good night, Molly. Good night, all. With lotions of love. God bless. We're a little late, so good night, folks. And thanks.